FILMS ON THE CAMPUS

Other Books by Thomas Fensch:

THE LIONS AND THE LAMBS
ALICE IN ACIDLAND

FILMS ON THE CAMPUS

By Thomas Fensch

South Brunswick and New York: A. S. Barnes and Company
London: Thomas Yoseloff Ltd

Library of Congress Catalogue Card Number: 70-104380

A. S. Barnes and Co., Inc.
Cranbury, New Jersey 08512

Thomas Yoseloff Ltd
108 New Bond Street
London W1Y OQX, England

ISBN 0-498-07428-5
Printed in the United States of America

For my brother Tim

and for Steve Osterlund.

Contents

Foreword

"I think I better go home," Tom Fensch said to me one day. "I'm working on three different books."

The remark was not astonishing, it was *astounding.* Named "Dick The Factory" by Ken W. Purdy in print one time, I nevertheless shudder at Fensch's production. It makes me feel as languid as Truman Capote and want to feel as sturdy as Norman Mailer. There was one weekend when I wrote, and rewrote, nine articles for *Cosmopolitan.* But that, as it was, could stand up only as a repair job. Purely mechanical.

Fensch was working on three books at a time. This is not a feat; it is Herculean labor. It accounts for the lack of fat around his bones and the hollows in his cheeks. His work and his cat that sleeps constantly on his bed are Tom Fensch's only companions. God grant it to others. Tom Fensch is a born writer.

This is being written in Iowa City, where Paul Engle established a climate for all the outcasts (writers) to work in. We work here and sooner or later talented kids show up to listen to our opinions, which we mainly work out as we go along.

Anyhow, here is Fensch. On the jacket, the publisher will tell you what he has done. To me it is an amazing volume.

No introducer-of-a-book ought to say anything like this but I must say, as I have said to Fensch himself, there is little point in this book's being written. Of course, there are kids all over the country making films. Of course, there is no book about student films. Of course, kids want to know what others are doing.

There is as much point in writing this book as there is in trying to teach the Beatles how to sing. The kids, to the delight and despair of all of us who are older, are going their own way, doing what their natural human conditions constrain them to do. Sometimes they fall. They always get up. Fensch himself has fallen, but I never have known him not to eject himself upward by his own energy.

The lot of us who are old enough to be his father had to go through a good deal before we finally began to make a living in what Wolcott Gibbs, who was old enough to be my father, called "this nervous business." This includes some of my colleagues here at Iowa: William Price Fox, Ben Santos, William Murray and others. It includes Norman Mailer, William Styron, James Baldwin, Capote, W. C. Heinz, Ken W. Purdy, Jimmy Cannon, Jim Bishop, et al; John McNulty, Quentin Reynolds, now both gone. Collie Small, still alive but unable to be found. Kyle Crichton, dead. Red Smith (known as Walter, still very much alive). Bill Davidson, perhaps the best magazine writer of all of us, also alive. Alva Johnston, dead alas. A. J. Liebling, and the fabulous Joseph Mitchell. Eli Waldron, Seymour Krim, Robert Benchley, Sr., and James Thurber.

Here I go making lists again and now I stop. If you want to read a pretty good book by a young man on his way, try this one.

Richard Gehman
Iowa City, Iowa

Author's Note

This book is the first complete, comprehensive analysis of film programs, student films, and film work in colleges and universities throughout the country. As a pioneer work, it has presented many problems and challenges. It is the result of many months of interviews, photography, screenings, and writing. I estimate that within the seven-month period, January through July 1969, I viewed over 500 student films on the various campuses discussed in the following pages. I have interviewed students and faculty members extensively and added background material from many other sources, both critical and general.

I hope to present an over-all view of the films students make—the personalities of the students and the various film programs. And I have attempted to achieve a harmonious balance between reportage of facts and figures and critical comment about the films and the programs. I wonder whether such a balance is possible, and if it is, whether I have achieved it.

I have only occasionally compared the philosophy of University X against that of College Y. Such comparison is a bit like suggesting "apples are better than oranges." The comment can't be justified. Film programs do not "compete" with each other, fortunately or unfortunately. They exist in worlds of their own, isolated by miles and philosophy from their peers. Nonetheless, I have attempted to describe the strengths and weaknesses of the major programs cited in this book. When a program fulfills its original philosophy, and most do, I have explained why. When a program fails of its purpose, or when the majority of film students are unhappy in that program, I have explained that, too.

In describing the films I have seen, I have usually commented upon them in general instead of critical terms. I believe that critical comment and aesthetic judgments must be limited to films that have a wide general release. Evaluative judgment does have a place in film writing, but only when the reader can view the film and compare his judgment against that of the critic. As most of the film cited in this book will never be available for general release to a wide audience, I have commented only in general terms. A few of the films mentioned are available for screenings, primarily to college film societies and other similar groups, and I have made critical judgments about those. In those isolated cases, the reader may have an opportunity to view the film and then judge for himself the accuracy of my criticism.

In some cases, I have let the film makers speak for themselves (Scott Bartlett, David Weinkauf, and others), believing rightly that their comments about their work may be more perceptive than mine.

The six scripts that I have included in this book will be interesting and valuable to other film makers. I think that student film makers can learn from each other, just as writers can learn from reading other writers. The scripts are excellent examples of student work.

When the cameras and choice of equipment used have a bearing on the outcome of a film, I have mentioned brand names; when the equipment has little bearing on the completed film, I have not.

A word about the photographs used in this book: student film makers usually do not take still photographs of scenes in their films. There is little reason for them to do so; because the films will usually not be distributed, there is no reason to take photographs for publicity purposes. The still photographs in theater marquees are taken by additional cameramen, stationed beside the motion picture cameras. It is the job of these photographers to take promotional photographs that will be sharp and clear. Because they were made from the actual student films some of the pictures are fuzzy or grainy. When students film in eight millimeter, the size of a single frame is less than that of a postage stamp; thus, when single frames are blown up to page size, they lose contrast and sharpness.

Using enlargements is, however, the only way to make printable photographs, when the students did not make still pictures for reproduction in book form.

Occasionally too, films are in color. Making a black and white print from an eight or 16 millimeter frame of color film involves a considerable loss of clarity, which unfortunately can not be helped.

The value of the photographs, I hope, will make up for the loss of clarity.

Although this book is comprehensive, it is not all-inclusive. There are some schools that perhaps should have been included which I was unable to visit. The University of Kansas at Lawrence began a Film Study program during the 1969–1970 school year, designed primarily for students interested in careers as teachers, critics, archivists, and historians. It stresses history, theory, and criticism, and requires only one production course and a minor in a related field, such as art, history, theater, or American studies. The Center for Film Studies at Kansas engages in a variety of projects in support of teaching and research. *The Cinema Journal,* a semi-annual publication of the national Society for Film Studies —the only U.S. organization of cinema historians, critics, and professors—is based at Kansas. *The Cinema Journal* is currently edited by Professor Richard Dyer MacCann, who recently published *Film: A Montage of Theories.* On the graduate level at Kansas, the student may take a non-thesis degree and make a film as part of his requirements.

During the production of his film *Short Story,* Frank Miller is at left holding black notebook. The film program at Ohio University at Athens is very selective, with a restricted number of film makers. In the 1968-1969 school year, there were only six students in the graduate film program and only 12 undergraduate film majors. (Photo by Carl Fleischhauer. Copyright © 1969 by Carl Fleischhauer)

Ohio University at Athens has a small, progressive program that should get better in the next few years.

Temple University in Philadelphia has begun one of the most selective and interesting programs in the country. Raymond Fielding, formerly a faculty member of the U.S.C. and Iowa film departments, now on the faculty at Temple, has described the Temple program as "emphasising film as communication, film as creative documentary, film as cinema vérité, film for political

Frank Miller edits his film *Short Story* on a Acmade editing machine with projection viewer. Ohio University has a small group of film makers, but they are active and enthusiastic. (Photo by Carl Fleischhauer. Copyright © 1969 by Carl Fleischhauer)

action, film as journalism. In other words, for those students in the country whose interest is in what, for lack of a better term, we might call 'creative documentary,' Temple is the place to be. On the other hand, for students whose interest is in theatrical film, audio-visual film, or experimental film, we advise them to go elsewhere. They wouldn't be happy here, nor would we be happy with them."

On the bachelor's and master's degree levels at Temple, the emphasis of the program is on professional production training. The aim of the Temple faculty is to turn out first-class professional people to take positions as writers, directors, and producers of film for the information-communications field.

As Fielding has said, "the films in which we are interested are

Ohio University film makers generally attend small classes. Here, J. L. Anderson, director of the film program, gestures during a graduate film seminar. (Photo by Carl Fleischhauer. Copyright © 1969 by Carl Fleischhauer)

in the public-information tradition of creative documentary. They also reflect the desire of young film makers to express their own opinions and feelings relative to the political, social, economic and cultural issues of the day. We are not interested in the so-called 'nuts-and-bolts' films."

The faculty at Temple consists of three exceptional professors: Ernest Rose, formerly head of production at the University of California, Berkeley; Fielding; and Ed McCoy, formerly head of film production at Michigan State University.

The Annenberg Building on the Temple campus, home of the film department, is a five millon dollar facility, containing studios, projections rooms, labs, editing rooms and complete color television studios. It is one of the most modern radio-tv-film buildings in the country.

In 1967, the Temple program had an enrollment of 217 undergraduate majors in film and about 35 graduate students. Within the first two years of the program, several exceptional students won national awards for their films. John Bartholomew won one of the two scholarships in the annual UFA/McGraw-Hill scholarship competitions for his film *Emma's Time* and Susan Klein won the first prize of $1,000 in the White House Press Photographers film competition for her beginning workshop film—which is quite extraordinary.

Temple has adequate processing equipment of their own to insure students 24-hour processing on all student film. The Temple program, more than any other program, expects students to make meaningful statements on film within the urban environment.

Within just a few months, the Temple program should reach the top four or five film programs in the country, and will certainly be the best program anywhere in terms of their concept of the creative documentary. It is the first really new and well-financed film program in many years.

The American Film Institute's Center for Advanced Film Studies, in Beverly Hills, California, opened in September, 1969, as a bridge between film study and film making as a profession. It is, strictly speaking, not a university film department, but has been patterned after the Czech, French, Polish, Swedish, Russian and West German national film academies. Each fall, the Center, under the direction of the American Film Institute's director, George Stevens, Jr., accepts 15 applicants, including young professionals and the most promising graduates of university film programs. These Student Fellows will study at the Center's Graystone Estate for two years. Ten will concentrate on writing and directing, two on cinematography, and three on history and criticism. A film making or research project will be tailored to each student, and these projects may be short dramatic films, experimental films, documentaries, educational films or critical and historical investigations.

"We are working to establish a tutorial tradition in American film such as exists in architecture, music, medicine and law," Stevens said, "The Center will serve as a bridge between film study and film making as a profession by providing a place where the finest practicing artists and craftsmen can dedicate time, experience and knowledge to the young film makers who will work and study at the Center."

Fred Zinnemann, Billy Wilder, and Robert Surtees have contributed time as instructors at the Center and the first-year faculty includes: James Blue, director of a number of documentaries, including the 1968 Academy Award nominee, *A Few Notes About Our Food Problem;* Kevin Brownlaw, British film director, historian, and author of *The Parade's Gone By,* is the first historian-in-residence; Richard Kahlenberg, member of the American Film Institute staff and Frantisek Daniel, Dean of the Czech National Film School, who is the first visiting professor.

The A.F.I.'s Center, along with the Temple program, are two of the most promising and selective film programs anywhere in the country.

Several universities I had hoped to discuss in this book were disappointments, to the extent of offering little either generally or critically. Neither the University of Rochester nor the Rochester Institute of Technology has taken advantage of the facilities of the George Eastman House in Rochester.

The George Eastman House was opened in 1949 as a museum of photography and cinematography and contains a priceless collection of motion picture material and a library of films exceeding that of the Museum of Modern Art in New York. The Eastman House also includes a 550-seat theater, where films are shown to public and private groups throughout the year. Thus far, neither the University nor the Rochester Institute have taken more than a token interest in this vast collection available to students, which would be highly valued as an adjunct by most film schools throughout the country.

The University of Minnesota in Minneapolis has a film program, but it currently is suffering from a leadership vacuum and is overshadowed by the Tyrone Guthrie Theater, which draws many from film work to the stage.

Readers of this book interested in enrolling at a film school described here are cautioned to remember that the philosophies and requirements for degrees in film are those of the 1968–1969 school year. The prospective film student should write to the appropriate program director for a conformation of requirements and guidelines, as the requirements and objectives may change during publication and release of this book.

Norman Mailer has said that authors should try their best with each book they complete; they should try to "hit the ball out of the park." This I have attempted to do. I hope the enthusiasm felt by student film makers is obvious, for students are articulate and intellectually honest about film. There may well be weaknesses and errors of judgment or fact in this book, but I hope too, there are salient judgments and interesting descriptions. *Films On the Campus* has given me happiness and frustrations. I have found continuing friendships with many of the film makers I met during the course of my research. It is a book that engaged a large part of my life for an extended period; I lived with it and sweated over it and nursed it along to completion. It demanded my time, energies, and creativity to an extent I never thought possible. It is a book I am proud of.

T. F.
Iowa City, Iowa

Introduction

THE STUDENT FILM WORLD

"Create a Film Revolution" the National Student Association urges, and throughout the country students have responded to that plea. They have dramatically changed film instruction and film making on college and university campuses everywhere. It is a cliché, but nonetheless true, that there has been an explosion in film interest on the nation's campuses that will not only continue, but increase, in the coming months and years.

It is a phenomenon not easily paralleled in the history of American higher education. Film-studies programs have proliferated at an amoeba-like rate. The demands for film courses and financing for equipment have come from students, instead of from university administrations. In the past, when a new department or area of study was needed on a campus, the word came from the administration. Committees were formed to study curricula and begin courses. Textbooks were compared and chosen by faculty members and degree requirements were established by executive fiat.

In the past few years, however, the impetus for film study has come from students. They have *demanded* to be able to major in film making. *They* have forced university officials to hire professors to teach film courses. And when deans claim that there is no room in the college or university budget to buy cameras, students have bought their own.

The statistics are surprising. Applications to the film program at the University of Southern California have doubled in the last five years; the film enrollment at the University of California at Los Angeles has more than doubled to over 450 students in the last four years. Boston University's film program had 125 students in 1965, 250 in 1967. Northwestern University has doubled its enrollment in film every year for the past three. The University of Iowa had 40 students in 1964; it now has nearly 100. Similar examples can be found at many other schools.

There are numerous reasons for this increase in campus film interest. Film is currently in vogue—and with good reason. In the past, students who wanted to be creative had to settle for writing or painting. They would squirrel themselves off in a campus apartment with a typewriter, cigarettes, and coffee and hope to create a lasting American classic. Alone, often discouraged, they had to work for months and months. Often their results were discouraging, pathetic, hopeless; their work, completed after months of solitude, was usually rejected by faculty members and refused by magazines and book publishers.

Now students can buy their own film and cameras, or rent the cameras, or borrow them and make short films in a matter of days —even hours. Instead of working alone, they can involve their roommates, their girlfriends. They can film bedroom scenes, if they like, blatant sexuality of the girl next door. Most don't however, as they are too interested in camera techniques and personal statements on film to waste time with sexual scenes. Best of all, in some cases, they can have their film processed overnight and judge the quality of their creative efforts immediately. It is not unusual to find an undergraduate campus film maker who has made dozens of short films in eight millimeter with his own camera.

The movies too have found an enthusiastic audience in college students. Movies that were formerly dismissed as cheap and unintelligent have changed. Films by such directors as Arthur Penn, Mike Nichols, and others have become increasingly popular on campus. And foreign films, by such men as Fellini, Antonioni, Godard, Truffaut, Bunuel, Polanski, have been easily and very profitably booked into college theaters. There is a language of film now that did not exist earlier, and it is to the credit of astute college students that they have helped to develop and sustain it.

Higher education, a dinosaur-like creature, not easily moved, has now begun to recognize film study, principally because the students demanded it. And films are not limited to film majors. They may now be found as an integral part of psychology courses, tracing human development. Sociology courses teach how films affect behavior. Films make history, art, and the social sciences come alive for students. No longer do teachers have to use the so-called "educational film" to instruct. They have discovered that they can well use regular feature films, distributed in 16 millimeter, and occasionally even in eight millimeter.

Faculty members of the emerging film departments often have backgrounds in non-film areas. Dr. John Fell of San Francisco State College holds degrees in English and sociology. Harry Breitrose at Stanford began his college work in English. Don Norwood at West Virginia holds a master's degree in music. Arthur Barron at Columbia has earned his doctorate in sociology; George Manupelli at Michigan earned a doctorate in art. Jack Ellis, head of the program at Northwestern, has a Ph.D. in education. Colin Young at U.C.L.A. has a master's degree in philosophy. All have moved into film easily; they have found their backgrounds in other arts helpful to film making and film instruction.

Students too, enter film programs from a panorama of other fields. Chris Parker at Iowa originally majored in comparative literature. His background can be seen in his films. George Lucas had vague thoughts of majoring in English or art before entering U.S.C.'s film program. Other students have come from anthropology, classics, mathematics, philosophy, even engineering. They have all been welcome in film. They have had a chance, in some cases, to use their backgrounds effectively as subject matter. Or they have just used their prior knowledge for a broader understanding of communications and aesthetics.

What then are these film students like? Can we chart some characteristics of them? From my work on this book, I can draw a rough outline of the average film student. First, it is likely that he (or she, although film study is primarily a masculine field currently) is highly intelligent. And articulate. And knowledgeable about himself and the world around him. Film students can discuss today's problems and conflicts intelligently. They know their own minds, they know the history of film, and they know the place film holds in communication.

They are leaders, not followers. They can write a script, direct a film, and edit it without help, without prodding from the faculty. They can often be found in various concerned groups—student action societies, peace groups, civil rights groups. They are concerned about poverty, disturbed about the war in Vietnam. But they are not propagandists in film. They are film makers. If they happen to make a social-problems film, it is apt to ultimately be dramatic, then problematical, like *Stasis,* done at Texas.

Almost none of them are members of fraternities or sororities. Most students, and especially film students, believe that the Greek system, as it now exists on the American college and university campus, is passé, impotent. Film makers do not feel a need to be part of the Greek system on campuses. If they pay any filmic attention to the Greeks at all, their film may resemble *And It Goes On and On,* done at U.C.L.A.

Film makers are knowledgeable about drugs, which are now part of every college or university in this country—large or small, liberal or conservative. Film makers, however, are not worried by drugs, and may only briefly touch on drug use in films, as witness the pot smoking in *A Beginning,* also at U.C.L.A. Although it is quite likely that many film students use drugs regularly (statistics show that a vast majority of college students in this country has tried drugs at least once during a four-year college education), film students tend to be blasé about grass (marijuana), acid (LSD), and the rest. Only a few, like Kee Dewdney at Michigan, admit to the use of drugs or acknowledge that drugs have a thematic part in their films.

If film makers happen to have long hair and resemble the stereotyped hippie, so what? Their long hours on location and their work in editing cubicles is not conducive to button-down shirts, rep ties, and sport coats. If faculty members can dress casually and look like the students (Doug Cox, Arthur Barron, and many others), who should care? No one should and no one does. Their excellence is in their product; clothes do not make the film maker.

Just as the film makers are different, so too are the programs. Each has developed (or is developing) a firm philosophy of film instruction, tailored to the needs of its students. U.S.C.'s emphasis is totally different from the program at U.C.L.A., although they are only suburbs apart in the Los Angeles area. The program at Iowa differs from the program at Northwestern and the two graduate programs at New York University are distinctly separate—in style and content.

This book, then, is the student film world as it exists today. The students in this book are indeed creating a revolution in film.

FILMS ON THE CAMPUS

by Thomas Fensch

I

THE WEST COAST SCHOOLS

1.

The University of Southern California

THE CREW CONCEPT; LUCAS AND THX

There are many criteria for judging the worth of a particular university department or school: the quality of the professors, the amount of equipment, the abilities of the student, prizes and awards won, lack of significant faculty turn-over, atmosphere of the department, and position of the alumni in the business. In all these areas, the University of Southern California cinema department stands at, or near, the top.

In 1929, the University offered, in co-operation with the Academy of Motion Picture Arts and Sciences, a course described in the general catalogue as: "*Introduction to Photoplay;* a general introduction to a study of the motion picture art and industry; its mechanical foundations and history; the silent photoplay and the photoplay with sound and voice; the scenario; the actor's art; pictorial effects; commercial requirements; principles of criticism; ethical and educational features; lectures; class discussions, assigned readings."

Guest lecturers in the late 1920s and early 1930s included Douglas Fairbanks, J. Stuart Blackton, Ernst Lubitsch, Irving Thalberg, and William C. DeMille.

In 1932, the University was one of the first in this country to offer a bachelor of arts degree with a major in cinema. In 1935, the University began offering a master's degree with a major in cinema. In 1958, students could receive a doctor of philosophy degree in cinema.

U.S.C. claims to be the oldest film school in the country,* and now in terms of enrollment it is the largest. There are about 350 majors in the department, about 70 percent of them graduate students. The faculty of the cinema department received an Acad-

* The University of Iowa first granted a master's degree for film work in 1916, but film interest at Iowa has been sporadic since then, until recently.

emy Award for *The Face of Lincoln* in 1956, and the students have won an enormous number of awards for other exceptional films. The walls of the departmental offices and secretarial pool are crammed with framed awards from festivals and exhibitions throughout this country and abroad.

Since the inception of the *Introduction to Photoplay* course in 1929, the cinema department has expanded until the 1969–70 course catalogue lists over 60 courses in film and related subjects. Some of these are worth noting:

Fundamentals of Film, introduction to cinematic elements, production techniques and equipment, audience evaluation, areas of film research and idea development . . . images and sound; *Visual Communication; Language of Film,* basic principles of visual and audio communication; idea development using image, movement, pace, the spoken word and other sounds, action and sound relationships.

Filmwriting, organizing and writing brief outlines, treatments, and scripts, training in elementary filmic vision and listening. Analysis of short films; *Image of the Film,* fundamental creative motion picture camera and lighting techniques; *Motion Picture Camera; Motion Picture Editing.*

Motion Picture Sound Recording; Film Directing; Documentary Film, growth, implications and use of the international nonfiction film in public service, propaganda, education and industry.

Literature of the Film; Filmic Expression; Analysis of Contemporary Cinema, trends in film philosophy and techniques from the postwar Italian neo-realism to the Cinema of the Absurd placed in historical perspective; *Advanced Writing; Advanced Camera and Writing; Photography in Scientific Research; Motion Picture Processing; Animation; Art Direction; Film Business Procedures and Distribution; Theatrical Film Symposium; Music in Motion Pictures; Seminar in Cinema History and Criticism; Creative Cinema; Seminar In Camera; Seminar in Film Analysis; Seminar in Film Distribution; Budgeting and Management; Seminar in Film Direction; Designing Large Group and Multi-media Presentations.*

The graduate catalogue lists exactly 60 courses, some of them undergraduate courses open to graduate students, others offered solely for the master's and doctoral students. These include: *Literature of the Film, The New Film Makers, The New Language in Film, Seminar in the Animated Film,* and others.

The department's practice of enlisting the aid of professionals has continued since the late 1920s. In the tradition of Fairbanks, Thalberg, Lubitsch, and DeMille, the department now calls on

Arthur Knight, author of *The Liveliest Art*, and Irwin Blacker, who has written a number of books, not only on film, but fiction as well. Jerry Lewis has taught a seminar and Norman Taurog and King Vidor are currently Artists in Residence.

Other friends and patrons of the department include Jackie Coogan, Irene Dunne, Ross Hunter, Gene Kelly, Ernest Lehman, Eleanor Parker, and Mary Pickford.

But catalogues and descriptive literature often do not present a true picture of the facilities of a department, as some students recognize to their chagrin too late. People make departments, and people alone contribute to the education of others, despite whatever platitudes are sent to prospective students and ancient alumni. Schools and departments, despite glowing information to the contrary, become unofficially known for one specialization or another. U.S.C., within the field of cinema, is known as a school that is practically oriented, producing students who can make films, technicians, workers, and sometimes drones with little imagination but plenty of craftsmanship.

U.S.C. is perhaps the prime example of a cinema school that is devoted to the crew concept of film making. In advanced courses, students usually shoot films in crews of four. One student will be the cameraman, another the director, a third the writer, and a fourth the editor. Or there will be variations on this concept. In theory, this concept forces students to work with each other, encourages feasible projects, and minimizes the mistakes of one student by a team effort toward perfection. Usually this works. Occasionally, with students like George Lucas, the team concept proves unworkable. The roles of editor, cameraman, writer, and producer are rotated from film to film; all students receive a sampling of the responsibility and creativity in each area of the productions.

One of the best young professors in the U.S.C. department is Douglas Cox, who usually oversees the student productions. Cox has been at U.S.C. for the past seven years; he received his master's degree in film from U.C.L.A., across town. He has participated in documentary film work in this country and abroad.

Cox is a likable man with a genuine love of working with students. He often dresses as they do—in wool work shirts and motorcycle boots; and he wears a full beard, which becomes him. He can also talk in the current language of the hip young film makers, which is an advantage.

"We believe that students find out about making films by making films," Cox says. "There are so many film students here that we do have an occasional logistics problem. Everyone wants to shoot

Professor Douglas Cox is one of the bright young film professors, and works with student productions at U.S.C. (Photo by the author)

on weekends. We also have a problem at the end of semesters, when everyone wants to use the editing booths and movieolas at the same time. But generally, if students plan ahead, there should be no problem regarding the equipment. We have come to believe that students should have their own equipment and we encourage them to buy eight millimeter cameras.

"The department has two Eclairs, one silent Airflex, one Auricon and several Mitchells. The equipment is adequate without being lush. We don't, however, have all the editing facilities that we would like to have."

It is easy to see why Cox says this. The Cinema department is located in an old, square barn, open in the center, with a picnic table provided for use during the California summers. Around the inside is a sheltered walkway and off of it are the various editing booths, screening rooms, the animation department, lecture halls, a sound stage (old and dirty), and the departmental offices.

"The students edit very well under the existing conditions, and

I guess that we have a reputation for making films that are slicker than some other schools. Faculty members from elsewhere have said that they can recognize a U.S.C. film by its editing and polish," Cox said. "I can't see it myself, but apparently the polish is visible to others."

Faculty members at U.S.C. tend to drift back and forth between classes and assignments. They sit in on the classes of others and take different class assignments each term, instead of teaching the same courses every semester. Consequently, Cox and others who supervise the practical production classes screen countless numbers of student films each semester.

"Several hundred films reach the exercise stage," Cox says, "and beyond that, we have about fifty or sixty films each semester that reach the composite or answer-print stage. The department encourages students to enter their own films in exhibitions and festivals and many students do."

The cinema department at U.S.C. is more conscientious than almost any other school, with the possible exception of U.C.L.A. regarding submission of student films at festivals and exhibitions. As a result, according to the late Herbert Kosower, U.S.C. receives in the vicinity of *300 awards each year,* some for the same films that have been entered in several categories (directing, camerawork, editing, and the like) in different festivals.

U.S.C. and U.C.L.A. are also the most aggressive schools in the country with regard to finding positions for their graduates. Exceptional U.S.C. students are assured that the department will do all it can to place them in the industry.

Melvin Sloan has been on the faculty of U.S.C. as a professor since 1948, and before that as a part-time lecturer. He teaches the senior workshop, which involves an interesting variation of the crew concept of U.S.C. film making: all the directors in the crews were members of a previous class, in a progression of production classes. Consequently, the directors have had at least one semester more experience than the other members of the class. The directors plan the idea and scope of their films. They must, however, then sell their idea to the prospective members of their crew. A director with an ill-conceived film, or an artistic film that would take more than the allotted amount of time during the semester (causing, in some cases, an incomplete grade report for the semester's work), will find that prospective members of his crew will veto the idea or join another team. This forces the director to choose an idea that will readily adapt itself to treatment that is artistically well-formed, feasible in terms of shooting and editing time, and at least nominally acceptable to other members of the team. Directors who, for one reason or another, find their

From *Dominator* by David Hanson.

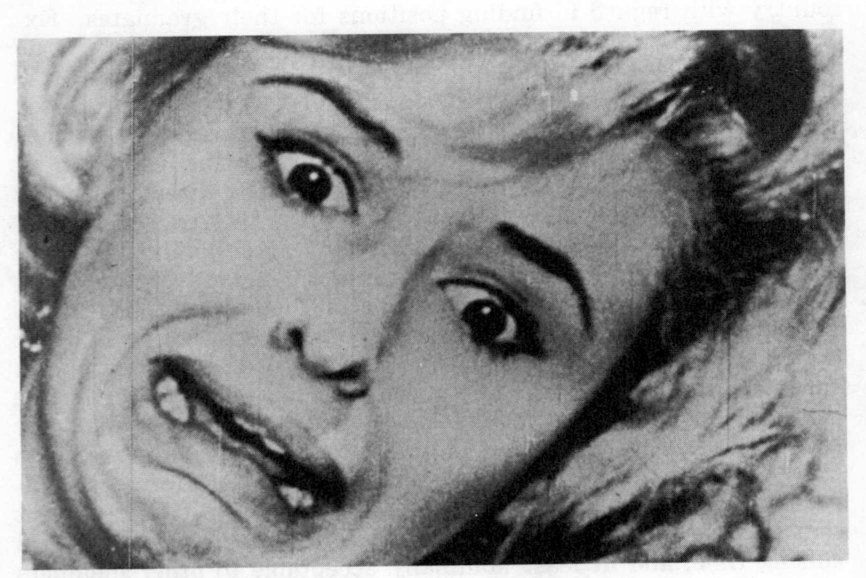

From *The Bug* by Hal Barwood and David Hanson.

ideas rejected out of hand—which happens occasionally—find themselves taking a lesser position on the crew of another director, with a subsequent loss of leadership (if not lowering of class grade).

"We don't feel that we have the ultimate idea about film making," Sloan says. "We try to break up our teaching patterns and don't usually believe in one teaching concept. The team technique fosters this; the students have to sell each other on the merits of proposed films and in this way they take the initiative in the course. The faculty members act as advisors and consultants when needed."

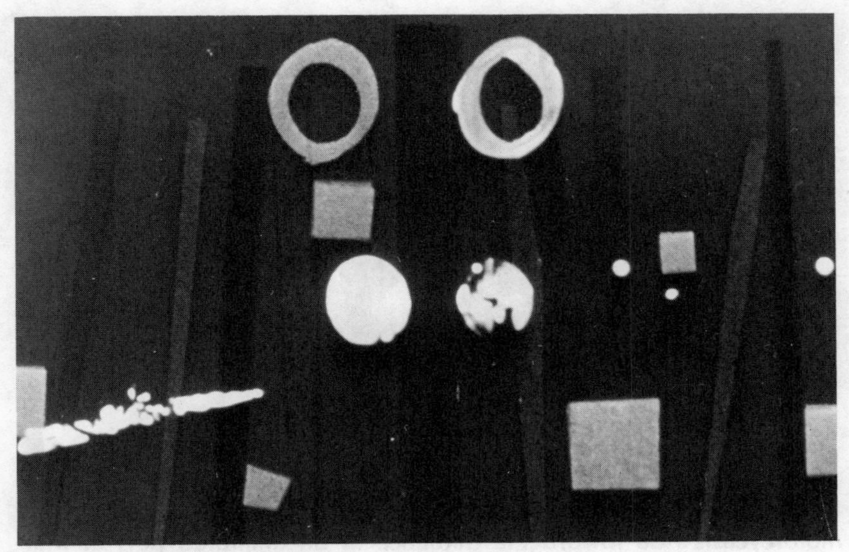

From *Cycle of Entelechy* by Jae Carmichael.

During 1968, the students and faculty chose 18 films that were thought to be a representative sampling of the superior work done during a year or so at U.S.C. Some of these films are:

Homage to Muybridge by David Hanson. Eadweard Muybridge, an early researcher, spent his lifetime studying human and animal locomotion with the use of series of still photographs. Hanson's film, which is two minutes long and in black and white, recreates the early photographic work of Muybridge. With the use of animation, he makes it appear that Muybridge's still photographs constitute a moving film. It is nostalgic and texturally reminiscent of the very early work in still and moving photography.

Baby Blue by Robert Dalva, Robert Steadman, Emmet Alston, Barbara Whitaker, and others is a dramatization of the conflicts of a young housewife whose husband is serving in Vietnam. As she does her household chores, her longing for her husband is verbalized on the soundtrack. Cuts to his framed portrait and cuts to televised news reports about Vietnam accompany her need for her husband. In part, a pet replaces her need, but at the film's end her longing is provocative: "I love you, I love you, I miss you . . ."

Marcello, I'm So Bored is an eight-minute animated film by John

Motorcyclists ride toward the audience in an animated part of *Marcello, I'm So Bored* by John Milius and John Strawbridge.

Milius, John Strawbridge, and George Lucas that attempts to mirror the current American landscape. The lack of emotional involvement between people is evident, especially in segments showing the *Playboy* bunnies and roving motorcycle gangs. *Time* magazine wrote: "*Marcello, I'm So Bored* . . . begins with an epitaph from the late Errol Flynn: 'I believe I'm a very colorful character in a rather drab age.' It then flashes through a quick-cutting kaleidoscope of mindless pleasure seekers—motorcyclists, teenyboppers, discotheque dancers—accompanied by a sound track of sighs and despairing screams. One judge (at the National Student Film Festival) saw in the . . . film a viable cinematic equivalent of pop art."

Poem of Rodia by Khosrow Haritash, Thomas Maxwell, and others is an excellent study of the Watts Towers. Simon Rodia, an Italian immigrant and tile mason, devoted his lifetime to the construction of the Towers of Watts, which were created out of the discarded junk of four generations. Haritash, a foreign student

From *Poem of Rodia*, a film about the Watts Towers, by Khosrow Haritash.

with a limited command of English, has, nonetheless, made an excellent silent study of the primitive beauty and geometric excellence of the Towers. The film seems much longer than its running time of four minutes.

Pulp by Bruce Green, Caleb Deschanel, Richard Walter, and Dennis Guyitt is a satire on the men's adventure magazines proliferating on the nation's newsstands. It studies leather-jacketed motorcycle riders who view themselves from the point of view of the situations and adventures they have read in the magazines.

Night Shift by Mathew Robbins, Deschanel, Walter Murch, and Robin Commagere shows a Negro attendant at a Chevron service station, alone and increasingly unnerved by seemingly sourceless sounds and actions of his station. The gas pump hoses writhe like snakes, the pneumatic alley bells ring when the camera plunges soundlessly over them, oil cans rattle in their stacks, and the neon signs swirl and twist. Eventually, the attendant, bedeviled by things that go bump in the night, runs frightened from

A frame from *Pulp*, a satire on the pulp magazines by Bruce Green, Caleb Deschanel, Richard Walter, and Dennis Guyitt.

A scene from *Night Shift* by Matthew Robbins, Caleb Deschanel, Richard Walter, and Robin Commagere. A Standard Oil station begins emanating eerie noises, the gas pump hoses dance like snakes, the bells begin to ring mysteriously, and eventually the lonely attendant is driven away.

the plagued station. The film is seven minutes long and is in color.

Bird, a kinestasis film by Bruce Green, is a one-minute study of Lyndon Johnson and the achievements of his administration. The film is accompanied by an old and unlamented rock 'n' roll song, "Surfin' Bird," by The Trashmen. Their lyrics are an idiotic repetition of "bap-bap-bap-bap-bird-bird-bird, bird-bird-bird . . ." Johnson is seen with open mouth, upside down, pulling his dogs' ears, backgrounded against Viet Nam action, and finally as *Mad* magazine's moronic mascot, Alfred E. Neuman. It is a wry commentary that goes to black on the screen when the song lyrics end "bbbbbbbbbiiiiiiiiirrrrrrrrrdddddddd."

The Bug is a three-minute black and white satire by David Hanson and Hal Barwood that shows that the eventual solution to the problem of a science-fiction invasion of beetles is not insecticide, or the palaverings of scientists, but the simplistic solution of a harried young man who simply stamps on and squashes the offending insects.

Ritual, four minutes long, by Michael Brown, is an exploration of women's penchants for embellishing their eyes and the elaborate paraphernalia that is involved.

Wipeout, one minute long, in black and white, by Paul Golding, is a study in forms and designs, of which it has been said: "What this film means to you will depend on your thoughts and ideas."

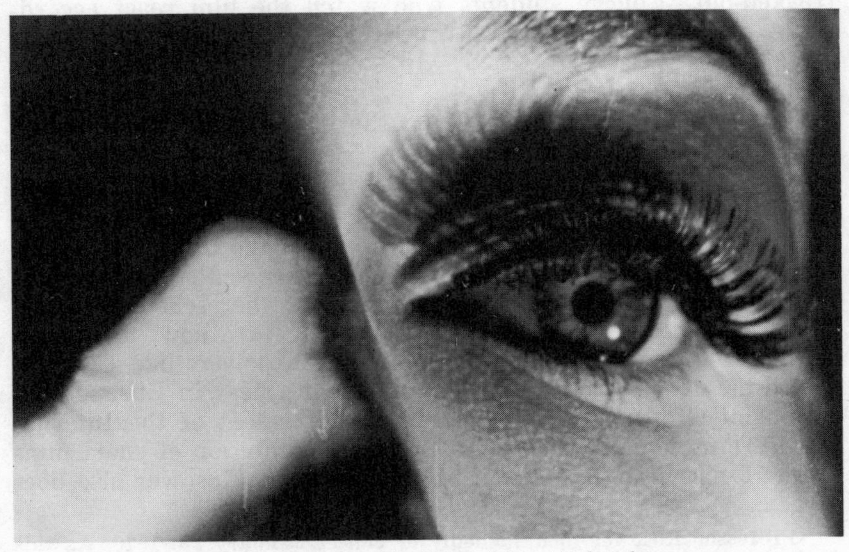

An extreme close-up from the film *Ritual* by Michael Brown.

From *Wipe Out* by Paul Golding. Understanding and appreciation of this film may depend on "where your head's at," in the phrase of the hippies, for it resembles a psychedelic experience.

This is an ordinary layman's term for being psychedelic and freaked-out. College students who watch the film react accordingly, or, in the hippie phrase, according to "where their heads are at."

In one area of film making, Southern California stands apart from any other school in the country. That area is animation, and U.S.C. is the only school to have a full-time professor of animation.

Herbert Kosower* has been at U.S.C. since the 1960 school year. It was then, Kosower explains, that U.S.C. showed great foresight in hiring an animation professor when no other school had one. Kosower's specific duties were then, as they are now, to build a separate sequence of animation courses. Kosower, like Cox, received his degree from U.C.L.A. and spent a year in Europe on a Fulbright Grant in 1958–59. He is the president of the International Tournée of Animation, a traveling exhibition of short films from 13 nations. In addition to his classwork, Kosower also does

* Professor Kosower died suddenly of cancer January 25, 1970. As this book went to press, no successor had been named to the U.S.C. faculty for animation studies.

an average of three or four films a year of his own, both animated and feature films. His most recent is *The Face,* a study of the variety and mystery of women.

Kosower limits the enrollment of the animators to six full-time students each year. He feels that more than six limits his teaching and limits what the students can do on the animation boards. There are, however, about 45 non-majors who take animation courses. Kosower generally offers five or six courses in various aspects of animation.

Each year Kosower's students shoot about 30 short animated films, each running one to two minutes. Longer animated films, running from two to eight minutes, are produced by his students at the rate of three or four a year.

Animation, however, has never really escaped from the influence of the Disney studios. Although it is true that animation has been developed for television, it is also apparent that television's only

The "Eleanor Rigby" sequence from The Beatles 1968 animated film, *Yellow Submarine*. This film has been termed "a new genre of animation art" by the late Professor Herbert Kosower, professor of animation at the University of Southern California. (Courtesy of United Artists Corp.)

use of animation is for children's shows and occasionally for commercials. Kosower believes that animation is a most important area of film making, and that one 1968 film single-handedly, as it were, sparked a revolution in animation.

The film? *Yellow Submarine,* featuring cartoon versions of John Lennon, George Harrison, Paul McCartney, and Ringo Starr—The Beatles—in their magic voyage to Pepperland, where they saved the citizens from the Blue Meanies. *Yellow Submarine,* from a song of the same name by Lennon and McCartney, was designed by Heinz Edelmann. Literally scores of artists (almost 200 by production's end) were involved in its production. *Yellow Submarine* has done boffo box office business and the sound track from the film has made several millions of dollars for The Beatles' record company, Apple Corps.

John Lennon fights one of the bad guys—the glove—in The Beatles delightful film, *Yellow Submarine*. The late Herbert Kosower, the leading expert in animation in the U.S.C. University community, has called *Yellow Submarine* "not Mod, Camp, Pop and for lack of any other label, I call it 'Sur-Mod.' The graphic adventures and powerful animation of the film bursts through into magical wonder, elevating this work of art into a surrealistic dream." (Courtesy of United Artists Corp.)

Kosower did the program notes for a benefit premiere of *Yellow Submarine* at the Los Angeles County Museum of Art, November 12, 1968. He wrote then:

> *Yellow Submarine* immediately establishes itself as a new genre of animation art. It is not a traditional animated film, but reflects the best in experimental animation, and generating it into something quite extraordinary and unique. Simply stated, *Yellow Submarine* is "where it's at" in animation. It makes Disney more classical and creates a fresh contemporary style of its own.
>
> *Yellow Submarine* is the first surrealistic feature and will no doubt go on and influence an entire generation of films. Eventually it will be seen as a landmark in the development of the animated film. The film is a mixture of Salvador Dali, Rene Magritte, Joan Miro and Max Ernst, as well as Francis Picabia's abstractions of reality. Surrealists have influenced animators such as Peter Foldes, Borowczyk and Lenica in Europe and

The Beatles classic *Yellow Submarine* appeared at the right time for animators. It may inspire college students to enter animation. (Courtesy United Artists Corp.)

From *Yellow Submarine,* with The Beatles. Professor Herbert Kosower, has said that "*Yellow Submarine* is the first surrealistic animated feature and will no doubt go on and influence an entire generation of films. Eventually it will be seen as a landmark in the development of the animated film." (Courtesy of United Artists Corp.)

these innovators of the animated film have more than paved the way for the extraordinary style of *Yellow Submarine.*

The graphics of *Yellow Submarine* are not Mod, Camp, Pop, and for the lack of any other label, I call it, "Sur-Mod." As in Surrealism, it looks for a truer reality in its synthesis of the exterior world as its interior model.

Four scores and 32 Bars Ago, the Forefathers of Pepperland —Along With the Foremothers—Had Sailed to This Land and Made It A Pleasant Place—In The Yellow Submarine.

Human figures and objects are divorced from their natural functions and placed opposite one another in a relationship which is unexpected and therefore gives each of them a new presence. There is the "sea of time," the "sea of consumer products" and the "sea of music" with the warning "there's treble ahead." Furthermore, there is the "sea of holes" and the "sea of green" leading to Pepperland, which is now at the heel of the tyrannical Blue Meanie and his despicable crew of music-loathing mercenaries. The graphic adventures and powerful animation of the film bursts through into magical wonder, elevating this work of art into a surrealistic dream.

In August of 1968, the 22nd Edinburgh International Film Festival was held in Edinburgh, Scotland. As a prelude to the main program of exceptional films from all over the world, Southern California presented three selections of student films: *New Directions in Student Cinema, Films 1967–1968,* and *"A Decade at U.S.C.* Thirty-three U.S.C. films were chosen on a non-competitive basis for the showings and all of them were presented certificates of excellence at Edinburgh. A full third were animated films.

Two of the eleven were:

A Child's Introduction To The Cosmos by Hal Barwood is a

From *A Child's Introduction To The Cosmos* by Hal Barwood.

wonderfully whimsical view of the birth of the universe, proving that the earth has an actual white polar cap, that we must distinguish what is (the daytime) from what is naught (the night), and that dragons and imps infest the night to plague mankind. It is in color and is a prime example of what the major animation companies *ought to be doing,* but often are not. *Cosmos* has won so many awards and certificates for excellence that the U.S.C.

From *A Child's Introduction To The Cosmos* by Hal Barwood.

officials stopped counting when all of them could not be listed on an entire page of typing paper.

Pollution by James C. Conrad examines, in color, the hazards of air pollution and features George Washington as father of his half-smothered country.

Scenes from *A Child's Introduction To The Cosmos*, an animated film by Hal Barwood.

One of the finest students to graduate from U.S.C. is a young man named George Lucas. Lucas is now working for Francis Ford Coppola, making independent productions, but he is still regarded at U.S.C. with mixed feelings of paternal pride and continuing exasperation. And he never thought of being a film maker in the first place.

George Lucas originally came from Modesto, California, and for two years attended Modesto Junior College, a dreary, small, insulated school. While at Modesto, he had two interests: working on high-performance sports cars and going to the single theater in Modesto out of sheer boredom. Lucas, who had been tinkering with cars for most of his teen-age life, eventually wanted to get into sports car racing. He was reasonably close to getting a license to drive on sports car tracks when he had an accident, which changed his mind about racing for a living. Then he turned to art and wanted to go to art school, but his parents wouldn't pay the tuition for him. Lucas, in the manner of so many college-aged young people, looked around and finally decided to go to San Francisco State and major in English. As he says, he "went through the ritual" of applying to the Cinema department at U.S.C., but he didn't even consider the possibility of being accepted. It's part of the college thing—you shop around, apply here and there, and eventually go *somewhere and major in something*—at least for a while.

Lucas had even less knowledge about film than he had about art, which was nil. But he had seen plenty of Hollywood movies in the Modesto theater and occasionally, in the dark, had realized that he could do better than *that.*

Lucas, to his amazement, was accepted by U.S.C. In his first year he was out of place. His feelings about films and film making were vague. He didn't make any films that first year and was not part of the cinema department establishment. During his second year, he woke up to film and discovered that there was more to film making than just shooting and screening. He discovered that there were some students who were just plain film nuts, just as he had known some people who were just plain sports car nuts. He began relating to the film people and, more importantly, he began watching films and understanding what he was watching. He discovered that he could talk to some of the film nuts, even though they had been living and breathing film for years and he had just begun film work.

During his second year, Lucas began hungering to make a film. He spent a lot of time hanging around the screening rooms and the productions and the editing booths. He wasted time *constructively.* By the time he got into his first real film class, he was ready for film making.

His first class was an animation class with Herbert Kosower. Lucas was limited to 36 feet of film, with the admonition: "That's all the footage that you can have but you can do anything you want with it." Lucas, believing that this was his big chance, instantly got into trouble by flagrantly going over the footage limits that Kosower had set. Lucas was not known in the department—he didn't have any kind of a reputation—therefore his disobedience was, as he now says, "a big chance."

Lucas's first film was called *A Look At Life* and was a breakthrough. Although primitive, it was the first time at U.S.C. that students had done anything like it; he used quick cutting, montages, and satire to show his view of international news and the world around him.

It only whetted his appetite for more work.

The next semester Lucas had three classes in the department;

two production classes and one film expression class. In the production classes he did *Herbie,* with Paul Golding. Originally Lucas had no title for the film. The eventual name was chosen for no other reason than that the student who did the original music for the sound track was named Herbie. Lucas has now forgotten what his last name was. *Herbie* was again a breakthrough and it still didn't endear him to the department heads. Lucas took a camera onto Hoover Street, which is near the cinema department building, and shot night scenes of reflections on automobile finishes, the blur of disappearing taillights, the reflections of on-coming headlights, and the flash and splash of neon lights. He edited the film to match the jazz track produced by Herbie whats-his-name. An exceptionally well filmed and scored project, it was runner-up at the National Student Film Festival the year of its competition (about 1966—Lucas is not sure).

From *Freiheit,* a statement in film about freedom and personal values, by George Lucas.

By the time Lucas had won the film award for *Herbie,* he had still further angered the cinema department faculty. His next film, *Freiheit* (German for freedom), added a new patina to the surface of their anger. Lucas knew what he wanted to say in the film, but "the idea looked silly written down," so he did not make a very adequate shooting script, which is anathema in the department.

Freiheit was Lucas's first experience at working with a Movieola and he considered the experience a disaster. He had 200 feet of film and the idea of making an anti-war statement; he did. He took a Bolex and several crew members into the Malibu Canyon, which is the "backlot" for U.S.C. film makers, where the old Republic Serials were made, and he shot a film of a freedom-seeking man running from East to West Germany. It was the "usual rebellious student thing," Lucas says.

It was also a poignant statement about freedom and the hypocrisy of some citizens who don't believe in freedom to the extent of dying for it. It too, was an exceptional student film.

At the beginning of Lucas's next semester, he knew that he was about to be drafted. He took the "480" film course, the crew class for film production, in which the students make two films, a five-week project and a ten-week project. Lucas discovered that the faculty was attempting to build the student's character by grouping individuals and forcing them to work together on a single production. Lucas found himself on a crew that was to make what was, in Lucas's eyes, a ludicrous project, a film titled *Herman Dink's Big Date.*

"Everybody thought small—and had little ambition," Lucas says. "They had no scope. I fought with that film crew again and again. I thought that it was senseless doing that film. The director didn't really know what he was doing or how to get the film finished, either. I was constantly in trouble with the authorities in the department because I objected to this senseless disaster. I finally reached an agreement with them—I'd take over the film and try to rescue it and in exchange, I'd get to produce a film of my own next."

Herman Dink's Big Date was never to be mentioned again, even with Lucas's job of attempting to salvage it. But with it, he bought his freedom to make a film *his way.* There were several things that undergraduates had never done at U.S.C.: they had never gone much beyond Malibu Canyon to shoot; they had never used color in an undergraduate film; and they had never attempted such additional liabilities as shooting from an airplane.

Lucas broke the rules and did all those things in his film *1.42.08.* It was a purely visual film that Lucas shot in three days in Willow Springs, California, over the hills of Malibu Canyon and 100 miles into the California desert. Lucas had the entire film storyboarded with polaroid pictures before he began to shoot. And he played the game the department's way; they would not buy him more color film, so Lucas went without lunch for several weeks and bought it himself. They would not rent an airplane for his overhead shots, so Lucas found a friend who had a plane and they shot out the side cockpit window. *14208* involves a sports car time trial; a practice run to see how fast a precision automobile will cover a rolling, twisting track. Lucas had problems all the way through the shooting. The desert light was wrong for color shooting, the sports car broke down during the shooting and the footage from the airplane was so blurred and bouncing that it had to be scrapped. Lucas shot 1,000 feet of stock, but what was more important at the time, he brought the edited film in at the ten week limit, which was unusual. Nearly all ten-week films in that course were in production well past the ten-week period.

As a result of his one-man production and completion of *14208*, Lucas flunked his draft physical examination. He had mononucleosis and aggravated diabetes.

Consequently, Lucas found that he didn't have to worry about the army. What he did have to think about was what he should

Film maker George Lucas relaxes on the deserted Warner Brothers' backlot in Burbank, California. On the basis of *THX—1138—4eb* and other films, he got a job with the Coppola Production Company, making films for release by Warner Brothers. These films include *Finian's Rainbow* and *The Rain People*. (Photo by the author)

do next. Prior to the date of his physical, he had not even considered what he was to do because he had assumed that he would be drafted.

Lucas found what he wanted in the U.S.C. cinema department. For several years the department had a working agreement with the Navy. The Navy would, yearly, send about a dozen career film makers to U.S.C. for additional study. The Navy cameramen had an unlimited supply of cameras, film, and equipment, but no one wanted to teach them. The problem was simple and not easily solved: the Navy men acted like junior high school kids. They already knew how to make films—the Navy way. They knew how to shoot but not what to film. They had technical knowledge but no imagination. They were positive that they were always right. Consequently, they interrupted the lecturers, slept in class, jeered, threw erasers at each other, and generally misbehaved scandalously.

Lucas offered to teach the Navies. His offer was gratefully accepted by the faculty members who were tired of trying to deal

Citizen 1138 runs from his society in the film *THX—1138—4eb*. George Lucas used white uniforms from the University of Southern California Dental department and shot the film in the University's computer center, the Los Angeles International Airport, and the U.C.L.A. parking lot. (Courtesy of University of Southern California Film Department)

with them. Lucas came into the class very much in trouble; he was smaller than the Navy men and weighed just about 120 pounds. He was younger than they were and he didn't command respect.

But Lucas had some ideas about how to treat the men. He quickly announced that there's be no tests and no papers required for the course, which delighted them. All they would have to do, for the semester, Lucas said, would be shoot a film and they wouldn't even have to worry about a script, because he had already written it.

Overjoyed at the prospects of frolicking through the semester, the Navy men agreed. So Lucas filmed *THX—1138-4eb*. He shot at night at the U.S.C. Computer Center; he shot at night in desolate sections of the Los Angeles International Airport; and he shot at night in deserted parts of the five-story U.C.L.A. parking lot. The Navy men were so amused at Lucas's shooting schedule that it became a joke. Lucas occasionally didn't have enough light to see the readings on his light meters. So the Navy men would shout "Open 'em up," and the cameraman would shoot with the lens open as wide as possible.

THX—1138-4eb has no special meaning as a title. It got to be an inside joke to pronounce it with a lisp, making it "thicks"—

An ingenious use of location shots. In *THX—1138—4eb*, this scene was shot at night in a deserted area of the Los Angeles International Airport, but it appears to be a futuristic city. (Courtesy of University of Southern California Film Department)

1138-4eb. Lucas went to the U.S.C. Dental department and "borrowed" white uniforms. Some of the Navy men appeared in the film, as operators of the computer equipment.

And Lucas completed *THX*—the best student science-fiction film ever made. In scope it rivals Stanley Kubrick's expensive

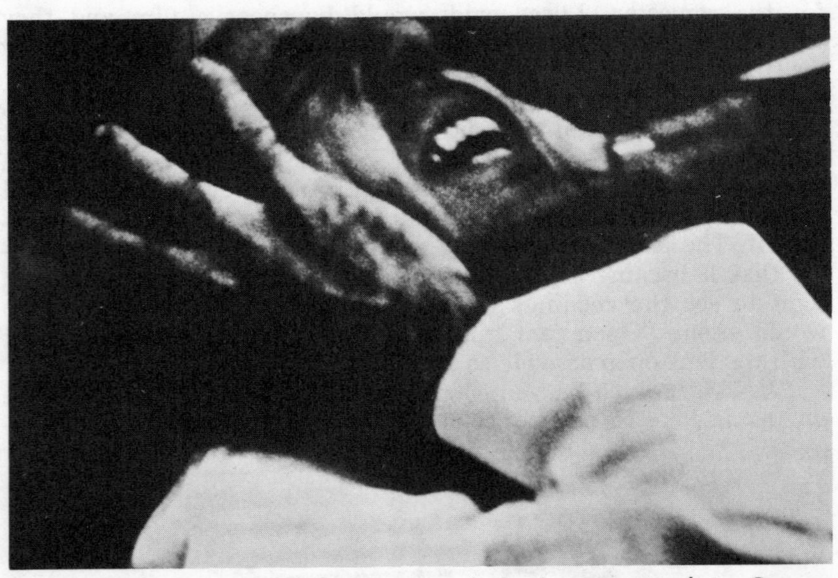

Citizen 1138 is numbed by waves of deafening sound in George Lucas's *THX—1138—4eb*. (Courtesy of University of Southern California Film Department)

2001: A Space Odyssey. In camera technique (he is best known as an excellent cameraman) it surpasses all of Lucas's previous work.

THX—1138-4eb concerns a citizen numbered 1138, not named, who attempts to escape from a futuristic computer-controlled society. He runs and runs, through the deserted airport passageways, attempting to evade the all-watchful eyes of monitor cameras. Constant checks are made on his whereabouts by programmed scanners, sequences that Lucas ran through a television screen and reshot. At one point in the film, 1138 takes an elevator and Lucas's crew shot down into the elevator through the open emergency door in the cabin ceiling. Citizen 1138 is nearly killed with high-frequency sound waves in the elevator, but escapes, and continues to run down passageways and through doors, into different levels in the city, and past monitor cameras. He kills

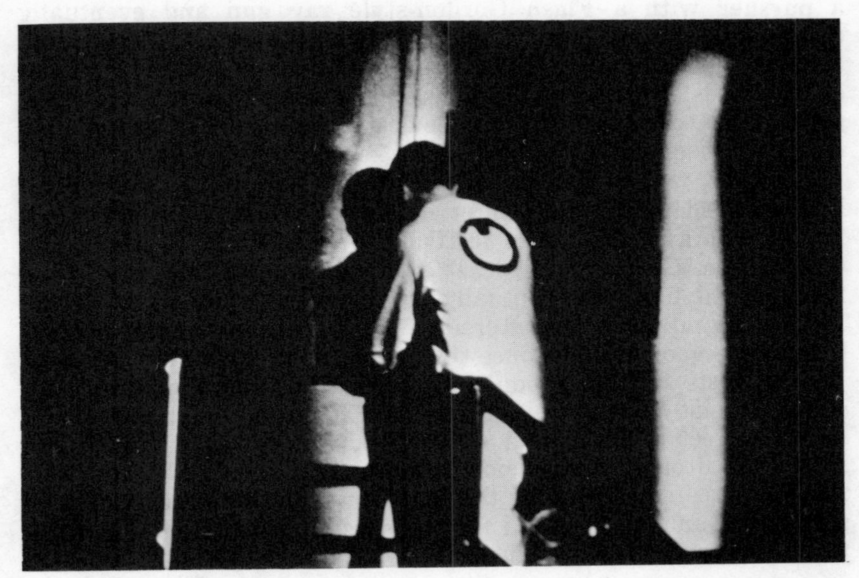

The hero, Citizen 1138, attempts to evade his electronic pursuers in *THX—1138—4eb.* (Courtesy of University of Southern California Film Department)

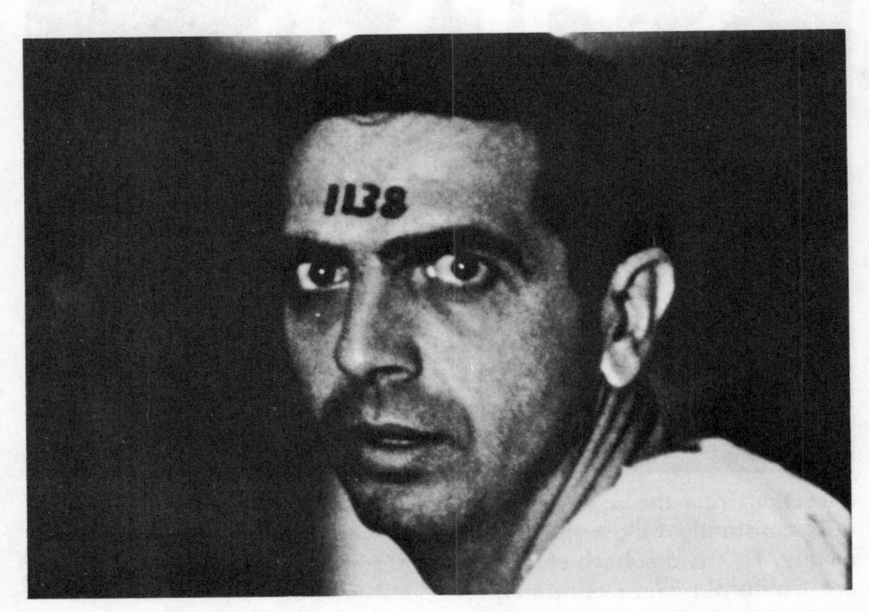

The frightened hero of *THX—1138—4eb.* This is one of the finest student-produced films done recently. (Courtesy of University of Southern California Film Department)

a pursuer with a Flash Gordon-style ray gun and eventually escapes his *Brave New World—1984* existence. At film's end, 1138 is shown in a low color telephoto lens shot, running across empty fields into the twilight. And the sound track announces, presumably to his wife, "1138 has destroyed himself. You are now free to choose another mate on level seven."

THX—1138-4eb won an award at the National Student Film Festival held in Lincoln Center in New York in February 1968. It also won awards at film festivals in Edinburgh, Scotland and Oberhausen, Germany. At least as important, to Lucas, was the fact that the film was eventually approved and appreciated by the Navy crew, all of whom offered to work with him again. Several became his good friends, once they understood what he was doing.

Film costs for the production were $700, and the completed, edited version runs 15 minutes in final form. At one point, Lucas shot 600 feet of black and white film, which was edited to 300 feet, run through a television monitor, and then reshot in color for the screening effect of the monitor. Five hundred feet were shot on an animation board for the special side timing and monitoring sequences seen in the film.

A section from the science-fiction film *THX—1138—4eb*. Monitor cameras constantly follow the hero, 1138, with readings like this. Technically, *THX* is a suberb student film. (Courtesy of University of Southern California Film Department)

A button is pushed and citizen 1138 becomes trapped in *THX—1138—4eb*. The scenes in the control center were filmed in the U.S.C. Computer Center. (Courtesy of University of Southern California Film Department)

Citizen 1138 looks for a way out of his trap. Note the number 1138 on the hero's forehead. (Courtesy of University of Southern California Film Department)

Time magazine commented on THX in a recent issue: *THX—1138-4eb,* by George Lucas, 23, of U.S.C., is a sci-fi chiller that looks at a cowardly new world where two varieties of humanoids, the "crosbods," and the "clinicbods," wander through dark corridors and light-pierced concrete caverns in pursuit of the only truly human character, "THX" . . . A vision of *1984,* it evoked in 15 minutes a future world in which man is enslaved by computers and TV monitors. Although portentous in theme, THX impressed the (National Student Film Festival) judges with its technical virtuosity: Lucas shot his future-oriented film entirely in present-day Los Angeles—much as Jean Luc Godard, one of his cinematic heroes, shot the nightmare *Alphaville* entirely in contemporary Paris.

On the basis of *THX—1138-4eb,* Lucas got a job with Francis Ford Coppola, the producer of *Finian's Rainbow* and *The Rain People.* (Coppola is another outstanding graduate, who will be discussed in the U.C.L.A. chapter). *THX* was bought by the Coppolas production company, American Zoetrope Co., to be written in full-length version by Lucas and Walter Murch for Warner

The hero of George Lucas's film *THX—1138—4eb* looks for a way out. The film, done on a smaller scale than *2001: A Space Odyssey,* equals it in technical skill and photographic effects. (Courtesy of University of Southern California Film Department)

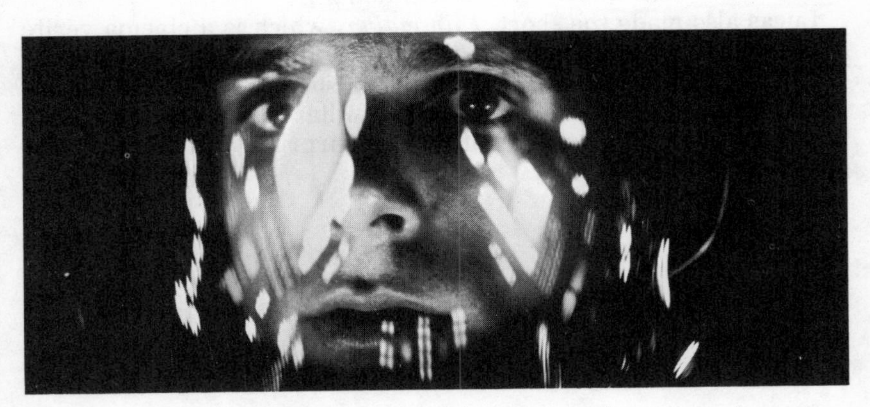

Commander David Bowman, played by Keir Dullea, goes through a time warp in the MGM film *2001: A Space Odyssey*. Naturally, no student could compete with the enormous time and money put into *Space Odyssey,* but some students produce excellent films on a lower budget and with less help—George Lucas and his *THX—1138—4eb,* for instance. © 1968 by Metro-Goldwyn-Mayer, Inc.

The 1968 MGM film *2001: A Space Odyssey* was a great favorite among college students. George Lucas's film *THX—1138—4eb* was a similar film done on a student budget. © 1968 by Metro-Goldwyn-Mayer Inc.

Brothers. The Warner version will be filmed in San Francisco, Los Angeles, Houston, and Toyko computer centers and will be directed by Lucas. Coppola will be the executive producer and the film will star Donald Pleasence and Robert Duvall, who was in Coppola's *The Rain People.* Lucas and Coppola expect to bring in the entire film under one million dollars.

Lucas also made the short, *Filmmaker,* which is a cinema vérité film about the production of *The Rain People.*

Although George Lucas's tremendous success with *THX* is unusual, the fact that there are many similarily talented people in film work at U.S.C. is not unusual or surprising. It is taken for granted.

2.
The University of California at Los Angeles

THE INDIVIDUAL FILM MAKER; OBERN; HIGGINS; COPPOLA

The two largest film schools on the west coast, the University of Southern California and the University of California at Los Angeles, couldn't be more dissimilar. Southern California, housed in an old barn-like building, is drab and tawdry compared to U.C.L.A.'s two and one-half million dollar buildings. The lack of suitable equipment at U.S.C. seems ridiculous compared to the million dollars worth of cameras, stages, and equipment that U.C.L.A. possesses. And the concepts that the two schools hold are completely opposite in character.

U.S.C. believes in the team concept of film making—the idea that a crew of three or four or five film makers producing a film together is a viable production technique. On the other hand, U.C.L.A., across town, believes in the individual concept—that one film maker learns how to make films by being his own writer, cameraman, editor, and producer. The U.S.C. students and faculty are convinced that their method is best. U.C.L.A. students and staff are no less convinced that they have the right attitude.

U.C.L.A. however, is a relative new-comer to film work on the west coast. U.S.C. has drawn on professional lecturers since the late 1920s. U.C.L.A., on the other hand, was not founded as a film school until 1947. It now offers bachelor's and master's degrees in film. On the master's level, students have the option of taking a Master of Fine Arts degree and submitting a film as a creative thesis, or they have the alternative of submitting a written thesis, usually in history of film or film criticism, and receiving the Master of Arts degree.

The University of California at Los Angeles suffers in ways that do not bother Southern California. U.C.L.A. is a part of the vast California college and university system and thus must accept any qualified student. U.S.C., on the other hand, is a private university and need not accept everybody who applies. And although the film departments of both schools are crowded, U.C.L.A. has the heaviest burden of students. As a consequence of state policy, U.C.L.A. now has 450 students who claim to be film majors. Hugh Grauel, director of production and a lecturer in theater arts, believes this figure may be high. All beginning University students must list a major, but the department only accepts juniors as actual film majors. So the exact number of film students in the department at any time may be hidden in two confusing sets of figures—the Registrar's and the department's. More than half of the majors in the department are graduate students and this percentage will increase in the next few years, while the percentage of undergraduate majors will remain the same or taper off. U.C.L.A., like most of the larger film schools, is becoming a graduate school of film primarily because graduate students are more articulate and older; they come equipped with a better film sense

One of the three sound stages at U.C.L.A. This is a western set during a pause in shooting. The stages at U.C.L.A. are among the few facilities on the west coast specifically designed for sound shooting, instead of being converted from silent film stages. (Photo by the author)

than undergraduates, and know better what they want to accomplish while they are in the department.

The department enrollment has jumped in the last four years from 175 students to the present 450 or so. This, according to Grauel, is too many; the equipment and facilities were designed for a student population of 200. Consequently, Grauel admits,

Students using the sound recording studios at U.C.L.A. It has the best equipment of any school in the country. (Photo by the author)

there is a tremendous logistics problem. All the students want to use the department's cameras and equipment. But there are only a limited number of cameras: two Eclairs, eight Aires, ten or twelve eight millimeter cameras, and twenty-three editing booths.

"We have to assign five or six students to each editing booth," Grauel says, "and this is a very bad situation. We have to keep the cameras circulating through small groups of students for maximum use."

The situation at U.C.L.A. has caused a peculiar problem that is very seldom articulated but often felt; the students—in the two and one-half million dollar buildings, Macgowan Hall, the

Macgowan Hall, the 2½ million-dollar home of the film department on the U.C.L.A. campus. (Photo by the author)

departmental offices, and Melnitz Auditorium, which houses the editing rooms, offices, and sound stages—are unhappy. They seldom mention it, but the problem of logistics and the concept of the individual film maker leads to a problem of separation and alienation. Macgowan Hall is a truly beautiful campus building. It is situated at the edge of the Franklin Murphy sculpture garden, a beautiful series of patios, plazas, and benches, with rolling grasses and huge modern statuary. But the students, inside the sterile atmosphere of Macgowan and Melnitz, feel isolated. Occasionally one can wander down the halls of Melnitz, past door after door of editing booths, and not see anyone. If one opens a door here or there, there may be students inside the booths, quietly editing film. There is less rapport in the modern U.C.L.A. facilities than there is in the old, dirty building at Southern California. This aspect of U.C.L.A. film production is recognized, but few really know what to do about it. And it is unfortunate because sometimes the atmosphere acts against the creativity of the student, instead of with him.

But still the students do seem to get their work done and the films eventually get into the cans.

U.C.L.A. does not pay more than a token amount for students' materials. As a consequence, many students spend much of their own money for film and equipment during their course work.

Production courses at U.C.L.A. are three: they are simply called Project One, Project Two, and Project Three. Only the first course is for undergraduates. In it students make eight millimeter films with 16 millimeter sound. The University has a budget of $100 for each film, but additional raw footage for up to about 800 feet may cost the student from $50–$150. The University provides $500 for film for the Project Two course, in which students make 16 millimeter sound films, which generally run 3–4,000 feet in raw stock. Additional film may cost the student upwards of $500 for these projects. Project Three films are designed to be lip-synchronization films and usually run 15–20 minutes. Again, students are expected to make up the difference between the departmental budget for the film and the final cost of the project. Students have been known to sink $500 to $2,000 of of their own money into a Project Three film. But since the students own the films, they can try to sell them for commercial distribution, if possible. Some do.

Richard Hawkins, former chairman of the department and now associate professor of theater arts, has commented, "the expectation of our students has risen sharply in the last few years. The department switched from Bell and Howell cameras to Airflexs in 1964 and for a while, the Airflexs were considered ideal cameras. But now the students are dissatisfied with them and are looking for better equipment. The Panavision Company, which has worked with us, has adapted their lenses to sixteen millimeter work, so that our students can work in wide-screen films. But we really don't know where to look for more equipment. A statewide bond issue for more equipment was voted down, so we don't know where we are going to get money and equipment. We have been turning to eight millimeter and urge students to buy their own cameras. We think of eight millimeter as a 'scratchpaper' medium, which is simple and responsive. It isn't as inhibiting as some of the larger cameras and fosters a flexible and personal approach. In the summer of 1969, we plan to switch to all super-eight editing equipment."

Ralph Sargent, who was formerly on the faculty at U.C.L.A., elaborated on this in an article "8mm at U.C.L.A.," which appeared in *Film Quarterly* magazine.

The Motion Picture Division of the Theater Arts Department of U.C.L.A. generally works in 16 millimeter. However, with the large enrollment of students, it is not possible to equip every student with a sixteen millimeter camera. It is for this reason that eight millimeter is being used to introduce students to film making. In effect, eight millimeter, because of its small cameras (requiring a minimum of accessories) and the low cost of film stock, is used extensively as the "sketch pad" of the beginning student.

Not only have we attempted to provide the students with a basic picture-recording device, we have also attempted to duplicate the sound-recording potential and editing flexibility of the larger and more expensive gauges. At U.C.L.A. it is possible to make an eight millimeter double-system, lip-synch., mixed, sound motion picture—and do it at a fraction of the cost of sixteen millimeter.

Of the many different types of film stock available, we find that the students tend to divide about evenly in their use of color and black-and-white. Though Kodak only retains eight millimeter color films, it does make many of its sixteen millimeter black-and-white films with eight millimeter perforations on special order. A number of companies, scattered throughout the United States, offer these films respooled for eight millimeter camera use. Dupont does likewise. Perutz black-and-white films is generally available directly from photo stores.

The University stocks five different types of eight millimeter cameras for student use. They are: Sekonic Micro-Eye F, Jelco Zoom Eight, Kodak Automatic Eight, Bell and Howell Type 134 and Fairchild Sound Eight. The Sekonic is the most popular with the students primarily because of its reflex viewfinder, fully automatic exposure controls (which may be locked out), single-frame devise and focussing zoom lens. The Kodak and Bell and Howell cameras are only occasionally used since they lack interchangeable lenses and are quite inflexible compared to the Sekonic and Jelco. The Fairchild is used for single and double-system sound work. It has been modified by the addition of a governor-controlled motor and synch generator for use with any of the well-known synch tape recorders (Nagra, Perfectone, Rangertone, etc.) but still retains its single-system recording capability. Whenever possible, tripods are checked out with the cameras as most students soon learn the value of steady camera support.

In most cases the eight millimeter films produced by students are screened and returned to the students. In a few cases, however, the films are of sufficient interest to show to a larger audience than within the film school. For this reason we print our best eight millimeter on sixteen millimeter for general exhibition at our semi-annual public screenings. This work is handled for us by Color Reproduction Company in Hollywood and the quality has been uniformly excellent. We have never dealt in eight millimeter-to-eight millimeter printing and none of our films originally photographed in any gauge are released in eight millimeter.

Recently we have been discussing converting to Super Eight as our standard "sketch" gauge. However, this presents certain specific problems which have not yet been solved by the manufacturers:

(1) The only film available is Kodachrome II. But our students make close to fifty percent of their films in black-and-white and when questioned on their choice fervently support black-and-white as being the best for whatever they did.

(2) Not until the introduction of the Beaulieu Super Eight camera did there exist a camera which really provided the flexibility and quality needed. The Beaulieu's high price, however, severely restricts the number of cameras that we may be able to make available to the students.

(3) Blow-up and print services are not yet available for Super Eight and this would make it impossible for us to exhibit our films publicly.

(4) The Movieolas we presently own for eight millimeter cannot be adapted to handle Super Eight and would have to be supplemented by new machines especially designed for this application. Once again we are hampered by budget.

In the average semester we make close to two hundred eight millimeter films of various lengths. Despite the effort that we have made to bring eight millimeter to the same flexibility of the larger gauges, students still insist upon using the medium as a "throw-away" and perhaps rightly so. Our basic aim is to teach film making. If eight millimeter, through its low cost, ready availability, and lack of mechanical impediment, contributes to a student's ability to test his ideas and visually learn from his mistakes, then its use, in any form, is justified.

There are two aspects of public screenings available at U.C.L.A. "Our semi-annual public screenings" that Sargent mentioned are the Royce Hall shows. Royce Hall is one of the bigger buildings on the U.C.L.A. campus and showings are held twice an academic year, usually in December and then again in late April or May. There are usually a dozen or so advanced films shown on four successive evenings and tickets are $1.75. Advertisements and reviews in the *Los Angeles Times* and the *Los Angeles Free Press*, the hippie newspaper, carry the word of special films. There are usually several hundred turned away from the shows.

The other aspect of student film showings is "Potluck at Melnitz," a weekly screening of whatever is available. Students may drop their films in a pick-up box for the shows, and show anything or everything that they have. They can also, if they feel like it, or have enough ego, show their films week after week at Melnitz. The auditorium in Melnitz is capable of seating only a few hundred, and these shows are mainly for the students themselves, as contrasted to the Royce Hall shows, which are as much a public event as a departmental show. The film people from the University of Southern California usually drive across town on the multitude of freeways for the Royce Hall films, but rarely drop in for Potluck, unless they happen to be in the vicinity for other purposes.

Some of the best student films of recent vintage from U.C.L.A. are:

A Beginning by G. Scott Heyman. In black and white, *Beginning* begins with shots of a hip girl smoking a joint of marijuana and gaily dancing along a sidewalk, window-shopping at night. She wanders off to an old rococo house, where her boyfriend explains that he is fed up with college life, uptight, can't take it any more, doesn't know who or where he is, and will join the Army the next day. The girl takes down a pop-poster of California Governor Ronald Reagan, dressed as a cowboy from one of his old western films, removes the boy's supply of pot from a hole in the wall, and offers him some. He refuses her silent invitation to make love. Cutting to the next morning, the boy finds a $20 bill taped to a bathroom mirror with an admonition written in lipstick to reconsider his threats to join the Army. The boy then leaves, and wanders downtown. He does try to enlist, but the local recruiting sergeant is busy and the camera watches through the window, noting the hazy enlistment posters. The boy wanders into a hillbilly bar where his bearing and general demeanor is enough to make him the butt of an attack from a bar bum. The boy attempts to avoid the attack non-violently by holding on to the attacker's leg and curling into a fetal position, but then goes berserk and hysterically attacks the aggressor, screaming, "why did you do that to me? Why did you do that to me?" The boy knocks the bully under a pool table, unconscious, and leaves the bar. At the film's end, the boy pauses and enters a theater, presumably to seek solace in the quiet afternoon matinee. And as he pauses to buy his ticket, the camera pulls back, encompassing the entire marquee and sidewalk and from across the street, the point of the film is made clear with the existential advertisement on the marquee: THE MAN WITH NO NAME . . . IS BACK.

Now That The Buffalo's Gone by Burton Hirschfield is a tour-de-force in color work. Free-lance writer Nat Freedland, in an article titled "Films At U.C.L.A.," in *Cavalier* magazine, noted: "Done mostly in tinted negatives of old stills and Western movie chases, the film was a hauntingly nightmarish evocation of North America's pioneer genocide of the Indian. The ghostlike quality of the montage of fast moving negatives made a stunning icon for the murder of a great native culture. The film was like a layout from the Haight-Ashbury *Oracle* come to life; certainly its freshness of imagery was as important as the way it revealed once more that the grandchildren of the cowboys would rather be Indians. Because Indians have more fun and aren't as uptight as Grandpa Barry Goldwater/John Wayne."

Technically, the film was a risky venture. The tinted negatives that Freedland refers to were "solarized"—a process of dying during development. This is risky because the chemicals must be exactly the right temperature; one or two degrees too hot or too cold will ruin the whole film. No commercial processor would guarantee the service; fortunately the processing *did* turn out well and the film is an extremely well done statement. The old prints are dyed orange, purple, pinks, blues, and the Indians are shown tending fires, hunting, living peacefully—until the Cavalry comes along. It is a powerful film, done in an extremely interesting and difficult technique.

The Labor And Anticipation of Abigail the Third, As Performed In An Antiseptic Miracle is a Project Two film by Don Guy. In color, it explores the pregnancy of Abigail and her dreams at the time. She is shown wandering down a beach. She is alternately alone on the beach or pursued by a crotchety old obstetrician, who pushes a hospital cart ahead of him in the sand. She wanders down a boardwalk and he follows. The film cuts back and forth to a hospital scene à la Ben Casey, in which she is rolled down a hospital corridor on the same cart toward the operating room. The film has a rare beauty, coupled with an intense study of a peacefully pregnant girl awaiting her baby.

Tangier Dream Cycle by Bill Kaplan Jr. is actually two different films with the same title because Kaplan is hung up on a motorcycle theme and on that particular title. His first film is a mixed media film, in which *Tangier Dream Cycle* is projected on an auditorium screen. The film surveys a wild motorcycle scene; the motorcycle involved is on the stage of the auditorium. The actors in the film, in the audience, get onto the stage to recreate and elaborate on their actions in the film. The motorcycle is started with a tremendous racket, and the sound track of the film is kept going. It is a visual and audio ménage, a cacophony of light and sound.

Kaplan's second film of the same title involves a motorcycle gang and a surrealistic dream sequence that a girl has with a motorcycle. The motorcycle gang are shown riding their "hogs," screaming around corners and roaring down streets. They are, in fact, a Hell's-Angel type gang. *Dream Cycle* begins with a normal screen size in black and white film. During the action, the screen is pulled back and most of the film is shown in Panavision. The enlargement of the film and the technicalities of the expansion to the wide-screen Panavision took Kaplan nine months to work out —but in final form, the film lasts only ten minutes. And at the end of the film, the audience is shocked; it has been caught off-guard: *the cycle gang are all lesbians.* There is no male in the film whatsoever. This fact is not only surprising on the screen, but was difficult for Kaplan to film. He had personality problems with the "girls" throughout most of the production of the film.

Laudate by Nicholas Frangakis was a summer workshop project. Frangakis based *Laudate* on Igor Stravinsky's Symphony of Psalms, and the film was made in color, with the aid of the Benedictine Community at Valyermo, California. It is 12 minutes long and follows the Benedictine monks praying, meditating, working in the community, and even joggling down country lanes. Frangakis intercuts this with quick flashes of the southern California megalopolis, with its frenetic rush. The quiet of the Benedictine community seems even more tranquil. *Laudate* is a very lush and beautiful film, breathtakingly so, particularly during sequences of the monks on retreat in the desert, lifting their communion cups against the rising sun and the rising symphony on the sound track.

Goldwater A Go Go by Michael Ahnemann and Gary Schlosser is a cinema vérité study of the teenage girls who wore boater hats and Goldwater sweatshirts and enlivened the crowds during southern California appearance by Goldwater during his abortive campaign against Lyndon Johnson.

Keinholz On Exhibit by June Steel was described by writer Freedland in *Cavalier* as:

> The most complete all-around film . . . , a satisfyingly thorough documentary about the big controversy over the "Barney's Beanery" artist's big show at the Los Angeles County Museum. A procession of museum goers—squares, hippies, even a nun—were interviewed as they passed the exhibit. Meanwhile, the camera was also catching the absurd restrictions that had to be put on the display when local rightist know-nothings began to howl.
>
> Keinholz's "1938 Dodge" with the drippy plaster casts of a couple balling in the back seat was only thrown open to view for a few moments at a time to explain the artist's Real Message. Ditto with the meticulous mock-up of a W. W. II Vegas whorehouse. Miss Steel's inquisitive camera poked about with the dead-center cathartic honesty of a Lenny Bruce monologue.

Incidentally, the film was only completed a year after the 1966 exhibit because June Steel had to drop it for a six-month full-time job before she could afford to go back and complete the editing.

And It Goes On And On was also a documentary done by Cheryl Hunter. Freedland, in *Cavalier,* wrote:

> Another documentary that hit home . . . *And It Goes On And On* . . . followed a cute brunette coed named Lynne Blaikie through a series of magnificently inane sorority-fraternity bashes—beer-belching, and pie-throwing extravaganzas. The sound track featured Miss Blaikie's ad-lib musings on the existential bummers of the Greek letter system. Film maker Cheryl, a busty blond California golden-girl, reports that she and Lynne quit the sorority two weeks after the film was safely finished.

The Season, an advanced workshop project by Donald MacDonald, is a 15-minute color examination of Christmas in California, which notes the palm trees, the wreathes, the department-store Santa Clauses, and the rest of the gimmickry.

William Lloyd Norton's *Coming Soon* is a parody of commercial war films. It is four-minutes long and features a hero named "Rock Balls," who is seen at the end of the film waving an American flag and running through a military war cemetery.

Imago by Richard Stanton is the study of a latent homosexual who has apparently been psychologically castrated by an over-protective mother. It is eleven minutes long, in black-and-white, and was a summer project by Stanton.

The Diggers is half-documentary, half-poetry—a study of a communal farm run by The Diggers, a California hippie-communal group. The highlight of the film, most commercial critics have noted, is a nude romp by the group in the grass of a rural pasture. It was done by Attila Domokos.

One of the few girls doing exceptional films is Pennelope Spherris, a dark, dusky, 24-year-old brunette who came originally from New Orleans. She is a very audacious girl, who has taken many risks during her film making that girls would not normally take.

One of her films, *Synthesis,* is a seven-minute, science-fiction film that took her three months to complete. It is concerned with a future civilization in which computers "talk" with each other. It was chosen second best film among 150 that were made and shown during one quarter at U.C.L.A.

But her most energetic film, and most risky, was a film titled *The National Rehabilitation Center.* When she first conceived it, the film was to be a "documentary about something that did not

One of the few interested in film is Pennelope Spherris, who has done several exceptional films while at U.C.L.A. She also contemplates graduate work in film. (Photo by the author)

exist," namely the possibilities that the government could, under certain circumstances, begin a political dragnet that would intern and hold political radicals in federal concentration camps. As she was discussing the idea with friends, they said, "oh, you mean the Internal Securities Act of 1959." Not knowing that such an act existed, and not realizing that she was basing her film on it, was a surprise to Pennelope. She began checking and found that her envisaged film did indeed correspond to the 1959 Act. Whereupon, she began filming a pseudo-documentary, projecting what might happen if the act was ever evoked. She began filming at a local Sheriff's Honor Camp, shooting scenes of prisoners wearing "county blues," denim work clothes. She gained access to the camp by claiming that she needed stock footage of camp scenes because she was filming a documentary about various prison camps. After finishing the stock footage, she claimed that she needed extra footage, footage that would correspond to the view from the narrator's eyes. With this excuse, she shot scenes that were supposed to be off limits to cameramen. She also gained access to secret western Army arms depots and shot footage within them. She had interviews with guards and workers at the camps, which she threw out in favor of the footage that she claimed was background material, "what the hero sees." She eventually had 12,000 feet of raw stock, and edited that down to 1,200 feet for a final composite print.

No less audacious is Vaughn Obern, whose *Hey, Mama* is an award-winning film. *Hey, Mama* was a Project Three film that Obern conceived, wrote, directed, and edited.

"It is a day in the life of a guy in a ghetto," Obern says. "That might be a cliché, but that's what it is."

Obern began production in the Oakwood district of Venice, California. At first, the negro residents disliked and distrusted him.

Vaughn Obern, who filmed *Hey Mama,* a documentary of life in a ghetto, paid for most of his own film. U.C.L.A. is one of the schools that do not pay for student's film. The students pay for their own films and consequently have the opportunity to try and sell them for commercial showings. (Photo by the author)

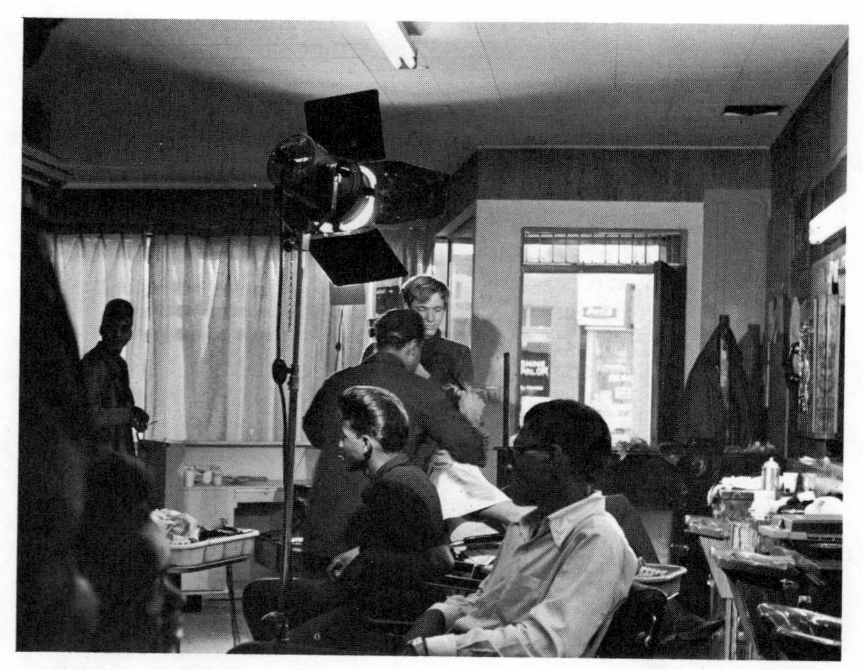

Vaughn Obern's crew on location filming *Hey, Mama* in Los Angeles.

They believed that he was "a big Hollywood producer" come to trick them in some way. But Obern had patience. He hung around, with his equipment, until he was an accepted part of the neighborhood. He became a local fixture and eventually was accepted and reasonably trusted. The shooting for *Hey, Mama* took six months, because even after Obern had the trust of the participants, he could never count on them. Fully half of the appointments that Obern made for shooting were never fulfilled—the blacks didn't show up. The filming was not without hazards either. One night Obern was filming at a party in the home of Leonard McAdoo, the hero of the film. Suddenly, another black became enraged at the lights and the equipment. He knocked over the lights, smashed a tape recorder, and pulled out a .38 revolver. "McAdoo chased the guy into the streets with a kitchen knife and that was the end of that," Obern remembers. "Everything was cool the next day. But a month or so later, the guy was killed in a street fight."

Another time during the filming, Obern was shooting outside, in a public park. McAdoo and some of his friends bought some wine and were drinking. Suddenly a fight started. To Obern's surprise, 12 police cars converged on the scene, lights flashing, sirens screaming. The filming ended with the arrest of several Negroes and a general mini-riot. Obern kept his cameras rolling as long as he could and in the final print, it *is* surprising: one moment the viewer is watching McAdoo and his friends relaxing and the next

Leonard McAdoo, the hero of Vaughn Obern's *Hey, Mama,* gets his hair straightened.

moment the viewer subconsciously counts the number of police cars that have magically appeared, as if on cue, and parked in lines down both sides of the street. "It was embarrassing," Obern says. "The police thought that I started the riot just for the sake of filming it. They were not happy about the riot at all. And later, they denied permission to another U.C.L.A. student to film in the same location. They told him 'Obern started that riot for himself. We won't let that happen again.' "

From a section of *Hey, Mama* by Vaughn Obern. Leonard McAdoo holds the dollar bill.

Hey, Mama won second prize for a documentary film at the Fourth National Student Film Festival, held at Lincoln Center, New York, in March 1969.

Obern likes cinema vérité; his other films that he is most proud of are an extended analysis of a Gestalt psychology session. They involved eight people and a psychologist. Obern shot 40,000 feet of film with three Eclair cameras and used synchronized sound. He made two separate films of the sessions for two different purposes. One film is a study of what a therapy weekend is like; the other will be used as a training film for psychologists, exposing them to what their role in such a project involves.

"We had the rooms lighted before the sessions began," Obern explained. "One cameraman shot the psychologist only. Another cameraman stayed with the patient. The third cameraman was free to roam around and film whatever seemed interesting at the time.

"We found that during the first half hour, everyone was aware of the cameras. After that, we could have stood in their laps for all the difference it would have made to them."

Obern paid for $5,500 worth of film and salaries to his cameramen by working as a cameraman on another film. He also worked as a sound technician on other crews to make money necessary for the project.

Students not only know what they should be doing well; they also know what glaring mistakes they must avoid. One U.C.L.A. student, Colin Higgins, has capitalized on this and completed a

Barbara Sammeth, back from her Mexican abortion, waits on the train station for her lover in the student film satire, *Opus One* by Colin Higgins.

satire on student film making titled *Opus One* (the shooting script and dialogue are printed beginning on page 88). Higgins's film begins at the end, with soaring seagulls, the end titles, and then—blackleader, while members of the audience discuss what they have seen in full: "GIGGLING GIRL'S VOICE 'I liked it. I don't know.' MAN'S VOICE 'I was somewhat confused with the opening shot, . . .' "

And of course, every possible student mistake was deliberately made by Higgins. He, as director, must lamely explain bad camera work and non-synchronized sound; "How many of you noticed that during the dialogue sequence there was no lip synchronization? That many, huh?" The participants appear in consecutive scenes wearing different clothes, the plot is not fully explained "Well, . . . (pause) . . . I thought I'd leave that a little ambiguous, . . . for suspense." The voice of the producer proudly proclaims that he has been influenced by French directors like Claudey Le l'ouch (sound track up with the theme from *A Man and a Woman*).

It is a wry inward view of the trials and tribulations of the learning process in film making.

U.C.L.A. is one of the top three or four schools (U.S.C., U.C.L.A., N.Y.U.) in the aspect of distribution and sale of student films, according to Bob Epstein, an assistant who has the job of distributing the U.C.L.A. films.

"The students have at least seventeen outlets for showings through Mike Getz, who runs the Art Theater Guild from Los Angeles. The students here have regular run rights to their films—for the sale of prints, television rights, and foreign sales, but the university retains the rights for non-theatrical showings (other university showings, etc.). Some times we have a buyer for a student film and the student-producer has graduated and we can't find him. That means lost money for the student. Usually, U.C.L.A. films win ten or fifteen awards each year for excellence," Epstein explained.

Students have sold their films or received national awards ever since the U.C.L.A. department was founded. *A Time Out of War* won an Academy Award for two brothers, Dennis and Terry Sanders in the early 1950s, and *The Season* was bought by McGraw-Hill after it was completed. Noel Black's first film after leaving the university was *Skater-Dater,* an award-winning short film. On the basis of *Skater-Dater,* Black got a job working for Twentieth-Century Fox and he was in on the production of an under-rated *Bonnie and Clyde*-type thriller, *Pretty Poison,* with Anthony Perkins and Tuesday Weld (1968). But perhaps two of the best known U.C.L.A. film makers who have made the step

Paul Kenworthy, who began *The Living Desert* as a master's thesis project, eventually completed it under contract to the Walt Disney Studios. © Walt Disney Productions.

into Hollywood (which of course, is the name of the game for most) are Paul Kenworthy and Francis Ford Coppola.

As a graduate student, Kenworthy had an idea for a thesis film that involved extensive production work in the desert. He began his film and was about half through the production when the Disney studios heard about it. They screened the footage that Kenworthy had finished and bought the film from him. He finished it under contract with Disney. It was *The Living Desert,* an exceptional film released a few years ago. The finished production pleased neither Kenworthy nor the people at U.C.L.A. "Disney took a great idea and made a typical Disney feature with it," one graduate student said. Kenworthy is still working for Disney, making essentially the same type of films.

More recently, Francis Ford Coppola has made an even bigger impression on the giants of the film industry. David Peoples, writing in the now-defunct magazine *eye,* said*:

From *The Living Desert*. © Walt Disney Productions.

From *The Living Desert*. © Walt Disney Productions.

From *The Living Desert*. © Walt Disney Productions.

Francis Ford Coppola is Hollywood's favorite skyrocket. A few years after graduating from UCLA Film School, he blossomed into one of the industry's most promising directors. When somebody in motion pictures wants to emphasize the change in the industry, he drops Coppola's name and waits for the fizz, as though he'd dropped Alka Seltzer into a glass of water. Coppola does look different. Slightly heavy, with a black beard and long black hair, he suggests a graduate student in history rather than an operator in bigtime movies. But not even Coppola, now only twenty-nine, skyrocketed into the industry. If his road seemed short—he directed his first feature at twenty-two—it is because he started early in the morning, kept his eyes on the road, his foot firmly on the pedal, and at times drove with what can only be called reckless abandon.

He was, he says, "a kid expert on Eisenstein," the brilliant Russian director who made *Potemkin* and other classics. At high school he made eight-millimeter films. In 1957 at Hofstra University, he tried to set up a cinema workshop, but that was before cinema was fashionable and a promised appropriation didn't materialize. So Francis turned his attention to the theater, managed to become president of two different drama groups at Hofstra ("it was very Machiavellian"), and then ap-

From *The Living Desert* by Paul Kenworthy. © Walt Disney Productions.

From *The Living Desert* by Paul Kenworthy. © Walt Disney Productions.

From *The Living Desert*. © Walt Disney Productions.

pointed himself writer and director of Hofstra plays ("it was very unfair, I suppose")—previously the directing had been a faculty job. "I really learned not only about doing plays and shows but also learned quite a bit about manipulation in a political situation." After all this exhilarating activity, Coppola found his next roadstop, UCLA Film School, depressing.

"They were very negative. And they would go around bowing their heads, saying, you know, "I could make a great film but no one'll ever give me a chance." Guys were working on their films but they had been working on them for years and they never finished them. That's that brief period of my life when I got involved in some nudie films which pure and simply were the only kind of filmmaking that I had access to."

Smalltime Hollywood promoters not infrequently use film students in the area for cheap labor and one of them persuaded Coppola to write a screenplay for a nudie film. He did, but when the promoter offered him two-hundred dollars for it, Coppola said there would be no deal unless he, Coppola, directed. No deal, so Francis found two thousand dollars' financing elsewhere and made the film himself.

Then he threw his energy into a student film, but was interrupted by a draft physical. In order to be in "perfect" condi-

From *The Living Desert*, the Walt Disney nature film, which was begun as a master's thesis project at U.C.L.A. © Walt Disney Productions.

tion for the physical, he stayed up all night, drank lots of coffee and, to pass the time, worked himself to a fever pitch writing a screenplay. It was ninety-nine pages long and won the two-thousand-dollar Sam Goldwyn award that year. He passed the physical but was never called.

Roger Corman, a struggling young producer-director of low-

From *The Living Desert* by Paul Kenworthy. © Walt Disney Productions.

budget films, was also using cheap student labor at the time and Coppola did some work for him for next to nothing. When Francis graduated, Corman took him on as an assistant for four hundred dollars a month. "It was a little film company and it was exciting and I wanted to get involved. I did everything, even cleaning the office," says Coppola. About six or seven months later, Corman asked his assistant if he knew a sound recordist at UCLA. Francis said he could do it. "It didn't know the first thing about it. I went home with the recorder and read the manual and brushed up on it."

He went to Europe and worked on *The Young Racers* with Corman, who, true to form, soon put him to work in other capacities such as second unit photographer. The plan had been to make another film in Europe after *Young Racers,* but Corman was called back to make *The Raven.* Coppola asked to be allowed to write and direct the second picture himself and Corman agreed, insisting that it be full of sex and violence. He left Francis with a projected budget of $20,000 and a check for $3,000. Coppola expanded the budget to $40,000 when he sold the English rights to the nonexistent film to a man he met in a bar. "I said I was making a big film for a big American company." The resulting film, *Dementia 13,* was shot in Ireland and released in 1963 by AIP.

On returning to the United States, he got a job for Seven Arts (on the basis of winning the Goldwyn award) writing a screenplay for *Reflections in a Golden Eye*. "They thought they'd hire some cheap writer, some young guy, and see what he could do with it." They were pleased and kept giving the twenty-three-year-old Coppola assignments and boosting his pay until he was making nine hundred dollars a week. "They were very, very nice to me, gave me a lot of money, but it was still not getting to direct a film." So he optioned the rights to a novel he liked, *You're a Big Boy Now,* and began adapting it for the screen in his spare time, at the same time pestering Seven Arts to let him direct.

Instead, they sent him to Paris to work as a writer on the giant production, *Is Paris Burning?,* a job he detested. "It was a real disaster and I finally quit and got fired over disagreements over how it should be done with the producer, who looked at me very pompously and said, "Mr. Coppola, I was making films twenty years before you were born." And I told him, "Yes, Mr. Graetz, but I will be making them twenty years after you die." And he died about a month later, so it's killing me that I didn't say forty years after you die, or sixty years after you die.

"There's a principle I've learned which is probably the most important thing any young person could learn about becoming a film director, and that's to treat the project you want to do as though you're already doing it. We went around and announced we were making this film and that's really, in principle, how *Dementia 13* was made. I went and told everyone I was making this big film and acted as though I was. I really had no deal. And the same with *You're a Big Boy Now*. By laying out those few hundreds of dollars necessary to make the trips and to rent a small office and generally saying, 'Hey we're making a film,' it got to be a going thing. And it's much easier to get a going thing than a nongoing thing going, obviously."

You're A Big Boy Now was released about 1965–66 by Warner Brothers-Seven Arts. *Big Boy* starred Elizabeth Hartman, Geraldine Page, Peter Kastner, Rip Torn, Michael Dunn, Tony Bill, Karen Black, and Julie Harris. The music for the film was written and performed by a rock 'n' roll group that has now faded from the public eye—The Lovin' Spoonful. The liner comments from the sound track album note:

It's a major American film. Produced by Phil Feldman for Seven Arts. Written and Directed by Francis Ford Coppola. With stars. With style. With sly, dark humor. If you've seen it, you may feel it's the most sophisticated American film comedy of this decade. And you're probably right.

It's the story of young manhood in New York, seen through a fine veil of madness. Peter Kastner stars as "Big Boy" Bernard Chanticleer, universal seeker and universal victim. Rip Torn as Big Boy's father, curator of the erotica collection in the New York Public Library. Geraldine Page as his loving, concerned mother from Great Neck—loving and concerned. Julie Harris as Miss Thing, the landlady of the rooming house his mother picked out for him. Elizabeth Hartman as Barbara Darling, the darling all little boys meet on their way to becoming Big Boys. Karen Black as Amy, the girl who loves Big Boy while he endures the growing pains.

Michael Dunn as Barbara Darling's diminutive biographer. Tony Bill as a co-worker roller-skating stock boy in the library, and a man of the world. Dolph Sweet as Francis, the talking cop. Michael O'Sullivan as an albino hypnotherapist whose wooden leg rests beside the bed of former patient, Barbara.

Greenwich Village. Times Square. Central Park and the Public Library as New York.

And you, dear reader. The amount of *déjà vu* you experience as you watch this film depends on whether you're a big boy now. If you're a big boy or a big girl—or on your way—there will be times you'll laugh until it hurts.

Press agent flackery that might be, but *Big Boy* was successful to Coppola in several ways. It was enough of a success to enable him to get more jobs producing Hollywood films. And, scarcely

Francis Ford Coppola is one of the very few university film students to break into Hollywood. It did take him ten years, however, to get to produce the film *You're A Big Boy Now,* which he submitted as a master's thesis film at U.C.L.A. He has gone on to produce *Finian's Rainbow* and *The Rain People,* and has hired George Lucas, bright young film maker from U.S.C. (Photo by the author)

noticeable at the beginning of the film, was the U.C.L.A. university seal. In final form, *You're A Big Boy Now* was Coppola's master's thesis film at U.C.L.A.

Coppola has since completed *Finian's Rainbow* for Warner Brothers-Seven Arts, starring Fred Astaire and Petula Clark. *Finian's Rainbow* was a reasonable film—it was not the worst musical ever released, but it did suffer from bad release dates. The nation was watching *Oliver, Funny Girl,* and several others at the same time and *Finian's Rainbow* was unfairly judged not-quite-the-best of a good crop of 1968 musicals.

Coppola has also finished *The Rain People,* a film which he wrote, directed, and produced. A press release noted:

The story of *The Rain People* concerns a pretty young housewife who quite suddenly quits home and husband and drives off in a station-wagon to nowhere rather than face the problems of marriage and children. She becomes enmeshed with a weak-brained ex-football player and a case-hardened motorcycle cop, is witness to a murder and at the end goes back to her husband.

Shirley Knight stars as the errant wife in *The Rain People,* James Caan portrays the childlike ex-footballer who complicates her journey yet helps her to find herself. Robert Duvall plays the tough motorcycle cop who tries to force a love relationship on the runaway wife and, thus, indirectly engenders a murder.

Coppola's script for this plot was so built that fortuitous accident could be embodied in the film. The producers of *The Rain People,* Ronald Colby and Bart Patton, evolved an eight-vehicle caravan which was a complete film-producing unit on wheels. Everything from editing equipment to a shower for the company was contained in a rolling stock ranging from bus to mini-bike. The caravan was staffed with a full crew of technical specialists, all the key actors and the director and producers, of course. Then it started out from New York City and filmed its way westward for 18 weeks, much of the time literally on the roadsides of America, and taking in mercurial life wherever it was encountered.

The Rain People company ran across a gala Italian wedding, a splendorous apple blossom festival, a grim mine disaster, a peppy street parade. These events were put on film with the actual participants; that is, the human beings who were making them happen or to whom they were happening. The caravan met the Amish of Pennsylvania, saw the great natural caverns near Chattanooga, rode through historic Harper's Ferry. These, too, were put on film. Actual bars, gas-stations, nightclubs, a wild-animal farm, kitchens, motels, boat-landings, bridges—in short, whatever was come upon that would yield interesting footage and the feeling of life as it is lived—were turned into settings for *The Rain People.* If something shot one day did not look good when viewed and edited next day in the caravan, the company simply moved on to another place and other conditions more exciting, provocative, impactful. *The Rain People,* as a result, has a level of vitality, spontaneity, warmth and naturalness that few pictures ever reach. And these were exactly the qualities writer-director Coppola wanted in what is, up to now his most personal film.

Coppola has plans to move The Coppola production company, which consists of himself, George Lucas, a secretary and "J. Rock," a stone outside their office door, to the San Francisco area and produce independent films from there instead of from offices on the Warner Brothers lot. Coppola and Lucas believe that better films can be made in an atmosphere that is not quite so heavy with the smog of the Warner productions.

Coppola and Kenworthy, *A Beginning* and *Opus One, The Season, Coming Soon,* and *Hey, Mama*—all have been exceptional. There is little doubt that even with the problems of logistics, the films and film makers from U.C.L.A. will continue to be exceptional.

OPUS ONE

by Colin Higgins

VISUALS	SOUND
1) Color shot of seagull, soaring in a blue sky. (All shots in this sequence are in color.)	The lush sounds of the "Spellbound Concerto" as it rises to its symphonic finale.
2) Shot of girl running along the beach.	
3) Shot of boy running along beach toward her.	
4) Girl running.	
5) Boy running.	
6) Medium shot of boy and girl coming in from the sides of the frame. They kiss and embrace.	
7) Shot of the soaring seagull.	
8) Hand-in-hand they walk towards the ocean.	
9) A breath-taking sunset with the sun sinking in the sea and the sandpipers scampering along the sand.	
10) Title card saying: THE END A Film by Colin Higgins UCLA Opus One 1968	Music climaxes with the title card.

11) Black leader—very long.

Silence.

Black screen
No picture

More silence

GIGGLING GIRL'S VOICE
". . . (*giggle*) . . . I liked it. I don't know.

More Silence

MAN'S VOICE
(SARCASTIC ALBERT)
(*clears throat*) . . . Mr. Higgins, what is the name of the film again?

THE AUTHOR
Eh . . . "The Abortion."

Black screen
No picture

SARCASTIC ALBERT
Thank you.

More silence.

MAN'S VOICE
(CONFUSED HAROLD)
I was somewhat confused with the opening shot, . . .

12) The movie begins, but it is now all in black and white. The same boy as before, now wearing a suit, is walking down a street. He pauses by the front gate of a house, and tries to ignore the two negroes who stand by the fence looking at him and at the camera.

the boy, the hero, is walking along the street, and, well, the two negroes in the foreground, what was the significance there?

13) The boy opens the gate and goes up the steps to the house. One of the negroes walks into frame and looks at him. He

THE AUTHOR
(*choke*) No significance. (*pause*) I was going to ask them to move, but, I thought they might be offended.

turns to the camera, scratches his head and breaks into a sudden grin.

14) Inside the house the boy looks around, emoting heavily. He is a very serious actor.

15) Shot of telephone off the hook.

16) Boy notices the telephone and walks towards it brushing past a vase which falls and smashes on the floor. Rattled and embarrassed, the boy looks sheepishly at the camera . . . QUICK CUT . . .

17) The vase is back on the table and the boy is continuing his serious walk to the phone. He picks up the receiver and replaces it on the hook with much meaning.

SARCASTIC ALBERT
Did you use student actors in the, eh, film?

18) The boy walks to the bedroom door and pauses.

THE AUTHOR
Yes, I did. Marty Veselich played the boy, and the girl was played by Barbara Sammeth. And I'd just like to take this opportunity to thank them. Eh, we were trying for naturalism, and I think they gave it to us.

19) Shot from inside the dark room. The door opens, silhouetting the boy. He steps into the room, and then closes the door slowly behind him, leaving the screen in total darkness.

20) Black leader.

Silence

GIRL'S VOICE (NEW YORK DORA)
(*authoritatively*) I'd just like to say that for me personally the film was beautifully done. And what impressed me most was your inspired use of silence throughout the film. It was so —right! Today's films . . .

21) The boy turns on a lamp.

22) The same girl as on the beach lies on the bed, her back to him. She opens her eyes . . .

23) . . . quick color insert of a seagull on the beach . . .
She closes her eyes.

THE AUTHOR

24) The boy gets up off the bed and puts the arm of the record player onto the turntable. He turns to look back at the girl.

(*interrupting*) Eh, about the silence, . . . Originally I had sound for the whole film, but during the transferring . . .

25) The girl slowly warms to the music. She gets up and kneels on the bed and the boy embraces her.

NEW YORK DORA

(*interrupting*) Oh, I know you have some sound in the film, some music and some dialogue, but my point is that for the most part it is a *silent* film. That's what I find so gratifying. So many films today are immersed in sound. Sound! What is sound? It is only a part of the cinematic experience. It's addition. It's extra. Therefore it should be used sparingly, as you do, only when you want to compliment, or highlight, or punctuate the visuals.

26) The boy breaks the clinch, and very seriously takes out a piece of paper and shows it to her.

27) Insert of the paper on which is roughly printed:

ABORTIONISTS

1) Dr. Clayton Quakenbush
2) Bozo Trip

28) The girl is momentarily shocked, but then with quiet resolve and courage she stands, walks over to her closet and swings open the door. She puts on her coat.

Music up as the Longines Orchestra and Chorus sing "Our Love Affair."

DORA

29) The boy opens the bedroom door and the girl walks past him. He stops her suddenly. She turns. He goes and takes the arm off the record-player. They both exit.

That's the creative use of sound, and you've done a first rate job.

30) Outside they walk down the steps of the house and out the gate. A Volkswagen, which wasn't there before, stands

waiting. The boy opens the door and the girl slips in. He closes the door, walks around the car, tries to ignore the two negroes standing by looking at him, gets inside, and drives off.	
31) The Volkswagen rolls up to a curb and comes to a halt. The boy gets out, walks around the car, and opens the door for the girl. She gets out, clearly wearing a different dress and coat, than before. He also is wearing a different suit. Together they walk up the stairs of an official looking building. We pan up to the top and see it is the Los Angeles City Hall.	Music continues: "Our Love Affair"
	Music ends.
32) A sign on a door reads: "DR. QUAKENBUSH"	
33) Interior of doctor's office. The boy and the girl are in their first sequence clothes. They sit in two chairs before the doctor's desk. The doctor is reading The American Journal of Gynocology. The book covers his mouth. He looks up and speaks.	A bleep begins the very badly recorded sound: DOCTOR: Good day. What can I do for you?
34) CU of girl.	BOY: Well, doctor, . . . perhaps you'd better tell him, Kathy.
35) CU of boy.	GIRL: Well, doctor, . . . no you tell him, Bobby.
36) CU of girl	BOY: Well, it's this way, doctor, . . . Go on, Kathy.
37) CU of boy	GIRL: No Bobby, I really couldn't.

38) CU of girl	BOY: You can if you try.
39) CU of boy	GIRL: No, Bobby, I don't . . .
40) CU of girl	BOY: Sure you can.
41) CU of boy	GIRL: No, I can't.
42) CU of girl	BOY: Yes, you can.
43) CU of boy	GIRL: I can't.
44) CU of girl	BOY: You can.
45) CU of boy	GIRL: I can't.
46) CU of girl	BOY: You can.
47) CU of boy	GIRL: (*with finality*) I can't!
48) CU of girl. She blushes and lowers her eyes.	BOY: Well, you see, Doctor, . . . Kathy's going to have a baby . . . an illegitimate baby, . . .
49) Quick color insert of the beached seagull, then back to sweetly blushing girl.	and, we want an abortion.
50) Medium shot of doctor. He stands up and covers his mouth with his hand in apparent shock. He keeps his hand there while he talks and then points to the door.	DOCTOR: Abortion! But that's illegal. Who told you to come to me? Absolutely out of the question. I must ask you to leave.
51) Shot of boy and girl as they stand up and leave the room.	Sound bleep ends this recorded section.
52) They come out of the doctor's office and are back in their second sequence clothes. They walk down the long hospital corridor. The hand-held camera follows them shakily from behind. An extended shot.	

THE AUTHOR
Eh, I'm just curious to ask, how many of you noticed that during the dialogue sequence there was no lip synchronization?

Silence.

Oh. That many, huh? Well, it is a problem when you're working with 8mm, but I think you can shoot around it.

53) Exterior. They leave the building, but it is a different building than the one they went into. Furthermore, they are in their first sequence clothes. The car is parked in front and the boy opens the door for the girl. She gets in and then he walks around and gets in. He turns on the ignition—but it won't start. He tries it again. Nothing. He keeps trying.

SARCASTIC ALBERT
(*dryly*) I do think you have a continuity problem.

NEW YORK DORA
Oh, Albert, really! This is not the type of film that begins in the beginning and ends at the end.

And trying.

SARCASTIC ALBERT
(*interrupting*) Well, I just think it's strange that the girl gets into the car in one costume and gets out of it in another. Or they go into one building . . .

And trying.

54) A long shot of the stalled car of long and boring duration intercut with shots of the boy, slightly piqued, trying to start it.

NEW YORK DORA
(*crushingly*) Oh, Albert, you're logic prone! You're bound up in linear thinking. That's out. It's passé. See Warhol. See Anger. Read McLuhan. This film deals in images, free-flowing images. What Colin has done is to use the medium cin-

ematically. He pictorially presents one of the pressing problems of our times—the unwed mother. And you are worrying about continuity?

THE AUTHOR
(interrupting) Excuse me, Dora, the girl is not unwed.

NEW YORK DORA
No?

THE AUTHOR
No. She's divorced.

NEW YORK DORA
Well, that makes no difference, . . .

THE AUTHOR
It does to her.

NEW YORK DORA
Yes. But the *relationship* of this woman to her lover . . .

55) The car remains immobile as the traffic streaks by it.

THE AUTHOR
Oh, that's not her lover. That's her first husband. You see she divorced him after her mother died, married her second husband, who ran away after the robbery, and so she turns to her first husband for support in her, eh, present crisis.

NEW YORK DORA
(*hesitatingly*) And *he* is the father?

THE AUTHOR
Well, . . . (*pause*) . . . I thought I'd leave that a little ambiguous, . . . for suspense.

56) The boy, quite frustrated, is swearing under his breath as he keeps turning on the ignition and pumping the gas. The girl, who has been pretending not to notice, caught up as she is with her acting, looks at him occasionally with muted disgust. The car remains still.

CONFUSED HAROLD
I must say that one sequence did seem to drag.

THE AUTHOR
Oh?

CONFUSED HAROLD
When he was starting the car . . .

THE AUTHOR
Oh, you thought that dragged?

57) Long shot of the car finally starting and driving off into the traffic.

CONFUSED HAROLD
Well, it made me wonder if you were using an improvisational technique or whether you had a script for the film?

58) Old Victorian house.

THE AUTHOR
Oh yes! There was a very detailed script, which I wrote myself, (*modestly*) based on one of my, oh, short stories.

59) Pan down from the pigeons in the gables, past a huge sign which reads "Bozo Trip" and end on the boy and girl in their second sequence clothes standing beside the Volkswagen. The boy turns to the girl and then resolutely walks up onto the porch and knocks on the door.

GIGGLING GIRL
(*giggle*) I liked it . . . I don't know.

60) From the porch we see the boy explaining to the person behind the door. He gestures back at the girl.

SEXY LISA
Mr. Higgins, did you do your undergraduate work in film?

61) Shot of the girl standing by the car. She blushes sweetly and lowers her eyes . . .

THE AUTHOR
Eh, no. I majored in Geology, you know—rocks. With a minor in Spanish.

62) . . . Quick color insert of the beached seagull . . . then back to her.

Silence

63) The boy turns back to the door and reacts as it is apparently slammed in his face. He turns around to the girl, empty-handed.

Des-ayo dar gracias a usted por pith-yendo la pray-gunta. (*proud little laugh*)

64) Shot of the girl. She bites her fist.

65) Shot of two pigeons on the roof. One moves away from the other.

66) Shot of a train waiting at the station.

67) The boy and girl are wearing their beach scene costumes. In addition both are wearing sunglasses. They walk along the platform and the girl steps onto the train. The boy hands her a suitcase on which four decals proclaiming "Mexico" have been stuck.

68) Five zooms from different angles in on the "Mexico" decals. After the third or fourth zoom. . . .

SARCASTIC ALBERT
Do you like the zoom lens?

THE AUTHOR
Oh yes. I think it's a wonderful technique.

69) The boy leaves and the girl sadly climbs up into the train.

SARCASTIC ALBERT
Very subtle.

70) Shot of train wheels as train moves out.

THE AUTHOR
Oh, yes. Actually I only found out what it was on the last day of shooting, but now that I've got the hang of it, I'll be using it more in my, eh, future productions.

71) Shot of train picking up speed and going off down the track. We hold watching the caboose getting smaller and smaller.

THE AUTHOR
Eh, the shots in Mexico didn't come out.

72) From the same angle and with a tremendous clanging of train noises and steam, an engine replaces the caboose and comes rattling down the track into the station.

73) The train stops and people get out.

74) In the doorway the girl appears minus her sunglasses and looking carefree and happy.

75) . . . Quick insert of a soaring seagull in color as the strains of the "Spellbound Concerto" fill the air . . . Then back to the girl as she steps off the train.

76) The girl puts down her suitcase and looks about for someone.

SEXY LISA
Mr. Higgins, what film directors have most influenced your work?

77) Shot of the boy coming up the station ramp. He too is looking.

78) Shot of girl looking. She sees him.

THE AUTHOR
Well, I've been very much influenced by the novel vague . . . particularly the French directors in it, . . . like Claudey Le l'ouch.

79) Shot of boy. He sees her, runs to her and gathers her up in his arms.

80) They embrace and the hand-held camera spins around them . . . and around, and around, and around, and around.

The theme from "Man and a Woman" comes in loud and strong.

81) The girl breaks from the embrace and looks up at the sky.

MUSIC from "Man and a Woman" continues

82) A long color shot of a seagull soaring in a blue sky.

—ALL COLOR SHOTS TO END—

83) Shot of the boy and girl, hand in hand and very happy as they run down a path and onto the beach.

Music fades.
Sounds of seagulls up.

CONFUSED HAROLD
(*wanting to say something nice*) I thought your use of color in the closing shots . . .

THE AUTHOR
(*interrupting*) Now that really wasn't my fault. That's the way it came back from the lab.

84) Four or five shots of soaring seagulls.

SARCASTIC ALBERT
Must have been on the same reel that you shot the seagulls.

	THE AUTHOR Oh, yes, the seagulls were in color. (*eagerly*) Oh, did you all get the symbolism of the sea-
—SAME SERIES OF SHOTS AS OPENING—	gulls, and the whole underlying bird motif? It wasn't too obscure?
85) Shot of girl running along the beach.	
86) Shot of boy running along beach toward her.	NEW YORK DORA It was beautiful. A visual metaphor!
87) Girl running.	(The "Spellbound Concerto," which began with the seagull
88) Boy running.	shot, plays underneath this speech till the end.) And that's
89) Medium shot of boy and girl coming in from the sides of the frame. They kiss and embrace.	why the film for me personally was such a moving experience. Because it dealt in pictures—moving pictures. But in no way did it slight its intellectual
90) Shot of the soaring seagull.	content. The film says something. A primitive statement, perhaps. But a personal state-
91) Hand-in-hand they walk towards the ocean.	ment. And where are we to draw the line? So few student films today come to grips with
92) A breath-taking sunset, with the sun sinking into the sea and the sandpipers scampering along the sand.	a contemporary social issue. Well, this one *does*. It cries out for understanding, but it does take a stand. And it is this concern for the human problem
93) Title card saying:	that pushes this film over the edge of greatness making it . . .
THE END	(The "Concerto" reaches its climax)
A Film by Colin Higgins UCLA Opus One 1968	. . . . the non-pareil!

BLACKOUT

3.
Stanford University

AND THE CANADIAN NATIONAL FILM BOARD

The film program at Stanford University is a very small, entirely graduate program. It does have some unique features, but it should not be considered one of the best departments in the country. The departmental brochures touch on the weak points, but do not go into detail:

> Stanford's film-making division is distinctive in several ways. It is possibly the smallest and most selective program of its kind. In 1967–68, there were 24 first year A.M. candidates, 13 second year. There are only two full-time faculty speakers, Dr. Henry Breitrose and Janet Voelker. . . . Because of its limited size, the faculty consciously tries not to do everything, but to do well what it does. The program stresses factual material—the documentary film—and aims at educating writer-directors. While students learn enough about equipment so that they can successfully express their ideas, the emphasis is on developing an approach to the use of film as a way to translate these ideas. Content and style, rather than merely technique, are the most significant factors of Stanford's method.
>
> Most graduate students in film making are candidates for an A.M. degree, which requires two years in residence, with production courses beginning their first quarter. By getting the course work out of the way during the first year, students are able to devote their second year to an independent film project.
>
> A shortage of Department funds for such projects has forced the students to compete successfully with professional film-makers for production funds to support their efforts. Students have been able to contract films for government agencies, corporations and other University departments. Speaking of their work, George C. Stoney, award-winning documentary film maker of New York, who spent the 1966–67 year in the Division says: "Sponsors generally get a fresh eye, a great deal more time spent on the project, and the chance to be more adventure-

some in their approach. . . . Of course, one takes a calculated risk in backing any student effort. We cannot guarantee a professionally competent film every time, though we have been amazingly fortunate. On the other hand, few films that are simply 'professionally competent' accomplish their purposes. The bright students we get these days bring a great deal more to their work."

The present projects cover subjects ranging from a film on computer parsing techniques for the Stanford Linear Accelerator Center to a television commercial for the Stanford Repertory Theater (being produced by first-year students). Currently in production are films on such diverse topics as a case study for the Graduate College of Business, a report on the field program of the Student Health Organization, and a vocational guidance film on careers in construction, designed for Negro high school students.

Stanford's approach to film making seems to answer directly a number of spokesmen for the film and television industries who have recently emphasized the need for fresh talent in writing and direction.

A university program in film making, by presenting an orderly and concentrated curriculum, is far more economical of student time than the traditional apprenticeship. However, the on-the-job training advantages of the apprenticeship are preserved at Stanford. Upon completion of the master's project, students must pass a comprehensive written examination, then spend a three-month internship with a professional film or broadcasting organization.

Stanford can train only a limited number of students in film making; consequently, it is important that these students be exceptional ones. If Stanford is to attract the best students, it must be able to compete with other universities in offering aid to gifted students who could not otherwise afford to study here. Of the 23 applicants accepted in 1967–68, only one did not ask for financial aid; about half did not come because they could not receive fellowship at Stanford.

In short, Stanford's film program is a small one; too small perhaps for an ideal situation, a school in which almost all of the students are on financial aids and grants, and a school in which students must fight on their own for outside projects to make money to complete their thesis projects and advanced work.

According to Henry Breitrose, "the film sequence was begun several years ago. Originally, film began as a radio, television offshoot and I came to teach films for television. We are now oriented away from television generally, but don't differentiate between films which are made as films and films which are made specifically for television."

Redwood Hall is the home of the Dept. of Communications (which includes the film program) at Stanford University. (Courtesy of Stanford University)

The department's equipment currently consists of six super eight millimeter cameras, a Bell and Howell and a Bolex, two Auricons and an Airflex, and an Eclair. They also have three Movieolas, a small "mini-studio," and some television equipment. According to Breitrose, "we don't teach students to push cameras around." A local Palo Alto laboratory processes all the Stanford student film.

One of the very few women in film work in Janet Voelker, who teaches a sequence of three courses titled *Writing for Broadcasting and Film*. The first course is simply an introduction to writing and beginning course work. The second sequence is split in half; part of the time students write for documentaries, and half of the time they write dramatic scripts. The third course in the series is devoted to writing for existing television series, such as a possible plot for *Star Trek*, or *Mission: Impossible*, or advanced student productions.

Miss Voelker, an attractive brunette with an easy smile, has a very good relationship with her students—a highly productive classroom technique. In the past, she has also taught *Film Criticism, Broadcast Film*, and, with Breitrose, *Survey of Broadcasting*.

One of the few women professors in film work is Miss Janet Voelker, who teaches script writing at Stanford. (Photo by the author)

As she says,

I was in the Stanford film program as a student in 1962, and went from here to Fargo, North Dakota, where I taught in a junior high school and later worked for a television station. I went from there to the Wolper Productions in Los Angeles, as an assistant to the producer, where one of our films, *Let My People Go,* an historical documentary, was nominated for an Academy Award. I eventually left Wolper, dissatisfied with some of the aspects of their work and was on the verge of taking a teaching job in Texas, when I was offered the job here. At first I was scared of film . . . and felt silly in taking up something that I enjoyed, but now I feel less and less worried about the old Puritan ethics problem. I simply love films, I asked myself "can I really study the movies?" said "yes," and here I am.

I have discovered several interesting problems teaching film. First, there is the question of whether you have to be a "film-maker" to make films. Secondly, students, particularly, have an inability to translate prose into film. In writing, you can say, "she had a gun in her purse when she walked across the room," but in film, you have to *show* her putting the gun there before she walks across the room or the audience will never understand that it is there. This is the kind of problem that some students don't find obvious in beginning film work. Students too, are uncomfortable with their peers. They tend to ask themselves "what of me is left if I work with others? How much of the urge to create is the urge to see myself"? It is tough to have your work —especially beginning work—criticized. Students also ask, "what is the work in the total of me as a person?"

Some new ideas are just bad gamesmanship, bad pedagogy. Students have what they think are new ideas and unfortunately they realize that these "new ideas" are the same things that someone else did in 1927. It's a hard way to learn, but that's not the idea—the way to learn is to learn . . .

Typical of the Stanford students is Todd Flinchbaugh, who received his bachelor's degree in philosophy from Gettysburg College in 1967, and decided to come to Stanford for film. He then spent two months just looking at films before beginning any work on his own. His first film was titled *Objects,* a study in animation with a ball, a stick, and a triangle. *Objects* is less than five min-

Working on a production are (extreme left to right): Urs Trepp, Todd Flinchbaugh, Martin Krasney, and Seth Finn. Kneeling girl is Harriet Gold. (Photo by Leo Holub, Stanford University)

Adjusting a projector is Todd Flinchbaugh, one of the members of Stanford's small department. (Photo by Leo Holub, Stanford University)

utes long, but it took Flinchbaugh three months to complete. Although pleased with *Objects,* he then decided that he had more learning to do and began working on animation literally by himself, by study, exercises, and individual work.

"I think that most students want to do the equivalent of painting the Sistine Chapel ceiling without first making preliminary plans and literally hundreds and hundreds of sketches. Now I am working on my 'sketchbook' before I feel ready to paint the ceiling, in film." While working on his own, Flinchbaugh did a lecture film for the University department of Astronautics-Aeronautics, a visual-aids film designed to accompany an advanced lecture. He received 200 dollars for three weeks work, 20 hours every week. Eventually, he says, "I'd like to do a number of animated films for a thesis. Exercises in cutting rhythms and graphic designs using pencils, pipe cleaners and whatnot, accompanying them with a sound track of computer music. I like teaching and would like to teach animation—but I never want to stop making films."

David Denby, graduate film maker at Stanford University. (Photo by Janet Voelker, Stanford University)

Also typical of Stanford's students' independent projects (though more extensive than most) is David Denby's *Summer Encounter,* which was made for the Office of Economic Opportunity. *Summer Encounter* was filmed in the San Francisco Mission District and the Watts ghetto of Los Angeles, and is a social documentary about the Student Health Organization, a liberal-left wing national organization of medical-school interns. For social services they organize clinics in ghettos, birth control information dissemination, neighborhood youth corps, and other related services. A grant of $7,600 from the Sears, Roebuck Foundation enabled Denby to make the film, which took five weeks to shoot and eight months to edit. Denby had 14,500 feet of film, which eventually was reduced to one thousand feet.

Summer Encounter is a half-hour long, in 16 millimeter, black and white. The shooting involved folk-singer Joan Baez, but eventually those scenes with her were cut out. *Summer Encounter* has been used by the Student Health Organization for fund raising and has been shown, as Denby puts it, "to the A.M.A. (Ameri-

David Denby and Bob Moore, shooting *Summer Encounter*. (Photo by Janet Voelker, Stanford University)

Bob Moore (standing) during shooting of *Summer Encounter,* a film made at Stanford for the Office of Economic Opportunity. At right, folksinger Joan Baez. (Photo by Janet Voelker, Stanford University)

can Medical Association) top brass." It was also planned for television screening, but as yet has not been shown because of ghetto sequences involving run-of-the-street profanity.

Denby has taught the undergraduate course in film criticism at Stanford, and has been Henry Breitrose's assistant. He has also written film criticism for *Film Quarterly* magazine and would

Filming a student production are: David Espar (left), Sheri Espar (right), and Ted Claire. (Photo by Leo Holub, Stanford University)

eventually like to teach film criticism, theory, and history at the university level.

David Espar, another Stanford film maker, has found himself involved with outside projects for Massachusetts Institute of Technology. Espar received his bachelor of science from M.I.T. in June of 1967, but found that he just plain didn't like business

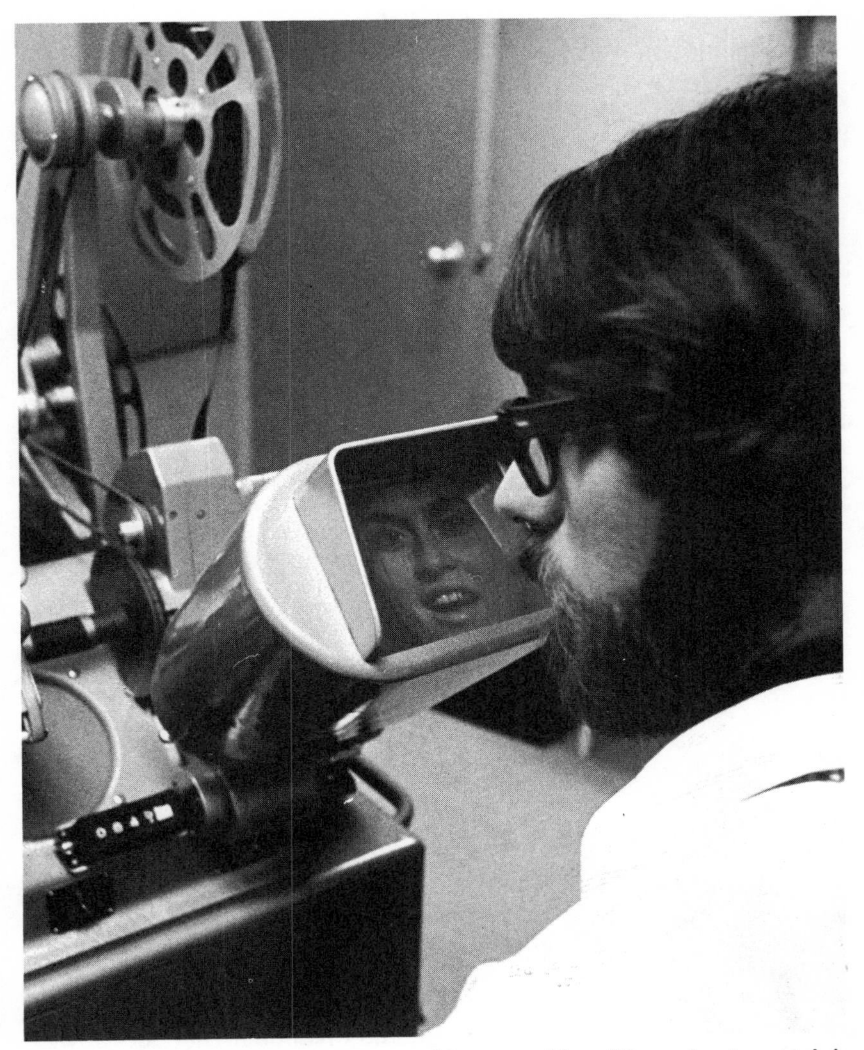

David Espar is editing a portion of his own film. (Photo by Leo Holub, Stanford University)

schools. In an undergraduate humanities course at M.I.T., called "20th Century Society and Consciousness," Espar made a short film, which he says, "was a sloppy production, but fun. It was 20-minutes long and revealed a sophomoric view of the problems of college life." The film, titled *The Ride,* had a motorcyclist as sustaining theme.

Now at Stanford, Espar is doing another film about college life, again sponsored by M.I.T. Untitled during production, the film is a half-hour long, and cost about $10,000, which M.I.T. is underwriting. The second film will portray the favorable aspects of college life and Espar will present a finished print of the film as his master's thesis at Stanford. His wife, Sheri, is also a film maker at Stanford and she is also working on a thesis film of her own.

Perhaps the most outstanding aspect of the film program at Stanford is the department's relationship with the Canadian National Film Board, a relationship that any other film school would

Martin DeFalco, a member of the Canadian National Film Board, was a guest lecturer at Stanford. The Film Board regularly sends guest lecturers to the University. (Photo by the author)

love to have. The National Film Board is a national council, and a leading world-wide producer of documentary films. For the past several years, the National Film Board has regularly sent a producer-director to Stanford for six month periods as a guest lecturer. The lecture program is actually a working vacation for the director, who has a chance to make American money, relax, talk with students, and generally take a vacation. Rex Tasker, a leading producer, has been to Stanford and during the 1968–69 school year, Martin DeFalco was there.

DeFalco has been working for the Film Board for 17 years; "the only job I've ever had." Prior to his stay in Stanford, DeFalco made a film about Don Messer, a "cowboy fiddler." The film was titled *The Happy Music.* After production of the film, Messer moved into his own show on Canadian national television. The film was shot in color, with an Eclair camera, half cinema vérité and half in studio sessions. DeFalco has also done films titled *Northern Fishermen* and *Trawler Fishermen,* documentaries about fishing and job opportunities on the Canadian Grand Banks.

DeFalco spent about 40 hours every week talking to students at Stanford, viewing their films and talking film with them. He also helped straighten out any film problems that they might have—

During filming of *Under The Volcano*. At left is David Stiers, at right, Mort Grosser. (Photo by Linda Moulton Howe)

"the technicalities aren't that difficult," he says. DeFalco sits in on the beginning and advanced film courses and helps the students with their working problems.

As DeFalco said, "all the students have a tendency to do more than they can handle. I don't advise them artistically, but I do advise them technically and explain to them whatever may be slowing them down in their own film work. I'm fascinated with the new American film makers. I am used to film as a folk art—it's now becoming a cult thing . . . I was getting ingrown in the Film Board . . . this sabbatical is fine because I can let it flow and relax in film for a while. I'm really surprised at the radical use of film in this country. Film is being shot in the streets and the accusations of police harrassment can now be proven, because cameras were there, witnessing riot scenes . . ."

The Film Board guest lecturers are chosen in conferences between the Board and Stanford. They are usually paid about $1,500 for each month's work at Stanford. So far, after several year's experience, the program has pleased both Stanford and the Film Board. It will probably continue as an integral aspect of the Stanford film program.

Robert Moore, film maker from Stanford University. (Photo by Linda Moulton Howe)

Preparations for shooting the film *Under The Volcano*. Adjusting his tie is Mort Grosser. At right is cameraman Bob Moore. (Photo by Linda Moulton Howe)

Preparing for shooting the film *Under The Volcano*. At left is Leonard Schwertz. (Photo by Linda Moulton Howe)

Working on the film *Under The Volcano* at Stanford are Mort Grosser (left), Kevin Burke, the director, and David Stiers. (Photo by Linda Moulton Howe)

Novelist-actor Mort Grosser (right) confers with director Kevin Burke during the shooting of *Under the Volcano*. (Photo by Linda Moulton Howe)

But generally speaking, despite Miss Voelker's work and the enthusiasm of the visiting professionals from Canada, Stanford bears serious consideration by the aspiring university film student. The size of the program and the fact that students are almost all on grants and fellowships, plus the fact that students must usually scramble for outside projects to finance their own films, indicate that the university student interested in film making might look elsewhere, especially if he has enough financial support for tuition, before he applies to Stanford.

4.
San Francisco State College

ENGULFED IN CHAOS; SCOTT BARTLETT AND THE RENO HOTEL

In theory, at least, San Francisco State has one of the best film programs of any college in its general size. The philosophy of the department emphasizes individual study, a small department, and the crew concept. The departmental brochures state:

> It cannot be sufficiently enough emphasized that the present film Division does not under any circumstances wish to grow to a scale which would impress by its size or its plant rather than through the accomplishments of its graduates and the excellence of their training. The faculty believes strongly that an undue size can only destroy the kinds of relationships among teachers, staff and students which have given the program its cohesion and its promise. Further, the teachers would far rather devote their support and their energies to creative executions and experimental research than to any program which would sacrifice these ends to impressive studio facilities or to commercial executions.

The phrase "grow to a scale which would impress by its size or its plant . . ." is a left-handed aside to the facilities and programs of the downstate schools, U.C.L.A. and U.S.C., both of which are larger and more expansive than San Francisco. San Francisco maintains a curious ambivalence toward the Los Angeles schools, at once rather proud of its small size and at the same time rather envious of the growth and equipment of the two bigger schools. A visitor to San Francisco State might eventually hear "well, of course, they are tremendously over-populated with students . . . but say, what are they doing down there now?"

The brochures would have prospective students believe otherwise:

The program is committed without qualification to every kind of motion picture and, therefore, every aspect of the production process which falls properly within the confines of a Liberal Arts education. Documentary films intended for both theatrical and television exhibition, news coverage, educational films, the low budget, non-studio theatrical film, animation, and experimental production are all considered Film's fair province.

The program is intended to serve the needs of the student whose interests are directed at crew experience and the student who is motivated toward the expressive aims of individual film making. Certainly, either student will experience both phases of work during his period of study. Some graduates will find employment in the film industry, but many will study film for other reasons.

The curriculum has no parochial or exclusive interest sympathy toward sponsored films, dramatic films or experimental films *per se*. It is indisputable that student interest may color with enthusiasm particular facets of any program, but the film curriculum assumes the obligation to provide the student with a collection of alternatives equally attractive in terms of course offerings, teachers and facilities.

The film faculty guides itself by these principles:

1) All students must be completely judged on their skills and craftsmanship vis-a-vis motion picture production equipment and a minimum body of technical knowledge.

2) A broad historic-social-esthetic perspective must accompany training in the technical skills.

3) We are not a conservatory and are committed to working within the pattern and the possibilities of the State College system.

4) We want to secure and maintain effective relationships with the creative community outside the discipline, beyond the school and into the community.

5) We are committed to excellence, however it be measured in different forms of film achievement.

The first film course offered at San Francisco State was during the 1938–39 school year. Titled *Motion Picture Appreciation,* it was then under the listings of the English department. The Art department offered *Cinematography* in 1958–59 and the Radio-Television department offered two courses in 1959–60. A separate major in film was established in the 1964–65 academic year and the department then changed its name to Radio-Television-Film.

Currently the department chairman is Dr. John Fell, who has a mixed background of anthropology, psychology, English literature, and communications. He came to San Francisco from Montana State University. Also on the San Francisco faculty is Lester Cole, whose Hollywood credits (as a scriptwriter) include *If I Had*

A Million, The Invisible Man Returns, The House of Seven Gables, and, more recently, *Born Free.*

James Broughton, who has done *The Potted Psalm, Mother's Day, Adventures of the Pleasure Garden,* and *The Bed,* a satirical and highly entertaining study of the uses and abuses of the bed throughout history, is a faculty member. Broughton is also a playwright and a poet, the author of six books.

David Crommie (also on the staff) was an associate producer and supervising film editor on the ABC network production of *Beauty and the Beast,* which starred Hayley Mills and the San Francisco Ballet Company. He has also done *Sound of Young America,* with Pat Boone, and *The Nutcracker,* with the Ballet Company.

Teaching part-time on the San Francisco State staff is Irving Saraf, whose credits include: *Poland, From Protest To Resistance, A Film About Fidel Castro, Louisiana Diary, Take This Hammer, Anatomy of a Hit, USA Poetry,* and *Report from Cuba,* all done for National Educational Television.

The film program currently lists 24 courses for undergraduates,

Home of the film department at riot-torn San Francisco State. (Photo by the author)

including an introductory course, two film history courses, a sequence of three production courses, three in film writing, two in animation, and several others, including *Applied Film Aesthetics, Film and Society, Film Distribution and Financing, Film Direction.* During the middle of the 1968–69 school year, there were approximately 135 students in the film program—100 of them undergraduates and 35 master's degree candidates.

But unfortunately, despite the list of course offerings, the departmental literature, and the availability of the faculty, the program at San Francisco State College has been seriously crippled by the riots and racial conflicts that have plunged the college community into chaos. The film department is largely an independent unit, with students coming and going as they please. The department itself has not been physically involved, either in proximity to the actual riot areas on campus or by the faculty or the students

Ralph Arlyck, a graduate student at San Francisco State, who holds a bachelor's degree from Colgate and a master's in journalism from Columbia, is now working toward an additional M.A. He, like any other film makers in San Francisco, is simply worried about whether the riots at San Francisco will disrupt his film work. (Photo by the author)

themselves. The department has tried, as one member put it, to "carry on with business as usual," difficult sometimes, when a Police helicopter is hovering over the campus throughout the day.

The department has been affected adversely. The students have had to be admitted to the campus past checkpoints of visored riot police and they have had to listen to wave after wave of charges and counter-charges. Quite a bit of the film making during the early part of the 1968–69 school year has been cinema vérité shots of the near-by rioting, and what quality appears in these films is difficult to ascertain. The students have just been too close to the combat to create cinema vérité masterpieces.

At the end of each semester, students and faculty gather for "Film Finals." These are sessions and screenings, gradings and criticism of the films completed during the semester. The finals for the first semester of the 1968–69 school year had to be cancelled because of rioting on the campus. The students and professors alike were unable to judge the products of several month's work and thereby all suffered. The rioting and general disorders on the

A girl jumps from a huge net in Robert Nagy's *The Landscape Is Part of the Trip,* which won an award in the 1963 International Film Festival.

San Francisco State campus need not be further elaborated here. The disorders should have been evident to anyone who has read any American community newspaper within the last year. Suffice it to say that the rioting has hindered the film department; exactly how badly the creative atmosphere has been crippled, members of the department will not admit or cannot judge. But the effect has been detrimental.

Nonetheless, there have been exceptional films done at San Francisco State, primarily before the rioting began. And many of these films received prizes and awards at various showings and exhibitions.

Carrie by John Broderick was shown at the 1967 Edinburgh Festival; *Atmosfear* by Tom DeWitt received the Zellerbach Award at the 1967 San Francisco International Film Festival; and *Nyala* by Glenn Donny won the Gund Award at the same festival.

Robert Feldman's *The Mattress* received an award at the Foothill College Film Festival, and *Chaos,* also by Feldman, was one of

A girl falls into a huge net in Nagy's *The Landscape Is Part of the Trip.*

three U.S. films shown at the Third International Week of 16 millimeter films at Evain, France.

William Furman's *The Stones of Eden* won the Golden Eagle Award, CINE, at the 19th International Short Film Festival, in 1966, at Salerno.

My House by Peter Simmons was an award-winner at the San Francisco International Film Festival in 1967, and Robert Nagy's *The Landscape Is Part of the Trip* was an award-winner at the San Francisco film festival in 1963.

Landscape is a most energetic film. Nagy recruited a San Francisco modern dance company and dressed them in outrageous costumes. He had them carry battered umbrellas and roll tires and carry trunks through the woods to a camp site. The company members, numbering more than a dozen, alternately rolled, walked, ran, rambled, danced, jumped, somersaulted, skipped, leaped, and crawled up and down through the woods to the camp, where they climbed up and through hanging nets, pushed each other about, danced, ran around, and swung back and forth on ropes. All the while Nagy's camera was as much a part of the action as possible, with extremely high and low camera angles.

A girl climbs into a net in *The Landscape Is Part of the Trip.*

Swinging through the trees in *The Landscape Is Part of the Trip.*

Sean by Ralph Arlyck won the first prize for a documentary film at the Fourth National Student Film Festival, in March 1969. Arlyck is one of those bright young people who got into film out of sheer interest, and was discovered by accident. He was originally from Sufferin, New York, and received his bachelor's degree from Colgate in 1962, with a major in English. After serving in the Peace Corps, Arlyck returned to the U.S. and received his master's degree in journalism from Columbia University in 1965. As he says, he was "turned on to film," during one course at Columbia, where the journalism students were shown some recent films. After his journalism work, Arlyck moved to the Berkeley area, where he got a job as a reporter and, almost incidentally, received a contract to make a film for the Berkeley Public School System. After that, which was his first film experience, Arlyck began working in the film department at San Francisco State, although never officially as a student. *Sean* was a study that Arlyck made of a youngster growing up on the edges of the ghettos of San Francisco. In completed and edited form, *Sean* runs 15 minutes in black and white. Arlyck shot 2000 feet of film in less than two weeks and edited that to a finished length of 550 feet. The editing took him two months. Arlyck hopes to become an independent film maker "if I can survive (financially)."

But perhaps the most interesting film maker associated with San Francisco State is Scott Bartlett, who has never considered himself a part of the college community.

Scott Bartlett talks with Ohio University students during a guest lecture at Ohio University. To the right of Bartlett is associate professor of film J. L. Anderson, director of the film program at Ohio University. (Photo by Carl Fleischhauer. Copyright © 1969 by Carl Fleischhauer)

Bartlett's first film, *Metanomen,* was an award-winner at the 1966 National Student Film Festival and his second, *OFFON* won an award at Oberhausen, Germany, in 1967.

Bartlett's life style can not be separated from his films; his life and his films are one and the same. More than four years ago, Bartlett moved into the Reno Hotel—an old, condemned hotel two blocks from the Hall of Justice in the Mission district of downtown San Francisco. The Reno Hotel, in the days of its glory, had been the center for the boxing crowd in San Francisco. All professional boxers who were in San Francisco for fights stayed at the Reno. But the Reno had stood empty until Dudley Knill bought it and partially renovated it for the use of artists, film makers, sculptors, and writers. The hotel has four floors and 400 rooms. Soon after Knill began his project, the San Francisco

A double-image sequence from Scott Bartlett's *OFFON*. This sequence, as most of the film, is in color and the doves are a bright red-violet. The figures in profile keep shifting back and forth.

City Health department condemned the top three floors and kicked everyone out who had been staying on them. Bartlett, who had his studios and equipment on the ground floor, was allowed to stay. The City Health Department decided that, in their august judgment, it was best to have someone in the building who could watch for fires and other signs of immediate disaster. As a consequence, Bartlett does have access to the top three floors and all 400 rooms, although official Health Department policy does not allow him to be there.

The former foyer and lobby of the hotel are now Bartlett's studios and working space. He also has equipment squirrelled away in other parts of the hotel. The former boxing practice ring is now his sound studio. Bartlett pays monthly rent of 100 dollars for the entire hotel. Bits and pieces of his equipment have been loaned by various friends, who can come and go as they please to use the equipment. Bartlett, who teaches one class for San Francisco State in mixed media productions, holds the class in the

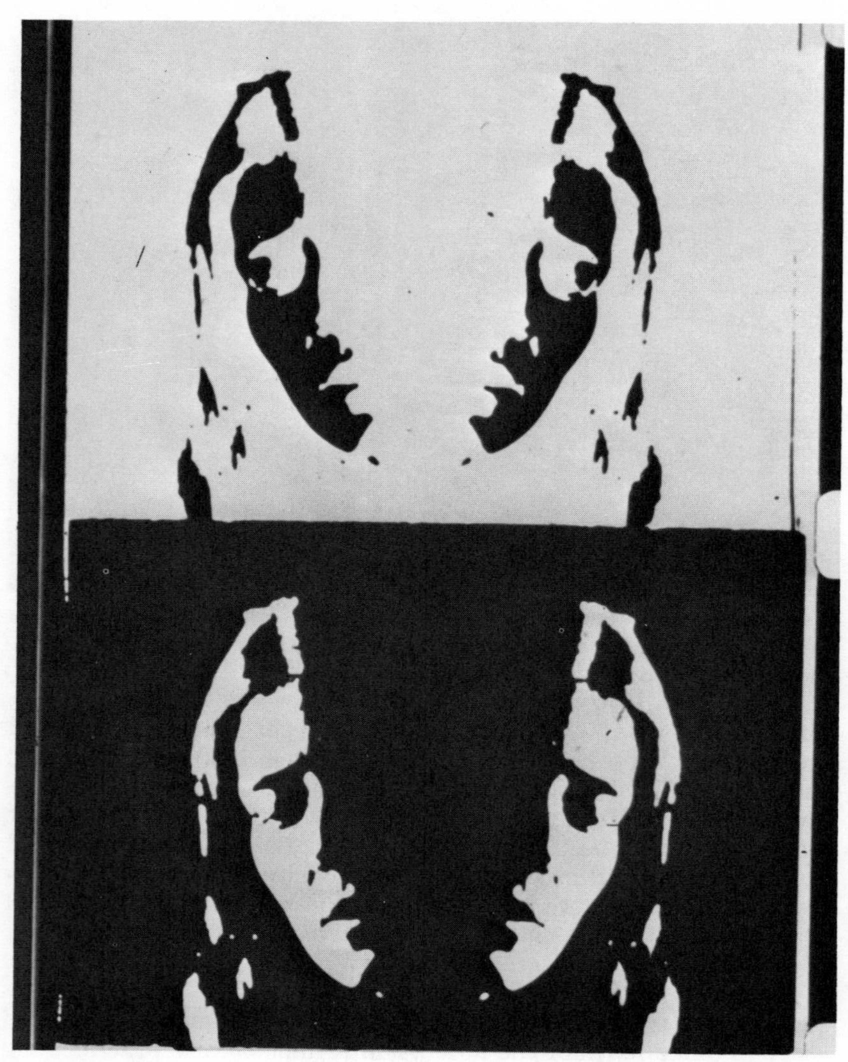

The negative (top) and positive (bottom) from Scott Bartlett's *OFFON*. Bartlett edited this sequence so that the positive and negative appear every two frames, an extremely time-consuming and difficult job. The switches between the positive and negative images at the rate of every two frames assault the viewer's perceptions.

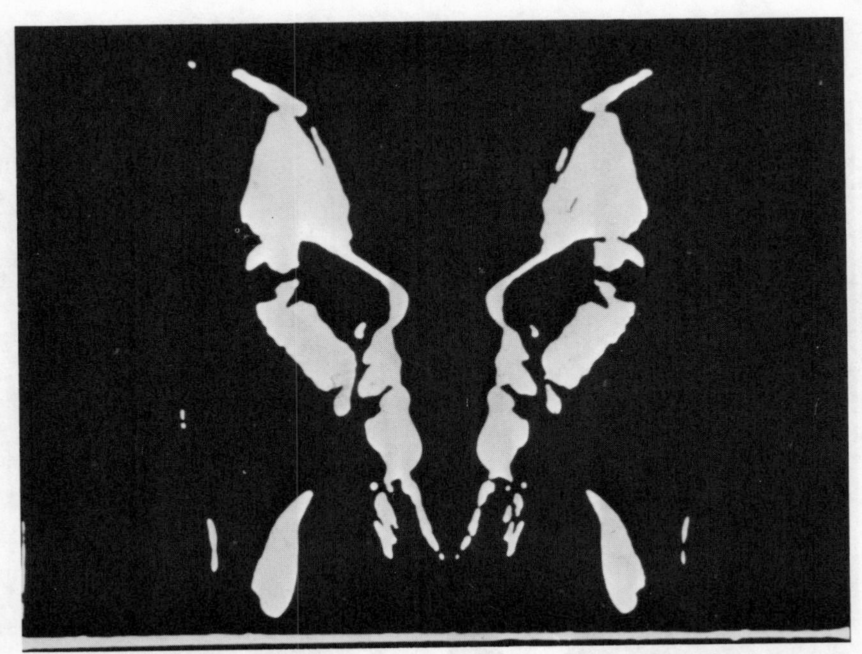

From *OFFON* by Scott Bartlett. Chris Parker had essentially the same sequences in *Cut*, made at Iowa, which was also an award-winning film.

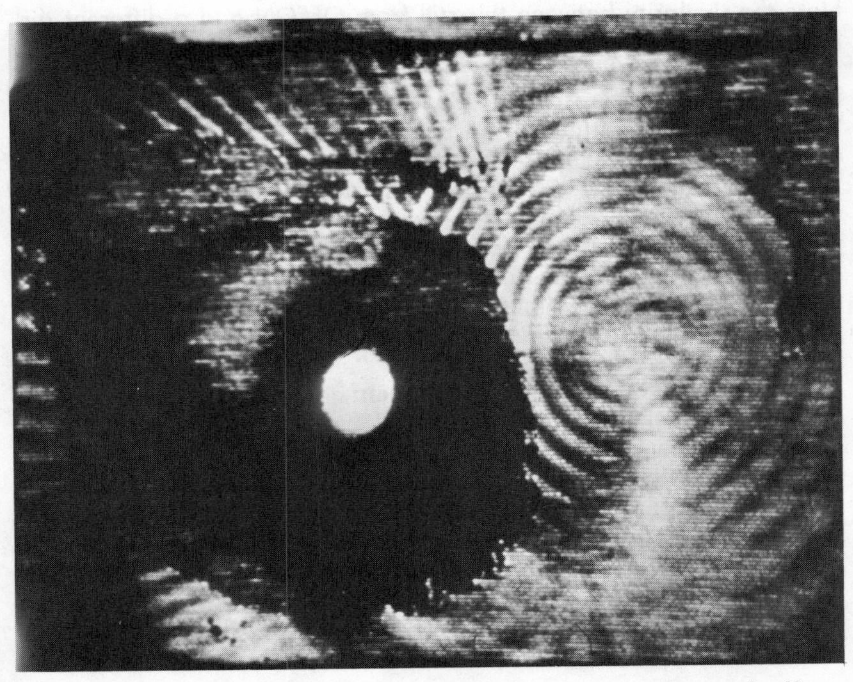

An eye, in an extreme close-up, is the basis for experimental effects in some sequences of Scott Bartlett's *OFFON*.

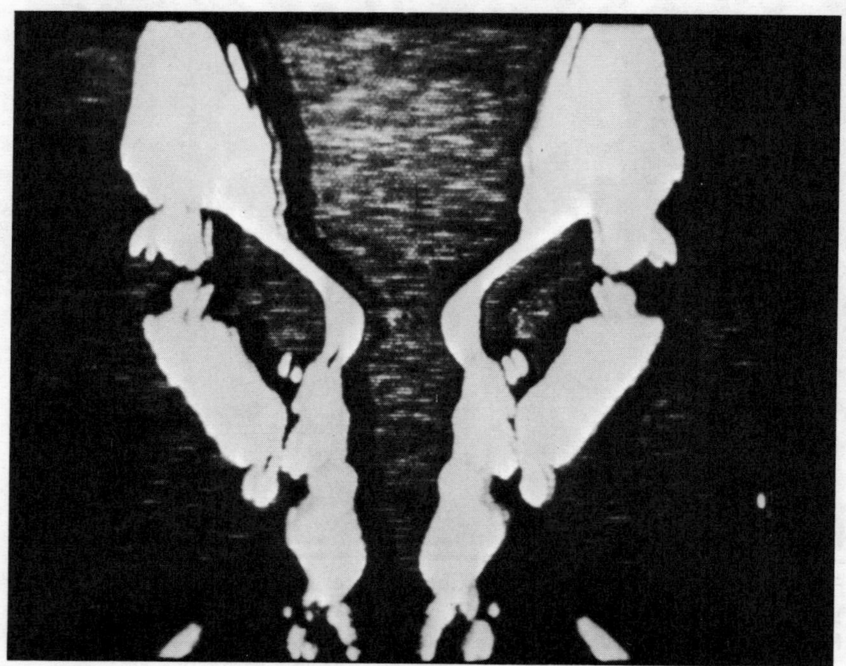

Note the similarity between this still from *OFFON* and a different girl in Chris Parker's *Cut,* made at Iowa.

hotel, when he holds it at all. Bartlett has gotten into trouble with the straight academicians and deans of the college in the past by cancelling class on short notice, which the students enjoy. Bartlett generally behaves in a manner that does not usually become a member of the academic community. He has had a brochure printed, *The Plain Truth Is I Love You,* which describes him and his films and in it, among other things, is a letter of recommendation, written by the superintendent of Colorado school district number 20, which includes Air Academy High School. It is also a glowing letter, describing Scott as "a fine student leader . . ." Above the letter is printed a comment, doubtlessly made by one of Bartlett's friends: "mr. bartlett, I notice you havent cut your hair for the last six months."

Bartlett could care less about the whole academic soiree. He was a color consultant with Richard Lester on the film *Petulia.* His students generally agree with his philosophy of film and academics. Bartlett has never made a "commercial" film and probably never will. The hotel rental is met by Bartlett's teaching salary, lecture

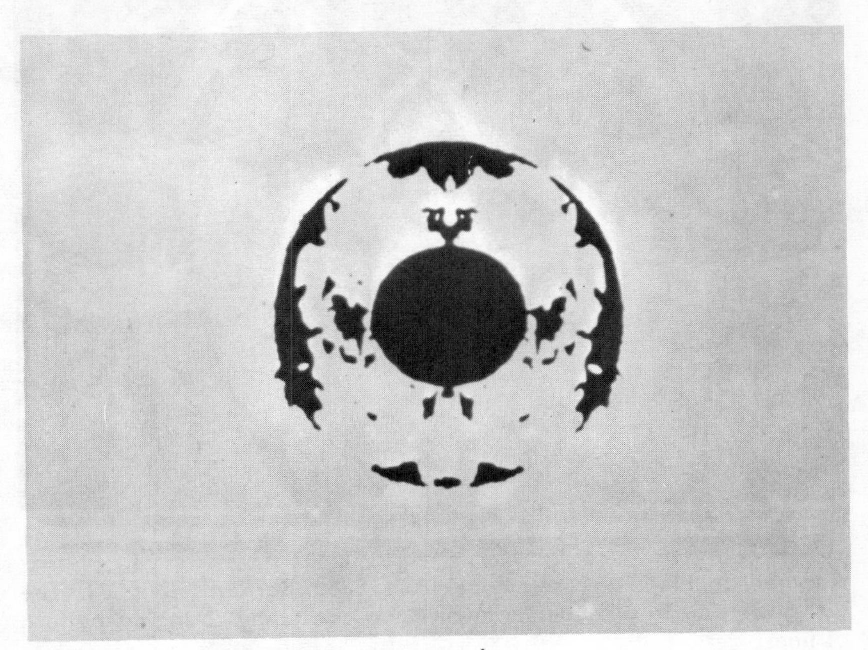

A sequence from *OFFON* by Scott Bartlett.

tours that he makes occasionally, and rental fees on the films that he has made in the past.

Bartlett's films *Metanomen* and *OFFON* are in The National Film Archives and *OFFON* itself has been purchased by: The American Film Archives, The Smithsonian Institute, the Museum of Modern Art, the Bell and Howell Corporation, Rochester Public Library, Yale University, San Francisco State College, Fairleigh Dickinson Film Archives, the Enoch Pratt Film Library, and the Pennsylvania State University.

All of which does nothing to explain what Bartlett's films are about, or even what he is about. *Metanomen,* which runs eight minutes, in black and white (with sound), has been described variously as "laboratory gothic," "study of a freight yard," "too fast for consciousness" (probably true), and "boy meets girl" (obviously false). It is simply a very metaphysical film that must be seen to be described. Bartlett himself describes it as "a graphic representation of the symbiotic nature of inter-personal relationships and the worldwide implications therein."

Another double-image sequence from Scott Bartlett's *OFFON*. The girl gives way to a sequence involving a constantly changing pattern of lines.

OFFON was described by Gene Youngblood* as follows:

The visual form of *OFFON*, says Scott Bartlett, "is too pure to make exclusively personal." He adds that the film explains something he is unable to explain with conventional words. "To project-express my time and my culture in its iconic forms," is one of those aims, as well as to "balance my time-culture between the beginning and the end of time."

With these words—but still more eloquently with this film—Bartlett expresses the essence of synaesthetic cinema. The geometric, iconic language of *OFFON* is indeed "too pure" to be exclusively personal because it reaches far beyond the concerns of one human being; more than self-expression, it is life-expression.

OFFON is suspended between realities. By "reality" we mean relationships. Reality often is impossible to comprehend because our perceptive capacities are limited. The history of art might be seen as man's progress toward manipulating reality itself as

* In *The Plain Truth Is I Love You*, copyright San Francisco, 1968, by Scott Bartlett and Freude Solomon, Reprinted with permission.

a language with which to create more realistic legends. Fiction, legend, parable, poetry, traditionally have been used to make comprehensible the paradoxes of reality. Synaesthetic cinema, whose very structure is paradox, makes paradox a language in itself.

It is this language which Bartlett speaks in *OFFON*. The interaction of the iconic forms establishes a sort of kinetic empathy with the inarticulate conscious of the viewer. By "inarticulate conscious" I mean something of which we are aware, but which we are unable to express in words. Thus frustrated, we seek some new language, some new mode of expression with which to communicate new dimensions of reality. In this way, synaesthetic cinema actually expands our awareness of the environment by giving us new "words" with which to conceptualize an abstraction. That these words are non-verbal does not lessen their effectiveness; in fact, their eloquence is increased.

The pulsating blue-red eyeball which opens the film is more than just an eye; it's the Third Eye, the mystic pineal gland, which sees within you and without you. *OFFON* is an approximation of the electrical-magnetic forces of the mind; it is concerned with directly delineating mind, rather than delineating mind by way of symbol patterns. The cosmic red-blue exploding-imploding force field which emanates from the eye is an iconic representation of this metaphysical concept.

The language of *OFFON* is evocation: the place between desire and experience; the interpenetrations and displacements which occur between various sense stimuli. It is expressive without self-consciousness, without an "idea" of expressivity, free in a process which liberates our intentions from our conceptions: that is, it speaks directly to our inarticulate conscious through the language of kinetic empathy. We gaze at these iconic forms hypnotically, much the same as we are drawn to fire or water, because they make us aware of fundamental realities below the surface or normal perception: forces and energies.

Freedom is the freedom of choice. In terms of choice, *OFFON* offers a proposition of both/and, rather than the traditional limited structure of either/or. It is structured of harmonic opposites through which we begin to understand the workings of our own mind, the architecture of consciousness. The mirror-images of the blue dancer, the blossoming lotus of Yin-Yang, up-down, black-white—all these harmonic opposites carry within them some universal logic that is simultaneously anti-logical.

OFFON speaks a total language of synergistic impulses. The history of art can be divided into four general styles: realism, super-realism, constructivism and expressionism. These are correlated, in several ways, to the four types of human consciousness: thought, emotion, intuition and sensation. *OFFON* communicates through all four types of consciousness simultaneously. In the past, trends and fashions in art have tended to concentrate on one style at a time, or one form of consciousness, to the exclusion of the other three. Thus, in a very real sense, *OFFON* creates its own total environment of psychical understanding. It is this total language which the child speaks before he is taught to think in symbols; and it is films like *OFFON* which will make children of us all once again.

Bartlett's third film, *A Trip to the Moon,* has been described as "a discussion of possibilities for man's release. Where in *OFFON* man travels into himself thru his senses to his soul, in *MOON* man steps out of himself into a hole."

Shortly after Bartlett completed *A Trip to the Moon,* in April 1969 (at the age of 26), he was awarded a Guggenheim Fellowship for his work in film.

But perhaps the best way to understand how Bartlett makes his films and why, is in the following conversation between Scott and his girl friend Freude Solomon, at dinner . . .

WORKING AROUND WITH SCOTT BARTLETT: A DINNERTIME INTERVIEW*

FREUDE: How did you make *Offon?*

SCOTT: What?

FREUDE: How did you get the color? I remember you telling someone once.

SCOTT: Do you know what I said?

FREUDE: It was one of those zzzzzzt explanations, you know & then two things got fused & squeezed. . . .

SCOTT: I wish I could remember. . . .

FREUDE: It was thru two things squished out the middle . . .

SCOTT: Well it was something about . . . wait til I finish cutting this . . . let's see, how did I do the color, well. Should we set the table first?

FREUDE: How did you do the color?

SCOTT: Right, right. I want what I say to say what *Offon* says. *Offon* is like what Youngblood said. *Offon* has so much to do with both the theme & the technique: they have so much to do with each other. I want to say it in such a way so that is clear.

FREUDE: Let me ask you another question. Can I ask you another question first?

---

* From *The Plain Truth Is I Love You,* copyright by Scott Bartlett and Freude Solomon, San Francisco, 1968. Reprinted with permission.

SCOTT: First let me ask you what is this? [*Holds up a squash*]

FREUDE: It's a squash.

SCOTT: Wow, OK, sorry, where are we?

FREUDE: Godard claims each particular shot, a dolly shot or a zoom shot, is the answer to a moral dilemma. Do you feel that's true for your effects? That each one of the effects in *Offon* represents, you know, some, some inexpressible thing?
[*much laughter*]

SCOTT: OK, great. OK, what? OK, I got it: The morality, sure. The morality. Wait while I get some cold water.

FREUDE: OK, well, no. Let me ask you another question. What are the electronic effects? How are those electronic effects achieved? I understand that there are television cameras & there are film cameras.

SCOTT: Oh, I see. OK. Here's the answer to the color. "How'd you get the color?" I filmed the images in black & white & made 16 millimeter loops of them. The black & white loop information was sent into a TV switcher. The color was induced by electronic television circuitry cross feeding white information in competition with itself where white light breaks into colors: Spectral breakdown. That's to explain it diagramatically.

FREUDE: When there were two black & white things feeding back into one another, did that actually create color? Color didn't suddenly, magically, appear, did it?

SCOTT: Yeah.

FREUDE: Really?

SCOTT: But also we were able to control color change color manipulate color.

FREUDE: Just out of black & white?

SCOTT: Just out of black & white. And I'm still trying to come up with a technical explanation. A television technician would be better able to tell about it. I have a feeling about it. A feeling of understanding. But its a natural thing to happen. It isn't so extraordinary.

FREUDE: It isn't magical?

SCOTT: It's a natural nearly organic thing to have happened. it isn't so amazing. . . . It isn't magical once you learn the rule. It's amazing. It's like when you finally figure the solution in geometry. You get to the understanding side & it seems so simple & its the spurt on to the next question & also a kick in the pants: Why were you so stupid so as to not see that. Do you eat this thing? Aren't those good? What was that?

FREUDE: Parsnips.
SCOTT: Oh, sweet.
[*Jim enters*]
SCOTT: Hi Jim, how are you?
JIM: What's that? A turnip root?
SCOTT: This? It looks like a turnip root. A big turnip. Taste that.
FREUDE: Color or black & white?
SCOTT: First we fed black & white film loops into the master circuit via the film chain in the television control room . . . then, let's see, cucumber?
FREUDE: Squash.
SCOTT: Oh, squash. Simultaneously we projected film loops on a rear screen on the studio floor and a television camera filmed that. The rear screen photage was constructed with a bank of projectors which included a lot of moire patterns and liquids of Glen McKays. That composite image was pumped into the system and crossbred with film chains. Usually the same image on both. The same loop or same loop that was chosen to relate. Then a second camera is recording the transmission of that combination. It filmed a television monitor on the control room floor.
FREUDE: What's on the monitor is the product of two things?
SCOTT: Right. The product of a crossbreed of two things and the product of itself since it's a circuit loop. That's the static diagram for what induced color from black & white light.
FREUDE: What are the images?
SCOTT: All of the images are alive things. Friends, all sizes. real, organic motion, natural motions of natural things, faces turning, bugs crawling, flames flaming & let's see, maybe I should cut up another parsnip & the other way the color was done was by dying the original stuff, the high contrast black & white stuff. Since the film original was an ab roll, one roll was dyed one color & the other roll was dyed another color.
FREUDE: How did you dye it?
SCOTT: With food color. I built a trough & filled it full of dye & rolled the film from one reel, through the trough & up along banks of heaters & I sat on top of a ladder & very slowly rolled the film thru this assemblage at a rate of about two or five or six inches a minute & it took me all night. A yoga dedication. One roll was dyed one color & another roll was dyed another color

& those two rolls were superimposed on each other. usually one roll was the negative of the other. It's a simple equation. A very easy discovery situation. "I see it all now."

FREUDE: Except that you're the madman who saw it first.

SCOTT: Except, except, yeah, except here's the thing. The *real* point is that the process got me to see it. You know, how one thing leads to another. There's a germ core inside both the meaning of *Offon* & the look of *Offon* & the approach to making *Offon* & everything & it's the same story that we're all telling . . . all the same—whatever it is—alternating current—back & forth & off & on & up & down or dualities of all kinds & so naturally my next film—the film I am working on—is sort of expanding into other dimensions that paradox a given so as to flip you thru a state of awareness—just like Escher. In other words, it's what Victor [Victor Moscoso] said about his drawing—that you have to have a rule & then you break the rule. You oppose the rule diametrically within the body of the drawing. That's part of it. The other part of it, just as a sort of general approach to this whole thing, is to let the movie make itself. To take changes, make leaps, just jump in & see what happens & trust yourself. Let the process itself dictate . . . since it's all unknown out there, it is stuff that's never been seen before & the only way to get there is to accept the fact that it's unknown & hurl yourself out into it. You never know what you'll feel like until you've done it. You can speculate only so far & then you must jump.

FREUDE: I think what you say about the process is true & works by itself—that germ—just as much as the film or any made up meaning does.

SCOTT: Yeah. People have a tendency when they discover something or when they stumble on to something new & fresh to hide the process away & capitalize on it. The only value in that, in the patent office route, is the value for the Caesar side of us—making more than the next guy. If you give it away freely to the world as a whole somebody else is going to pick up the next step—the "it" of it—and the "art" of it is going to benefit & that's a whole lot groovier for the whole of it than the Caesar side which is better for the separate part of it—the man who has by virtue of his secret, by virtue of the hidden process, made himself a magician when anybody else has potential for the same magic.

FREUDE: Yeah, except magic is different all the time anyway. I mean each person who picks it up . . . has different results . . . depending on the story of *their* life.

SCOTT: Right. Any anyone who is really interested in how I did it outside Hollywood is interested more in what to carry on. Hollywood would be interested in how to duplicate it & yet Hollywood rents my films & tries to figure it out but no one ever came to ask me. They just assume right out front that I wouldn't tell them. I've said all this before, in fact, it's all in *Technical & Thematic synopsis.* [published *Filmagazine,* issue #1].

FREUDE: No, no it isn't. I mean it is. Yr right. It is there but all the connecting links aren't there. "Themecream" says it better than any longer explanation. A longer explanation, the words just stumble all over themselves & get in the way: but "Themecream": there it is.

SCOTT: Yeah.

FREUDE: Everything you said before is connected & it goes you see one deer right after another &

SCOTT: One what?

FREUDE: Deer, deer, you know, hit the road. You know you just cut the road out of that & just left all the deer, boom, boom, boom.

SCOTT: Yeah.

FREUDE: Well, I think you've answered all my questions.

SCOTT: What? There are still more bridges to the technical process: the way working works. Yr tied & bound in yoga—meditative, repetitive binding to a still calm center locked into the center of centers—the center of inspiration & that's part of the process too.

FREUDE: & that's part of *Offon*—what you learned sitting up there on the ladder. Tho it's part of the process, it's not part of the imagery—it came later—it's just part of the *process.*

SCOTT: Well, the process & the imagery they're all so bound together—they're all reflections of each other & the movie is a reflection of itself, finally. Like face after face after face receding into infinity & *that's* precisely what it's about. [*Laughs.*] I don't know. Shit.

FREUDE: [To him]: People are continually trying to make Scott feel responsible for his films. [*To Scott*]: "Would you please tell us what you've done, Mr. Bartlett?"

SCOTT: Right.

FREUDE: People ask all the time what does it mean & a lot of people say it doesn't mean anything.

SCOTT: & they get uptight about it . . . they don't understand it & yet, obviously they sense that it must mean something or else they wouldn't bother to ask me what it does mean.

FREUDE: What does it mean?

SCOTT: Or else they wouldn't be uptight enough to tell me that it doesn't mean anything. There's a lot of movies all over the place that don't mean anything. [*To Jim*]: How do you feel when you see an abstract mandala pattern? Do you get pissed because it doesn't mean anything?

JIM: No, in fact I try to go on sensory trips with it.

SCOTT: There are forms in *Offon* & there's a relationship of forms that does imply a meaning. They are images that were collected over a year's time while I was making light shows & the light shows were based on the same principles as the film: follow the technique, follow the image. The images were ikonic images & they fit into different groups. Zodiac ikons, theological ikons, this kind of ikon, that kind of ikon, psychological & emotional reference points. I played with 200 of them for a whole year. I presented them in nightly light shows & they were combined spontaneously & I had immediate audience response & I had an immediate, continuing, ongoing feeling of what was happening & half the time without even thinking I was *choosing* images—where do those images come from? Assuming, I mean, why do I go out & film a guy going like that or why do I film a bug tied over itself? The choice was like masturbating, working with what you got. Most choices were made by relating themes to themes similar to the themes of *Offon*: deep down inside of whatever yr looking at. Emotional stances—floating or getting inside of or warming up & cozy, tied up or breat out, open up, blossom, burst, close all those different emotional stances, different energies that would express different feelings: anger, fear, uptightness, pain, boo-boo's baa-baa's, you know, harried, nervousness & brrrrr. You know just the way you shake the projectors can have a lot to do with triggering emotional response. In fact, maybe at times we were nervous so we got the nervous loops out & just reflected & in the reflection we brought ourselves together again. The arrangement of the material for *Offon* was just, OK, themecream. There's a pattern in *Offon* that can be the pattern of a 100,000 movies & what it is simply, ah, repeat & purify, repeat & reduce, repeat & synthesize—abstract, abstract, abstract. Take this thought, undercut it: take that thought, undercut it: find the meaning inside the meaning inside the meaning: peel the real rind all the way down as far as you can & you end up with the rorschach blot burning & that's what it is & that was the movie, as simple as that. In *Offon* there's no attempt to duplicate specifically on film some vision but rather to reflect on film a process that would precipitate some vision. The meaning that most people who don't accept the film are looking for is a story meaning, a narrative statement you can translate into words. If you could translate it into words there wouldn't be much sense in making a movie about it & filmakers say this over & over again: the reason I make films is cause I can't say it in words. I'm through talking. Dinner's ready. Eat it.

II

MIDDLE AMERICA

5.
The University of Texas

WHITAKER, KOORIS AND STASIS; A BEGINNING

Film work at the University of Texas in the past few years has very much resembled the outlying Texas landscape—barren, scraggy, but showing promise of future development.

Before 1966 and the arrival at Texas of Rod Whitaker, the films being produced in the Austin area were almost completely independent with no particular connection with the University film department.

In 1965, an English major at Texas, Greg Barrios, began a film series based on New York's Cinema 16 program. In reference to the local nickname of the Texas campus ("The Forty Acres"), Barrios named his program Cinema 40. He began initially with films by Andy Warhol and Jonas Mekas, and expanded to a format that includes other types of films as well. Warhol's *Chelsea Girls* drew three sell-out audiences totaling 1,350 recently. Barrios has now left the campus to teach English at Dime Box, Texas, but his Cinema 40 and another venture that he began, the Gulf Coast Film Distributors Co-operative, continue to operate. Gulf Coast brings films from other sections of the country to the Austin area, submits Texas films for national circulation whenever possible, and manages to make a slight profit. The Co-op occasionally shows films at various locations near the Texas campus, such as the University YMCA or the Jewish Hillel foundation.

The current operators of the Co-op are a married couple, Howard and Cynthia Smagula, who run the operation from an apartment near the Texas Capitol grounds, between the campus and downtown Austin. They are both film makers in their own right; Cynthia Smagula has completed *American Health Series,* which contrasts "official" footage of a space shot from Cape Canaveral with footage of a bulldozer pushing garbage into a burning dump. It is a not-so-subtle reference to American technology and what it leaves behind. Howard Smagula has done *A Vision of Art,* which consists of a collage of the 1940s, of newsreels, film clips, and other ennui, backgrounded with a sound track of the Requiem High Mass. Both Howard and Cynthia have been fine-arts majors at Texas.

Jim Kellough, also a fine-arts major, has done several films, generally in color, but usually unspecific in content. His films have occasionally been shown at the University Union, accompanied by tape-recorded music by The Rolling Stones, Moby Grape, and other psychedelic rock 'n' roll groups. Kellough's films are combinations of local wanderings, with campus restaurants and local parks predominant, interspersed with cuts to vague lights and strange forms. With The Stones in the background, completely unsynchronized with the film, his films constitute visual "trips," short odysseys with few reference points.

Others, with even less connection with the University, have done a variety of films with a variety of equipment and wide ranges of professionalism. Stan Bowles and Fred Clark have experimented with short films. And a crew of untrained film makers, Bonnie and Haden Kaden and Bill Gruben, have finished a satire on hero-thriller films, titled *The Return of the Green Fart.* Gruben, who is an economics major, was the "hero" who had the ability, aided by numerous cans of beans, to devastate any villain and break the bonds holding him to the tracks of an amusement-park kiddie train. Not only was this the Kaden's first film (contradicting the title: *Green Fart* had no other film to make a return *from*), but they reputedly borrowed all their equipment from a local camera shop on a 30-day trial. They managed to complete the film and return the equipment within the months' time. *Green Fart* runs slightly more than a half-hour.

Perhaps the best-known of the Austin independent film makers is Ronald Perryman. He has made several exceptional films. *The Heisters* involves two arch villains arguing between themselves, while a third in a dungeon builds a monstrous beetle from a dimestore kit. The climax of the villains' struggle is a classic pie fight, with a six-foot pie, that is trundled from the side of the set with weights. *Heisters* resembles the larger, more expensive Hollywood film, *The Great Race,* and audiences usually make a connection between the two and assume that Perryman patterned *The Heisters* after *The Great Race.* However, *The Heisters* was made first. It has been shown in Sidney and Melbourne, Australia, and opened the San Francisco Film Festival in 1966. Perryman was also invited to submit it to the 1965 Academy Awards, but it was deemed ineligible because it had not been seen first in the Los Angeles area.

Perryman has also completed *Pandora's Easy-Open Pop-Top Box,* which was commissioned by the American Institute of Planters and paid for by the U.S. Public Health Service. *Pandora's* begins with slow landscape footage of green trees and blue skies and quickly cuts to a noisy Interstate highway. It continues to cut between the blessings of nature and the plagues of encroaching civilization. Although filmed on commission, in style and technique, it is easily a campus art-type film.

Dr. Rod Whitaker, faculty member at the University of Texas, was co-producer of the film *Stasis* at Texas. He is shown here in front of the University of Texas Student Union. (Photo by the author)

But the most influential film maker and teacher on the Texas campus is Rod Whitaker, who began teaching in the School of Communications in 1966. Whitaker has a doctorate in film from Northwestern University and came to Texas not because of any great enchantment with the film program, but because of the University's salary scale. Whitaker has been variously described as a "great Renaissance teacher" and a "fantastic professor." He is one of the few film professors who has had theatrical training and, as a consequence, is now involved in an extensive, $10,000 project in conjunction with the Department of Humanities. He is working on a "transmediation" filming of *Thyestes*. "Transmediation" is a word that Whitaker coined, meaning a translation and restructuring of a stage play into a screen drama. Two experts in the Humanities department are involved with this project, and the problem, according to Whitaker, is not just adapting a stage play to the screen, but also filming it so that the climacteric aspects of the drama are resolved in cinematic terms, rather than conventional stage-theater terms.

Soon after arriving on the Texas campus, Whitaker discovered that he had walked into a seriously under-equipped department. The editing booths and screening rooms are located in a converted home at 2621 Speedway, a side-street about three blocks from the main Radio-TV-Film building on campus. The house is literally fronted with bramble bushes and one has to edge carefully through them and up a flagstone walk to the door. One editing room has been converted from a bathroom, and to get to it students and professors alike must walk out the front door, down a steep hill, and into the cellar. Whitaker and the students now have two 16 millimeter Bell and Howell cameras, two Cine-Specials, one Auricon, one Eclair, and two Bolex cameras, with attendant equipment. It is still not enough, for the radio-television-film department has grown in two years from 40 students to over 200, with about half of them majoring in film work.

So far, Whitaker has been surprised at the caliber of Texas film students. They have similarly been impressed with *him*; he is a young, gifted intellectual who never loses his cool, a requisite for college professors these days. He has, according to his students, always remained challenging. His theatrical work has been an added facet in the classroom and while supervising student film making.

Film courses are taught to juniors and seniors and, as is the case with many similar departments, they are structured on introductory, intermediate, and advanced levels.

Beginning students are required to show competence with the technicalities of the equipment; they shoot 200 feet of film, demonstrating, in whatever manner they choose, that they have mastered focusing, exposure, panning, and visual structure. These films are the equivalent of writer's scratchpaper work, intended as exercises and nothing more. They are screened in class and criticized.

Whitaker recently attempted an interesting, but ultimately unsuccessful, classroom experiment. Students who began film work were tested on their abilities. Those who did well received an "A" on the test and moved to the intermediate class. Those who did not pass the tests received a "B" and had to take the tests over again, either failing again and receiving a "C," or passing into the next class. Thus, in theory, even a "C" student at Texas was ultimately the equivalent of a superior student anywhere else. The system, for all its merits, failed; there was just too much misunderstanding, complaints, and criticism. Thereafter Whitaker returned to the traditional "A," "B," "C," scale, with no requirements of repeated testing.

At the intermediate level, students work in crews, usually with four students to each production. Crew members assume the role of editor, cameraman, soundman, and director. Each crew shoots four films, rotating assignments to give each student a chance at the different jobs. Whitaker again grades on the technicalities exhibited, and not necessarily on artistic brilliance or aesthetics. Classwork on this level is concerned with what the students are doing, or doing wrong, with the cameras, sound equipment, actors, and laboratory work. Students finishing this course have edited a film, sent it for processing, and submitted a composite print with sound synchronization.

On the advanced level, students can, and are expected to, concentrate on any level of film making that interests them. This work may take the form of film theory and criticism, leading to an M.A. or Ph.D. degree in film, or it may take them toward commercial film making for various companies that need short promotion, industrial, or instructional films. Richard Kooris, for instance, is a graduate student who received his B.A. degree from Carleton College, in Minnesota. Kooris, under a contract awarded to his own company, Artemas Productions, did a film for the Texas Aeronautics Commission. He completed the film, added a synchronized sound track, had the film accepted, and even made some money on the project. Other companies have offered similar projects to advanced students, usually through Whitaker's office.

Late in December of 1967, Whitaker had reached the point of wanting to make a film that would represent Texas and the abilities of Texas film makers. He wanted a film that "would put Texas on the map" as University film makers. By January 1968, one-fifth of the script was done—a dramatization of Jean Paul Sartre's short story, *The Wall.* But Whitaker, who had enlisted the aid of Kooris for the project, wrote, filmed, re-wrote, and shot some more, constantly keeping only a few script pages ahead of the shooting, and eventually the film bore only slight resemblance to Sartre's story. Their title, *Stasis,* means "the state of equilibrium or inactivity caused by opposing equal forces," and

At the end of *Stasis,* by Whitaker and Kooris, Ray Bazemore screamed in anguish. The scream continued but the action was frozen on the screen and the title of the film was imposed—the first time the title had been seen. It was a very effective end to the film.

the film was made without professional actors. It eventually cost Whitaker and Kooris $1,700, which Whitaker had termed "lunch money in a regular Hollywood film budget." It would have cost over $11,000 had they used professional union-scale actors.

Whitaker and Kooris had the film edited by the summer of 1968 and a final print by the fall of the same year. They shot 7,500 feet of film and eventually edited that to a final version of 2,000 feet.

"Hollywood can't afford to lose money on dramatic films," Whitaker has said, "but if they can be made under $2,000, then University film departments can make them. Films like this are often rare opportunities. We used 'found' locations for the shooting and the politician (as the character Mason) was a local liberal who we filmed in three hours. The sequences that I am in (as the Leader) were also filmed in one night of shooting. The gift of failure without financial ruin is the only gift that universities can give students—the chance to experiment. Writers have to

Pamela Clark, in *Stasis*. The nail on the post plays an important part in the climax of the film.

James Hill in a scene from *Stasis,* which was based loosely on a story by Sartre.

be taught what they want, otherwise the director will take over, and the directors have to be taught to film what the writers produce, rather than shooting a visual film without a script."

Stasis is an excellent film. It is nearly an hour long and begins abruptly, without titles, credits, or sound track. The opening scenes are *cinema vérité* shots of an Austin riot, which had been filmed by a student with a hand-held camera. The scenes are actually in the vicinity of the film building. Unexpectedly, a title appears: THESE SCENES ARE ACTUAL RIOT SCENES. And more are shown. Students are half-carried, half dragged to police vans. Some are clubbed and the cameraman is jostled as he follows the action. Again another title appears: NONE OF THE PARTICIPANTS IN THIS FILM ARE PROFESSIONAL ACTORS. And then the dramatization begins.

Stasis is the story of a black civil rights group, led by a pacifist, which is caught on the edge of a major urban riot in an un-named northern city. The leader, William Turner (played by Ray Bazemore), has made tentative arrangements for mutual help with a liberal white politician, but Turner and the politician know that when riots occur neither can much help the other.

The group is caught by a mob of white hoodlums who demand to know the whereabouts of the politician, forcing on Turner an

Sam Clemens (left) and Raymond Bazemore confront each other in *Stasis*.

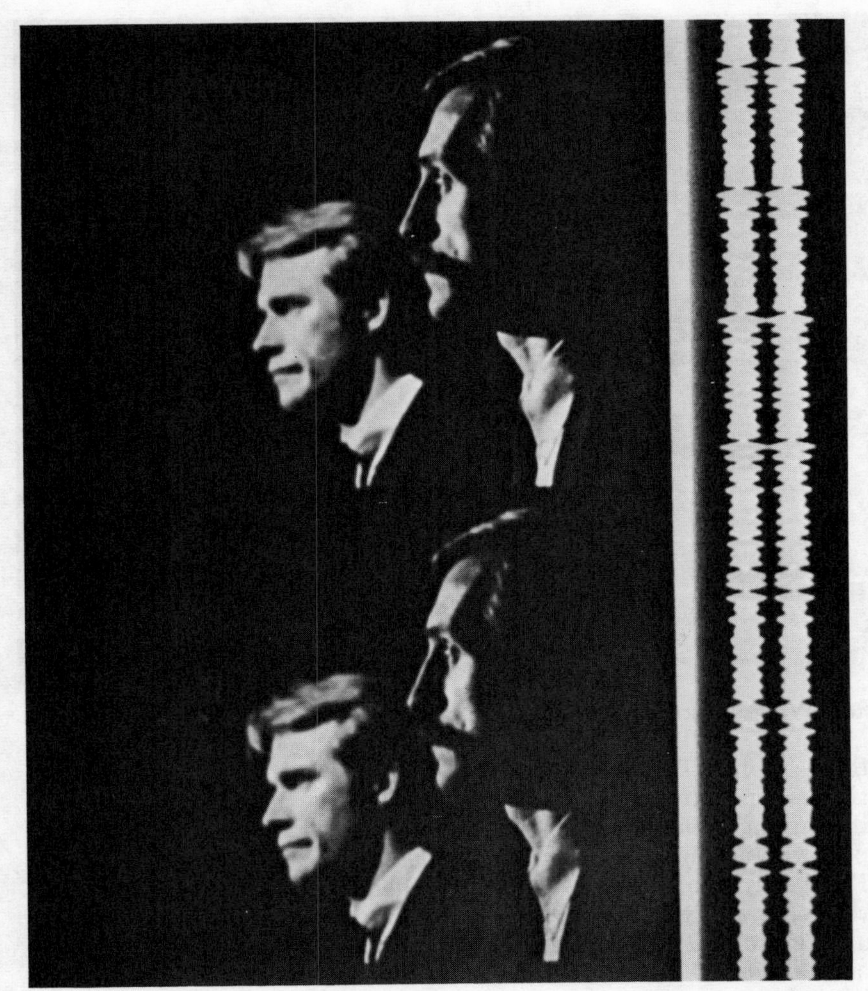

Rod Whitaker (left) and Bill Scott in *Stasis*. The sound track can be seen at right.

existential decision: whether to reveal the politician's location and risk death, or remain mute and risk not only his life, but as it turns out, the lives of his friends.

The film is paced very well and it is tightly edited. The scenes with the politician speaking to the off-camera (but recognized leader—Turner) were shot with a backlighting ratio of seven-to-one, surpassing the general Hollywood ratio of no more than a

Rod Whitaker kneels during direction of *Stasis.*

three-to-one. The lack of professional acumen is noticeable at times—lines are not picked up as quickly as they should be—but the acting generally remains on a high plain, with a notable performance by Whitaker as the leader of the mob: "William, I've been unfair to you. I realize when I was upstairs talking I really haven't given you a fair chance at all. I mean, I say to you, uh, either you die or he (the politician) dies and you make a normal sort of moral decision, because you are a noble man . . ." Whitaker plays the role with remarkable sophistication in the Steve McQueen-Paul Newman style, with professional movements, speech inflections, and command of the role.

The editing of the film by Whitaker and Kooris is excellent throughout. Toward the end, the camera moves in for a close-up of James Hill and slowly pans across a brick wall to Ray Bazemore. The pan across the wall effectively indicates both the passage of time and the hopelessness of the blacks' situation. Dissolves from a dripping water faucet to the characters' faces are also remarkably effective.

The crew of *Stasis* relaxes during the shooting.

Richard Kooris in preparation for camera work in *Stasis.*

At the end of the film, Bazemore inadvertently kills Hill in a scuffle by swinging him into an exposed nail on a beam, which the camera had touched and discarded intermittently throughout most of the film. This sequence was filmed in slow motion by five stationary cameras and the fight and swing into the nail is overlapped into a grim *danse macabre,* not unlike the death throes of Warren Beatty and Faye Dunaway in *Bonnie and Clyde.* Then, Bazemore comprehends that all his friends have died fruitlessly. When he also hears that the politician has been slain in the rioting, he screams in anguish. The frame is frozen. His face is con-

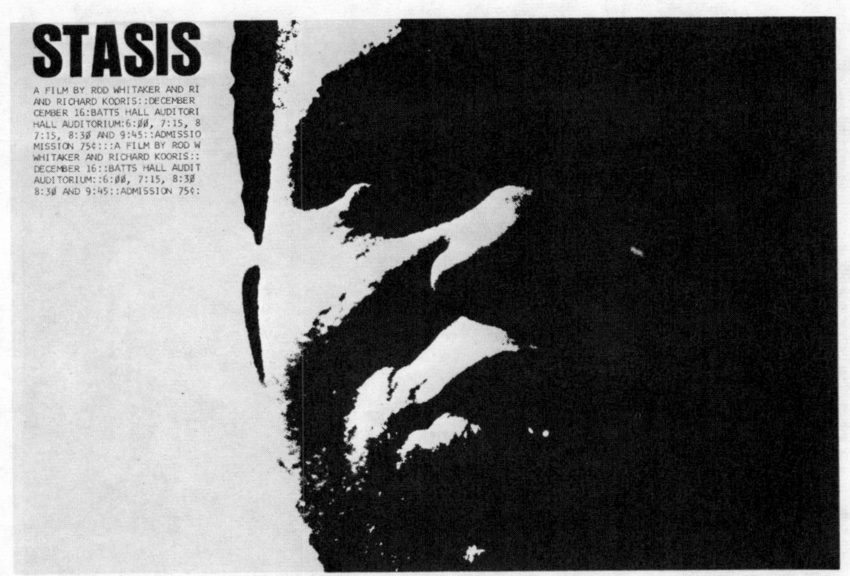

Display poster for the Whitaker-Kooris film *Stasis*. The design itself was so successful that students took down posters as fast as they were put up (apparently the students wanted them to decorate dormitory walls). Consequently, few students saw the film.

torted, the scream continues powerfully, and the title appears overprinted for the first time.

If anything, *Stasis* seems to be a slightly self-conscious film. Whitaker and Kooris, who wanted a showcase, made a film that continually reminds the audience that it *is* a showcase. *Stasis* is the equivalent of a Tiffany diamond, cradled in velvet, turning on a pedestal, reflecting light in its many facets. It is an exceptional film and the criticism of its self-consciousness may, to others, be a minor or non-existent point. It has been described by Robert E. Miller, the director of *Any Wednesday, Sweet November,* and *The Heart Is a Lonely Hunter,* as "quite an accomplishment considering the limited budget." And an article in the University of Texas student newspaper, *The Daily Texan,* termed the film "impressive."

It is, particularly in script and camera work and editing. The script tells most of the story and is herewith presented, reprinted with the permission of Whitaker and Kooris.

Stasis: a good beginning for a growing department.

Richard Kooris, one of the most able film makers at the University of Texas, explains a detail in *Stasis*. The still he is holding is from the same film, which he and Rod Whitaker produced. (Photo by the author)

STASIS

*Transcription of sound track**

NEWSCASTER #1: . . . The President's response to the problem has not gone without criticism. Many people within and without the government have expressed doubt that his actions will have the needed effect on the beleaguered city. Indiana's Senator McPherson, in a press conference this afternoon, said. . . .
SENATOR MCPHERSON: The police are hopelessly inadequate to the task of establishing order. The city is in the hands of the mobs and our President, our President, has convened a committee. The action, gentlemen, is analogous to lightening a falling airliner by emptying the ash trays.

NEWSCASTER #1: In other action, reliable sources report that an attempt has been made on the life of Congressional hopeful, Jake Mason. Mr. Mason has been a leading and controversial force in the civil rights movement. This reporter attempted to contact Mason to verify the report but was unable to locate him within the city. As the battling subsides for the evening, here is Dan Meyer downtown.

DAN MEYER: The streets are strangely empty and foreboding; no traffic moves in the heart of this city except for an occasional police car crawling slowly, apprehensively, through a tangle of overturned, burnt-out cars. But there are people here—unseen in the humid heat of the night. The mobs make their existence known through sudden angry bursts of gunfire. Here and there in the dark city there are centers of confusion and activity. The hospitals are crowded with the hurt and wounded. Red Cross centers have been established for the lost and confused—many are children. Fire alarms sound in the empty fire station; all available fire fighting forces are battling the blazes that threaten all corners of the city. Mayor O'Connor remains in constant contact with the Governor and the President. Earlier today he had these brief remarks to make to reporters:

MAYOR O'CONNOR: When the Negro rioting began ten days ago I warned everyone that white backlash wouldn't be limited to legislative reluctance this year. . . .

BACKGROUND: Put them here with the rest?

MAYOR O'CONNOR: . . . I warned this. Well, it happened. It's lynch law out there and our police can't handle it. There aren't enough of them. Now last year I asked for more funds for . . .

NEWS REPORTER: Mr. Mayor. Could you place the blame for this thing on any group of persons?

MAYOR O'CONNOR: Outsiders. Outsiders are to blame.

OLD MAN: Hey, Bo. Give me a hand here. [*Telephone rings. Radio continues in background.*]

WILLIAM TURNER: Turner. . . . No, we're waiting for you here. . . . Well, look David . . . I don't know. Do what you think is best. I'll have him call you when he gets here. . . . Turn off the radio. . . . Alright! Alright! We know. . . . We're just about ready to pull out. . . . No, we'll wait a while. Look, if Mason shows up there instead, have him contact me.

YOUNG BOY: It's locked.

YOUNG GIRL: No, just open the top drawer.

YOUNG BOY: I just did that.

YOUNG GIRL: Like this.

YOUNG BOY: Oh, yeah? You know, maybe you'd be happier if you weren't so smart.

YOUNG GIRL: I don't like waiting around here like this.
YOUNG BOY: Our leader says wait.
YOUNG GIRL: I still don't like it.
YOUNG BOY: I don't either.
YOUNG GIRL: Hey! Got a cigarette?
YOUNG BOY: Did I take your last one?
YOUNG GIRL: I guess. Why don't we get out of here?
YOUNG BOY: Aw, the big pacifist leader from the East says wait. You know, pack up everything and run around. And just wait.
YOUNG GIRL: I guess we are waiting for Mason.
YOUNG BOY: Yeah, I guess so.
YOUNG GIRL: What if he doesn't come? What if they got him already.
YOUNG BOY: I don't know what if.
YOUNG GIRL: What if they just bust in on us?
YOUNG BOY: I wish to hell they would. I would be on them like ugly on ape.
YOUNG GIRL: Yeah. . . . I hate it hanging around here like this.
YOUNG BOY: Yeah. . . . Hey, how about it, big noble pacifist leader imported from the East. What are we going to do if they bust in on us? Huh?
WILLIAM TURNER: I don't know.
YOUNG BOY: How about Mason? Why isn't he here?
WILLIAM TURNER: I don't know.
YOUNG BOY: Man, is there anything you do know?
WILLIAM TURNER: Why don't you go help Ray?
YOUNG BOY: Yes sir, boss . . . go help Ray. [*Singing*] We shall overcome . . . Hey! The boss says I ought to help you.
OLD MAN: Good.
YOUNG BOY: Well, what are you doing?
OLD MAN: Waiting.
YOUNG BOY: You need any help?
OLD MAN: Sure. Two can wait twice as fast as one. Put your finger there.
YOUNG BOY: My finger put right?
OLD MAN: Okay. Say, what did Mr. Turner say?
YOUNG BOY: Aw, he don't know. [*Telephone ring.*]
WILLIAM TURNER: How do you know? Was anyone hurt? What makes you think that . . .? Well, we need something more than just a guess. . . . You're sure they didn't get Mason? He'll probably come here. . . . What are you going to do . . . ? Well, that is up to you. . . . No, I can't. . . . They're your people. . . . You have to decide. . . . Alright! Alright! We will try to be there. . . . Good luck. [*Hangs up telephone.*] David at headquarters. Trouble at First Street Station. Phone is dead.

YOUNG BOY: What are they going to do?

WILLIAM TURNER: Packing up . . . Leaving the city.

YOUNG BOY: Is Mason with them?

WILLIAM TURNER: No. He will probably be coming here.

YOUNG BOY: If some gray dude don't shoot him on the way.

WILLIAM TURNER: You go ahead and get our mailing lists and let's get out of here. And don't take anything we really don't need.

YOUNG BOY: Yeah, man. Way to go. Right! Right! Right!

WILLIAM TURNER: Didn't I tell you to go get the mailing list.

YOUNG BOY: Yeah, I think you did.

WILLIAM TURNER: Get it.

OLD MAN: You know what everyone is going to say if we leave Mr. Mason behind.

WILLIAM TURNER: We can't risk it. You all packed up?

OLD MAN: They are going to say we wouldn't have left him if he wasn't white.

WILLIAM TURNER: I know.

MILES (bearded boy): William! Will! Will! We got to get out of here! Will!

WILLIAM TURNER: Get ahold of yourself, Miles.

MILES: Okay. I am alright.

YOUNG BOY: Did anybody follow you?

WILLIAM TURNER: Give him a minute will you?

MILES: Will! You have got to get out of here. You got to get out of here.

YOUNG BOY: Did anybody follow you?

MILES: No.

WILLIAM TURNER: Did Mason?

MILES: I don't think so.

WILLIAM TURNER: Was Mason with you?

MILES: He was earlier today. I think he left before they came.

WILLIAM TURNER: Did Mason . . . ?

YOUNG BOY: How did you get away?

MILES: Out the window.

YOUNG BOY: Oh, he just said excuse me while I leave out this window, right?

MILES: I don't remember.

WILLIAM TURNER: Were they honkies from across the bridge?

MILES: No, these men were different. I never saw them before.

YOUNG BOY: Anybody else get away?

MILES: No.

WILLIAM TURNER: Alright. . . . You come with us.

YOUNG BOY: Jumped out a window. Yeah.

MILES: No, I told them I had to go to the bathroom.

YOUNG BOY: Oh.

MILES: And then I got out the bathroom window.
YOUNG BOY: Never occurred to you they might have let you go and then followed you here, huh?
MILES: No.
YOUNG BOY: Some kind of dumb. You are some kind of dumb. You know it? Listen fellow. If they bust in here . . .
WILLIAM TURNER: Forget it, Bo.
YOUNG BOY: Listen, if . . .
WILLIAM TURNER: I said forget it.
YOUNG BOY: You know the world doesn't come to an end when you talk.
WILLIAM TURNER: Go get the Ditto machine and put it in the car. [*Telephone rings.*] Yes. Where are you? It is Mason. . . . You alright. You're not hurt, are you . . .? Yes. . . . Uh-huh. . . . Well, can you get out of town . . .? Well, what do you want us to do . . .? You want me to come and get you . . .? Alright. Alright! Well, could we . . .? Alright. Be careful. [*Hangs up telephone.*]
LARRY (Gunman): Good evening. Put that down slowly. Over there.
BILL (Gunman with mustache): Turn around. Put them right in there.
LARRY: Right there, son.
BILL: See what you can find over there.
LARRY: Alright.
BILL: You ain't going to be doing any moving or any talking or my friend is going to kill you. . . . Just a formality with you, beard. [*Radio in background.*] You haven't got anything worse than a packet of leaflets on you anyway, huh?
STANLEY (Big gunman): Hey, this bottom door is locked.
LARRY: Open the top one first.
STANLEY: Oh.
LARRY: You are really dumb.
STANLEY: Huh?
LARRY: You are really dumb.
BILL: When was the last time you changed your shirt, huh . . .? Okay, he's clean. . . . Now you are a different kind, altogether, aren't you. Nobody pushes you around do they, huh? Naw. You are a real fierce one aren't you, huh . . .? Now what's this . . .? A taped bicycle chain, huh? What's the matter, you afraid it will rust?
YOUNG BOY: Yeah.
BILL: Don't talk. Now I said you people would just be listening. Keep your eyes on that wall, honey. . . . Now I am sure you don't carry any chains or razors do you, huh? But I am going to check

you out very carefully just the same. Alright. . . . Ah, yes. That's real nice, uh-huh.

LARRY: Seems to enjoy his work doesn't he?

STANLEY: Uh-huh.

LARRY: I wouldn't mind that job myself.

STANLEY: Huh?

LARRY: I said, I wouldn't. . . . Forget it.

STANLEY: Uh.

YOUNG GIRL: Stop it.

BILL: Don't talk. Boy, you people are compulsive talkers, aren't you? Get your eyes back on that wall, man.

LARRY: You really get your kicks out of listening to that stuff?

STANLEY: Uh?

LARRY: What does it get you?

STANLEY: Do you have something that you want me to do?

LARRY: No.

STANLEY: Then don't nudge me.

LEADER (of gunmen): If we have to we can lock them down there. . . . Hey, it is only a couple of hours before the Army moves in. . . . We'd better get this thing over with. Oh, by the way, remind me to call our patron. He'll be worried about us. Wondering how we're doing. . . . He worries a lot that way. . . . It's perfectly possible, people, that you may leave here unhurt. I certainly hope that's the way it turns out.

LARRY: I didn't find any. . . .

LEADER: Just sit down. . . . All we need is a little cooperation. I guess I'll be talking to you mostly, William Turner. . . . Turn around. Face me, please.

BILL: Move.

LARRY: I didn't find anything. They pretty much cleaned the place up.

LEADER: Thank you. You know, I know something about you, William. Read about you in the papers. "Pacifist joins the movement. Hopes to bring reason and moderation to city violence" or whatever it was. Well, I know. We've been on those streets all night long and I don't see much reason and moderation out there. . . . Can't change the world.

WILLIAM TURNER: What do you want?

LEADER: Where's Mason . . .? Oh, come on, William. We are not the enemy. We are not rednecks. We have already achieved integration. . . . Look William, you tell us where Mason is and, who knows, you might be free to go practice your non-violent approach in some more likely city. . . . Come on William, we don't have a lot of time.

YOUNG BOY: You won't tell him anything, huh?
LEADER: Who is he?
BILL: Nobody.
LEADER: Yeah, looks the type. . . . Didn't you tell him?
BILL: I told him.
LEADER: Next time. You hear that, son. Next time you talk. . . . Alright. Now come on William. Where is Mason?
WILLIAM TURNER: I don't know. Why do you want him . . .? I don't know where he is.
LEADER: Oh.
BILL: He was talking to him on the phone when we came in.
WILLIAM TURNER: I don't know.
LEADER: Hmmm. Now look, you come right over here. Stand here. Now, William, it is very important to us that we find Mason tonight. Our patron wants it. And we don't have time to persuade you, so here is how it goes. You tell us where Mason is or we are going to kill you. Now, you are an intelligent man. You know we are not fooling, don't you? Where is Mason? Alright. There's a place down in the cellar. You can lock them up there. . . . Okay, I'll give you five minutes to think about it, Will. [*Noise of people exiting.*]
BILL: Take those stairs one at a time.
LEADER: No, we don't have him yet. How would you know that from the suburbs? Okay. Right. Down here . . .
LARRY: Okay. Right down here. . . . Alright, come on. Let's move it. . . . Hey, give me some lights down here.
BILL: Come on, step it up. Right there. . . . Come on . . .
LARRY: Hold it right there.
BILL: Take your gun and cover them.
STANLEY: Okay.
BILL: Why the hell did you bring that radio?
STANLEY: Because I want to hear my program, that's why.
LARRY: Get over here. . . . Hey, what about this room in here? [*Pause.*]
BILL: It is going to have to be cleaned out some. . . . Yeah. . . . Okay. Strip it and we will use it.
LARRY: Okay. . . . Clean the room out. Clean the room out. [*Music from radio.*] Hold it there. Get over there. . . . Get off of him Stanley. . . . That's enough, big boy. Get off of him. Get up. Come on. . . . [*From outside room.*] That was really good, you hear me?
STANLEY: What am I supposed to do . . .? [*Talk continues outside room.*]
WILLIAM TURNER: You all right?
OLD MAN: You okay, man. . . . Take a deep breath. That hurt?

You keep screwing around, man, and you are going to get us all killed.

YOUNG BOY: Had to do something, man.

OLD MAN: I know.

YOUNG GIRL: What are we going to do?

MILES: It is all a bluff. They won't kill you.

YOUNG GIRL: How can you be so sure.

MILES: They can't kill William. He is the only one that knows where Mason is.

YOUNG GIRL: Is that true. I mean they wouldn't kill . . .

WILLIAM TURNER: They must have followed him here.

MILES: No. I don't think so. I don't know.

YOUNG BOY: You don't know! You let them follow you here and you say . . .

OLD MAN: Take it easy.

YOUNG BOY: You take it easy. I told this man I would kill him if . . .

OLD MAN: Take it easy. . . . Take it easy.

MILES: It doesn't matter. They can't kill William anyway. He's the only one that knows where Mason is. That is all they are after is Mason. As long as William is alive, they have got a chance to find out. They won't kill William.

YOUNG GIRL: I wonder what they will do with us. I wonder how long Mason will wait for us.

MILES: That's right, William. If we can stall them long enough . . . then Mason might be gone. Mason is the only one they are after.

WILLIAM TURNER: I don't know how long they will wait.

YOUNG BOY: Well, what are you going to do . . . ? Hey, pacifist. What are you going to do, just let them kill you?

WILLIAM TURNER: What would you do?

YOUNG BOY: I sure as hell wouldn't die for no white politician.

WILLIAM TURNER: You wouldn't now?

MILES: You would let Mason die just because he is white?

YOUNG BOY: Climb off it.

MILES: You are a racist.

YOUNG BOY: You bet your ass.

YOUNG GIRL: Did they hurt you?

YOUNG BOY: Well, what do you think?

BOTH: I'm sorry.

MASON: I am glad you are here William. I thought for a while that your idealism would obstruct your better judgment. I see it hasn't, and I need you. More precisely, I need your reputation as a pacifist. How about some coffee? No, no. I don't mind that question, Bill. But I can't give you the answer you want or expect. I can promise you my intent, but promises are cheap. Getting into office is what I expect out of it. Is that honest enough? If things go well this summer, I'll be in D. C. But in the long run, the only man you can trust is a selfish man whose motives and objectives coincide with your own. That's life. That's the way it works. No, it's simpler than that. One, I need the black vote, but two, I'm not a thief. I'll pay for your vote by supporting the sort of legislation you want, but not because I'm noble or excessively fairminded. I have a second term to look forward to. No. No. We don't have that choice. Violence is coming to this town this summer. It's not going to be another Watts. No one-way street this time. Your people are going to get hurt. Gun sales are up 146 percent. The honkies are ready. This is going to be ugly. That is the picture. Are you going to be with me, Mr. Turner?

OLD MAN: Mr. Turner, you don't think they are bluffing do you? Mr. Turner.

WILLIAM TURNER: Huh?

OLD MAN: You know they are not bluffing, man. If it was me, I would tell them. I really would. I would tell them.

LEADER: William. William. Made up your mind? Will you let me talk to you, William? Open the door, will you?

STANLEY: Get over there.

LEADER: Let me talk to you. . . . Terrible place. Terrible place to be. William, I've been unfair with you. I realize when I was upstairs talking I really haven't given you a fair choice at all. I mean, I say to you, uh, either you die or he dies and you make a normal sort of noble decision, because you are a noble man. That isn't the case now and I want to be honest with you. That isn't your real choice, because he is going to die, William. Even if we don't get him he is going to die. I mean that. Now, don't look away from me. We are not the only people looking for him you know. All of the redneck society is looking for him. On every road leading out of here we have the little kids in the cars with the stars and bars in the back and the can of beer and the shotguns and they are going to get him, in two hours, or maybe tomorrow morning. He's got. He's a had man. So really, what is your choice? Either you tell me and you live or you don't tell me and he dies anyway. How about it William?

WILLIAM TURNER: I don't know.

LEADER: You are lying. Oh well, I mean, we know you are lying. That's part of your noble gaff. Okay, how about this, how about who Mason is. Now do you see Mason? Do you really see Mason like a great big noble white savior. What is he? Is he a vote getter? What is he going to do when this is all over? What is he going to do to you? Drop you? Move on? Get him now or you have to get him later. . . . Where is he? Man, I don't have all day. Where is he?

WILLIAM TURNER: For the last time, I don't know.

LEADER: You are lying. Okay, I am going to make it easy on you. I am going to do it like this, William. It's not you or him anymore. These people. This one. . . . This one. . . . These people. All five. One at a time. All five. Up to you. Now, where is he? Do you believe I'll do this, or do you not believe I'll do this? Do you believe I'm a violent man or not? [*Slap.*] Do you believe me, William? Okay, you got about two minutes, William. . . . Okay.

BILL: Hay.

LEADER: Yeah.

BILL: What do we do if they don't talk?

LEADER: Well, I guess you will have to do it then, won't you?

BILL: Take the tough kid first?

LEADER: Yeah. . . . No. No. Save him for last. He's breakable.

BILL: Okay. [*Water dripping, music from radio is turned on.*]

YOUNG BOY: Well, what are you waiting for man. Are you going to. . . .

WILLIAM TURNER: Leave me alone. . . .

YOUNG BOY: Come on man. . . . Hit me. Do it. Come on. Yeah. Come on. Right here. Come on. Hit me. Hit me . . .! You can't do it, huh, you are a coward. You know, if I was a coward, I wouldn't call myself a coward. I would be a pacifist.

YOUNG GIRL: Why did you do that?

YOUNG BOY: Oh. He's the whole problem, huh? I mean, if he was dead, then they would not want us. And even Mason would be safe.

MILES: They're not going to do it; they're just putting us on. It's all a set-up. I mean it's obvious, they can't just—they can't kill us. That wouldn't make any sense. I mean it's not logical. They tried to bluff before, they said they'd kill William, but they knew he wouldn't talk. This is just another bluff. I mean, he wouldn't talk, so they said they'd kill us, but they won't. It wouldn't make sense. They won't do it.

YOUNG GIRL: You don't really think they're going to kill us, do you?

OLD MAN: No, no, they can't do that.

MILES: They're only bluffing. They bluffed before with William; they're bluffing again, that's all.

YOUNG GIRL: Hey, got a cigarette?

OLD MAN: Sure. [*Door opens; door slams shut.*] No, hell no, not her. . . . Man, tell them what they want to know. Come on, tell them, man. Stop them, man.

LEADER: There's still time, William.

OLD MAN: Tell them what they want to know, man. He's not worth it. Man, that man's going to do you no good. That man's not worth it. That's nothing but a kid, man.
YOUNG BOY: Well, how about it?
MILES: They're not going to do it!
OLD MAN: Tell them! Come on!
YOUNG BOY: Well, how about . . .
BILL: Take it easy; you'll be okay. Right here.
OLD MAN: Why don't you tell them? He's just not worth it, man. Aw, tell them what they want to know. . . .
YOUNG BOY: Come on. [*Old Man, Young Boy, and Miles keep repeating the lines to William until all three are shouting at the same time. Gunshot.*]
OLD MAN: You sorry son of a bitch. [*Radio turned back on.*]
MASON: Of course, it's going to be ugly. People are going to be shot up. People are going to be hurt. Some will die. They're your people. Many will not even know what's going on. . . . No, you're not going to get any help from the police. First of all there is a manpower problem. Most of the force will be assigned to the fire groups, simply watching them. And there is another problem involved in it, the whole tradition and concept of American police enforcement. You know, our police are not like Bobbies, they're more like cowboys. They have a long tradition of pursuit and punishment. They don't protect the citizen. You might as well face it, you can't buy a philosopher for three-fifty a month. . . . Let's not have any of this Ivory Tower concept of massive insurgent people, walking behind some banner in the name of some cause. . . . They can be frightened. And whenever they get frightened, they hurt someone. . . . This is the way it is going to be, and if you can't handle it on these terms, get out. No one is going to hold it against you.
MILES: Why her? I mean, why would they kill her first? That wouldn't make any sense. Besides, we don't even know she's dead. I mean, we saw them take her out and we heard the shot, but that's easy enough to fake. We don't know he killed her. Besides, if they were going to kill us, I mean, they would save her for last. That would put the most pressure on. That would be the logical way to do it. But if they weren't going to kill us, then taking her first would make sense. I mean, if it is a bluff, and we think that they did kill her, it doesn't make sense. So that would be the logical thing to do if they are bluffing. I mean, it has to be a bluff. If they did kill her, then you'd never talk. I mean, you're responsible. . . . If they killed her, you'd be guilty and you could never talk . . . they're . . . Mason's all they're after. And if she is dead, I mean that's it, they'll never find out. They're not that stupid.

They wouldn't do that. They didn't kill her. They want Mason and he's the only one that can tell them. They didn't kill her. They won't kill any of us.

OLD MAN: I remember once when I was a kid. I sneaked off to the circus. It had come to town. And my uncle had told me not to go. But me? I mean nobody was going to tell me what to do. I had to go. I went down there . . . no money . . . couldn't get in. Funny. Then I just. . . . Well, if you can't go on, you got to go back home. So what do you do? I take off. I start home. And man, I realized what time it was and started running. And you look up, looking at that moon and it would follow you. You stopped; it stopped. You run some more—it would run wtih you. So, you know what you got coming; you know what you're going to do. So go ahead and get it. It's kind of funny. And then, uh, you really can't figure what you supposed to be getting all this for. But. . . . You know, not really. It's a little tough, little rough. . . . I don't guess it's going to work.

BILL: Okay, Beard, let's go. Come on!

MILES: This won't do you any good. If you kill me now, Will will never tell you where he is. I mean, Will won't talk anyway. And if you kill me, he is responsible for us. And to Will, that's just like he killed us. He's not going to tell you anything. This . . . this won't help you at all. [*Gunshot, water dripping, radio turned on.*]

OLD MAN: Man, there was this girl I met in a place. It was a beer joint, that's what we call them. And we used to dance together. And boy, did we dance—we could dance. We were just kind of, you know, kind of made for each other. And uh, this man, he decided he wanted to start him a contest. He set it up, got it started. And mister, we danced, nobody beat us—but nobody. So when the contest was over, we had won. What did we win? A trip to San Antonio—to the zoo, yet. And that's . . . that's tough. I don't know what happened to her. We parted. She went her way. Then I met her brother. He said, "she's still sick." What's wrong, man? "Tuberculosis. TB, man." Man, that killed me.

RADIO ANNOUNCER: . . . the latest developments in the current rioting crippling the city. The National Guard, called in by the governor earlier today, now has gained control of a reported two-thirds of this city. The commander of the National Guard stated that the Army should be in complete control of the city. . . .

YOUNG BOY: You hear that? All we need to do is stall them a little —just a little time.

OLD MAN: You know there was this girl. We used to dance and dance. And we did some kind of dancing. Well, this guy gets the idea he wants to start a contest. So, uh, he set it up. And we won.

[*Pause.*] Hey, man, I've been this route! What's wrong with me?
YOUNG BOY: We've got to stall them. We need a little time.
MASON: Now, you'll be on your own, of course. I won't be there when the fighting starts. It's not a matter of hiding. But, if anything happens to me, the whole thing would be pointless. [*Radio in and out.*] I know what you're thinking, Bill. You think I'm an opportunity. Alright. But you have your job and I have mine, and my job's to get elected. . . . Got a match? You know, I can keep a thousand names and faces on my mind and can't find a match sometimes. I'm not really a coward, Bill. I suppose I'm as brave as the next man. But perhaps you don't know the feeling a man gets standing on a platform at night. You can't see beyond the lights. And sometimes I get a tingling in my head, I get a feeling someone's taking an aim. . . . Okay, that's it. I'll try to keep in contact with the cell if I can. If the thing goes wrong, they're coming after me. In that case, I'll hide out at Hill's. Remember Hill, he was the big blond fellow here yesterday. If things go bad and I can't stay with Hill, then I'll have to get out of town. Okay?
LEADER: Where's Mason?
MASON: In that case I'll hide out at Hill's. [*Radio in, radio off.*]
OLD MAN: You know, I remember when I had my first cigarette, I was about ten years old. I stole one from my uncle. And of all places, I went under the house. There were cracks in the floor and up went the smoke and out came my grandmother. And boy, I'm telling you. . . . [*Door opens.*] Well, it's been close before. Nothing ever has happened. [*Gunshot—loud scream from old man.*]
LEADER: Shoot him again! Shoot him again! Shoot him! [*Gunshot.*]
YOUNG BOY: I wish . . . I just wish I knew where that bastard was. I'd tell them. I'd tell them where he was even if they killed us anyway. Because he's responsible for this just as much as you.
WILLIAM TURNER: It's not my fault. If I had told them and they had killed Mason, that would have been my fault. But this. . . . This isn't my fault.
YOUNG BOY: Please, man, please, please, we need time, we need time. Then I'll tell them. I'll make up something. They'll have to check it out and that will give us some time. I'll tell them he's hiding with, uh, what's the name of that guy he was with the other day? Hill. Yeah.
WILLIAM TURNER: No! [*Door banged open.*] No! Anybody but Hill.
YOUNG BOY: Hey! Hey! Hill!*

* (*The boy is killed during the next lines—author*)

RADIO ANNOUNCER: . . . life of Congressional hopeful, Jake Mason, was found just moments ago in the downtown section of the city by Military Police. . . .
OLD MAN: . . . you sorry son of . . .
LEADER: . . . now, where is he . . .?
RADIO ANNOUNCER: . . . again, Jake Mason was found shot to death. . . . [*Repeat of last three lines three times.*]
RADIO ANNOUNCER: Repeating once again, Jake Mason was found shot to death in the streets of the city just moments ago. More information as it is available. Please stay tuned. [*Radio music up.*]
WILLIAM TURNER: [*Scream.*]

Stasis ***won the "Publisher's Award" in*** Esquire ***magazine's first International College Film Festival, as announced in the August 1970 issue.***

6.

The University of Iowa

CHRIS PARKER'S CUT AND WHITEY

Halfway between the two major centers of film industry, Southern California and New York, the University of Iowa is quietly gaining ground in the area that *Cavalier* magazine recently incorrectly labeled as "avant-garde" film making. Film making at Iowa is not "avant-garde," but creative and not typed, like Southern California and New York films sometimes seem to be. Surrounded by the ubiquitous cornfields, a source of constant amusement to out-of-state students, Iowa has produced some major student films and claims to be one of the best-equipped film centers in the country.

The fact that Iowa recognized film from its beginnings is generally not known. Doctorates from Iowa in film and related subjects now number 19—more than twice the number from any other film school. The earliest Iowa M.A. degree in film was awarded in 1916, for *A Social Study of the Motion Picture*. Often neglected since then, film is now being appreciated at Iowa and the Film Department is beginning inter-departmental work with the famous Writer's Workshop and the Center for New Music.

Unlike other film centers, Iowa has shown little interest in commercial Cinema 16-type showings. There has been no theater in Iowa City with courage to consistently show art-type or foreign films. With a population of 40,000, and half of that university students, there is little to do in Iowa City except study, drink beer, or go to the theaters. The three theaters, the Iowa, the Astro and the Englert, are satisfied to show whatever commercial films come their way. (At Academy Awards time in the spring of 1968, the film *The Graduate* had not been seen in Iowa City.)

As a consequence of theater policy, the only art films seen in Iowa City are shown in the University Memorial Union, part of a Cinema 16 program that fluctuates between the mediocre and the just-plain-awful. Occasionally the Film Department shows films itself in the departmental screening rooms.

One of the best films to come out of Iowa in the past several years is Christopher Parker's *Cut*. Parker, like most of the other film makers, is a product of Iowa's interdisciplinary program. He is a Ph.D. candidate in Comparative Literature, lured to the studios in the old Armory Building by Fellini, Antonioni, and particularly Godard.

Cut won first prize in the Second Annual National Student Association competitions in January 1968, and it has been shown in Lincoln Center in New York.

Directing the film-within-a-film in Chris Parker's *Cut*. Richard Killen is the film maker here.

"Film is like the snake, the worm Ourbouros, and like all continuous forms can be symbolic of evil." That, from the film, is essentially the plot. *Cut* is about a man making a film and his relationship to a professor who wants him to study Herodotus instead. The film constantly cuts between the lives of the five main characters to the shooting, the editing, and the screening

Chris Parker (back to camera) in a minor role in his own film, *Cut.*

of the film-within-the-film. Parker himself reads the shooting directions to constantly remind the audience that they are watching a film: "Medium shot: . . . wife on ferris wheel, seat five. Closeup to wife's frightened face." Parker's debt to Godard is direct and proportional: in one sequence the film maker is editing his film-within-the-film. In the editing booth, on the wall, a poster appears briefly. The scene is so short that the poster is not readable. But on second and third viewings it appears to be an acrostic. Reading down and sideways, the poster is a reference to Godard: G-O-D, down the first line, A-R (and a small "t" on the second line), and, on the third line, g-o-D. Few members of the audience ever notice it.

Cut, although skillfully edited and paced well, is chaotic at times. In several sequences Parker has used two tracks, one of the film maker's wife and one of the heroine of the "inside" film. At one point, he has edited them frame by frame, each doing her make-up. The sequence is run so quickly that it appears to be only one girl. At another point in the film, one of the characters talks to the director about the "inside" film. Parker again uses two

Chris Parker's subtle reference to Godard on the poster.

From Chris Parker's *Cut*, a very successful film.

Chris Parker in a minor role in his own film.

tracks and double images, with the synch missing by seconds. The sequence is difficult to follow; the camera continually pans back to the director who is attempting to follow the gibberish from the two sound tracks. It is instant *déjà vu* and impressive.

Parker throws his audience off guard from the beginning of the film. The first segments of the sound track seem meaningless: "Click . . . click . . . clickckck . . . clickck . . . click . . . click . . . click . . ." but the audience eventually realizes that the film maker in the film is editing his own film with a viewer, frame by frame.

Parker shot the whole film on less than 2000 feet of film, casting, in addition to his wife, the neighbors at the University's married student housing project, Quonset Park. "*Cut* is a missed chance," Parker says. "It is like a preliminary sketch one wants to conceal, hang on to, before making the painting public . . . I wanted to make a film which would appear to be making itself, putting itself together on the screen. I didn't do it. I got distracted with other aspects of film metaphysics. I am very concerned with

The film-within-a-film in Chris Parker's *Cut*.

the relation of the film maker to the people, the life, the world he cuts up on his bench, and the audience he bombards, shoots, anesthetizes, on the screen. A film which does not reveal itself to be aware of the implications of its existence is for me no longer permissible. It is a dangerous medium, it is no longer innocent, an illusion. We must recognize its partial responsibility in creating our self-parodying pseudo-existence. That is what the title 'Your End' is meant to suggest at the end of the film."

Time magazine wrote: "*Cut* . . . is the difficult abstract work, with no apparent plot or sequence, which talks elliptically of Greek myths and their significance to film makers . . . Montages of images cascade across the screen for 21 minutes . . . The Chaos is astonishingly well photographed and edited—and . . . displays a debt to the non-styles and nongoals of the cinematic underground."

As successful as it is, *Cut* is not satisfying to Parker. "I want to make films which will make audiences feel the same way, cut off from their spectres at least momentarily, so that they will leave

The film maker examines his own film in *Cut*.

the theater having their egos annihilated, not reinforced, their eyes turned inwards, not outwards." And he adds, "one wonders if such a thing is possible, can happen, in the United States, in the Twentieth Century, to us . . ."

Parker's second major film is titled *Whitey* and he worked on it from September 1968 through June of 1969. Parker prepared introductory notes for the American Film Institute, and on the basis of those notes he won a grant of $2,500 to finish the film. In most aspects, *Whitey* picks up where *Cut* left off. Parker wrote:

> I want to make a film which will probe what I take to be the central dynamics, the nerve center, or primary dialectic of our world (in 1969)—what it means to be a human being in our time, and the meaning of those tensions, contradictions and ironies which make that simple goal so extraordinarily difficult to realize. As a film maker, this means that I must ask myself, and invent a form that will ask itself, what it means to make films (in 1969). In order to unite form and content, medium and message, I have decided to build my film around one of the

Cameraman Robert William Rowley (left foreground) ready for shooting Chris Parker's *Whitey*. Seated with his hands behind his head is David Sundance and wearing earphones is John Benvenuto. During one scene in *Whitey*, there is no sound until Benvenuto threads a recorder on camera. When he turns on the recorder, the actors can begin their normal on-camera conversation. (Photo by the author)

most basic oppositions in our society, in the natural world, and in the film medium—the opposition between black and white, day and night, Nigger and Whitey. My aim is to make a film in which this controlling principle will be present in every image, and operating on different levels within every frame of the "story."

This will not be a film "about" the Negro problem, nor will it express any political or social sentiments in general. That is not my aim. My objective is to make a dramatic-experimental film, as close to a work of art as I am able, which will be relevant to our times in so far as it pushes, broadens, and expands these public concerns into a new perspective. The point of the film will be that every man is both black and white. What is being derogated by the epithet "whitey" is a frame of mind—and another point of the film will be that this frame of mind

Chris Parker directs his wife Clarissa in a scene during the shooting of Parker's *Whitey*. Parker's soundman, Victor Landweber, is in foreground. (Photo by the author)

does not "belong" to any one man or group of men, but that it is a kind of all-pervading beast (symbolized most dramatically by mass media) which infiltrates and controls the lives of all men (even those who think they are controlling the mass media). The film will expand the black-white dichotomy into the larger confrontation of man and "beast," but always with the awareness that the film itself, *Whitey*, is by its very nature, the product of precisely such a dichotomy. As a form, the film will pose itself the dilemma: how can a high contrast medium approach uniform grey? What is the alternative, can there be an alternative, to seeing in terms of black and white?

I have tried to invent a form which will allow me to incorporate "history," and cinema vérité footage, into the film in such a way that it will be impossible to distinguish between fiction and reality. One will never be quite sure in the film whether the action is taking place in the hero's world, in the world of a TV set he is watching, or of a TV set which is watching him. One will not be sure whether some of the people

Victor Landweber, wearing earphones, and Chris Parker during production of Parker's *Whitey* at the University of Iowa. Behind Parker's hand is Mike Lally, who had a small part in the film. This scene was shot in the offices of *The Iowa Defender,* an independent campus-oriented newspaper. Note the ancient handpress in the background. (Photo by the author)

> in the film are "actors" or just people. One will not be sure whether the action really happened or whether it was staged. Or if in fact it might have been real, whether it was supposed to be happening in the present, or was a film, or instant replay, or something that happened in the past. My aim is not simply to create confusion by doing this, but to capture something of the incredible complexity of our contemporary experience of events and pseudo-events.

A massive project for a student film maker? Doubtlessly. But Parker has outlined exactly how he will complete it:

> Perhaps the quickest way to indicate the basic nature of tone of a film is by comparison. Whitey will fall into the same gen-

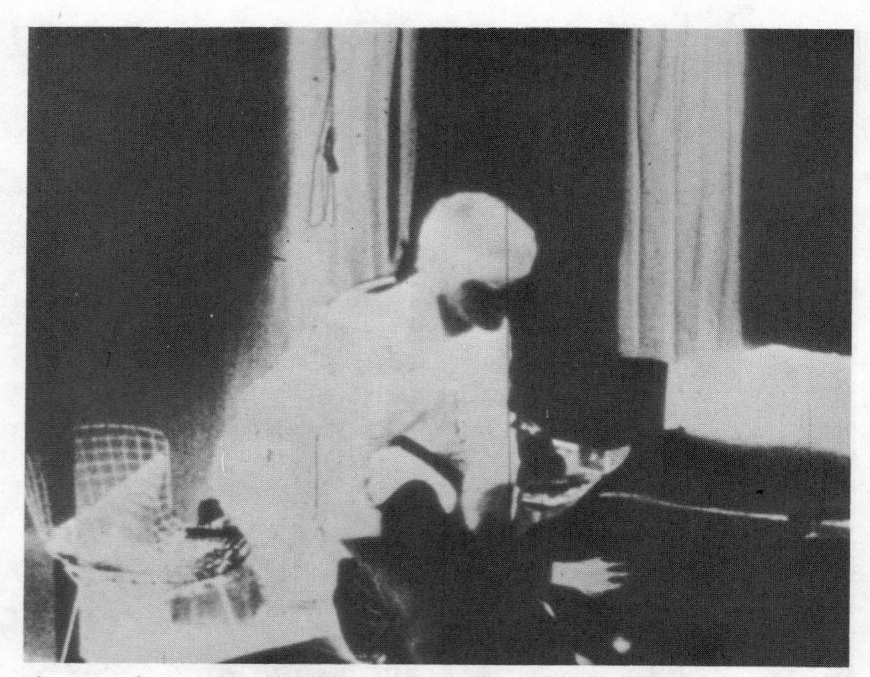

The rape-lovemaking-murder scene that begins *Whitey*. The man here appears to be negro, but is white. The white hand shown in the lower center of the photograph belongs to the girl, who appears white in this sequence, but is actually negro. The scene is a graphic and stunning beginning to an exceptional film.

eral category as Godard's *Alphaville* or William Burrough's *Towers Open Fire,* except that the element of fantasy in my film will be more closely confined to the mechanics and phenomenology of the film itself. Nor will I be trying to suggest a futuristic state, but to make metaphors, myths, and poetry out of our present state. What was "alpha 60" in Godard's film will be the film itself—the actual soundtrack, the structure, the piece of emulsion on which the action takes place—in my film. That is, the hero will discover that the anonymous powers controlling and threatening him and his friends are in fact the film he is in, and that this film is actually an extension of himself. He will discover that he is just as much a part of the anonymous power (perhaps called ITT) as anyone, or anything, else. He is a stockholder. He is both Whitey and Nigger, alpha 60 and Lemmy Caution, Iago and Othello.

On the narrative level, this will be the story of an under-

John Benvenuto as Martin Luthar, the hero of *Whitey,* is a hippie reporter-photographer, trapped in the film by the film itself.

ground reporter-photographer-cameraman who has a threefold objective: to discover and annihilate ITT, to rescue his girl from ITT, and to discover the four frames (now in the possession of *Life* magazine) which he thinks contains the secret of the Kennedy assassination. The three basic groups of characters in the film will be:

1.) the hero (perhaps called Luther, or maybe Che) and his friends.

2.) ITT, who we will come to know only as a voice, a noise, or a manipulating and sinister presence.

3.) the captive girl (perhaps called America, or maybe Desdemona, or maybe not.)

Luther is white and his girl is a Negro. He knows only that she is being kept away from him, but he doesn't know whether she is in the hands of Negroes or whites, nor will the audience know until the end when they discover that it is neither. The film will begin with rapid flashes of black and white under the title and credits accompanied by female screams; and will be followed by a scene in negative showing a white man and a Negro woman who will, of course, appear as a black man and a white woman. This will actually be Luther and his girl, and the audience may suspect this later on, but will not be sure. It will be a rather violent scene, both in sound and image, suggesting simultaneously torture, rape, love-making, and murder. The girl could be either in pain or ecstasy. It will also be rather abstract and dance-like, ritualistic, shot in high-contrast positive, perhaps in slow-motion.

After this we will move into the actual world of Luther as a white man whom we learn is looking for a girl (the audience will not know whether she is Negro or white at this point) who he is afraid has been tortured or raped. Throughout the film and Luther's search for the girl, we will return to the negative scene of the ritual act. It will be the most beautiful part of the film. We will also hear the voice of his girl talking to him throughout the film, a personal voice, intimate, as if she were writing him a letter trying to tell him where she is and what he must do to save her. She will represent something like the lost soul of America, the emanation of our somnambulant culture. The audience will hopefully suspect that Luther and his girl are the same couple as the black man and the white woman in the negative scenes, but this will be withheld until the end, when Luther breaks into the control center of ITT and processes the negative film.

ITT will be in control of, hovering over, every aspect of the film. We will see it operating constantly as a TV monitoring devise, following Luther and his friends. ITT will have the ability to select a particular gesture or scene and loop it, so that we see a repetition of the same action over and over as ITT analyzes it, files it, computes it. When ITT moves in to eliminate some of Luther's friends, ITT will simply freeze the action, turn it negative, over-expose it, at which point the freeze will be released, the film will switch back into positive, and the person in question will drop in his tracks. The voice of ITT will be pure rhetoric in addition to pure noise; the realm of cliché and double talk abstracted from political speeches, advertising, industrial propaganda, and newspapers. When Luther says something questionable, ITT will have the ability to instantly censor it, garble it, slow it down to half speed, erase it, or splice in something else. At times the camera work will assume the random scanning pattern of ITT, moving from Luther to take in all the details of his environment, as if making a visual note of potentially useful information. Luther will of course not know that he is in a film, but he will wonder about it. He suspects that someone is watching him the way he is trying to watch everyone else. ITT will also be able to make use of instant replay, and in fact, prevent Luther from doing certain things by cutting his action short just before he achieves his end, like putting a piece of food in his mouth. In the end,

ITT, the black rapist on negative film, and Luther himself on positive film, will be revealed as one and the same. They are all part of the syndrome of "whitey."

The base of Luther's operations will be the editorial office of his newspaper. Here he will collect with his friends to plan his strategy and plot his tactics. Here he looks at photographs related to the assassination, trying to piece together evidence and discover the connection between the missing four frames of the Zapruder film and his missing girl. He looks at the photographs and the film he has shot in the streets—interviews with people, shots of riots, shows of after the riots. He looks through memorabilia of his girl, sorts information, and writes out his editorials. He watches things on TV. We will see him in many different situations; at home, in bars, cafes, the library, on the streets, in stores, always looking for and collecting information, taking pictures and asking questions, searching for the secret, trying to see through the veil of mystery, the film, which surrounds him. He is approached by a prostitute hired by ITT who tries to find out how much he knows. Throughout all this, we will be constantly aware of ITT watching him. He will look for his girl in Negro neighborhoods at the same time he is there taking pictures of the riots. The audience will probably assume that his girl is white (except for the recurring hint of the negative scene) and that therefore he is looking for the Negro rapist. Actually, his motive will be that he is looking for her parents, thinking that she might have returned home to hide with them, to riot with them, or to protect them from the rioters. Finally, he will find the parents and they will tell him that she is not there.

At this point the audience will know that his girl is Negro, Luther will realize that she is definitely in the clutches of ITT, and that ITT is in some way the entire medium which surrounds him. He begins to realize that he is part of a film he didn't know about. He goes to the production studio, the recording lab, the sound stage—no one is there. But he seizes the tapes in the tape room and degases them, wiping out the rhetoric of ITT. The girl's voice gets stronger, closer, more intimate. Finally, he breaks into the processing lab where he sees the piece of negative film running, and the ritual being performed. He takes the negative film and runs it through the processor, and we see that piece of film change through a very long lap dissolve from negative to positive. When it reaches positive, there will be a slow zoom in on the white man, now recognized as Luther. At this point, Luther realizes that he is his girl's captor, that they are trapped on a piece of film, and that he must break into the projection room and stop the film. That projection room is of course similar to, and might well be, the same as the one located behind the audience watching the film *Whitey*.

Luther gets into the theater, but can't break into the projection room. He runs down the aisle towards the screen to tear it with a knife, but before he gets there, the Luther within the film, on the screen, shoots him, six times. Luther dies in the aisle with the audience, possible perverts, standing around and his girl's voice talking in the background. The film will end with an interview with this girl, very straight and realistic, possibly by a newspaper reporter asking her why Luther shot himself, what his relationship was to her, whether these decapitated fingers were his, where he and she had been for the last week, etc. The film will end with something like this exchange:

"His name was Martin Luther?"

"Yes."

"How do you spell that?"

"LUTHER."

"Race?"

"White."

"Your name?"

"America."

"I don't believe you."

"It's true."

The shot of the girl's face will then be terrifically overexposed as she repeats, "It's true," until the screen is washed white. Over that will appear the word THE. Then the screen will switch to black over which will appear the white word END.

. . . a large portion of the film will be cinema vérité footage. One of the exciting and essential things about the project is that it will enable me to make use of news and documentary footage—and sound. I have specific ideas about what I want, but I can only trust my luck in getting them. And one thing that I want from my actors is spontaneity. This means that I will try to impose as little as possible upon them within a given framework. Many times I will ask them to improvise. And this will mean of course, shooting until I get what I want. I did not do a script for *Cut* before I made it, so I have had some experience working this way. I found the script in my first film, *Beginning,* restrictive. I like to start with a general body of ideas leaving myself open to new possibilities which may occur at any stage of the process. Hence the ending I present here is tentative. I'm not sure that I'm satisfied with it, but I can't think of anything better at the moment.

And Parker adds:

This film, I think, can't help but have an audience. It is the sort of thing which could be made into a feature as well as a short, cheaply or expensively. The central motif has many levels, variations, and ramifications. My limitations as a student film maker will be as usual, in addition to my own, the availability of competent actors, sophisticated portable equipment, and most of all, access to controllable locations. My objective is to make a film . . . which is both in touch with

John Bovey and Loren Bivens, independent film makers, have worked and studied at the University of Iowa. (Photo by Harold Eastman)

what's going on, and yet stretches out awareness of that beyond the obvious to the essential.

Another film maker, working more independently than Parker is Loren Bivens. Bivens first became interested in film in 1964, when he knew Beverly Grant (now the wife of actor Tony Conrad). Bivens and Miss Grant were acting together in an off-Broadway production and, according to Bivens,

> she kept telling me "film, film film. You've got to meet film makers." She was working with Ron Rice and Jack Smith. So I got into film making and was fascinated. For a while I was assistant to Gregory Markopoulos and even appeared as a werewolf in the film *Dracula,* which Jack Smith produced and starred in, for Andy Warhol.
>
> I eventually paid eight dollars for an eight milimeter camera and began making films. My first film was *The Chastening,* a mystic film, allegorical, about a girl who was a prostitute and who somehow was engulfed in darkness and came into the light and was re-born a virgin. That was in 1964 and it was forty-minutes long. There were a lot of double-exposures in it. I then made *Unjeweled,* a film about what a hassle the city (New York) is to live in. But I am most proud of . . . *Shall Statues Overturn.*
>
> *Statues* is the reversal of the Narcissus complex; and is about a man (Bivens' partner John Bovey) who makes statues of mud on the bank of a stream. The man gazes at his reflection in the water to pattern the statues. At the end of the film the man suddenly goes joyfully berserk, and smashes the statues, jumping up and down on them, as if to say "piss on it" . . .

After *Statues* Bivens was drafted, and after serving in the Army he came to Iowa City to enter the University. He bought more equipment and worked as a bartender to pay for it. Mentally he has moved forward and sees an entirely new type of film:

> Many film makers are doing "visual" films. They are using new images, new experiences and new language. They tend to believe that if a certain subject or treatment has been done before, it has no power or influence if it is done a second time. I don't really believe that. Unlike most other film makers, I think of film as an actors' medium. In my films, I want very strong photography and very strong sound. I haven't found form as fetching as dramatic conflict to a resolution. I am now working on a new type of film, which I call the "highpoint" film. These films are series of highpoints in emotional conflict. The highpoint emotionally is that instant in which all circum-

Loren Bivens works on a Movieola. Bivens has developed what he terms a "highpoint" technique of film making. He has made several films in New York and Iowa. (Photo by Harold Eastman)

Jim Lusher appears as a professor in *The Moral Timbre* by Loren Bivens.

Howard Weinberg appears in Loren Bivens's *The Moral Timbre*.

stances of a situation are seen clearly by the participant. It is the crucial moment, which is all important. It would be like that instant in a pole vault when the vaulter is at absolutely the top of his vault; before he begins falling over the bar. In my films, I pile these highpoints one after another, like Joyceian epiphani. The highpoints develop one after another instead of the traditional plot development. It is, perhaps, a technique of poetry, although most film makers don't like to use any literary references when speaking of film.

Biven's first film with this technique was titled *The Moral Timbre,* which was concerned with ideas and morality. Unfortunately, when the footage was returned from the lab, Bivens found that the processing had put scratches down through the middle of all the footage and the project had to be scrapped.

His second film, *Pipedream,* is a short six-minute film dealing with a man's inability to cope with the bottom of thought. Bivens did the filming in one month, but had to put the film in his refrigerator to keep it fresh because he couldn't afford immediate processing. And because of his independent film work, he dropped

Loren Bivens (right) shoots an extreme close-up of Howard Weinberg for Bivens's film *The Moral Timbre.*

some courses at the University and thus lost his G.I. Bill because he didn't take the minimum course work. Bivens has turned to commercial films, solely for the purpose of financing his own projects.

"Films have to have a sense of rhythm and film makers have to have an understanding of rhythm, in life and in film," Bivens says. "Film makers must cut their films as if they were music—they must have regular measures and phrases and movements—beats and counterpoint. You can use this to be very strong—to run a very precise rhythm. But if the film maker wants to jangle the nerves of the audience, he can chase the beat. This is, I think, a jazz principle—to chase the beat and build tension and then revert to a regular beat and release the tension."

An award-winning film maker at Iowa, Ted Perry (who moved to the University of Texas for the 1969–1970 school year), joined the department faculty after graduation. As a student at Iowa, he won the first annual University Film Producers/McGraw-Hill

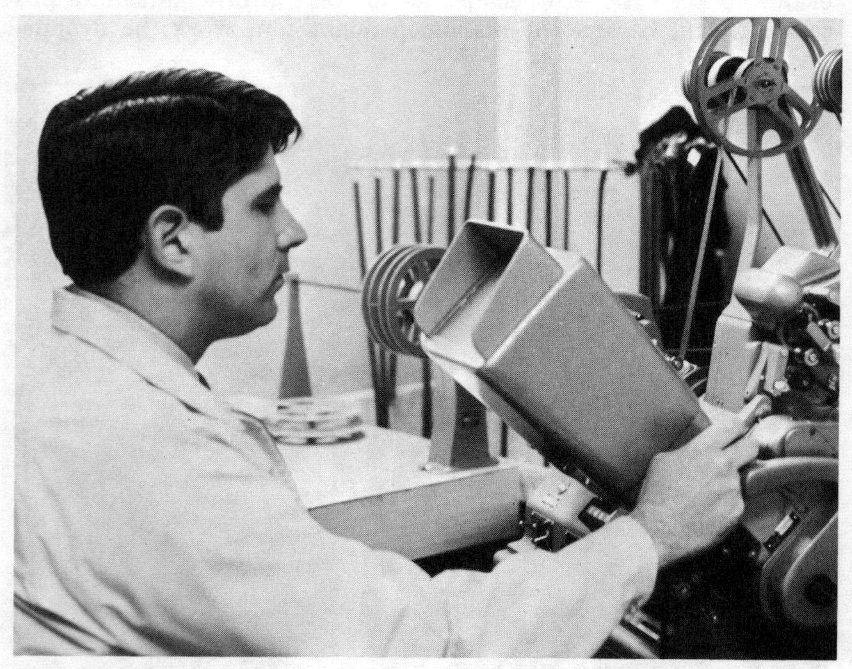

Editing film is Ted Perry, who, as an undergraduate at the University of Iowa, won the University Film Producers-McGraw Hill $1,000 prize. Perry is now on the faculty at the University of Texas. (Courtesy of the University of Iowa News and Information Service)

Scholarship of $1,000 for his film, *The Quiet Desperation*, about Texas drug-addicts. He teaches the beginning classes in Cinematography Techniques.

"Iowa, away from the East and West Coasts, is free from specific orientations. Here we can try what others have not—and we can do what others are not doing," he says.

"Currently no one here is fiming documentaries. The students are breaking up the conventional story patterns. The better films are those in which the students do not plot; they ignore the temporal and concentrate on the real world.

"The students are ignoring the sound stages and are continually carrying the equipment outside. I am constantly re-excited by films here. It's an excitement that I don't find in other mediums, other forms. The student films here, even the beginning ones, are as exciting as anything I have seen."

Raymond Fielding has taught at the University of Southern California before coming to Iowa. He has been past president of the University Film Producers Association. He left Iowa for

Working on an editing machine is Ted Perry and standing behind him is Raymond Fielding. Fielding, former president of the University Film Producers Ass'n, has been on the faculty of U.S.C. and Iowa, and is now teaching at Temple University. Perry, an outstanding film student at Iowa, is now on the Texas faculty. (Courtesy of the University of Iowa News and Information Service)

Temple University for the 1969–1970 school year. He says: "The films here are generally very polished. The students are very stylistically conscious. I think that here, the students are working in cinema vérité, and the students *are* in control of the medium and are very competent.

"I think a mark of their work is that the student films don't look like student films. I think that this is due to the inter-departmental connections. Chris Parker is interested in art and literature and film; Ted Perry was in drama before beginning his film work—there are several others who have begun film work after courses in the Writer's Workshop, or in the Art School or in the Music School."

One student in film, working with the Art Department, is Joe Anderson. With the help of Hans Breder, art professor, Anderson has completed an interesting study of nude forms, and he is working on the transposition of two-dimensional work collages into the film medium.

Anderson's best film to date is *Inter-Media Rehearsal,* a study

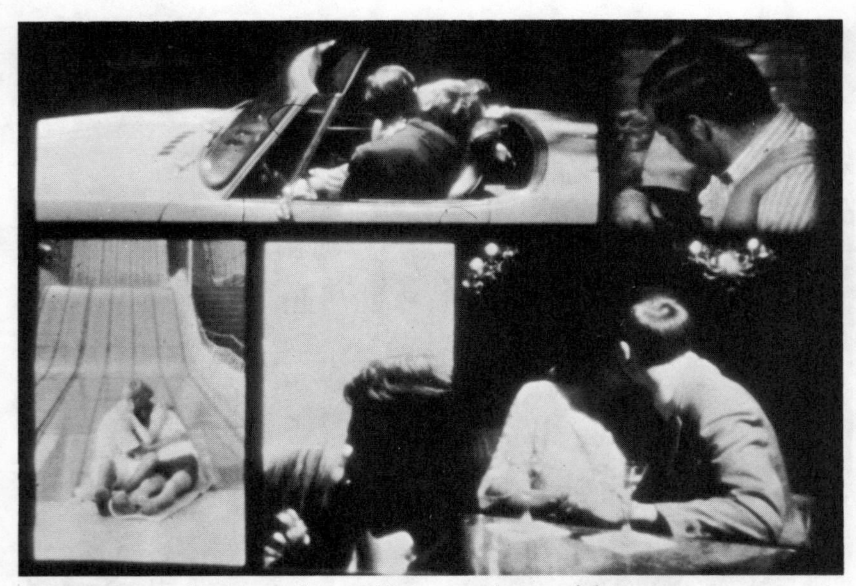

Five different kisses in five different styles and locations are seen in one scene in the multiple-image film *Marmalaide* by Terry Taylor. Taylor is a doctoral candidate in the mass communications program at Iowa and his *Marmalaide* is a 16 mm film in color and black and white. It is a comment on the current social situation in various forms and styles.

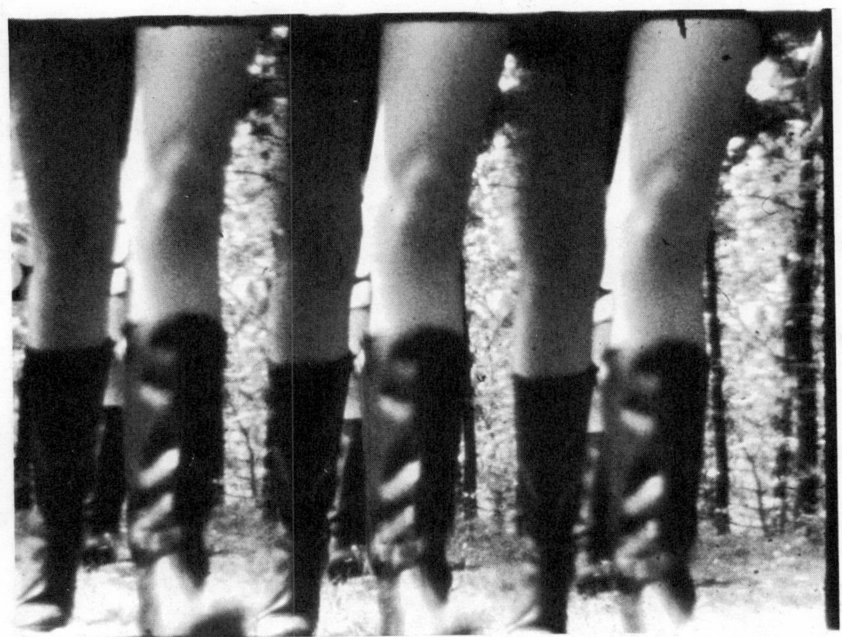

Legs á la Busby Berkeley are seen in *Marmalaide*. The film is in black and white and color.

in contrasts between the University Center for New Music and the Art Department. Anderson cuts from a rehearsal of oriental-sounding contemporary music to the run-through of a photography session, involving two nudes wrapped in Saran Wrap and illuminated by a psychedelic crystal reflecting ball. It is a highly sensual and intriguing work. Anderson says of the nude scenes, "We all had a ball doing it," reflecting Iowa's position of permitting nudity as long as the scenes have a relevance to the subject of the film.

"We have a problem here that is being faced at other schools," Ted Perry has said. "We try to meet two demands. First, we have students from the Journalism School in the film courses. They are primarily interested in the rules, the technicalities. Most of the other students are from the arts and crafts areas—music, literature, film, and for them, we concentrate in the experimental areas. As a consequence, we have found that most of the journalism school students are dropping out of the sequence. And I think that is good. The death of a university comes when it is nothing more than a training school—full of rules."

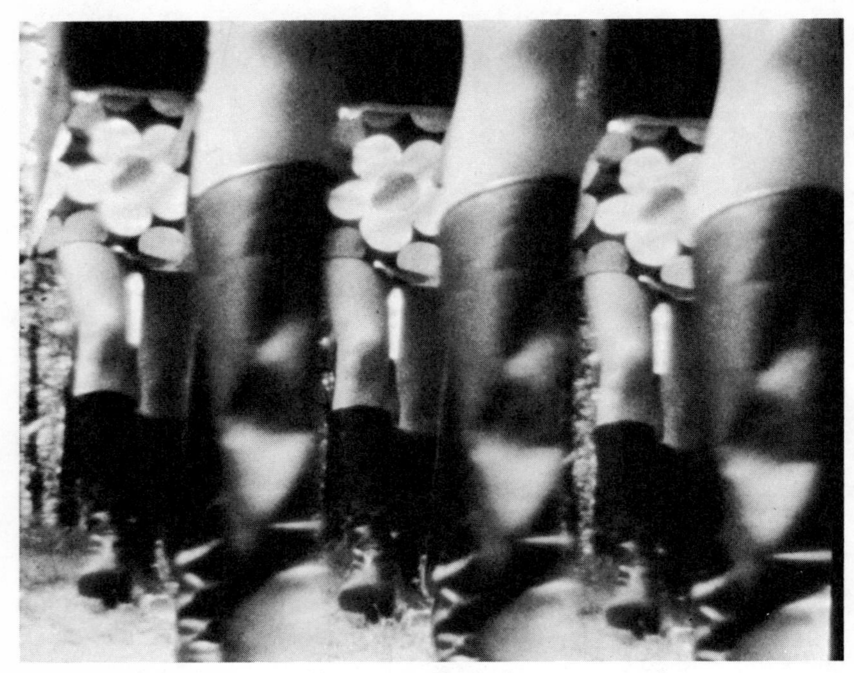

Legs and legs from the film *Marmalaide* by Terry Taylor.

Although Iowa claims to have one of the best student-equipment ratios of any film school in the country, this statement lends itself to statistical juggling. There are only about 40 students in the beginning classes each semester in *Cinema Techniques;* 12 or so in the following class in *Cinema Production* and four to six in the last class, *Cinema Workshop.* The beginning class must make four films during the semester with a three-man crew for each assignment. Their longest film runs ten minutes. The *Cinema Production* class adds sound to the basics, and the last class, the *Workshop,* can do whatever they wish with black-and-white film and sound. The beginning classes shoot their films with Bell and Howell cameras; the advanced classes use Airflexes. All classes have enough lightmeters to go around and there are several Movieolas. Unfortunately, the editing cubicles, which should of necessity be dust-free, are located under a wooden corridor. Whenever classes change and the corridor is crowded, dust rains down onto the film, the Movieolas, and the film makers. However, there are no logistics problems at Iowa that plague other schools like

Highway signs are shown in five different frames in one sequence of the film *Marmalaide*. Taylor uses the split-screen technique effectively in the film.

An extreme close-up of a girl from the film *Marmalaide*.

U.C.L.A. Students can generally use the equipment whenever they want to.

There are about 36 film scheduled each year in the advanced classes. For one reason or another, only about 20 are finished. Of those 20, usually two or three, not more, are exceptional.

"The people here are very hip," Raymond Fielding has said. "We have found a new generation of film makers. They are educated—they know where their own art form comes from and they are politically educated. And they haven't been corrupted—yet. I think that this is because the medium is still young and college-aged people find a young medium exciting.

"The only restriction we place on the students is a practical one of production. We have found that frequently the student will have a well-designed film, that from a production standpoint could not be completed during a particular semester. Otherwise,

An abandoned limestone quarry was used for segments of Diane Peterson's fantasy, "Nine O'Clock in the Afternoon." Here, Dick Tibbets at right conducts a rustic revival. Playing the guitar at left is John Bean. Cameraman Mike McKay is at extreme left and soundman Harry Kroyer kneels at right (back to camera). (Photo by the author)

we have no restrictions on film subject. Students are working on animation, the problems of two-dimensional art, experimental films, light and movement. We don't necessarily look at these films as end products, but as experiments in the medium.

"We are less production oriented than we are scholarly—and experimentally oriented. We are trying to teach the film teachers."

The highlight of the film year at Iowa, although not officially a part of the film program, is REFOCUS, a student and professional film festival held annually, late in March, in the Main Ballroom of the Iowa Memorial Union. During the 1968 program, Godard's *Masculin-Feminin* was one of the highlights, as was the Japanese film *Yojimbo.* Peter Weiss's *The Mirage, Wholly Communion,* and *A Woman Unashamed,* based on a poem by Iowa poet Paul Engle, were also shown. Several films from the Canadian National Film Board were presented.

REFOCUS attracts standing-room-only audiences for some programs and during the longer programs, which last until almost midnight, students are free to get up and get coffee, stand around, and smoke. The 1968 program was something of a hassle. The Film Department, which in theory ought to run the program, only advises from the sidelines. Gung-ho student government kids actually handle the program, which accounts for the sometimes-seen lack of film acumen.

The 1969 program featured Andy Warhol's *My Hustler,* Ingmar Bergman's *Persona,* Kenneth Anger's *Magick Lantern Cycle,* and a series of Bruce Conner films. Norman Mailer's film *Beyond The Law* was shown, and Rip Torn and Buzz Farber, friends of Mailer's and participants in the film, made guest appearances during the program. Wynn Bullock, a still photographer presented lectures on still photography and Stan VanDerBeek presented a multi-media show and lecture.

Award-winning films from the 1968 National Student Association were presented during one evening's showings. They included *Keinholz On Exhibit* by June Steel, *The Latter Day* by Donald MacDonald, *An Idea,* a color cartoon by Walton White, and *Now That The Buffalo's Gone* by Burton Hirschfield—all from U.C.L.A. Several 1969 National Student Association entrants from Iowa were also shown. REFOCUS is more of an exhibition than a contest; although certificates are presented to the participating film makers, the awards presented at the end of the week's program do not carry the weight that similar awards do at the Ann Arbor Film Festival, for instance. The walls of the departmental offices at U.S.C. particularly are covered with REFOCUS certificates.

With the emphasis on the experimental and the free-wheelin',

Ken McCullough sits disconsolately in a corn field in the ambiguous and frenetic film, "An Invitation to Time" by Iowa film major Edgar Grana.

with small classes, adequate equipment, and an emerging spirit of film making among the cornfields and puritanical locales of Iowa, the University is taking definite steps forward. They include the design of a multi-million dollar arts complex of glass and brick that will include art, music, theater, and film and that will occupy a two-block area along the Iowa River, which bisects the campus. This multi-level, plaza-type complex should be ready for the film department sometime during the 1970–1971 school year.

Despite the loss of Fielding and Perry, there is little doubt that Iowa will continue to be one of the better film schools in the midwest.

7.
The University of Michigan

GEORGE MANUPELLI AND THE ANN ARBOR FILM FESTIVAL

For those interested in film as an art form and for those interested in independent film making, the University of Michigan offers a unique combination of showings. Although deficient in film courses on campus, the Ann Arbor community has two fine film programs—the annual Ann Arbor Film Festival, conducted by George Manupelli, and the weekly Cinema Guild program.

Admittedly, the offerings of film courses on campus leave something to be desired. Robert Davis taught two film courses within the speech department and, for several years, attempted to base his program on the University of Iowa's three-course sequence. Unfortunately, Michigan offered little in the way of film making on which Davis could base a program.

Until 1966, the film sequence within the speech department had one Bolex camera. During the 1966 school year, additional equipment was obtained: two Bell and Howell cameras, four editing benches, one homemade animation stand, splicers, four quartz lights, and one footage counter. After 1966, there were three courses offered within the university: one in the speech department, *Introduction to Cinematography,* and two courses in cinematography in the art department.

In the fall of 1969, *Advanced Cinematography* was offered, but students had to work without sound. But Davis left in the fall of 1969, after several years at Michigan, to direct a similar department at Southern Illinois University at Carbondale. The official film sequence at Michigan is practically non-existent, compared with other midwestern universities, like Iowa, Northwestern, and even West Virginia.

On their own, however, students at Michigan have made some exceptional films in the past few years. One of the best is *Inevi-*

George Manupelli, founder of the famous Ann Arbor Film Festival and producer of several award-winning films. (Photo by the author)

tably by Ida Jeter and Doug Vernier. *Inevitably* was filmed entirely in an old-age home, cinema vérité, with telephoto lens, so that the patients were not aware of the camera. It is a harrowing coda of despair. Jeter and Vernier have achieved a stark statement of age, with close-ups and little sound track. *Inevitably* is such a strong psychological study of old age that most college-aged audiences refuse to watch it.

Another excellent film, shot with the assistance of the speech department, is *Mime* by Ed Van Cleef and James Onder. A pantomime artist, safe within the confines of his stage, wanders outside and begins to play innocently with a six-year-old girl in

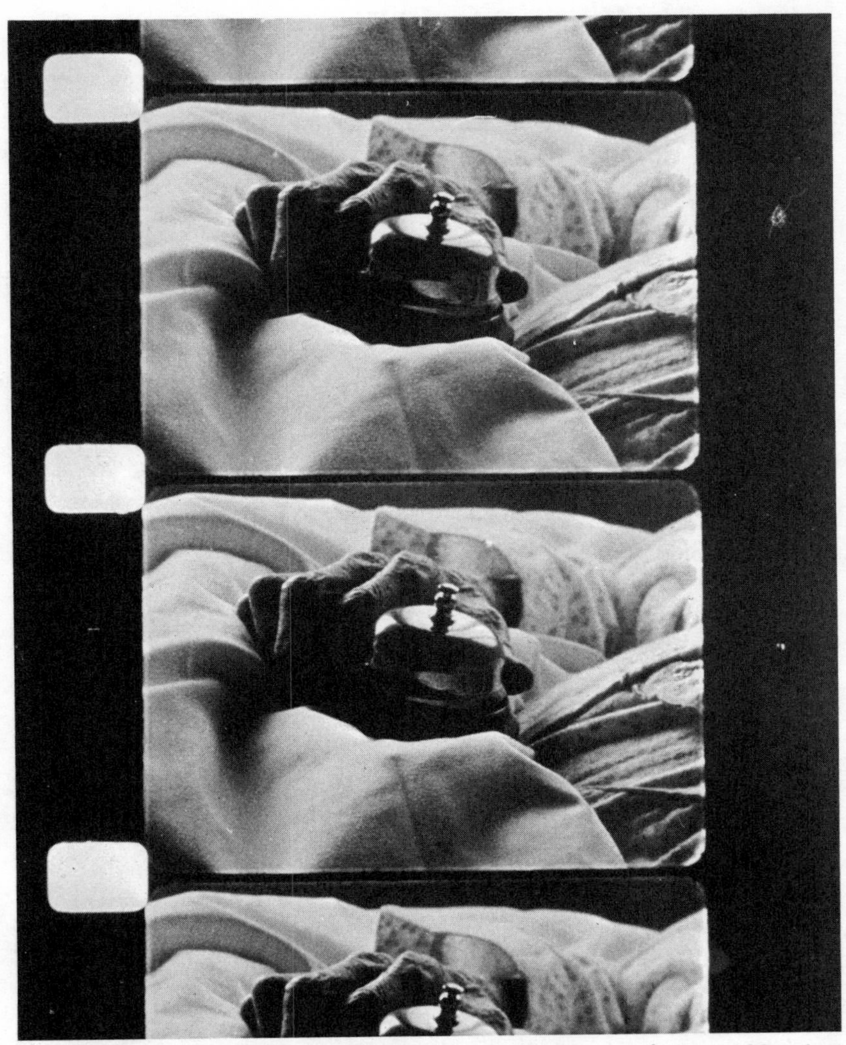

From the gripping film *Inevitably* by Ida Jeter and Doug Vernier. *Inevitably* was filmed in an old-age home and none of the patients knew they were being photographed. Most college-age audiences find the film unnerving.

a public park. He comes to realize that society considers such a relationship unnatural, and he returns, disconsolate, to the safety of his stage, where individual pantomime is "safe." *Mime* was filmed entirely without sound and the artist uses his craft of pantomime with the little girl very effectively.

Exposure by Morleen Getz and Terry Jones involved a facts-

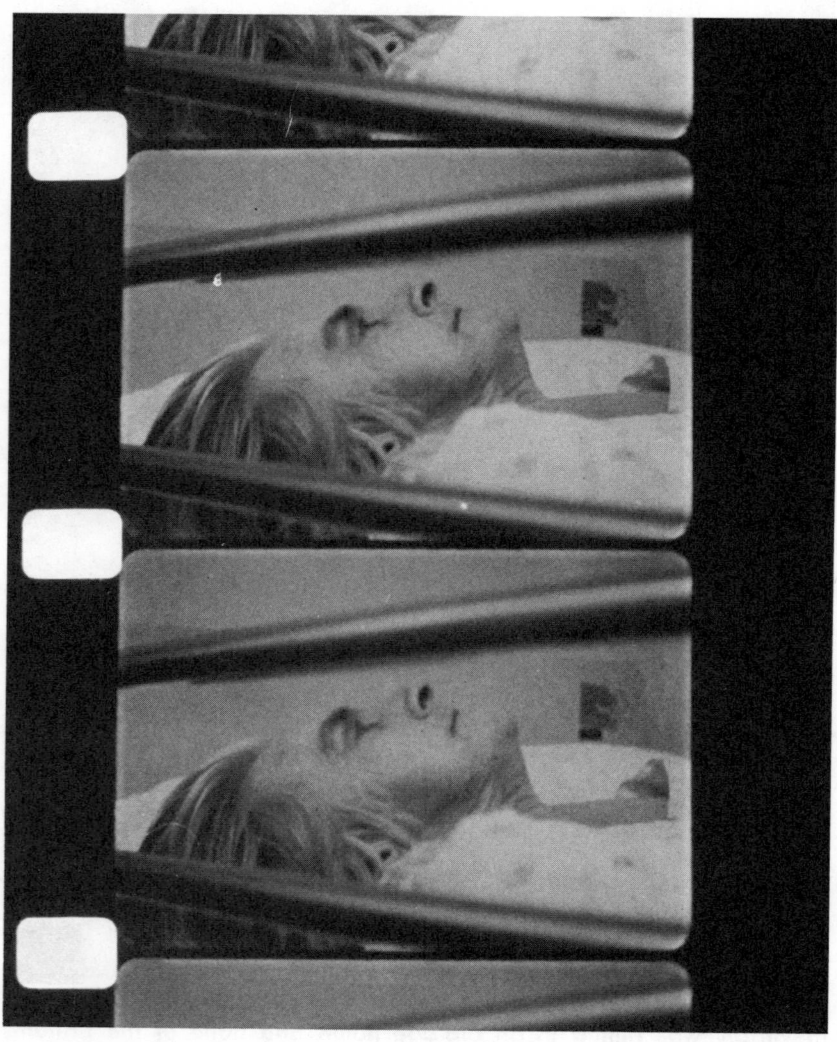

From *Inevitably,* an excellent cinema vérité film done in an old-age home, by Ida Jeter and Doug Vernier.

of-life encounter of a young girl who begins modeling for a photographer. She falls in love with him and the film becomes a travesty of the high-fashion photography usually associated with the fashion magazines.

Kee Dewdney, a young Canadian who has been working on his doctorate in mathematics, has produced three fine films independently. One, *Scissors,* is an animated study of scissors *as people,*

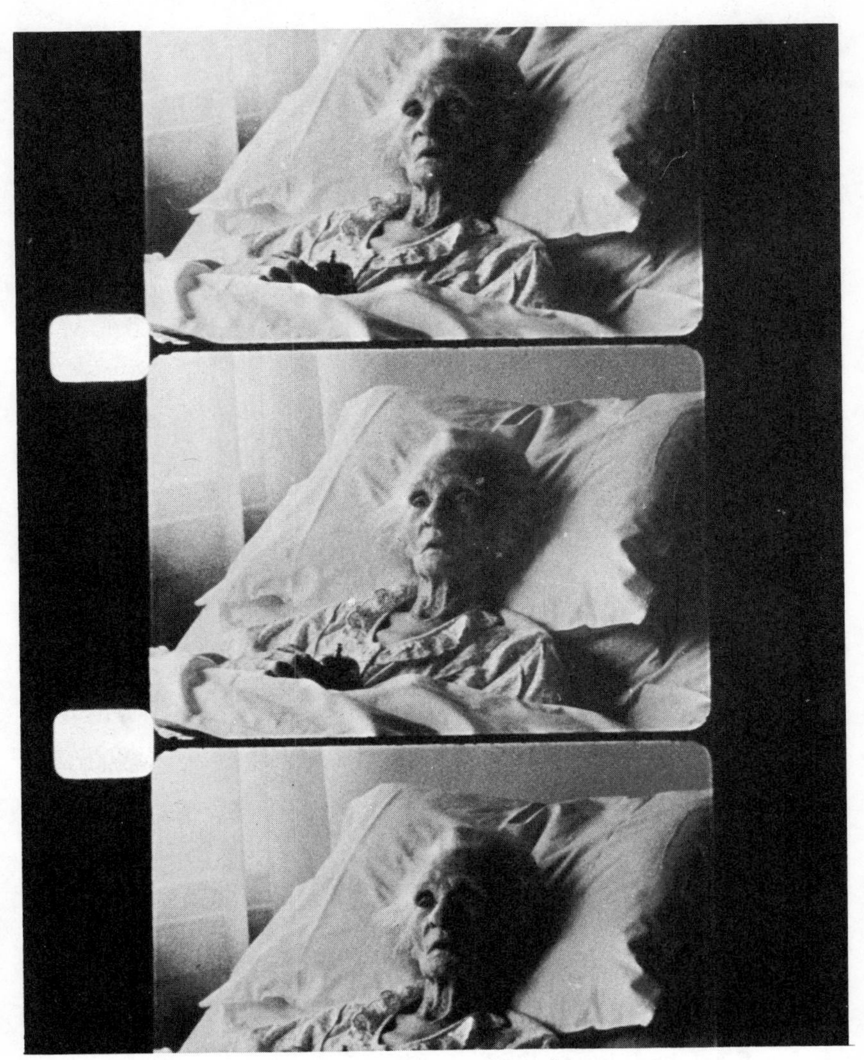

From *Inevitably* by Ida Jeter and Doug Vernier.

giving birth to young, growing up, and dying. Another film, *The Maltese Cross Movement*, is at once cryptic and hallucinatory.

Maltese Cross is partly animated and partly in color. The Maltese Cross reference in the title refers to the mechanism that pulls film through a projector. But Dewdney's film actually represents a "trip" he made on the chemical DMT, similar to, though more

The mime artist enjoys an innocent afternoon with a girl in *Mime* by Ed Van Cleef and James Onder.

powerful than, LSD. The Maltese Cross is a sustaining theme for various sequences within the film.

"It's actually my whole life," Dewdney has said. "All the experiences I have ever had, all the emotions that I have ever felt, are in the film in some fashion or another." Dewdney's *The Maltese Cross Movement* was so successful as a film that he de-

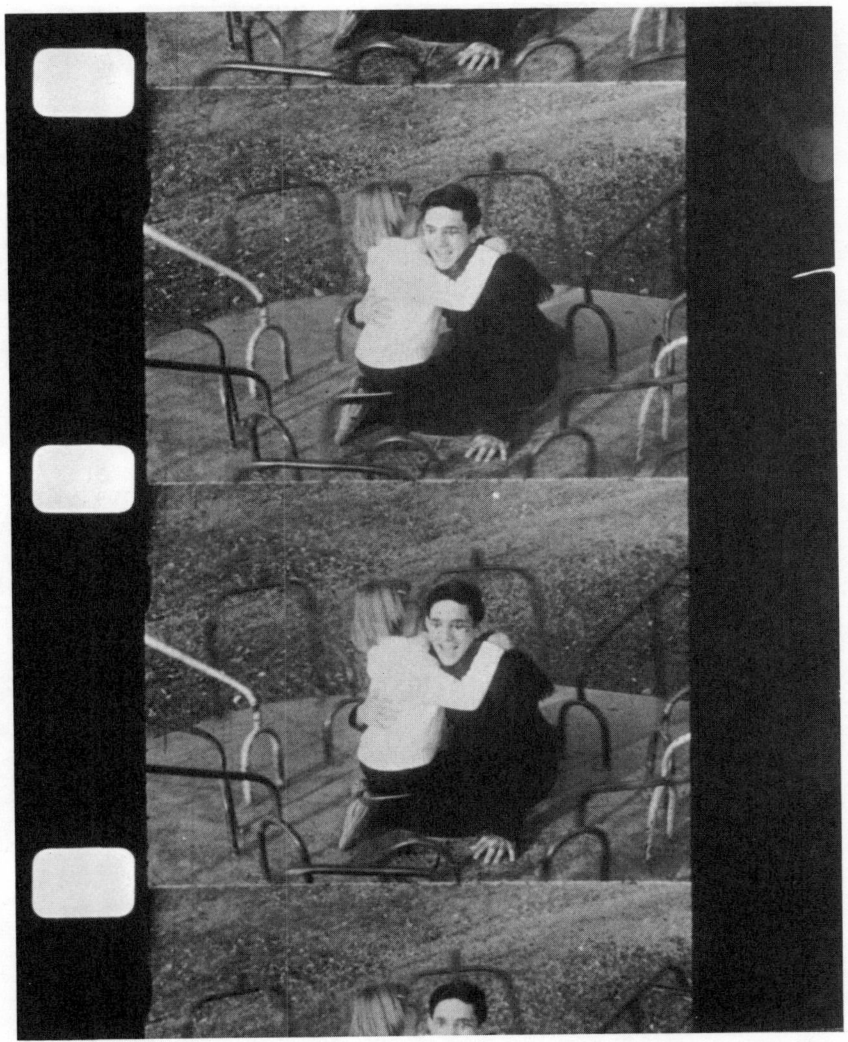

The mime and the girl enjoy an afternoon in a park. Note the theatrical make-up over and under the mime's eyes.

signed and printed a book describing the action on the screen. The book is written in arcane language and shows, among other things, Alice Liddell, the model for Alice in Lewis Carroll's *Alice's Adventures In Wonderland,* and Adolf Hitler as a baby, playing with a maltese cross. It also includes a picture of "the first girl that I ever fell in love with," as Dewdney says, which is

A stranger with a knife waits in the bushes for a child in *The Package* by B. G. Cross and Rich Wood.

a lingerie model from a slick woman's magazine. "People tripping on acid (LSD) have told me that to read the cryptic book and figure it out is a fantastic experience," Dewdney says.

Dewdney returned to his native Canada in the fall of 1968 to help establish a film program at the University of Western Ontario at London, Ontario.

Before returning to Canada, Dewdney also experimented with

From *Exposure* by Morleen Getz and Terry Jones.

Illustration made in conjunction with *The Maltese Cross Movement* by Kee Dewdney.

Illustration made in conjunction with *The Maltese Cross Movement* by Kee Dewdney.

Illustration made in conjunction with *The Maltese Cross Movement* by Kee Dewdney.

Kee Dewdney, young Canadian who made several excellent films, notably *Scissors* and *The Maltese Cross Movement,* while studying at the University of Michigan. In front of him is a keyboard that he is wiring for sound so that he can play radio stations like piano notes. (Photo by the author)

loop films. He became so intrigued with the idea of continuous film and synchronized sound that he became involved with a massive project of wiring a clavichord keyboard with *radios*. Eventually, he had a keyboard which he could "play" like a piano keyboard, with each key tuned to a different radio station.

Michigan's most famous program is George Manupelli's Ann Arbor Film Festival. The reference book *An Introduction to the American Underground Film* (Dutton) credits the Ann Arbor Film Festival as being "one of the most durable (of the film festivals)." Begun in 1962, the Festival is a week-long showcase for films submitted from throughout the country.

The 1969 Festival was a 40-hour competition and for that, Manupelli received over 250 films (double the number submitted for the 1968 contest). Of those, almost 100 are shown. During the week-long program in March, two different programs are presented each day from Wednesday through the next Sunday. The highlights and the award-winning films are shown on the last day of the festival.

"In Ann Arbor, we present the program to about 4,000 people and every showing is sold out. We don't view the program as a local event; rather we believe that it is a showcase for talented young film makers throughout the country," Manupelli said.

The awards jury, which in the past has included critics like Pauline Kael, reduce the program to 12 hours of films that then tour throughout the country.

The film tour generally includes: The University of Illinois; Northern Illinois University; Kenyon College in Gambier, Ohio; Denison University; Kent State University, Kent, Ohio; The University of Cincinnati; The Vermont Film Festival; Bowling Green State University; Chicago; Madison, Wisconsin; the Yale Film Festival; Xavier College; San Francisco State College; the University of California at Berkeley; and other locations.

Each film is eligible for up to $300 in first prize awards at Ann Arbor. The various stops on the tour also have prizes for the best films shown. Consequently, a film maker who enters the Ann Arbor Film Festival and has his film chosen for the tour may make as much as $15,000 in total prizes from various stops on the tour.

After the tour, the films are syndicated by Mike Getz, of the Cinema Theater in Los Angeles. He usually selects 17 theaters throughout the country, and the films are then shown in: San Francisco, Los Angeles, Columbus, Denver, Tempe, San Diego, Champaign, Memphis, New Orleans, Fresno, Sacramento, Albuquerque, Dayton, Toledo, Akron, and Youngstown. Getz pays the film makers a dollar a minute for their films, with a minimum of $250.

"There are no restrictions placed on the films submitted at the Ann Arbor Film Festival," Manupelli says. "The only thing that we ask is that the films must be in 16 millimeter and be in good condition. Otherwise, the film makers are free to submit what they wish. We like to think that we represent no 'school' of film thought."

Some of the films shown first at Ann Arbor are now thought to be classics of the genre. Kenneth Anger's sadio-masochistic motorcycle study, *Scorpio Rising,* was first seen there, as were the works of Bruce Bailey; Ed Emshwiller's *Relativity* was an entrant, as were films by Robert Breer and Stan VanDerBeek.

A few of the films entered in the 1966 program, for example, included two by Yoko Ono, now married to Beatle John Lennon;

Oh Dem Watermelons by Robert Nelson; George Manupelli's *Jennie and the Poet;* and two, *Lupe* and *Vinyl,* by Andy Warhol. Warhol's rock group, The Velvet Underground, also made an appearance during the 1966 festival.

The 1968 program included: *Christmas Is Naked Turkey* by Benjamin Hayeem; *Cayuga Run* and *Peyote Queen* by Storm de Hirsch; *Alla Ricera Del Miracoloso* by John Milius and John Strawbridge; and (from Michigan) *Sandlewood* by Onder and Van Cleef, *Malanga* by Dewdney, and *Inevitably.*

Some of the winners in the 1969 program were: *A Personal Statement by Robin Farbman* by J. L. Cassidy; *F U N R* by John Chon; *Hollywood Here I Am* by Bill Clark; *Selected Quotations From Chairman Mao* by Bruce Hentsel and Ellen Frank. They were all from Ann Arbor.

Ralph Arlyck's *Sean* from San Francisco State and an entry from U.S.C., *Last Days On The Sand* by Richard Robertson, were winners from universities.

Brandy In The Wilderness by Stanton Kaye, *Akran* by Richard Myers, *Nuptiae* by James Broughton, and George Manupelli's *Dr. Chicago* were 1969 winners from independent film makers.

Manupelli has gone to great lengths to keep film interest high. In June of 1967, Manupelli and Joseph Wehrer built two nearly full-size World War I Scout biplanes and one Fokker triplane. The planes were sold at Robert Rauschenberg's New York studio by Christie's auction house of London. The proceeds were used to help collaborate work between artists and industry.

Manupelli has also done several exceptional films on his own. Some of his best are: *Bottle Man* and *The House,* 1959; *My May* and *Jennie and the Poet,* 1962; and *L'Historie du Soldat,* 1963.

Writing in *Filmagazine,* he said:

> In my films I am concerned very much with the camera—a precise use of the machine. I have tended to use the camera even self-consciously although the consequences for having done so were never very painful.
>
> As far as what I chose to film is concerned—at one point my themes were very romantic/poetic/dramatic. Now my themes are likely to become more obscure—vague . . . of little interest to anyone except myself (or so I am projecting).
>
> I have filmed those things I had a desire to see on the screen —in the same sense a painter (and especially the surrealists—) constructs those pictures that occur in his mind and that he would like to have a look at for what they may be worth.
>
> PARIS (ANGENIEUX 12-120), for example, is a two-minute shot of a little red schoolhouse. But it is also a portrait of many things: a portrait of the schoolhouse in which I live; a portrait

of the two zoom movements that occur during the two-minute run; a portrait of the markings on the lens from which the film takes its title; a portrait of two minutes, et cetera.

I like the photographs in *Vogue* and *Bazaar*. They are among the most provocative images being produced today.

I also like harness racing as a source of imagery. I like the straining little machines who obediently snake by the stands at the half and who charge by four abreast at the finish. I like the broken dreams of horseplayers that are so much like the broken dreams of unsuccessful artists.

(Manupelli once owned a harness horse named Diane's Debby, whose lifetime earnings through 1967 were $1,381.)

More recently, he finished *Portraits, Self Portraits and Still Lives,* after working on and off of it for five years. *Portraits* is a gauzy, soft-edged daydream that expands into lesbian dream sequences.

For the next few months, and even perhaps the next few years, Manupelli's *Dr. Chicago* project will encompass most of his time, equipment, and finances. *Dr. Chicago,* the Film Festival award-winning film, is the first of a projected 20-film series—each two hours long.

When he completed the first film, *Dr. Chicago,* Manupelli had definite plans for the next three: *Dr. Chicago Goes To Sweden; Ride, Chicago, Ride;** and *Dr. Chicago Steps Out.*

Essentially, the series follows the adventures of Dr. Chicago, an abortionist and sex-change scientist—the latter claim a fraud, the former true—whose plans include a sex clinic in Sweden.

In the title film, Dr. Chicago is run out of Lima, Ohio (which all the participants consistently mis-pronounce as *Lee-ma,* instead of *Lie-ma*) by the local police. Because he wants eventually to get to Sweden, he steals a Volvo (a Swedish car) that breaks down in the midwestern woods. There Dr. Chicago meets a deaf-mute, a child of nature, who can perform mystic rites and make potions with herbs and berries. Dr. Chicago finds himself surrounded by Negro detectives, who for sympathetic reasons won't close in on him and the deaf-mute. The deaf-mute eventually stabs himself and Dr. Chicago and his cohorts escape.

In the sequel, *Dr. Chicago Goes To Sweden,* half the actors speak only in foreign languages and Dr. Chicago wins the Nobel Prize by operating on himself.

The Dr. Chicago films are full of strange digressions and bits of by-play and Jewish ethnic humor. Jokes about race, love, and sex are injected by all the films' participants. And Dr. Chicago

* On July 19, 1969, the American Film Institute announced Manupelli had won a $13,000 grant for the completion of *Ride, Chicago, Ride.*

himself is played by an actor who stutters in real life as well as well as on camera, thereby adding additional bits of unconscious and accidental humor.

Dr. Chicago, for all its professionalism and award-winning characteristics, was filmed in a frantic seven days, according to Manupelli. The second in the series, *Dr. Chicago Goes To Sweden,* was filmed in four days, with all the cast and crew contributing bits of dialogue and shooting directions. Manupelli wrote about 60 percent of the dialogue an evening ahead of the shooting schedule, and the remaining 40 percent was contributed during the shooting.

The films are in 16 millimeter and are black-and-white. Manupelli wanted the character of Dr. Chicago, to "establish a New American Folk Hero, the equivalent of Dickens' heroes. I think that Dr. Chicago will eventually become the equivalent of Hamlet or Dick Tracy," Manupelli says.

Manupelli teaches in the art department at Michigan, with side trips to Bowling Green State University in Bowling Green, Ohio (not far from *Lee-ma,* Ohio), and the Center for Advanced Studies at the University of Illinois, at Champaign-Urbana, Illinois. Not surprisingly, he holds a doctorate in art.

In addition to the Ann Arbor Film Festival, the area also offers the Cinema Guild program, one of the best film programs of its kind in the country.

The program is run weekly, throughout the year, by a 12-member board of directors. Two paid staff members, usually graduate students at the University, are responsible for the operation of the program.

The Cinema Guild encompasses the whole spectrum of film from early silent films, through films of the 1930s and 1940s, to foreign and experimental films. The Cinema Guild is one of the oldest programs on the University campus—dating back almost to World War Two—and it has been established particularly for students and film makers who want to know more about film. Cinema Guild's philosophy is, if you want to see the development of film as an art form, you have to see films. The program is considered a dynamic library of entertainment or study, depending on the view and the objectives of members of the audience.

The Cinema Guild selections are shown in the 400-seat auditorium of the Art and Architecture building on campus. The Guild counts on a hard-core of about 150 or so regulars, with packed houses of 400 (and more) for special showings. For years the price of admission was 50 cents. Recently that was raised to 75 cents to cover rising costs of film rentals and projectionists' salaries.

Usually the Guild tried to feature a special program at least once a year. In 1967, there was a two-week program devoted to the works of Eisenstein. In 1968, there was a one-week program of the films of D. W. Griffith.

One of the highlights of the 1967 film year was the confiscation of Jack Smith's *Flaming Creatures.* Originally made in 1963, *Flaming Creatures* is usually considered patently illegal, bordering on the pornographic. Most theater groups that want to show it have to order a print delivered by R.E.A. Express to avoid violating the obscenity-through-the-mails laws. It is full of shots of strange creatures whose sex is certain only when their genitals are exposed. The film has been described as "going too far . . . on purpose." The third International Experimental Film Competition in Europe "recognized the aesthetical and experimental qualities of the film, but ascertained that the showing would violate Belgian laws."

When the film was shown in January 1967 by Cinema Guild, the police stopped it after ten minutes and arrested Hugh Cohen, one of the staff members and several members of the board of directors. Their trial began almost a year later in December 1967. The Ann Arbor police made a deal with the Guild, over Cohen's objections: One member of the Guild was convicted on a minor charge and the rest were released.

"Technically nothing came of the whole thing," Cohen says, "It was a stand-off. I think that eventually, the police realized the seriousness of the Guild. I don't think that there was anything wrong with showing that film. After all, if the Guild had wanted to screen pornography, there are plenty of films more obscene than Smith's *Flaming Creatures.*"

Although Cinema Guild has prospered since that encounter with the authorities, *Flaming Creatures* is still a sore point in Ann Arbor.

And as a postscript to the Ann Arbor brouhaha, in 1968, when the United States Senate was investigating pornography, one of the films that the senators saw in the pompous serenity of the Congressional offices, was the print of *Flaming Creatures,* which the Ann Arbor police had been holding. The Senators were, of course, embarrassed, shocked and indignant, even outraged at the lewd qualities of the film.

At the same time, the University of Iowa's Cinema 16 program screened a different print of *Flaming Creatures.* Iowa's Cinema 16 directors knew of the problems that had been encountered at Michigan and consequently there was little publicity on the Iowa

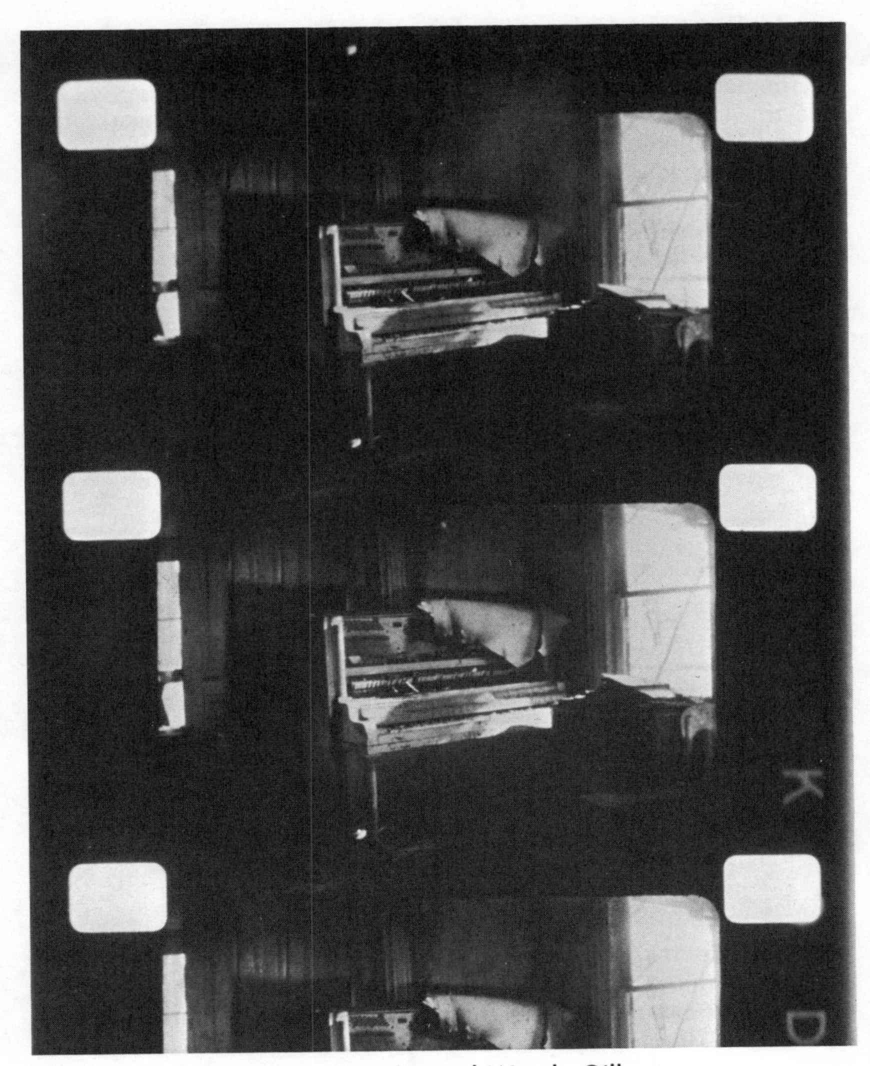

From *House* by Margaret Freathy and Wendy Gilbert

campus before the showing. Cinema 16 established a double system of identification for the occasion: students had to present their University identification cards when they bought tickets and then when they entered the Union's theater (presumably to prevent Iowa City police and local conservatives from viewing it). Most of the audience was also shocked at *Creatures*, but the Cinema

Guild needn't have bothered with the double system of safeguards. What the University of Iowa audience saw was a heavily edited version, with most of the offending portions deleted. Who did the editing no one knows, perhaps Smith himself.

If the University of Michigan has sense enough to insure that George Manupelli will not be pirated away by some other ambitious film school and take the Ann Arbor Film Festival with him, and if the University finds someone to replace Robert Davis and enlarge the course offerings in film, then the area's reputation for film should rise higher than it is now.

Professor Robert Davis was involved in the two courses on film within the speech department at the University of Michigan. He moved to teach similar courses at Southern Illinois University at Carbondale for the 1969-1970 school year. (Photo by the author)

8.
Northwestern University

JACK ELLIS AND JAMES LEAHY

Film work at Northwestern exists within an excellent Speech department that numbers among its past students professionals like Warren Beatty (who never graduated), Charleton Heston, Jennifer Jones, and Patricia Neal, who have all won Academy Awards; Ann-Margaret; Tony Randall; Virginia Graham; Walter Kerr, drama columnist for *The New York Times;* Tim Kiley, director of the Smothers Brothers show; the husband and wife team of Richard Benjamin and Paula Prentiss; the late Jeffrey Hunter; and others.

The work in film has been best described by Jack Ellis, chairman of the film program, in *Film Quarterly* magazine (Spring, 1963):

> At Northwestern film education is relatively new (inaugurated in 1956) and small. We expect to grow older and wiser; not necessarily much larger since our goals, teaching methods, and admission standards conspire against numbers. Set within a Department of Radio, Television, and Film, which is in turn part of a School of Speech, the film section has lately begun to move along lines that seem most proper to it. With increased autonomy has come clarification of objectives, and the first satisfactions as some of them are achieved.
>
> On the undergraduate level the training is conceived as preprofessional, for entrance into the film industry. Though there are pressures for increased "practicality"—from the students, of course, and from local producer-employers as well—the program maintains an equal balance between production and history-criticism. How to conform 35mm negative to 16mm work print, sell a sponsor on a film, and like matters, can be learned faster and better on the job, we feel. A university can, however, teach supremely well and consistently within its general aims of higher learning what a particular medium of art and

communication is, the special qualities inherent in it, an understanding and knowledge of past achievements that are valuable in themselves and suggest the range of its possibilities. In short, all of the matters basic to appreciation and creation. With this approach even film production, which we do a good amount of, is thought of as a way to learn how film works, what can be done with it, rather than a way to learn how to be a film editor, a script clerk, an assistant cameraman. Though we of course hope ours is also the best preparation for specific jobs.

On the graduate level production continues but here the basis is firmly that of artist-film maker in control of his work. Much graduate and upper division production is done as independent study for credit by individuals or small groups who meet in tutorial fashion with the instructor throughout the phases of production. This film making is experimental in the sense that solutions are attempted for certain problems of technique and subject; e.g., use of available interior light, fusion of fictional narrative with documentary description, shifting the point of view through changing camera set-ups. But most of the graduate study consists of advanced theory and research, much of it original and independent. Though it's not always clear how film scholars and critics will earn a living, it has finally seemed to us that film scholarship and criticism can't wait any longer on the answer to this question. It is our hope, too, that practicing film makers may gain most from this sort of intellectual muscle-stretching and freedom to experiment.

A discussion as brief as this is limited to general approach. Courses in film, as well as those in important complements such as theater, television, communication theory, and mass media research, are described in material the writer will be glad to send. The remaining space can best be devoted to our "products"—people, films, writing—and recent developments.

Several of our alumni are teaching university courses in film—at Stanford, Massachusetts, Alabama; a number are script writers, assistant directors, production managers, and the like in Chicago, Boston, Detroit, and elsewhere. Others are doing film work with ad agencies or with business firms or the government. Our student productions have been at their best in the story-documentary (e.g., *Good Night, Socrates*—about a 12-year-old boy in Chicago's "Greek Town"), the free-cinema essay (e.g., *A Place to Go*—about a campus-area coffee house), and in a kind of whimsy (e.g., *The Bulb Changer*—about a Tati-esque character whose job is replacing stoplight lamps)—the first and third are distributed commercially. Recent research and criticism, completed and in progress, has included a study of Bergman's theology (published in Northwestern's *Tri-Quarterly*), D. W. Griffith during his last 20 unproductive years (to appear in *California Historical Quarterly*), an M.A. thesis on James Agee's criticism, Ph.D. dissertations on the changing myth of the American Indian in the Hollywood film, and on the social-political-economic reflections in the French films of the 'thirties.

Current developments which seem particularly significant include substantial additions of space and equipment, an increasing number of students attracted to film from other departments in University, plans for additional courses (particularly at the graduate level) and teaching personnel. If the Northwestern film program were rated as in those personality evaluations where you check the adjectives that seem to apply, I would expect to find: intellectual, scholarly, critical, analytical, creative, aesthetic, experimental, free, individual. But this may seem like being for virtue and against vice. In any case, the aspirations are suggested and the goals, if not unique, continue to challenge.

An article written in 1963 might well be out-of-date for most film schools. However, this is still accurate. Northwestern's program is still small (though larger than it was then) and the ad-

Northwestern's students appear before the cameras in addition to behind them. Here Marianne McAndrew (right) is seen with Barbra Streisand and Walter Matthau in the 20th Century-Fox production of *Hello Dolly!* (Courtesy of 20th Century Fox)

jectives of intellectual, scholarly, critical, analytical, creative, and the rest still apply.

A more recent article than that was written for the October 1966 issue of *Film Society Review* magazine by then graduate teaching assistant Richard Kahlenberg. He wrote:

> Northwestern, like many universities, is experiencing an enormous upsurge of interest in film on the part of its students. Majors in many departments of the University—music, journalism, advertising, literature—as well as those within the School of Speech, in which Northwestern's film program is located have begun to take film courses or have become active in extracurricular film activities. They explain generally that they have come to realize that film is important to them for reasons of personal enrichment and career planning.
>
> In the last few years . . . enrollment in the film program has doubled. Adjustments have been made within the existing curriculum structure to accommodate this new interest. To stimulate and make possible increased film research and criticism, the number of films shown has been raised. Extra screening hours were added after consultation with the students, who are encouraged to borrow and screen films on their own for research projects. Groups of students are assigned the task of preparing complete scripts from classic films for study purposes when such texts are otherwise not available.
>
> For the beginning course, *Introduction to Film,* a history-aesthetics-basic production course for sophomores, eight millimeter production equipment has been introduced. Aside from the considerably lower costs of eight millimeter, the use of single-lensed zoom cameras with built-in light meters has brought about a wonderful burst of creativity among sophomores. Their films are much more fluid, and the film makers seem to take themselves less seriously now that they are freed of the poundage and calculations of sixteen millimeter. A problem is assigned whereby each student must script, shoot and edit a three-to five-minute silent film on a given theme; e.g., in the three recent quarters, all students made films on a card game, a chase, or an encounter between two characters. Classmates are generally used informally as crew.
>
> In the advanced production courses this year students have been assisted in securing film making contracts from "outside." They shoot in sixteen millimeter with equipment supplied by the Department, and they work in crews. Presently underway are films on old age, American Indians in Chicago, the University sororities, fashion advertising, the Austrian painter Gustav Klimt, and an orientation film on the University health service. Students in the film editing course are making compilation films from footage collected in the Chicago area from industrial and advertising film companies.

This year's M.A. candidates (1966) have chosen written rather than filmed M.A. projects. Last year, an M.A. candidate, wanting to do an animation film using still photographs, built a full-scale professional animation stand for his project and later donated it to the film program.

The film program serves as a center for Northwestern's thriving extracurricular film activities. The University's student-run Film Society operates three independent film series, choosing films in consultation with the film faculty to complement the curriculum. Forty features and almost as many shorts were shown by the Society last year. Burgeoning student interest in films has left the Society with sufficient cash to hold a short-film script contest with a $600 production budget as prize. The winning script is now in production. The sophomore class at NU has held a creativity contest with student-made films as a major category and cash prizes offered. For the past two years the Northwestern University Symposium, an annual think-talk event involving visiting speakers, has commissioned a film on the theme of the conference. Film program students made both films.

Throughout, the goal of the film program is to develop within the students an increased sensitivity and discernment toward film and an ability to put into practice as film makers the ideas gained through exposure to good models.

The Radio-Television-Film program at Northwestern had about 180 students during the 1968–69 school year. About one-third of them were in film; 40 to 50 as undergraduates, and 10 to 12 as graduate students. Northwestern is known primarily as a criticism-history film school and outstanding alumni like Rod Whitaker at Texas and Don Staples at Ohio State credit the excellence of the program to Jack Ellis. Should Ellis leave Northwestern for some other school, the program would practically fall apart. Northwestern discovered this several years ago, when Ellis left to become a visiting professor for a year at New York University. While he was gone, the program stalled and administrative decisions were not made. When he returned, he discovered that he had to make all the decisions and get the program back on its feet again, which he promptly accomplished.

According to Rod Whitaker, "Jack Ellis is the ultimate reference point for communications throughout the country. If you have a question about film and if you call Ellis, he can probably answer it immediately. He is, I think, perhaps the most knowledgeable man in film anywhere. His students are now professors in almost every film school in the country. His greatest innovation has been the mode approach to film. Instead of breaking down film into writing, editing, camerawork and so on, Ellis devised an

Professor Jack Ellis (right) and a moderator on a television show about student film on Chicago's educational television station, WTTW.

entirely different approach. He breaks film down into various modes: the documentary mode, as a whole; the art mode; the narrative mode and the persuasive. It works quite well. And," Whitaker added, "he is quite special," which he is. He is rather the Grand Old Man of the Young Men in film.

Some of the best courses offered in film recently have been listed in the Northwestern catalogues as:

Introduction to Film, which includes sections on "the aesthetics of film," "the technology of film," "history of film," "the business of film," and "the social function of film." Students in the introductory course, in addition to classwork, also plan their own films, write and revise shooting scripts, and screen the films for grades.

Film Script Writing and Production Planning is described as "theoretical considerations and practical experience in the conceptions suited to film in communication and expression, the form and the function of the film script and the planning growing out of the script and preceding production."

Film Direction and Cinematography is described as: "the theory and practice of directing and photographing motion pictures including the interpretation of the script, the handling of actors and action, and the camera in relation to them."

Film Editing and Sound Recording is "the final phases of the production processes including silent and sound editing, recording of narration, music and effects, sound mixing and conforming of original work print."

The course listed as *The History of Film,* included classwork in "the international birth and childhood of a new medium of art and communication; the rise of the American film, 1915–1919; the great German silents, 1919–1925; art and dialect in the Soviet film, 1925–1929; Hollywood in the Twenties, 1920–1929; sound comes to America, 1929–1935; the golden age of French cinema, 1935–1939; documentary in Britain, 1939–1945; Neo-realism in the Italian film, 1945–1952; the contemporary scene, 1952–."

Modes of Film Communication includes: "Introduction to Modes of film communication; film in the theater—35 millimeter; film in the community—16 millimeter; film in the home—television; the philosophy of film; the psychology of film; the technique of film; the experimental film; the documentary film; and the changing form and function of film." During that course, students are required to write a major term paper on any film of their choice.

The Documentary Film includes: "the sources of the documentary; man and his relation to nature; man and his relation to society, Great Britain; and his relation to society, United States; the conflict among nations; influence of the wartime documentary on the fictional film; post-war documentary emphasis; documentary film for television; the documentary as personal essay, 'Free Cinema' and cinema vérité."

Also teaching at Northwestern and working with Jack Ellis is James Leahy, the author of *The Cinema of Joseph Losey* (A. S. Barnes—Zwemmer). Leahy is a young Englishman, a native of the Amersham area near London. He received his bachelor's degree from Cambridge in 1960, majoring in English literature. At Cambridge, Leahy was a part of a very active film group that included Peter Cowie, who now edits the *International Film Guide* (A. S. Barnes—Zwemmer). Leahy, Cowie, Peter Graham, and Charles Barr all worked on an undergraduate film magazine titled *Broadsheet,* a mimeographed weekly journal of film and theater criticism that unfortunately was never circulated much beyond the Cambridge campus.

Leahy received his master's degree from Cambridge in 1966 and then came to America to work on his doctorate at Northwestern, under Ellis. Before his arrival in America, Leahy gained

James Leahy, author of *The Cinema of Joseph Losey* (Barnes-Zwemmer), standing in front of the Northwestern libraries. Leahy teaches film at Northwestern and finds the climate for film making there very good. (Photo by the author)

some appreciation of the day-to-day workings of the film industry as a third assistant director during the production of one of the "Carry On" series of English comedies. (He forgets which one it was.) Unfortunately, his work came during a labor squabble. He found that the unions made work unpleasant. At Northwestern, Leahy teaches a series of production courses: the first course in script writing, the second course in directing and cinematography, and the third course in editing and sound recording. In the past he has also taught the introductory course, a seminar in film criticism, the history course, and the modes of communication course.

"Here," Leahy says, "the film students are very good. They seem to have an interest in the same subjects that I do. I am free to do virtually what I like in the film. In class I try to pull film apart and put it back together again. I try to reveal, on one hand, the world that the artist has created in the film and, on the other hand, the implications of that view of the world."

In class, Leahy works with films by Lang, Godard, Hawks, Hitchcock, and Losey, among others.

Northwestern professor James Leahy (left), author of *The Cinema of Joseph Losey* (A. S. Barnes), with Bosley Crowther of *The New York Times*.

During the spring quarter of 1969, Ellis taught classes in: *Introduction to Film, Internship in Film Production,* and *The Documentary Film.* Leahy taught the course in *Film Editing and Sound Recording.*

Students under Ellis's and Leahy's direction have made many fine films at Northwestern. Some of them are:

Alleluia by William Grisham and Howard Smith was made for the St. Scholastica Priory in Duluth, Minnesota, on the occasion of its 75th anniversay. *Alleluia* has been described as "a lyrical appreciation of a community of nuns active in the fields of science,

Howard Smith, who began film making when he was 12, is an award-winning film maker at Northwestern. (Photo by the author)

music, photography, teaching and medicine, who combine good works with a resolute and cheerful faith." It is 33 minutes long, in black and white.

The Bulb Changer is an experimental film made early in the history of the film program (1960). Produced by Tom Smith, Fred Mumm, and Ed Swanson, *The Bulb Changer* is whimsy about a man whose job it is to change lamps in traffic signals. It is part of the University Film Producers Association Outstanding Films archives.

Casey Jones, made in 1968 by Thomas White, studies a 98-year-old man who has, for decades, entertained on the streets of Chicago with his accordion and *trained chicken.*

Cause Without A Rebel, done in 1965 by Peter Kuttner and Sheppard Ferguson, examines the contrast between typical campus frivolity and apathy and the dedicated activity of the civil rights movement through impressionistically counter-pointed sights and sounds. It received a Recognition of Achievement citation from the National Student Film Festival.

A scene from George *Lincoln Rockwell Visits Northwestern,* directed by Ron Abramson.

The world of a Chicago teen-age Negro gang, the Vice Lords, as it looks to them was the subject of the film *The Corner,* completed in 1963 by Robert Ford. *The Corner* received the Golden Eagle award from CINE, and is also in the University Film Producers Association Archives of outstanding films.

George Lincoln Rockwell Visits Northwestern is a cinema vérité study of a visit to campus by the late leader of the American Nazi party. It was directed and produced by Ron Abramson.

The Golden Haze is the name of a rock 'n' roll group that is seen and heard in performance, in bull sessions, with their agent, posing for publicity photos—trying to get into the big time of rock music without quite knowing how. It is 30 minutes long and was completed in 1968 by David Coynik. It has been described in the film brochures as: "Done as an M.A. thesis, this film represents an attempt at capturing the mood of a rock group trying to 'make it big.' It was Coynik's first full sound effort and he feels that is one 'clue to understanding what's good and what's bad' about it. Produced in cinema vérité style, rather than being preconceived and scripted, *Golden Haze* tries to emphasize the immediate, the

The late American Nazi George Lincoln Rockwell from the film *George Lincoln Rockwell Visits Northwestern.*

David Coynik, who produced *The Golden Haze* as an M.A. thesis film at Northwestern University.

From *Good Night, Socrates* by Stuart Hagman and Maria Moraites. Completed in 1962, *Good Night, Socrates* is one of the most poignant films ever made by a university film team.

chance. This is a modern style of filming, appropriate for a story about young men trying to succeed in a business just as chancy and just as real as the photographic style used to tell their story."

Good Night, Socrates by Stuart Hagman and Maria Moraites is perhaps one of the most poignant films ever made by Northwestern students. Completed in 1962, *Socrates* is a study of the last days of "Greek Town" in Chicago, which was almost completely razed to make way for a superhighway. The film follows the experiences of a 12-year-old Greek boy who watches with interest the bulldozers and the construction work, but cannot understand why his mother and grandfather are unhappy. *Socrates* won first prizes at the Venice International Film Festival, the Producers Guild of America Intercollegiate Awards, and the Midwest Film Festival. It is 34 minutes long, in black and white.

The Great Bicycle Chase by Richard Sterne is an experimental film that follows a thief who steals a bicycle. He, in turn, is chased by its owner, who steals another and follows frantically. Final justice is administered by a moppet with a six shooter. It is only four minutes long, in black and white, and is silent.

Have You Seen Jenny Gilbertson? is also an experimental film made in 1967 by Jerold Sider. Sider has said that the film was "made from an illegible script . . . shot on location in thirty or

The youngster can not understand why his parents are unhappy; they know that their Greek community will be destroyed by a superhighway. From *Good Night, Socrates*.

From *Good Night, Socrates.* The old man weeps because a superhighway will destroy Chicago's Greek community.

forty obscure places." It has also been described as "the most sneering view of life. . . ." It was made on assignment during a week in spring as a study of systems, though Sider admits that is not readily apparent. He adds, "anything that interacts or contains interaction is a system, so the assignment was fulfilled; for that matter, *Valley of the Dolls* would have fulfilled the assignment."

The High Up Doll was a 1962 experimental firm by Robert Ford and is a fantasy about a little girl who desperately wants a large and expensive doll. When she gets it, through feminine wiles, it somehow loses its splendor.

Home For Life, completed in 1966 by Gerald Temaner and Gordon Quinn, is a documentary in cinema vérité, depicting the experiences of two elderly people in their first months at a home for the aged. *Home For Life* was selected for screening at the Edinburgh and Chicago International Film Festivals.

The Homing Pigeon was a nature study by Robert Ford, made in conjunction with the U.S. Army Signal Corps. Ford is now vice president in charge of the New York production of Wilding Pictures.

Arthur Dahl's *A Nice Place To Live* is an 11-minute film con-

During production of *The Homing Pigeon* (1963) by Robert Ford. Ford, a graduate of Northwestern, is now vice president in charge of the New York production of Wilding Pictures.

cerned with a woman who is attacked and murdered in a quiet suburban community while her neighbors scarcely heed her cries and fail to come to her aid.

Nothing is images of Chicago and sad young love in the summer, set to Petula Clark's recording of "I Who Have Nothing." It was completed in 1966 by David Acomba and Richard Robertson and runs three minutes in black and white.

A Place To Go is a "free cinema" essay on an expresso coffee house, the patrons and the proprietors—the way they look and what they do. *A Place To Go was* completed by Jay Kaufman and Donald Murie.

Regus Patoff is a satire on success in business as portrayed by a Jacques-Tati-like employee who invents a tomato juice squeezer. *Regus Patoff* was done by Clifton Witt and the title comes from the abbreviations found on most inventions: *Reg*istered, *U*nited *S*tates *Pat*ent *Off*ice.

Shulie is an intimate study of a young Chicago art student whose individualistic attitudes about her own independent life are

During production of *The Homing Pigeon* by Robert Ford.

stated with extraordinary articulateness as she moves through her days, according to Northwestern's brochures. *Shulie* was completed in 1967 by Jerome Blumenthal, Sheppard Ferguson, James Leahy, and Alan Rettig. It is 29 minutes long, and in color.

Some of the Boys by Dennis Johnson is a soldier's view of the Civil War, composed largely from 180 photographs in the Mathew Brady collections of the National Archives, the Library of Congress, and state historical societies. The narration is based on authentic letters, diaries, and journals from Union soldiers and presents a year in the life of a soldier in the Civil War. Experiences shown are common to both Union and Confederate soldiers. *"The war fever is in our young men,"* wrote Oliver Wendell Holmes, *"and patriotism is the fire of it. . . ."*

The Way Back is a view of the Rehabilitation Institute of Chicago's services, and is organized around the therapy given one young paraplegic woman. *The Way Back* won an Oscar at the American Film Festival in 1964 for "best medical documentary of 1964," and has been shown on BBC television. It was produced as a university project in conjunction with Robert C. Ford Productions. Some of the crew were Ford, who has won five awards for films, including *The Corner* and *The Homing Pigeon;* Mrs. Antone Gregorio, a member of the film department; and Jack Ellis. Curiously enough, the role of the crippled young woman was played by a professional actress, Audrey Pollock, who had been a psychologist. All the other roles were played by disabled persons at the Rehabilitation Institute.

"The measure of rehabilitation is not taken in days and weeks, but in the succession of little physical and psychological victories. It is measured in the restoration of a sense of personal dignity," Ford said.

The Film Festival judges' comments ranged from "excellent

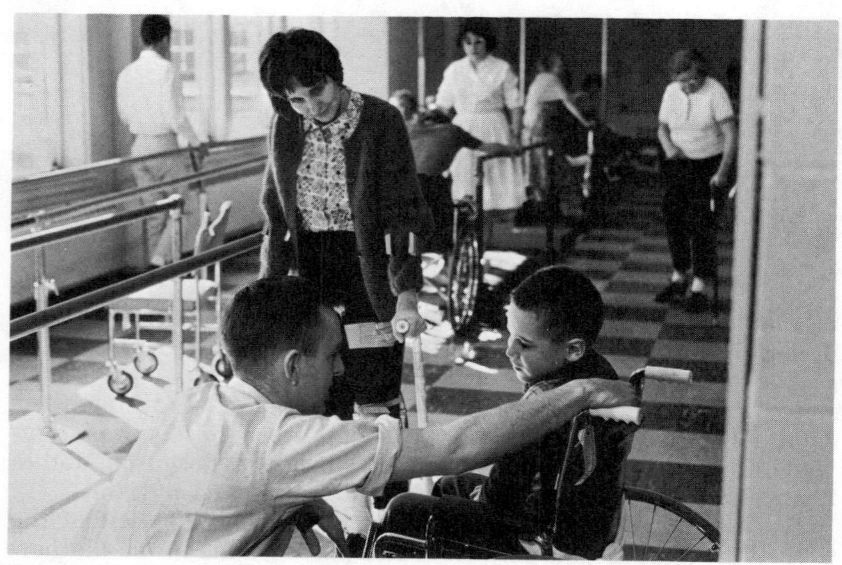

Robert Ford during the production of *The Way Back.*

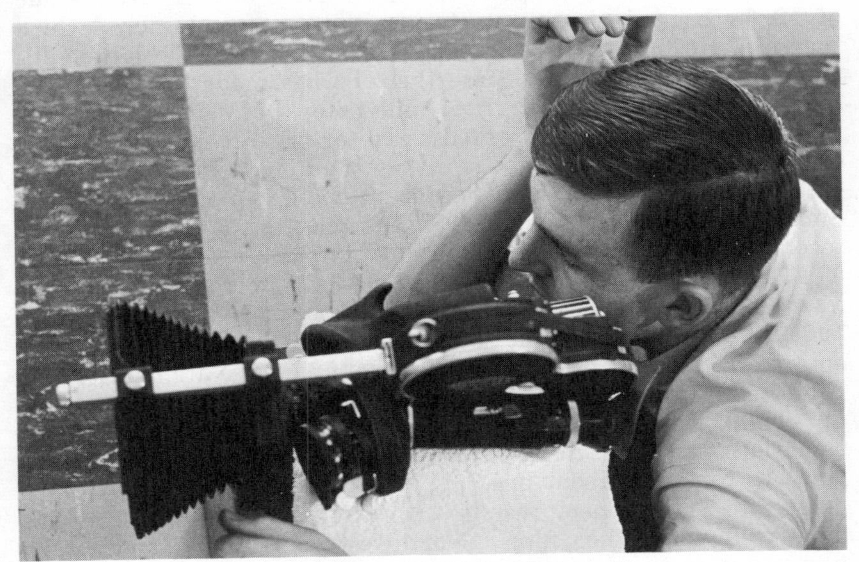

Robert Ford during the production of *The Way Back*.

presentation; rare straightforwardness," "honest and unsentimental," to "sincere and realistic. Excellent human interest details."

What Are Lonely Girls Made Of by Stephen and Elinor Karpf is a drama of the loneliness and frustration of single-girl office workers in a big city, centering upon an anti-heroine's attempts to escape from the troubling realities of herself and her life. *Lonely Girls* runs 41 minutes.

Yes was written, produced, directed, and edited by Ronald Fridell. It is a surrealistic tale of a teen-aged girl nearing a breakdown in a room filled with a television set, other teenagers who wander in and out, and hallucinatory images. It is 70 minutes long, in color, black and white, and negative, with disembodied narration dialogue and a continuous sound track. As Fridell says, "*Yes* was made in two springs, one summer, one fall and one winter in a large white room, a garden of lilacs, the Civic Center, Maxwell Street and three forests in Illinois and Wisconsin, inside a television set, the heads of four people and a camera." It was selected for screening by the Chicago International Film Festival.

Two of the finest film students at Northwestern during the 1968–1969 period have been Howard Smith and David Turecamo.

Smith has had virtually a life-long interest in film. At the age of 12, he begged his parents to get him a movie camera, which they did. He began "playing the scales," in film with eight millimeter films at that time. Since then, he has made over 50 films, most of them short, a few in 16 millimeter, but some a half-hour to 45 minutes long. He worked as editor on *Alleluia* and has recently completed *Still,* which is in color and black and white, based on the last eight lines of Theodore Rhoetke's poem, "The Lost Son." Smith has commented, "*Still* is the first of a trilogy. The second film is titled *Born* and the third is *The Eventual Feeling of You*. These films are an attempt to get back to the emotions and away from the mind. *Still* took from May of 1968 until January, 1969 to complete, although it only runs for 13 minutes. It has been entered in the Ann Arbor Film Festival and the National Student Film Festival and bombed both places—never got past the screening committees. Professor Ellis thinks that all my films are about essentially the same thing—that you have to view several before you can comment about one."

Despite Smith's poor results with *Still* at the festivals, he has done well with other films. Northwestern annually sponsors a film program titled "Orgy of the Arts." In 1966, one of Smith's films, *Epic,* won a prize of $100 for first place. *Epic* involves a central character seen wandering through the city. The camera follows and it is obvious that the character is tormented or looking for someone. Two other characters are also involved in the film—eliptically—Smith says. The film is black and white and runs for ten minutes. In the 1967 "Orgy," Smith won second place with a film that is second in another trilogy, begun with *Epic*. That film is titled *Boredom* and concerns three girls and four guys in an apartment; the girls get bored and eventually leave. It is as close to a pure documentary as Smith ever gets. In the 1968 "Orgy," Smith completed the submission of the trilogy with the third film *Stop* and he dropped down a position, winning third prize with it.

Stop is a super-imposition film with a circular structure. The film begins at a point in which the circular structure is later obvious. It has a mythical quality—a bizarre game involving five guys and a girl with a cape. The girl is captured by the men, who are apparently members of a gang, or group. Several members vie for her; she has an opportunity to leave but doesn't, and one of the gang members eventually runs off with her. At the end of the film, she is shown returning to the group with him. Smith has shown the film to Adolphus Mekas, who called it "amazing." It has very little sense of editing or cutting.

David Turecamo, an award-winning film maker says "I live for movies. I'll work to make money to make films, and I'll do anything: edit commercials, television, even make stag films if necessary." To this date, Turecamo hasn't found it necessary to make stag films. (Photo by the author)

David Turecamo is one of the most humorous film makers currently in college; his humor is self-centered with a very wry touch. He began making films when he was seven, and has continued ever since. As he says, "No one took me seriously until I came to Northwestern. Then it was :"Wow!" You're a film maker! A young film maker just like in *Time* magazine! . . ."

He also admits, "films are an extension of my life or maybe my life's an extension of films. I've wanted to make films for as long as I can remember, at least since *Blackbeard and the Pirates.* Remember when they bury Blackbeard up to his neck in the sand and leave him for the tide? I'll never forget it."

Turecamo has made *Anytime,* sponsored by The Little Brothers of the Poor, in Chicago. It is a sensitive cinema vérité study of the Brothers' work with the old and the poor living alone in the inner city of Chicago. *Anytime* is similar to, although much more pleasant than, *Inevitably,* made at the University of Michigan. *Anytime* is 29 minutes long, in black and white.

Turecamo has also completed *Ghet,* an intensely personal por-

Dennis Gordon, Trisha Harding, Henry Mitchell, and Erica (?) in David Turecamo's *Ghet*. (Courtesy of Beall Turecamo)

trait of a group of young people whose fun and games seem only occasionally to enliven their world of boredom and latent violence. Turecamo says about it:

> Perhaps the key to understanding *Ghet* is to let it happen. It must be taken, initially, at face value; whatever you derive from it must reflect your own attitudes. It is only a story of today, conceived in terms of today. My prime motivation is to turn you on to the sights and sounds of our generation. Forget about *your* days, your nights, your world, your life, and let the film work for you to replace your expectations of reality.
>
> Shot in two months, eighteen versions of the script were written. Edited in three months, it was largely unstaged except to place the characters in a particular setting or situation. About a year and half from the time it was conceived it was finally finished. Music was written almost a year before the shooting began. It's interesting that the music was not structured to the film, nor vice versa; Paul Sohmer (who did the music) and I feel so similarly towards our generation, our predicament, that the marriage of our world could be affected with almost no alteration in either."

Ghet was made with scraps of film left over from *Anytime*. It was processed with *Anytime* because the two could not be processed separately. Turecamo had shot *Ghet* on the end of rolls of film used in *Anytime;* it had to be completed, so he reacted agreement with the sponsors. *Ghet* would be processed along with *Anytime* and Turecamo would repay to the sponsors the processing costs of *Ghet*. "Ha!" says Turecamo, "we couldn't really separate the two costs." So he was able to complete *Ghet* free.

Ghet, which has no particular meaning as a title, won an award as the best experimental film at the San Francisco Film Festival in 1967. It is 40 minutes long, in black and white.

Turecamo is now working on a film titled *Toledo Rex,* which involves Lola Montez who cheats on Donald Duck by dating Andy Hardy. It is not a comedy. Donald Duck's real problem begins, Turecamo says, when Donald begins making a film titled *Derek Knight and the Metal Monsters,* which takes over his life completely.

Says Turecamo, "*Toledo Rex* re-creates minor incidents to recreate a love affair. Lola becomes confused between Donald and Andy Hardy and at the end of the film, everything dissolves.

He has also completed a film titled *Paul's Case,* based on a short story by Willa Cather, which ties in with Salinger's *Catcher In The Rye*. A boy runs away from home, gets an expensive room that he can't pay for, and eventually jumps in front of a train.

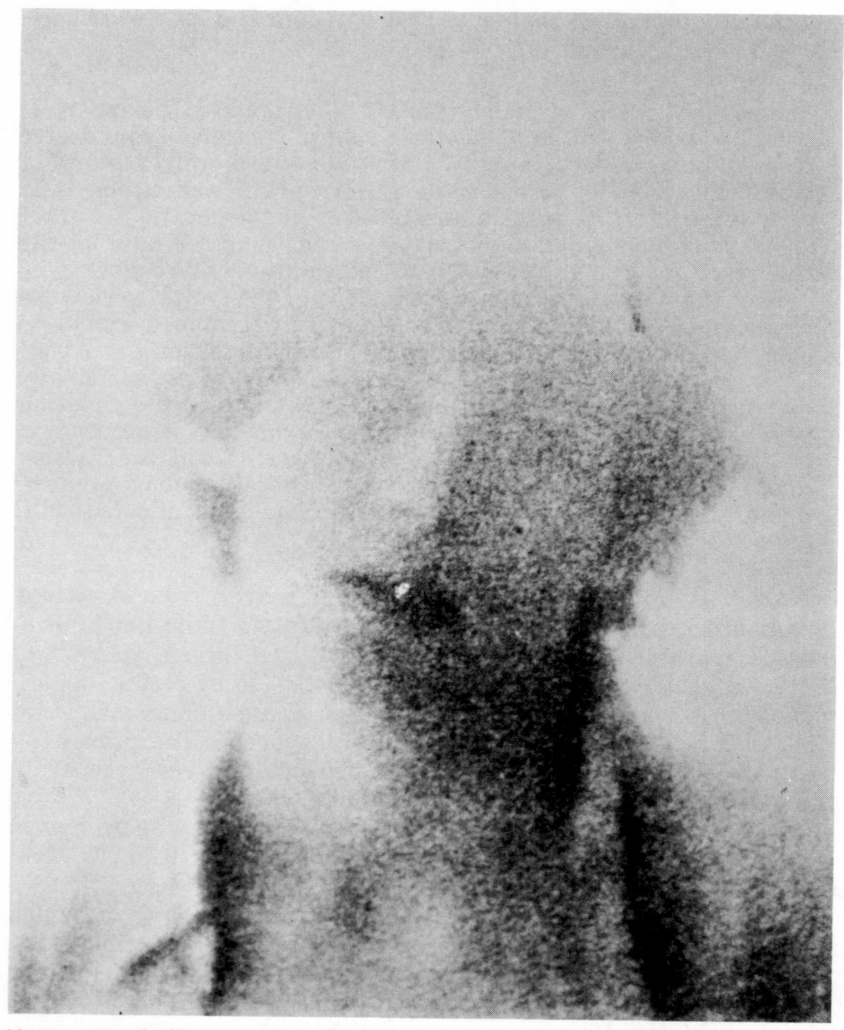

Henry Mitchell appears in a hazy sequence in David Turecamo's *Ghet.* (Photo by Beall Turecamo)

Before coming to Northwestern, Turecamo completed *My Daughter Loves A Rolling Stone,* which was influenced by Lester's *A Hard Day's Night.* It told the story of a high school-aged boy who liked to dance to Beatles' records and who cheated on his girl friend. "Everything turned out OK in the end," Turecamo said complacently.

An unknown girl appears in *Ghet*. (Photo by Beall Turecamo)

Vicki Loveness appeared in *Ghet,* produced at Northwestern in 1968. (Courtesy of Beall Turecamo)

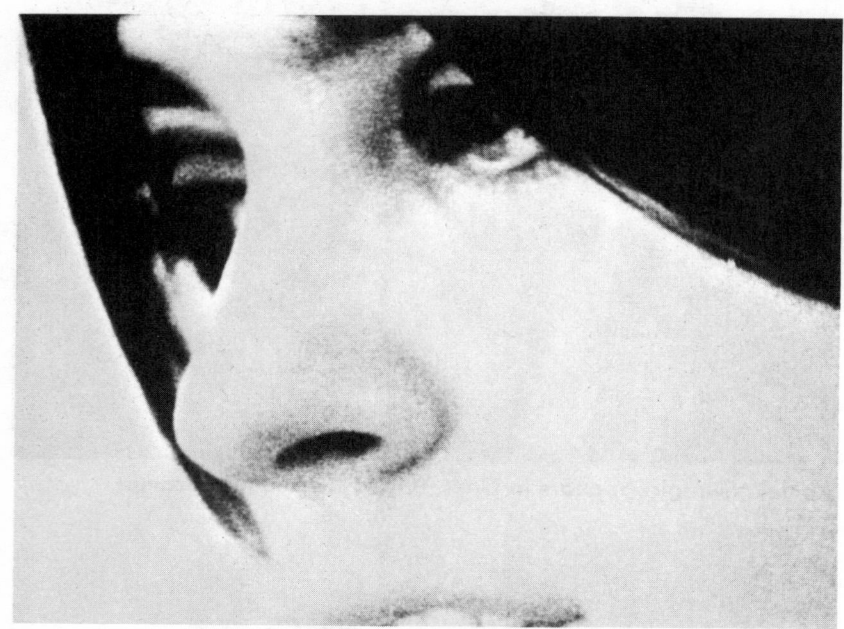

Susan Pinsker in *Ghet*. (Courtesy of Beall Turecamo)

An article titled "A Serious Young Filmmaker Speaks Out," which appeared in *The Chicago Daily News,* quoted Turecamo as saying "People think film makers are freaks, oddities, weirdos—but we're just other people who happen to make movies . . . I live for movies. I'll work to make money to make films and I'll do anything: edit commercials, television, even make stag films if necessary." To this date, Turecamo hasn't found it necessary to make stag films, although he admits that he'd *like* to make a *campy* stag film.

The Daily News analyzed *Anytime* as "A quietly moving essay on sympathy and loneliness," and said that *Anytime* took Turecamo a year's time and 24 hours of footage, edited down to 35 minutes. "I did it for the $500 the Brothers (of the Poor) gave me," *The Daily News* quoted, "But then I got caught up in it. For a long time, I looked for objective tragedy, such as one old lady who lived in a coal bin, but then I realized that the major difficulties of these people are not in their circumstances but in their attitudes."

The *Daily News* reported:

And it is their attitudes—the cramped tedium and compulsive rumination imposed by old age—that come through in *Anytime.* Never offensively charitable, but always attentive and respectful, Turecamo's camera moves among them, at a party, at the summer camp, in the drab shelter of their homes—always coming to rest on faces which, however lively, seem full of penultimate things, things which deeply affected the director:

Professor Jack Ellis has single-handedly made Northwestern one of the finest film schools in the country. (Photo by the author)

"I'm fascinated by loneliness, though one reason I love films is because they help dispel our solitude for a little while. And also by death, the inescapable feeling that everything heads towards an end, and not a beginning. Characters in a film are always trapped in the last reel, like we are in life . . . violence and sex? Dull in themselves, interesting in the way they go together—and they always do.

Turecamo said, "I love Renoir and Fellini, but I can never equal them. I can't write dialogue and I hate shooting, mainly because working with actors is almost impossible. And of course, I'm never satisfied with a picture; I always tell myself: It could have been great, if I'd only had another six years or so . . ."

Northwestern also has a Film Society that varies, like Iowa's Cinema 16 program, between mediocre and excellent films. During the 1968–69 school year, it was good, with showings of: *Jules and Jim, Far From Vietnam, Boudo Saved From Drowning, A Day In The Country, The Elusive Corporal, The Devil Is A Woman, Personna,* and *Orphee,* among others.

Guest speakers at Northwestern have included Jack Valenti, president of the Motion Picture Association of America, and former *Esquire* magazine staff members David Newman and Robert Benton, who wrote the script for the fantastically successful *Bonnie and Clyde.* Bosley Crowther of *The New York Times* has also spoken at Northwestern and Jean Luc Godard was scheduled for an appearance, but cancelled at the last minute to remain in France for film work.

In the language of college students, with Jack Ellis on campus, Northwestern rates an "A." If, for any reason, Ellis would leave Northwestern for some other school, the program would flunk.

9.

The Ohio State University

MIKE CLARK AND THE $64,000 QUESTION; THE KEMP NIVER RESTORATION PRINTER

Mike Clark became interested in movies at an age at which such an interest is unusual; he began going to the movies when he was six years old. He was just beginning elementary school in Ashland, Ohio, and he'd read the *Cleveland Plain Dealer* movie columns and wait for films to come to Ashland's only theater. Sometimes they'd get there, often they wouldn't; for Ashland, a small town about 60 miles south of Cleveland, has never been much interested in first-run films. On Saturday afternoons, Mike's parents would drive him to the theater and he'd watch, fascinated, whatever was playing. Sitting in the dark, with his feet barely touching the floor, Mike began remembering names, titles, credits and roles, although occasionally he couldn't understand the plot of an adult film.

At the age of eight, Mike's parents moved to the Columbus suburb of Upper Arlington. By that time, Mike was reading all the "trashy movie magazines" that he could get, and, with a variety of films playing in the Columbus area, Mike's interest grew. The films always arrived in Columbus sooner than they had in Ashland, and Mike and his friends would go to the Saturday matinee together, chauffeured by a cooperative parent.

By the age of nine, Mike was "knowledgeable" about films, but did not, by any means, have a photographic memory, as was reported later.

When he was ten years old and in the fifth grade in the Upper Arlington schools, *The $64,000 Question* had been on the air about three years. Mike's father wrote to the program staff, advising them of Mike's unusual interest in the movies. He didn't tell anyone, not even Mike's teacher, for fear that the whole thing would be considered a joke by the staff. Months went by and no word

Mike Clark examines stills during his appearance on the ill-fated show, *The $64,000 Question*. Clark won $16,000 at the age of ten answering questions on film.

from the program. Then a call came; could Mike meet with officials in Cincinnati? He did and they asked him a few questions. They were quickly satisfied that Mike did indeed know the facts and dates of American films.

Just before New Year's Eve of 1958, Mike was asked to travel to New York and meet with the show's producers. He and his father made the trip and on New Year's Eve Mike appeared on *The $64,000 Question*—at the age of ten.

He appeared on the show for the next five weeks and the questions asked of him weren't tough—he thinks now. "They played it straight—for a ten-year-old the questions weren't so bad—they could have made things a lot tougher if they had wanted to."

Mike Clark answers questions about American movies during *The $64,-000 Question*.

At that time, *The $64,000 Question* was still untarnished by the scandals that would plague it later. Interest in Mike's appearances was high, especially in Ohio. On the $1,000 dollar level, Mike was asked to identify four Academy Award winners, name two pictures in which they starred, and pick William Boyd from the middle of a group of bit players. He did, easily.

The week after, Mike also answered easily the $2,000 question and then, on the same show, the $4,000 question. The questions began getting tougher then. For $4,000, Mike was asked:

What were the titles of the films that launched James Dean and Doris Day into stardom?

Who was George Gobel's co-star in the film *Birds and the Bees?*

What was the name of the original film on which *Birds and the Bees* was based?

Who were the stars of that original?

(To judge how well you compare with Mike Clark at the age of ten—and for $4,000—the answers are listed at the end of this chapter.)

Mike rattled off the answers without hesitation.

"You're right, for $4,000, M.C. Hal March* said.

During the next weeks' shows, Mike won the $8,000 question, then the $16,000 question.

And the week after that, Mike appeared on the show with Zsa Zsa Gabor. Their conversation with Hal March was as insane as any quiz show dialogue. Hal March began it:

"Who's the lady I see you with?"

"Mr. March, this is Zsa Zsa Gabor, the movie star. Miss Gabor, this is Hal March, the master of ceremonies for this program.

"Delighted, Miss Gabor," March said.

"A pleasure Mr. March. You look exactly as I imagined you would."

"You look better," March replied. "Mike, let me get something straight. You've only reached $16,000. You're not entitled to an expert yet . . ."

"Oh, she's not my expert, Mr. March, she's a friend."

"Mike, I underestimate you. How long has this friendship been going on?"

"Since two o'clock yesterday afternoon. I had lunch with her."

"You seem no worse for wear. How did you happen to have lunch with her?"

"She invited me."

"I'll get to the bottom of this yet. Zsa Zsa, will you help me clear up this mystery?"

---

* Hal March died in the spring of 1970, as this book went to press.

The late Hal March interviews Mike Clark on *The $64,000 Question*. At left is Zsa Zsa Gabor.

"It is no mystery. I have been watching Mike on the show and I am a great admirer of his, so I invited him to have lunch with me and after that we went to the screening of my lastest picture, *Queen of the Universe.* Then he, in turn, invited me to be his guest on your program."

"Some fellows have all the luck. How did you like the picture, Mike?"

"Oh, it was swell. I recommend it highly to everybody, to people of all ages."

"Man, that's a friendship," March said, "what's the picture about?"

"Oh, it's a science fiction picture and Miss Gabor plays the Queen of the planet Venus. She has blue hair but she has no king."

"No king," March said, "why not?"

"Because there aren't any men around."

"What a waste of blue hair. No men at all, Zsa Zsa?"

"In the end there are men," she said, "I import them from the planet Earth."

"I'm relieved," March said, "just between us men on Earth, Mike, I have a feeling you like Miss Gabor . . ."

And after *that,* with the approval of his parents, Mike played it safe, took the $16,000 and quit. The government immediately took $4,400 for taxes and Mike deposited the rest for his college tuition.

Mike didn't have any outlet for his film knowledge through high school. When he became old enough to drive, he was able to attend any theater in the Columbus area. He did want to write a film column for his high school paper, but wasn't given the chance. Upon graduation from high school, Mike entered O.S.U., majoring in Journalism (the best major for film-oriented students at Ohio State).

Most journalism students work for *The Ohio State Lantern,* the student-run daily newspaper. During the winter of 1968–1969, Mike became Arts and Entertainment editor, which gave him a chance to write a regular review column and run features on films. His reviews were accurate and penetrating. Some of the headlines were:

SHAKESPEARIAN DRAMA
A CINEMATIC TRIUMPH
—about *Romeo and Juliet*
Jan. 7, 1969

DELECTABLE BLONDE 'CANDY'
WEARS OUT FILM WELCOME
—Jan. 9, 1969

'HELLFIGHTERS' IS SADDLED
WITH SCRIPT OF THE '40'S
—Jan. 13, 1969

McQUEEN LIMITED
IN ROLE OF 'BULLITT'
—Jan. 17, 1969

'FINIAN'S RAINBOW' IS GOLDEN
—Jan. 21, 1969

'PETULIA' MARKS RETURN;
'ONE OF LAST YEAR'S BEST'
—Feb. 2, 1969

STORY OF A FALLING 'STAR'
—Feb. 10, 1969

'PRETTY POISON' IS AMBROSIA
—Feb. 11, 1969

'CHITTY CHITTY BANG BANG' BOMBS
—Feb. 18, 1969

STREISAND SAVES 'FUNNY GIRL'
—Feb. 18, 1969

'LOCAL SHERIFF' HITS ITS MARK
—April 18, 1969

Mike has also worked for a Columbus television station, WBNS channel 10, the CBS affiliate, as their film expert. For several months, Rod Serling, who was a guest lecturer at Antioch College in Yellow Springs, Ohio, south of Columbus, had been the regular film critic on channel 10. When his work at Antioch was completed and he left WBNS, Mike applied for and got the job. He worked in the traffic and promotion departments and prepared the scripts for the introductions for the movies. He appeared on "Eyewitness Noon News" in February 1969 as a reviewer and also made appearances during the Ohio State Fair, with Flippo The Clown, interviewing fairgoers and answering questions on the short program, *Stump The Expert.* He was seldom stumped, except for several gimmick questions, which he learned to recognize.

This writer interviewed Mike Clark in May 1969, and at that

Mike Clark, who has graduated from The Ohio State University, was something of a problem to his professors. What could they say to him after he won $16,000 as an expert on film? (Photo by the author)

time he was about to graduate from Ohio State University. He said then that his plans were vague; he was excellent draft material. After the service, he planned a long-range career as a critic, writing primarily for magazines like *TV Guide*.

There is little doubt that Mike Clark will become an excellent film critic. His memory for film facts, dates, and plots, if not photographic, is remarkable. If and when he does become a regularly published film critic, few will know that he began learning films in the dark of the Ashland Theater, in Ashland, Ohio, at Saturday matinees.

Other than Mike Clark's notable achievement, the programs, facilities and films at Ohio State are not outstanding. They are relatively mediocre in most respects. Ohio State, commonly nicknamed "The Big Farm," is such a huge school that it is almost impossible to accomplish anything well. There are now nearly 45,000 students on the main campus in Columbus. Recently, a reporter asked one of the deans what the optimum size of a university should be. "We've passed it long ago," he said.

Students are not able to major directly in film at Ohio State. They may major in journalism and take film courses as part of that program or they may major in the colleges of behavioral science or fine arts and take film courses. The Department of Photography and Cinema offers four courses in still photography, four in film, and three involving both. Thus the undergraduate may take courses leading to the B.F.A. degree (Bachelor of Fine Arts) or, on the graduate level, may receive an M.A. or a Ph.D. in an inter-departmental program involving other subjects, with film as supplemental material.

The University prides itself on being the largest producer of educational films of any university in the country. Ohio State employs a staff of 50, half in still photography and half in film, who make photographs and films for the university, governmental agencies, and other similar programs. The staff and students expose over two mililon feet of film each year, according to Don Staples, a faculty member of the film program.*

The film students often work with the film unit as crew members on projects. The students gain some experience from this and are occasionally paid for their time. The department thinks this an ideal arrangement, but the students are not overly happy about it. They see little point in working on films with titles like: *Better Living Through Research and Education; Crisis And The University; Factors In Visual Depth Perception; Development of a Frog;*

* Staples left Ohio State for New York University in the fall of 1969.

Futures in Welding; Nesting Redwing Blackbirds; Story of a Dam; Ohio Maple Syrup; or, for that matter, an award-winning film, *Football As It Is Played Today.*

The program on the graduate level was described in *The Journal* of the University Film Producers Association (Vol. 19, No. 1, 1967) by Don Staples, in an article titled "An Approach To Cinema at the Graduate Level." He said:

> One of the major problems of cinema instruction arises from the students' lack of experience in visual communication. They may have begun formal instruction in writing at the elementary level; many have had some speech training at either the secondary or university level; but the majority have not learned even the fundamentals of communicating visually.
>
> The motion picture program at The Ohio University offers graduate students a unique minor in cinema. They come from major programs in varied fields—biology, theatre, education, physics, English, telecommunications, dance, sociology, painting, design, psychology—and a motion picture class is a group of people that have very little in common other than a desire to study the film medium. They distribute themselves along the entire spectrum of motion picture interests—from what might be called "pure information presentation" to "pure art."
>
> The program at the Ohio State University attempts to meet some of the needs and solve some of the problems that arise, collectively and individually, when university students discover film. The program involves the student in a series of experiences that will be worthwhile for the mass communications major, the senior in anthropology, or the teacher in training. It has two primary functions: 1) to develop an understanding of the medium, and 2) to develop the capacity to create within the medium. The program encourages the student to think about, and in terms of, "moving images" as he reads, discusses, writes about, and most importantly, makes and views motion pictures. Viewing is stressed because films themselves are the visual "literature" of the field.
>
> In learning to create within the medium, the student is involved with "camera sketching" or what might be called "visual note-taking," experimentation, and, finally, complete sound motion pictures. The program is concerned with the needs of the student who believes that film is the medium by which he can best express what he wants to communicate.
>
> This approach allows the student who has never seen a camera to move alongside the student who may have been making home or semi-professional movies. At points the two come together on the same level to investigate the art and technique of creating and using moving images. This theory of moving images—what they can do, what they cannot do, how they re-

late to each other, how they are apprehended, and how they fit into a history of moving images—is of primary importance to the student whether or not he has had prior technical orientation. And it matters little whether these images are thrown on a wall, a bed-sheet, a sensitized tube, or a beaded screen or whether or not the image is sent by light waves, micro waves, laser beams, or wires; nor does it matter whether the image was originally recorded on film, tape, IBM cards, or thermoplastic materials. Solid theories of how to understand and create moving images will still be useful.

The other day I was introduced to a professor in the social sciences, who, upon finding out what I taught, asked me "Does it really take a whole quarter to teach someone to load a camera and push the button?" I stated that we would certainly hope that the student would have learned that much in high school and could progress from that point onward. To me, teaching "how to load the Bell and Howell camera" in a graduate class would be like starting a graduate English composition class with the first two weeks devoted to "touch typing techniques."

Currently, we are trying to convert the mechanical details that a film maker must know into self-instructional units using teaching machine principles to allow the student to learn the technical phases of loading, exposing, and splicing, etc. on his own time at his own rate. This relieves the instructor of many tedious tasks and on the creative end he can teach "how to handle equipment." Many people, including the professor whom I mentioned earlier, are not able to differentiate between the two.

Just as recent technical innovations have helped the film maker, the film teacher has benefited by these scientific advances. One of the most important in solving graduate cinema instructional problems is the advance of the 8mm field. UCLA, State University of Iowa, and Ohio State are just a few of the universities which are availing themselves of this new "visual pen," or "pictorial brush." Taking the automatic 8mm camera the student can now, economically and physically, do rough sketches and take pictured notes of his random ideas and his film plans. He is able to experiment with new and different thoughts which involve composition, texture, relationship of images, light and shadow, perspective, plot progression, information presentation, fact retention, and emotional response.

With a camera in his hand—set to "automatic"—he can explore his environment, probe his relationships and come up with original ideas from which his finished film will be born or from which significant research and writing may develop.

After living their lives in the "Gutenberg Galaxy" as Marshall McLuhan calls it, students must be allowed to see the world anew, through the end of a focused view-finder . . . it may not be the same world that they have experienced through the written word.

We've also been experimenting with students using automatic 8mm cameras for "visual note-taking" from the screen itself. This provides individual reference to meaningful screen experiences which could not be captured in words or adequately recreated by the memory from sketchy notes. The student can then refer visually to something which he has seen.

Eight-millimeter films are also of increasing importance in the area of film history—our visual literature. Film classics are available to the buyer on 8mm for about the same price it would cost to rent them for one showing on 16mm. Most of our film classics are not really classics in the traditional sense of an art classic, but historic milestones in the scientific and stylistic achievements of film. Thus it is important to have these available for the student to study and restudy during the quarter as he would a library book. The potential of this type of "visual reference center" for motion pictures and television has not even been considered on most campuses at this time. We need to provide the student with adequate facilities for studying and evaluating all types of moving images that might relate to his future creative or critical function as a professional man in his own field of specialization. He needs to learn to read, write, speak, and *visualize*.

On the more advanced level where complete productions are involved, sixteen millimeter is still the standard gauge of film and equipment at the Ohio State University. Sixteen millimeter films are viewed in the classrooms, restudied on an independent basis, and produced as individual and group projects. During the production stage and while in the production learning process the advanced students work with the facilities of the professional motion picture division and under the guidance and supervision of the academic motion picture staff.

In addition, all the members of the professional staff in the department become at one time or another film teachers. They may participate as lecturer, critic, advisor, technician, or master craftsman while the student is involved as a learner in either the audience, research, or apprentice category. This cooperation and interplay covers the fields of writing, direction, cinematography, animation, editing, management, sound, and research and is intended to be mutually enriching—both for the professional staff and the student.

One of the first graduate courses centered around the production process emphasizes the relationship of film and television. Each student is required to make a 60-second sound film with a public service message. Many of these students are television majors with TV production experience, to which the film course is linked. They will have seen the use of closed-circuit television in the presentation of Department of Photography courses both as a tool for amplifying lectures and as a demonstration medium in the laboratory sessions. In the course, he will make a film for the electronic medium. Although short in time, the graduate student who needs a film making capacity finds the prospect of creating a perfect minute of film as challenging and generally more demanding than a comparable three hour course in other studies.

After completing this first production course, the student may enroll in the advanced production course which requires the cooperation of others—with a film crew of three or four graduate students who work together and create a complete sound motion picture, usually seven to ten minutes in length.

After this group experience the student may engage in a series of independent film studies and select specific theoretical or production problems to explore. These often take the form of theoretical study, research, writing, and analytical problems; however, they more frequently are complete film production problems where the student will make a motion picture of his choice challenging him to produce a film in which he makes his most personal statement. If the graduate student elects to make more than one of these "problem" films in his program, the faculty usually insists that one be a "sponsored" film. This affords the setting for that demanding and critical situation in which he has to meet the needs of a sponsor while maintaining his integrity as a film maker.

Whenever several graduate students want to investigate the same general area of film research and analysis, and if discussion is necessary to the investigation, special seminars are arranged so that the chosen topic may be thoroughly explored through group effort. In the Spring Quarter, 1967, two such seminars were arranged. One in the experimental film and another, in cooperation with the Department of Speech, on film and television.

Throughout the curriculum there is constant evaluation to provide a flexible program of education about motion pictures tailored for the individual graduate student. Therefore change and adaptation are an integral part of these flexible curricula.

This has been an attempt to reveal some of the problems in graduate instruction in film and to suggest a few of the ways in which we at Ohio State are making an effort to help the student in his need to communicate visually in a variety of fields.

New problems will arise; some of the old ones will disappear. We will be presented with new, undreamed-of media and new methods for using the old media. But we must remain constantly alert to the visual communication needs of the modern graduate student and be prepared to program flexibly and creatively for those needs.

Some students do make exceptional films, almost privately, at

Ohio State. Of the 150 or so films that are begun each year, only six to 12 get to the composite print stage.

The Ohio State faculty is "anti-film-festival," as one student put it. They take the peculiar attitude that a film-is-a-film-is-a-film; that a good film is a good film whether or not it was student-produced. Consequently, the faculty feels the term "student film" is misleading. And thus, they do not share the students' enthusiasm for entering films in festivals.

One of the finest films to reach composite stage recently is *331—204–3171* by Chuck Nelson. The title of George Lucas' science-fiction film *THX—1138–4eb*, from the University of Southern California, is completely meaningless as a title. Nelson's isn't. It is his social security number. The film has been variously de-

From *331-204-3171* by Chuck Nelson. The title is Nelson's Social Security number and the film expresses a state of mind, a college-aged view of man and his problems.

A Dali-esque view of time is a sustaining theme in Chuck Nelson's *331-204-3171*.

The hero carries a cross during *331-204-3171*.

The hero batters a wall á la Don Quixote while spectators applaud in Chuck Nelson's *331-204-3171*.

The hero of Chuck Nelson's *331-204-3171* solemnly drives an abandoned bus in one sequence of the film.

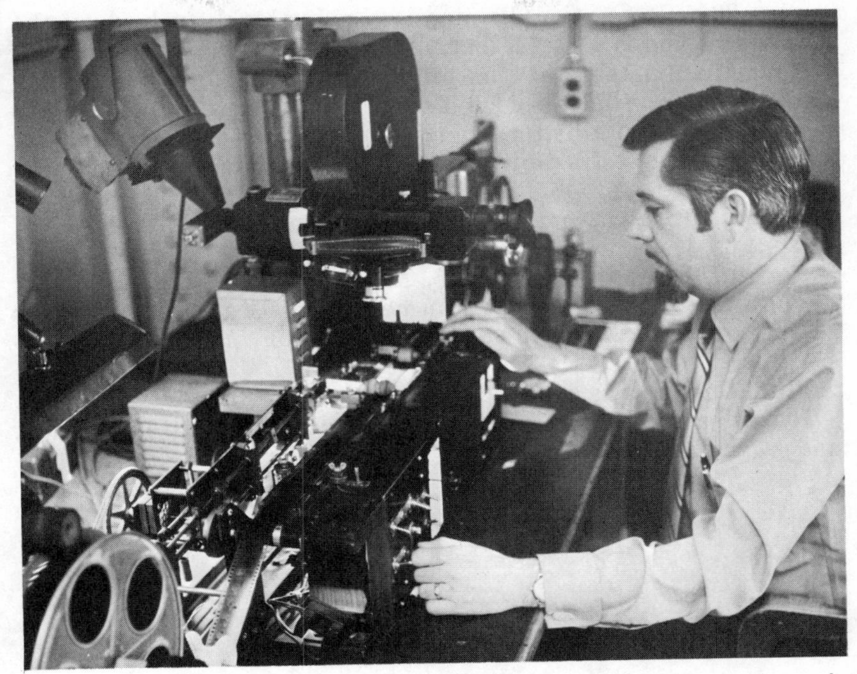

Richard Long operates the Kemp Niver Restoration Printer, the only machine of its kind in the country. Originally designed to reprint the Library of Congress paper print collection, the Printer is now used by Ohio State to copy all old, fragile films. (Photo by the author)

scribed as "a man and woman relationship," a state of mind," and "young people's feeling about man and his problems." *331–204–3171* is highly unconventional; it contains scenes of a man being beaten, viewed by a sadistic, applauding audience, a political murder, a Dali-esque view of time, and a man carrying a cross.

"I only film what I feel," Nelson has said. "My films have no main themes."

Of some importance in film history, but little importance to the students at Ohio State, is the Kemp Niver Restoration Printer, the only machine of its kind in the world. Originally used for restoring the paper print collection held by the Library of Congress, the Restoration Printer is capable of recovering, by copying, any type of motion picture film. It is primarily used to copy extremely flammable antique film onto safety base film. The dangerous old originals may then be destroyed and the new copy filed in the vaults. The Restoration Printer is a prize highly valued by the department and is a useful machine, historic in its own right.

But unfortunately, the film program at Ohio State is sadly behind the times. Students soon discover that if they'd like to major in film, they have a better chance at Ohio University, in Athens, which has progressive view of film. Most students acquainted with the film offerings at Ohio State are disappointed with the shallowness of the program and the limited opportunities it presents.

For $4,000, at the age of ten, Mike Clark knew that:

The titles of the films that launched James Dean and Doris Day as stars were *East of Eden* and *Romance on the High Seas,* respectively.

Mitzi Gaynor was George Gobel's co-star in *Birds and the Bees.* It was based on the film *Lady Eve,* which starred Henry Fonda and Barbara Stanwyck.

10.
West Virginia University

AND A 19TH-CENTURY ADMINISTRATION

Of the many problems that university film departments face—logistics, equipment, and film philosophy—a problem seldom encountered is that of an uncooperative, short-sighted, or adamant university administration. But that is exactly the problem facing the film department, faculty, and film majors at West Virginia University.

The film program at Morgantown is relatively new; basic film courses were begun in the 1966 school year. The courses now include:

Appreciation of the Motion Picture—three hours credit. An introduction to the appreciation of the motion picture and the television film as art forms. Principles of aesthetics involved in evaluating films. Attention given to the various types of film as art forms: documentary, entertainment, experimental, instructional, etc.

Techniques of Motion Picture Production—An introduction to basic film making principles, with considerations given to motion picture directing, editing, lighting, cinematography and sound recording.

Documentary Motion Picture Production—a detailed study of the documentary as a film form and social commentary. Students will write, produce and exhibit a 30-minute documentary using 16 millimeter Bolex camera equipment.

The courses open to graduate students only at West Virginia are listed as:

Problems in Motion Pictures. Discussion and research into various issues and problems . . .

Film Directing and Cinematography. An advanced study of motion picture production from the directional and cinema-

Frank Wudorsky films with a Bolex camera outside, during work at West Virginia University.

graphic standpoint. Students will be expected to complete the full production of a motion picture as their term project.

Despite these course listings, students at West Virginia are not able to actually major in film. Students must register as Radio-TV majors and specialize in film. During the 1968–69 school year, there were about 20 majors in Radio-TV, and about half of them were disguised film majors. This lack of an actual film major is the fault of the university administration, via curriculum committees, deans, and the like, who still don't consider film and film study a relevant aspect of university life.

The director of the film program is assistant professor Don Norwood, who came to West Virginia from television work on station WWVE in New Orleans. He has a master's degree in music from Tulane University. Norwood, after careful study in the deficiencies of the film program, recently proposed several new courses to be added to the film curriculum. The courses were rejected by the university, with the general comment, "we don't consider these as the sort of thing a university should offer." They were not additional courses in film production, or experimental film, or even basic film criticism. For the most part, Norwood has hoped to add courses in film history. When he heard that the administration had rejected his proposed courses, he asked himself, Why do I stay here?" But he felt that even though the film program lacks the necessary courses for a full major, he can, at least, help the

Filming *The Couple* are: Ross Whitney, Richard Dematteis, Larry Baker, and Don Norwood (at camera).

students who are at West Virginia and who *are* interested in film. He hopes that eventually the program will be strengthened sufficiently to include course work and facilities not currently offered or available.

The film department is housed in the former Music department building. Sound-proofed practice rooms have been converted to

Shooting in a downtown Morgantown street are Larry Baker and Don Norwood.

editing rooms that are clean and adequate. Some of the larger rooms have been converted to screening rooms. But all the rooms and offices are in the basement of the building, making film seem psychologically a neglected cousin to the better situated Radio and TV facilities. West Virginia, typically, has just completed the establishment of an educational television station, affiliated with the National Educational Television network. The station, WWVA, is immaculate and beautiful, but currently no Radio-TV students work in it. The station is staffed by professionals on a full-time salary basis.

Although film students can not officially major in film, Norwood has found ways to side-step the scructures of the course catalogues and the requirements. Graduate students can take three nebulous courses, variously described as "Independent Study for Graduate Students," "Special Projects," and "Special Topics." Some graduate students have gone semester after semester, carrying a full academic load of the three courses and have worked throughout the semester solely on making a film. This is alright with Norwood and alright with the Registrar, because what he doesn't know about the loopholes in the requirements benefits the film makers.

The film makers do have adequate equipment: two 16 millimeter Bolex cameras, one Cine Special, six super eight millimeter cameras, one 35 millimeter Mitchell, and two Moviescopes.

The university only officially lists the films made in the courses listed in the catalogues. Recently four films were completed and shown:

A Man and His Art, produced by Ronald Harman, Joe McCausland, Elliott Oshry, and Ross Watne, tells the story of a University photography instructor and his endeavors to disseminate and cultivate an appreciation for the art of photographic expression.

In Their Hands, produced by Stewart Burge, Tony Gusic, and Harold Hendsley, is an attempt to bring into focus the poor physical facilities present in the Monongalia County public school sytem and provide some direction in which parents and taxpayers might proceed.

Rock Music: Only A Reflection was produced by Tom Burger, Richard Dematteis, and Reginald Humphrey. "Rock music carries a message: sing it like it is. In this film, we see a panorama of rock music in a university community and explore many facets of the popular music of today's young generation," according to University brochures.

R.O.T.C. At W.V.U., produced by Dave Hark, Larry Baker, Marvin Born, and Kevin Orr. A film made for high school seniors, showing both Air Force and Army R.O.T.C. programs at West Virginia University. This film is used in the spring and fall recruiting programs of the University's R.O.T.C. detachments.

All very interesting and all very bland. The real film work is done by Norwood's students in the "Speech 189: Techniques of Motion Picture Production" class and in the three "Special Projects," "Independent Study" and "Special Topics" courses.

Two Types In Stereo by Parke Johnson, Rhoda Shaw, Tom

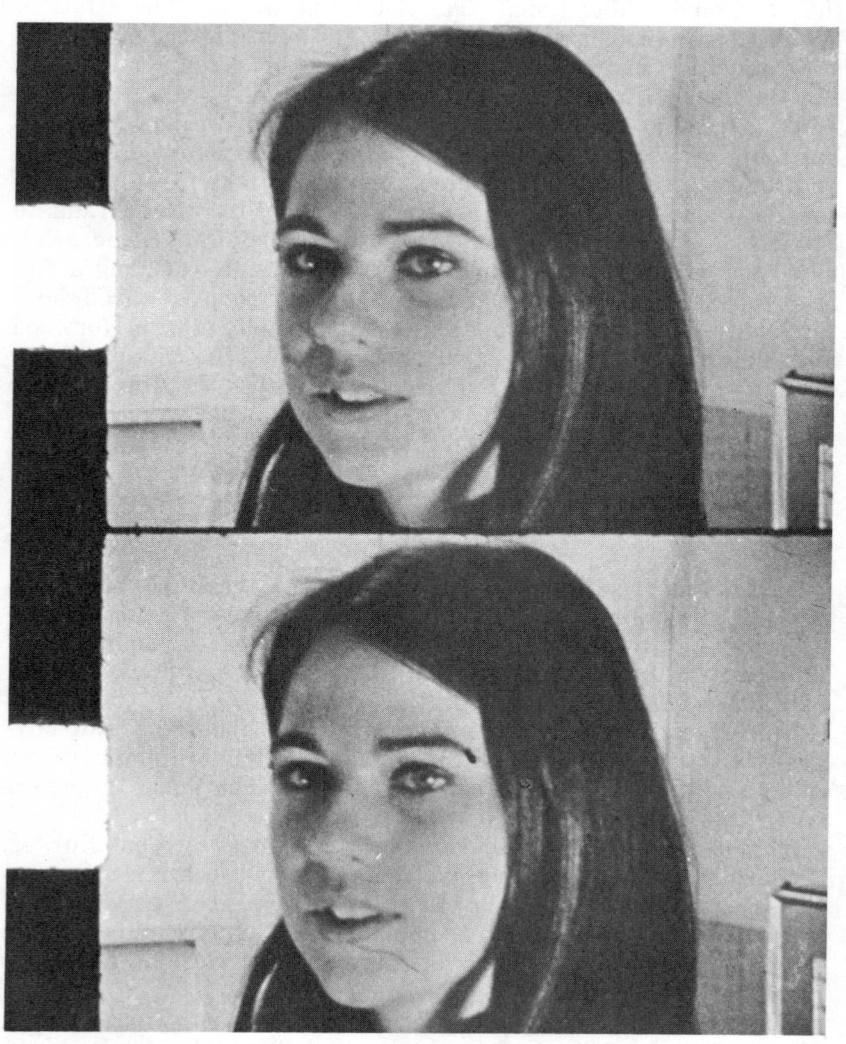

Evy Andrews in *The Color of the Heart,* produced by Dave Anderson, Barbara Tsoucaris, Al Martine, and Charles Hollingsworth. (Photo by David J. Hark)

Rodak, and Ken Hall cuts back and forth between two rather stereo-typed students—a clean-cut fraternity boy and a bearded hippie. Each leads a rather empty and pointless existence on the fringes of the campus community.

The Color of the Heart is one of the better films made recently at West Virginia. *Color* was produced by Dave Anderson, Bar-

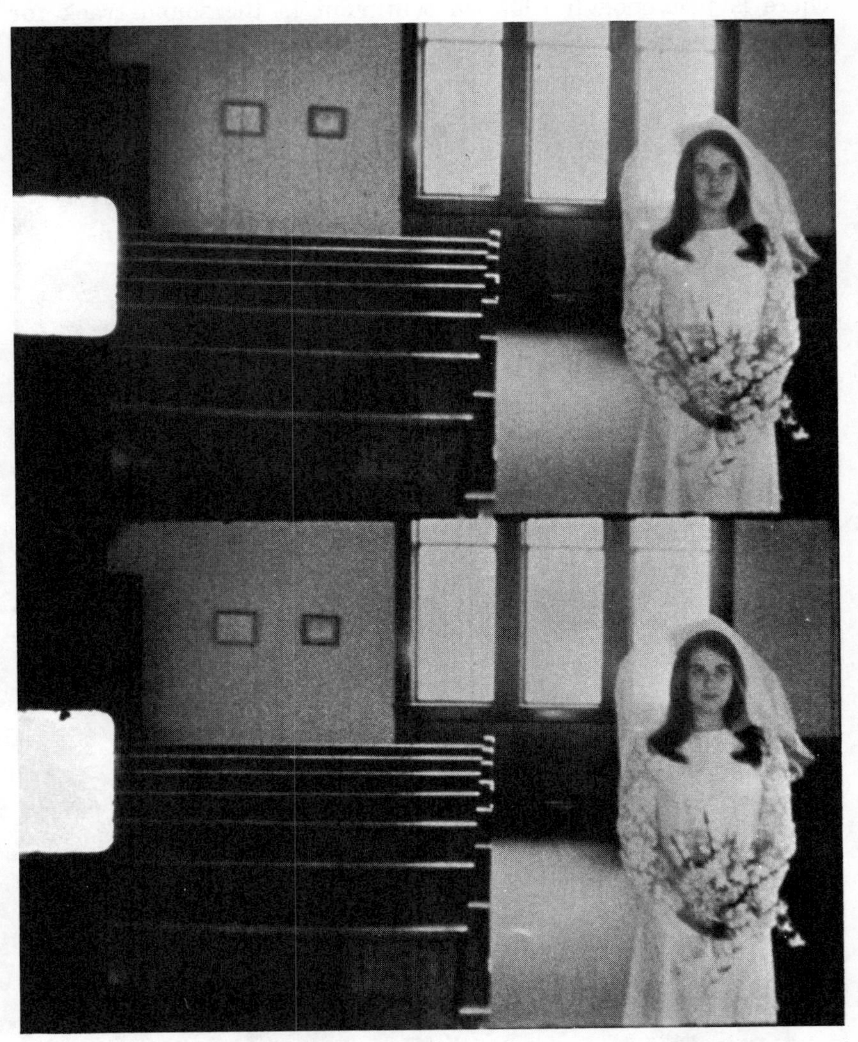

Evy Andrews walks to the altar in an empty church in *The Color of the Heart,* a study of sentimentalized inter-racial love. (Photo by David J. Hark)

bara Tsoucaris, Al Martine, and Charles Hollingsworth. It is a highly sentimentalized film about an inter-racial couple—a white girl and a black guy. The girl hears soaring violins and waltz tempos whenever she thinks of her fiancé, but all he ever hears and sees are the racial slurs and the inhospitality of others. The film could have been mawkishly handled and maudlin, but was not. There is just enough 1940-ish sentiment in the sound track for

From *The Color of the Heart,* a sentimental but highly successful film. (Photo by David J. Hark)

effect. The heroine, Evy Andrews, plays, but does not over-play, her role. *Color* is a fine statement about two viewpoints of love in a bi-racial setting.

Squirtguns, Balloons and Other Violent Thoughts is perhaps the finest film made at West Virginia; surprisingly, it was a team production for the 189 beginning film course. The shooting script is reproduced at the end of this chapter. *Squirtguns* is a 15-minute color film in super eight millimeter. It comments on the violence in urban areas and in the countryside and, as a sub-theme, notes that the tendency toward violence is present in all of us. *Squirtguns,* produced by Brett Falkenstein, Cathy Wirtz, Frank Wudorsky, and Jon Hall, is a charming film; it is good enough to stand favorably beside the beginning film work done at any other university.

Innuendo by Larry Baker is a statement about the emotional state of a man who has lost his wife. Photographically, it is very fine, crisp, and hard edged when it should be, soft and dreamy when it ought to be. But it is also somewhat pointless, marred by a cliché-ridden poetic sound track, somewhat reminiscent of Edgar Allen Poe's *Annabelle Lee*:

> Soft malice of the silence when barely is heard, subtle and light the voice in the night of the moistened leaves and listen vaguely the voice of water murmuring in the grass . . . there are voices of the past, links of a broken chain. Wings that cannot bear me back to times that cannot come again. Yet God forbid that I should lose the echoes that remain. One day in the blue month of September I held her there. My pale and silent loved one and like a gentle dream. Within my arms was she and over us in the fair summer heavens was a cloud that fleetingly I saw, very white and terribly far about us, and as I looked up it was there no more.

The role of the protagonist in *Innuendo* was played by Professor Norwood, who tried to talk his way out of the role, but did not succeed. In the script it is clear that the man eventually commits suicide to be near his lost wife, but that is never made clear in the film. Pictorially, however, it interesting.

As We Forgive Those is a shocker produced by Stewart Burge. The camera follows as a driver picks up a hitchhiking Negro on a deserted road. As the night falls, the driver suddenly, and with a considerable amount of violence, kills the Negro. At film's end, we watch a severed hand and arm being fed into a machine that processes food for a state prison. *As We Forgive Those* is one of the most violent films made in a university in recent months.

The Color of Respect was produced by Jeff Bowles, Bill Campbell, Jim Rightmire, and Jim Walton and involves two Negroes who rob a Jewish grocer. As they flee, the grocer fires a pistol shot that wounds one of the robbers. The two hide in a cellar, and as one dies in one corner, the other cowers in another, all for a few dollars from the grocer's till.

Blessed, by Bruce Hollen, Jack Pollard, and Ken Stoner, is a bit dis-jointed but interesting study in quick cutting techniques between a psychedelic group playing Bach-rock, to a church choir singing the real thing.

In April of 1968, the film program held a general film festival and showed the film equipment to the public. Shown during the festival were the four documentaries, *A Man and His Art, In Their Hands, Rock Music,* and *R.O.T.C. at W.V.U.* At the time, the *Dominion-Post,* the local newspaper, noted:

> Originated last year, the motion picture program at W.V.U. is now nearing the end of its fourth full semester of operation. "And yet," Professor Norwood said, "the average citizen both

The 1969 West Virginia Student Film Festival included showings of: *Two Types in Stereo; Blessed; The Color of the Heart; Squirt Guns, Balloons and Other Violent Thoughts; A Way To Begin; Innuendo; As We Forgive Those,* and other films.

at the University and in Morgantown is unaware of the extensive activity in film production undertaken by film students here during that time."

Norwood brought in, as a guest lecturer, Raymond Fielding, then at Iowa. Fielding was appalled at the film techniques being used in the West Virginia student films. "They were using techniques and styles that everyone else had used and discarded during the 1930s," he said.

A year later, Norwood was planning to have as guest lecturer Pare Lorentz, one of the early documentary film makers. Norwood was positive that Lorentz would not see the out-dated techniques that Fielding saw. "The students have matured tremendously during the last year or year and one-half. When Ray Fielding was here, the students *were* behind the times. Now some of them go to New York and come back and tell me what they saw in Antonioni films and Godard and Fellini."

No doubt they have matured as critical and practical film makers, but until the West Virginia University administration changes its mind and joins the 20th century, cinemagraphically speaking, West Virginia University will continue to be a doubtful and rather risky choice of aspiring university film students, despite whatever Don Norwood might like to do there.

SQUIRTGUNS, BALLOONS AND OTHER VIOLENT THOUGHTS

by Brett Falkenstein, Cathy Wirtz,
Frank Wudorsky, and Jon Hall

SHOT

1 *Exterior. City of Pittsburgh. Day.* E.L.S. of Pittsburgh. Zoom into a L.S.

2 *Exterior. Ghetto. Day.* M.S. Flash.

3 *Exterior. Pittsburgh. Day.* L.S. of the city. Zoom into M.L.S.

4 *Exterior. Ghetto. Day.* M.S. Flash.

5 *Exterior. Pittsburgh. Day.* M.L.S. of the city. Zoom into M.S.

6 *Exterior. Ghetto. Day.* M.S. Flash.

7 *Exterior. Downtown Pittsburgh. Busy street. Day.* M.S. High angle. Protagonist walks into view. He stops. He starts walking again and camera pans him to street corner.

8 M.S. ¾ view of protagonist as he rounds the corner and the camera pans him as he walks down the street.

9 C.U. of cars whizzing by revealing full figure, head-on shot of protagonist as he reaches the corner. He walks into a C.U. and looks toward traffic sign.

10 C.U. Low angle of traffic sign.

11 *Exterior. Pittsburgh. Street corner near park. Day.* L.S. of protagonist crossing street into park.

12 Full figure, head-on shot of protagonist walking in park.

13 C.U. High angle (front) of protagonist's feet walking in park.

14 *Exterior. Field in valley. Day.* C.U. reverse angle of protagonist's feet as he walks in the field. Tilt up to a tail-a-way shot of protagonist as he walks away from the camera.

15 E.L.S. High angle of protagonist walking in field.

16 *Exterior. Ghetto. Day.* M.S. Flash.

17 *Exterior. Field in valley. Day.* L.S. of protagonist walking in field. (Diff. angle from shot 15)

18 M.S. Side angle of protagonist walking by stream. He stops and picks up a pebble and tosses it into the stream.

19 M.S. of water rippling, made by rock.

Go out of focus.
Come into focus to

20 *Interior. Staged. Cameo setting. Day.* L.S. of a keystone cop standing on corner. People in costume walk by and keystone cop hits them over the head with a balloon.

21 C.U. of balloon.

22 M.S. of a doll with a balloon

23 M.S. Head-on of approaching robot. Shot in single-frame action.

24 M.S. of doll. Robot comes into picture and pulls out doll's hair. (Also shot in single-frame action.)

25 C.U. Low angle of robot's hand coming down. (Also shot in single frame.)

26 C.U. of politician's hand hitting podium.

27 M.S. Politician speaking behind podium. Man walks in from side and shoots politician in head with water pistol. Politician falls to the ground.

28 C.U. High angle of toy soldier on ground. Tilt up the low angle C.U. of man behind wall with toy soldiers on wall. He flicks toy soldiers off wall and they fall into the camera. Tilt up to nothing.

29 M.S. Side angle of girl walking in from right side.

30 M.S. Head on of man walking toward girl.

31 M.S. Head on of girl walking toward man.

32 M.S. Head on of man walking toward girl. He reaches out his hands toward camera.

33 C.U. of girl with frightened reaction.

34 M.S. Side angle of the two people continuing to walk on in opposite directions.

35 L.S. Slow Motion of paper buildings. Match enters picture and lights bldgs. Bldgs. burn.

36 *Exterior. Field in valley. Day.* Full figure shot. Slight angle of protagonist standing against tree. Hold for three seconds.

37 *Exterior. Ghetto. Day. M.S. Flash.*

38 *Exterior. Field in valley. Day.* E.C.U. of protagonist's eyes.

39 *Exterior. Ghetto. Day.* M.S. Flash.

40 *Exterior. Field in valley. Day.* M.S. of protagonist shrugging off thoughts and yawning.

41 *Exterior. BBF (Hamburger Stand-author) on High Street in Morgantown. Afternoon.* C.U. of protagonist yawning.

42 M.S. of protagonist standing on balcony of BBF. He looks at his watch and glances down street. He waves his hand at someone.

43 L.S. of friend down street acknowledging recognition.

44 L.S. of protagonist walking down steps. Camera pans him shortly as he begins to walk down street.

45 M.S. ¾ angle of friend walking toward protagonist.

46 Two-shot of protagonist and friend meeting and starting to walk down the street. They walk out of the side of picture.

47 L.S. of protagonist and friend at box office theatre. They buy tickets and walk in the door.

48 M.S. Low angle of theatre marquee.

49–51 C.U.s of still scenes from movie board.

52 M.S. Slight angle of protagonist and friend walking out of the theatre. They hesitate and discuss film for five seconds. They walk off in opposite directions.

53 L.S. High front side angle of protagonist walking up the street and stoping in front of window.

54 C.U. Head on of protagonist's face face looking in the window.

55 C.U. of window. Gun is in sight.

56 E.C.U. of protagonist's eyes.

57 *Exterior. Mountainlair Plaza (West Virginia University Student Union Building—author). Day. (Use vaseline effect).* M.S. Low angle of man shooting another man on steps with water pistol. Man falls on steps. Tilt down to reveal two kids on bottom of screen looking up to man lying on steps. Tilt down further to show the two kids, also shooting each other with water pistols. Nothing happens.

Swish Pan to

58 M.S. Low angle of man and old lady struggling.

59 M.S. High angle over man's shoulder showing him and old lady struggling.

60 M.S. High angle over old lady's shoulder as she beats the man to the ground with her umbrella.

61 M.S. Low angle of man on stomach. Old lady bends over and steals his wallet. She looks around and runs off.

62 M.S., head on of old lady standing, counting the money.

63 C.U. of the umbrella over old lady's arm.

64 *Interior. Downtown Morgantown. Met Shoeshine parlor.* M.S. of man sitting reading newspaper with umbrella over his arm. (Also with vaseline effect.)

65 M.S. ¾ angle of man and boy. Boy finishes polishing man's shoes and reaches up with his hand for a tip. Man folds up newspaper and looks at shoes disgustedly. He beats boy over the hand with the newspaper.

66 L.S. of bystander in foreground and previous action in background. Bystander gets up and starts to walk out.

67 C.U. of bystander in doorway looking across street.

68 L.S. of telephone booth. As seen from the bystander's point of view.

69 M.S. of bystander starting to cross the street.

70 M.S. of telephone booth where one man is struggling with another man. Bystander walks into booth and tries to use phone.

71 *Exterior. Morgantown. High Street. Day.* E.C.U. of protagonist's eyes.

72 *Exterior. Ghetto. Day.* M.S. Flash.

73 *Exterior. Morgantown alley. Day.* L.S. of protagonist walking down alley, looking around at surroundings.

74 Cut-away of alley scene.

75 Cut-away of alley scene.

76 E.L.S. of protagonist walking down alley with his back to the camera.

77 *Exterior. Field in valley. Day.* E.L.S. of protagonist walking in field.

78 Full figure ¾ angle of protagonist walking in field.

79 M.S. low angle of protagonist walking in field.

80 M.S. ¾ side angle of protagonist stopping to sit down in field.

81 C.U. side angle of protagonist's face.

Go out of focus.
Come in focus to

82 *Exterior. Morgantown. Tennis court. Late afternoon.* L.S. of a group of white men surrounding a Negro and pushing him around.

83 M.S. same scene as 82.

84 C.U. of white member of gang laughing.

85 M.S. of Negro gang approaching the white man who is laughing.

86 C.U. over white man's shoulder. Negro hands reaching into camera. (Man) Black out.

87 *Interior. Living room of house. Day.* M.S. high angle from behind a television set. Boy in front of T.V., imitating the violence he is seeing.

88 M.S. high side angle. Girl enters picture and she tries to switch the channel. The boy hits her and she falls on floor.

89 C.U. of television picture.

90 *Exterior. Boreman Hall gutter. Dusk.* Girl walks into the gutter with her back to the camera.

91 M.S. of girl rounding corner in gutter and she hesitantly looks back.

92 M.S. side angle of a man creeping out of the bushes. He grabs girl and they fall into the bushes. Tilt up to the sky.

93 *Exterior. Twin Towers. Day.* L.S. of Twin Towers.

94 L.S. of entrance of Twin Towers.

95 M.S. diff. angle from 94 of student coming out of the entrance. Camera follows him to bus stop. He looks at his watch and then up toward towers.

96 M.S. low angle of man standing on window ledge.

97 L.S. high angle of ground. Shot from the top of towers. (Man on ledge point of view)

98 C.U. of man waiting at bus stop. He looks down at his watch again, being more concerned about getting to class.

99 M.S. of bus pulling up to towers. Camera follows bus until it stops. A couple gets off the bus and the man who was waiting gets on. The boy and girl stop and the boy points up to the man standing on the ledge.

100 C.U. low angle of man on ledge.

101 M.S. from behind couple. The boy and girl look at each other, shake their heads and start to kiss.

102 *Exterior. Woodburn Circle. Day.* M.S. of protagonist sitting in grass in the circle.

103 *Exterior. Ghetto. Day.* M.S. Flash.

104 *Exterior. Woodburn Circle. Day.* C.U. of protagonist getting up off the grass.

105 Full figure Tailaway shot of protagonist as he starts to walk towards Woodburn Hall.

106 M.S. ¾ low angle of protagonist as starts up stairs outside of Woodburn Hall. Stops when he reaches top of stairs.

107 C.U. side angle of protagonist's face.

108 *Exterior. Ghetto. Day.* M.S. Flash.

109 *Exterior. Woodburn Circle. Day.* C.U. of protagonist's face.

110 *Exterior. Ghetto. Day.* M.S. Flash.

111 *Exterior. Woodburn Circle. Day.* E.C.U. of protagonist's face.

112 *Interior. Shot of still photo.* C.U. of violent photo.

113 *Exterior. Ghetto. Day.* Camera pans right, across ghetto scene.

114 M.S. Camera tilts up on ghetto scene.

115 M.S. Camera pans right on ghetto scene.

116 *Interior. Still shot of photo depicting violence.* C.U. of violent photo.

117 Different C.U. of a photo of violence.

118 *Exterior. Ghetto. Day.* M.S. camera pans left across ghetto scene.

119 M.S. Camera tilts down on ghetto scene.

120 M.S. Camera pans left across ghetto scene.

121 *Interior. Still shot of photo depicting violence.* C.U. of violent photo.

122 *Exterior. Woodburn Circle. Day.* C.U. of protagonist's face.

123 M.S. of protagonist standing on top of stairs outside of Woodburn Hall. Students jostle him as they pass and he is swept inside the door.

124 L.S. of Woodburn Hall, as the last few students rush into class.

125 *Interior. Woodburn Hall. Day.* M.S. of empty hallway. Then students start coming out of the classrooms.

126 *Exterior. Woodburn Circle. Day.* M.S. of protagonist coming out of Woodburn Hall.

127 Tailaway shot of protagonist walking towards Martin Hall.

128 ¼ side angle view of protagonist at corner of Martin Hall, where the sidewalk splits. He turns over his shoulder to look at Woodburn clock. He turns back, and then thinking that he sees something in the tower, he turns up to Woodburn tower again.

129 C.U. of startled protagonist's face.

130 L.S. of sniper in Woodburn Tower. From protagonist's view. Zoom into bust shot of sniper.

131 M.S. of protagonist, as he looks around for cover and then he runs to the side of Martin Hall.

132 M.S. of protagonist standing against wall.

133–137 C.U.s of people reacting to protagonist's unusual behavior.

138 C.U. of protagonist's face with a tired look.

139 *Exterior. Open highway. Day.* Full figure, head on shot with protagonist running with background out of focus. He glances back.

140 *Exterior. Woodburn Circle. Day.* M.S. of sniper in tower.

141 *Exterior. Open highway. Day.* M.S. low angle head on of protagonist running with BG out of focus.

142 *Exterior. Pittsburgh. Day.* L.S. of the city.

143 *Exterior. Open highway. Day.* Full figure ¾ angle of protagonist running with BG out of focus.

144 *Exterior. Ghetto. Day.* M.S. Flash.

145 *Exterior. Open highway. Day.* M.S. side angle of protagonist running with Bd out of focus.

146 *Interior. Still photo of violence.* C.U.

147 *Exterior. High street in Morgantown. Day.* C.U. of gun in window.

148 *Exterior. Open highway. Day.* Full figure ¾ angle of protagonist running w/BG out of focus.

149 *Exterior. Morgantown alley. Day.* M.S. of alley scene.

150 *Exterior. Open highway. Day.* M.S. side angle of protagonist running w/BG out of focus.

151 *Exterior. Ghetto. Day.* M.S. Flash.

152 *Exterior. Open highway. Day.* M.S. ¼ angle view of protagonist running with BG out of focus. He glances back.

153 *Exterior. Woodburn Circle. Day.* M.S. of sniper in tower.

154 *Exterior. Open highway. Day.* Full figure, low angle head on shot of protagonist running with BG out of focus.

155 *Interior. Still photo of violence.* C.U. of still photo.

156 *Exterior. Open highway. Day.* M.S. ¼ view of protagonist running with BG out of focus.

157 *Exterior. Field in valley. Day.* L.S. of empty field.

158 *Exterior. Ghetto. Day.* M.S. Flash.

159 *Exterior. Woodburn Circle. Day.* M.S. of protagonist slowly sinking to ground in corner of steps on side of Martin Hall.

160 *Exterior. Field in valley. Day.* L.S. of field. Protagonist comes into picture. Tailaway shot of him running and starting to slow down. (Slow motion)

161 M.S. of protagonist falling to ground. Shot in slow motion.

162 C.U. of protagonist's face as he lies on the ground.

163 *Exterior. Woodburn Circle. Day.* M.S. of protagonist sinking slowly in corner against Martin Hall.

164 C.U. of protagonist's face.

165 C.U. of sniper in tower.

166 M.S. high angle of protagonist sinking more into the corner.

167 C.U. of protagonist's face.

168 L.S. Extreme high angle of protagonist completely sunk in corner of steps, in background. In foreground, people start falling in slow motion. After they fall, tilt up to trees.

169 Credits shown.

III

THE EAST COAST SCHOOLS

11.
Columbia University

ARTHUR BARRON'S BIRTH AND DEATH

In February 1969, Erik Barnouw, chairman of the film division of the Columbia University School of the Arts, announced that he wished a leave of absence from his position. He stated that within two years he would retire and he asked that Columbia appoint a new chairman of the film division.

Arthur S. Barron, the man Columbia selected as Barnouw's successor, has had a remarkable career in film. Barron holds a doctorate in sociology from Columbia and has been Executive Producer of Documentaries for Metromedia, Inc. He has also been Supervisor of Creative Projects for NBC News and staff Producer-Director-Writer for CBS News.

He is also the president of his own film production company, Verité Productions, and has completed *The Rebirth of Jonny, The Rise of Labor, My Childhood: Hubert Humphrey's South Dakota and James Baldwin's Harlem, The Burden and the Glory of John F. Kennedy, The Berkeley Rebels, Sixteen in Webster Groves, The Great American Novel: Babbitt and The Grapes of Wrath,* and *Johnny Cash! The Man, His World, His Music.*

That Columbia made an excellent choice in Barron should be readily apparent from the reviews and articles about *Birth and Death,* the film Barron had completed just prior to his appointment at Columbia.

In the article "A Document of Birth and Death"* in *New York* magazine, Barbara Kevles said:

> *Last June Arthur Barron resigned from CBS where he had earned a reputation as a brilliant, iconoclastic young documentary producer and became an independent filmmaker or "indie." Having behind him such extraordinary programs as*

---

*Copyright (c) 1968 New York Magazine Co.

Arthur Barron is the new director of the film program at Columbia. He has made several exceptional films with his own production company, Verite Productions. (Photo by the author)

"16 in Webster Groves" and "The Great American Novel," Barron turned down a well-paying offer to make a routine medical series and convinced the Public Broadcast Laboratory to provide an $85,000 budget for a major documentary to be produced by his new company, Verité Productions, which he had formed with his wife Evie. . . . The documentary, called "Birth and Death," would explore simultaneously the last month of a man dying of cancer and the last month of a girl's first pregnancy. I was able to watch the production process from its beginning and kept the following journal.

"*June 6.* The immediate problem was to locate subject material: a man who is dying and willing to talk about it, a girl willing to share one of the most important and intimate experiences of her marriage.

"I am waiting for the Barrons in the offices of a lung cancer specialist in the East 50s. On television, a Los Angeles cop is saying, 'No one in the world knows the identity of Robert Kennedy's assassin.' The same is true for these cancer patients

Johnny Cash, seen in a pensive mood during the film *Johnny Cash! The Man, His World, His Music*. This film was first conceived by two Columbia University students, Roy Hykin and Harry Wiland, who interested Arthur and Evelyn Barron in the project. The Barrons eventually produced the film, and Hykin and Wiland were associate producers. The film was released successfully by the Walter Reade Organization. In addition to Cash, the film also features Cash's wife, singer June Carter, Bob Dylan, Carl Perkins and The Tennessee Three.

Johnny Cash and Bob Dylan record a song together for *Johnny Cash! The Man, His World, His Music*. The film has done very well at the box office, especially in the south and in college towns, where interest in Cash and Dylan is high.

Johnny Cash and his wife June Carter sing their hit "Jackson," in concert during *Johnny Cash! The Man, His World, His Music*.

just steps away from me whose nameless assassins are mutilating their bodies a little more every day. When the Barrons arrive, a nurse in wide WAC shoes cancels their appointment. The excuse: 'behind schedule.' Evie crosses the doctor's name off the list.

"In a nearby restaurant over a snack, Art vows to take all rudeness and rebuffs in order to create a film CBS rejected as 'morbid and not newsworthy.' I ask why he's so determined to make *Birth and Death.*

"He answers, 'Making this film is like exploring a loose cavity with my tongue. I'm so afraid of dying. This film is to master my fears of death. . . . Recently I realized my films were a way to express and experience emotions I've been fearful to have in life.'

" 'You mean fantasy was more real than life?'

"Evie says, 'Only Art knows whether the interviews for his Ph.D. thesis are real or made up.'

"Art described his childhood: the bright Jewish kid in a tough Irish community and an intolerable family. All week he lived for Saturday and the movies. 'It's no accident the first film I produced myself was about a schizophrenic who never spoke till a therapist unlocked his world.'

" 'How do you feel after interviewing patients with advanced cancer?'

" 'Life is beautiful, food tastes good, colors are lovely. I wanted to tell an uptight cabbie today, be gentle, we're all going to suffer the same agony. We're all brothers. How ridiculous life is to fight over a $5 raise or a promotion. I have a strong desire to stand up in this restaurant and shout, why are you pretending? The fact of death is so immutable.' He paused. 'This film is a crucible of what life means, what is of value. The film is so universal and dramatic. I don't want to be a crusading reporter. My heroes are Bergman and Fellini. I want to be a novelist in film.'

"*June 19.* The Barrons meet an East Village couple already the parents of twins. They are expecting again, and this time they are married.

"*June 20.* Art and Evie interview a pregnant ex-Miss Summer Festival Queen—a beautiful girl. Mournfully Art sums up her personality: 'flat.'

"*June 25.* Alone, Evie starts attending a week of classes given by Mrs. Elizabeth Bing, New York City's guru of natural childbirth. Fifty-five prospective parents to choose from.

"*June 25, Evening.* After class, Evie has coffee with Bruce and Debbie North, both late 20s, first child due August 5, a clinic delivery. Debbie designs promotion materials for a national magazine to support Bruce's ambition to make it as a landscape painter. On instinct, Evie invites them home to meet Arthur.

"The Barrons' living-room of a West 90s brownstone duplex. Art probes the Norths gently, but incisively, asking Bruce, 'How does it feel to be supported by your wife?'

"Bruce's fingers play with black curls that spill from his head: 'Almost no guilt about it. I told Debbie how it would be from the start.'

"The air is hot and sticky. The producer sheds his shirt and continues the interview stripped to his waist. Bruce is not noticing. His face wears a blissful smile, probably imagining the untold publicity a film could give if Debbie would consent. Finally his wife voices the pivotal question for her decision. 'We've waited six years to have this child. It's a very intimate, personal thing. Are you going to spoil that closeness between us?'

"Art reacts as he does with Columbia students, with complete candidness, perhaps at the cost of the film. He explains the two-man crew will follow Bruce in the front door at the end of a day, out in the morning to sketch, to the supermarket with Debbie, to the clinic to watch and hear the baby's heart beat amplified. 'If you want a film of the birth of your first child to have as a family album, you're going to have to compromise some privacy.'

"The Norths leave, promising to think it over.

"*July 1.* The Barrons surprise Debbie at work and take her to lunch. 'The Norths really want to make the film.'

"Memorial Hospital gives its delayed decision: 'No time or facilities to make *Birth and Death.*' Art knows of five films done at Memorial. Furious he hollers into the receiver, 'When this is one of the masterpieces of all time, you'll regret your refusal.' Only a dial tone answers.

"*July 2.* Four doctors at Lenox Hill promise to put the film on the October staff meeting agenda. 'But our cameraman goes on payroll this week,' the Barrons reply.

"*July 3.* A friend knows a dying man who talks about it. The man is spending his last vacation in Florida. On *Moby Dick,* Arthur dared to ship a full union crew to Alaska to film a Captain Ahab he hadn't found yet. The Barron luck prevailed in Alaska, but the risk was on CBS' money.

"The Norths, lovingly, are standing very close to each other as the Barrons enter a 53rd Street restaurant. 'They're it,' Arthur resolves.

"*July 4 weekend.* At the Catskill home of Bruce's parents, the Norths are initiated to *cinema vérité* filming by cameraman Gene Marner and his pregnant wife and soundman. Carol, and their assistant, Mitch Smith. Bruce's mother tells them, 'Eat, eat, you're eating for two.'

"By choice the Barrons remain in the city. Art, 39, a latecomer to film, has never learned to shoot or take sound like most young filmmakers today. 'I don't particularly enjoy location work,' he admits. He maintains remote control by meetings with the Norths and the Marners and by screening rushes with Gene.

"*July 22.* Art switches on the moviola . . . and watches footage from Coney Island. Growing sound of a buzzsaw: camera reveals a tractor huffing past a group of old ladies at cards and pans to Bruce North sketching with teacher, the cartoonist-painter David Levine. Medium shot of the lady cardplayers *smoking cigars.* 'It has the quality of life. Unbelievable!' Art gasps and nuzzles Evie with kisses. 'Like Fellini. No Walter Cronkite, life! Art is not journalism.' He is as turned on as any cameraman watching his own footage.

"Now a close-up of Debbie North walking from bus stop to New York Hospital entrance, and the camera is steady all the way. 'Nice . . . Niiiiiice!' Art exclaims and gets so carried away this time that he bends down and kisses the moviola. It is Art Barron's finger drumming, feet stamping editing dance.

"The door opens and moustached Gene Marner, gesturing like the man in the 'heavenly coffee' ad, enters. 'You are realizing my fondest dreams,' Arthur slurps.

"The Coney Island rushes once more. Art questions, praises, hints, orders hesitantly, trying to direct Gene toward the themes of *Birth and Death* that at this point exist like so many undiscovered galaxies in Art's mind. '. . . I'm interested in showing the community of life through generations—that behind Bruce North and every human being stands 30 ghosts . . . I want the Birth people talking of the terror of Death and the dying talking of life.' Gene should not just follow an event, but manipulate it, stage confrontations, plumb the themes. The Marner Coney Island compromise: Bruce North, not Gene, will get the ladies.

"The reel ends. Art and Evie give the news about Calvary Hospital, a hospital specializing in advanced cancer patients who have a life expectancy—according to the admissions application—'of more than one week and less than twelve.'

"*July 22.* Morning. Run by an order of Dominican Sisters, Calvary Hospital sits on a hill separated from the neighborhood by a curving stone wall. Ironically, the Bronx Savings Bank advertises with big baby booties on a billboard opposite the hospital which averages two deaths a week. Today the Barrons meet with assistant administrator, William Oliff, for permission to shoot at Calvary. If Calvary refuses to cooperate, the Barrons must start from scratch to find a hospital willing to allow a dying patient to be filmed. The importance of this pivotal meeting has forced Arthur into the unaccustomed outfit of suit and tie.

"Mr. Oliff turns out to be quite amiable for such grim surroundings. As he inquires into the whyfors for *Birth and Death,* Arthur replies like a professional con man touching all the right keys—the spiritual reason—'the kinds of grace and compassion that motivate the hospital'; the promotional aspect—'to show the care given even the dying'; the recruiting advantage—'the fund raising possibilities . . .' Art capitalizes on the smallest vanity, the smallest motive to win permission. Mr. Oliff has only one objection—the interference with his staff and wheel traffic. *That* is his only hesitation. Art dispenses with that easily. Only one obstacle left—the approval of the Monsignor of the Diocese.

"*July 25.* The Monsignor gives his blessing. The Barrons have seven weeks of shooting to go—49 days to find and film their dying man as well as complete the shooting of the Norths delivery of their first child.

"*July 29.* The Barrons start daily visits to Calvary. Unobtrusively they wander through the corridors where patients pass the time between meals, never talking of their all-consuming illness, afraid to voice the unspeakable fear. The endless charade. In one room, the Barrons confront a woman who asks, Will I be home to register for social security?' more as a prayer than question. Each visit for Arthur is like moving a little further into the cold sea of death, first toe, then ankle, then knee. He plans to be at Calvary for every day of shooting to purge his fears, his old aching cavity.

"Evie suggests the possibility of following two or three patients as an insurance policy.

"*August 1.* On film a grocer hands Debbie North a bag of peaches and weighs another as outside his Brooklyn store Hasidic Jews with *tallith* bags and *tsisis* pass on Sunday walks. One man religiously covers his face when the camera points at him.

"The assistant editor locks another reel into place. An on-camera interview with the Norths. In her voluminous pleated dress, Debbie is a live dirigible, a balloon stretched to capacity grounded to the couch by her husband's hand. 'Now that I'm married, I don't think about death,' she says, 'I'm too alive. There's too much to be done yet.'

"Art stops the moviola. He is ecstatic. The Marners are giving him the themes of *Birth and Death,* just as he requested. Art dances his editing dance throughout the entire screening.

"*August 5.* This week's doctor at the New York Hospital Clinic reverses the decision of last week's doctor. This doctor will not induce Debbie's labor as she shows some signs of imminent delivery. The Barrons are crestfallen. For the past five days, they have paid a second cameraman to do nothing but stand by for added coverage for the delivery. Now, they must keep the cameraman on payroll and depend on nature to take its course, knowing that due dates for first babies are as reliable as official New York City weather reports.

"Like doctors on call, the Barrons, the crew and I lead a minimal personal life, meaning we all stay home by our phones.

"*August 8*. It is a costly wait for Verité Productions. The Barrons schedule the first day of shooting of the dying at Calvary for the following day. *Birth and Death* production resumes.

"*August 9*. I stand with Evie in a Calvary nursing station as Art and crew follow a doctor on his morning rounds. As the doctor is having an on-camera interview with one patient, another dies in a nearby bed. Quickly, the nurses come and cover the body with sheets, as easily as slipping a letter into an envelope.

"Art introduces me to the people from whom one will be chosen as the main story for the second half of *Birth and Death;* Mrs. F., a Puerto Rican housewife who treats us as if we were guests in her home kitchen; and Mr. T. who carries death in his bloated belly, as large as Debbie North's carrying life. He is sitting up awaiting his family to go home for *Shabbas*. Down the corridor, Mr. M. just over 60, lies eyes glazed with pain. He hardly pays any attention to our 'Hello' for his lustreless eyes look inward, as he faces the inevitable with no distraction.

"From time to time, Art asks the doctor, 'Have I antagonized anyone?' and receives the reassurance that Calvary is behind him.

"Mrs. T. arrives. As she tells the camera what good care the hospital gives her husband, as she plays the charade of wife hoping for her husband's recovery, she breaks down, crying and screaming. The film makers flee the room, afraid they are causing a heart attack. But not before her husband reaches over and gently strokes her head. And they know that he knows he's dying, that he hangs on because his wife needs him, that though he fears death, he is distracted by love and the living.

"*August 15*. At 2:45 a.m. the Barrons' phone rings. Debbie is in labor. Art taxis to the New York hospital. A not-to-be-believed bureaucrat at the front desk refuses to let him pass. Finally, Art dons a scrub suit and arranges for the largest delivery room. Forty-five minutes later, a nurse adds Mrs. North to a wall-size chart—the production schedule of the baby factory.

"Minutes later, Debbie, Bruce and crew are positioned in a tiny labor room and Art wanders in and out handing Gene film and whispering suggestions. As the pain of contractions builds, Bruce North like a practiced coach orders, 'Breathe in, blow, blow, blow. Now relax. Remember the class, remember Mrs. Bing . . .' Debbie's eyes scrunch down like a pneumatic drill.

"Not the usual one, but *three* doctors, all aching to be filmed, appear for the internal examination. Prudishly, Bruce says, 'Arrrrrthurrrrrr.' The producer leaves but the cameraman stays behind and films everything.

"Evie arrives in time to see Debbie wheeled to the delivery room.

"With contractions coming every two minutes, the baby about to emerge, Gene's film runs out. He drops his camera and picks up another on hand for such an emergency. The batteries of the second camera are dead. He must reload the first one. Carol Marner drops a clamp to her tape recorder. She, too, must take time out to reload. Evie appears at Art's side and says, 'Keep your cool, darling.'

"At 9:52 a.m. all cameras rolling, Thursday, August fifteenth, a doctor's fingers draw out the shoulders, one arm, then the other. And Andreas Marco North yells the yell of selfhood.

"Art, father of two, weeps, Evie, mother of three, weeps, and the Marners, too, are teary-eyed at this rehearsal of the birth of their child a month away.

"*August 27.* Calvary Hospital. The Barrons and crew are filming Mr. T. at a birthday party for two ladies whose next namedate will be celebrated with the lighting of a candle *in memoriam,* a contribution to the church, and a cemetery visit. In one corner under the arcade of gay streamers sits Albro Pearsall with a strange, other-world look on his face, here-but-not-here. The Barrons are wondering whether to interview Mr. Pearsall, whether there is any purpose in exploring another character when they have invested so much time and footage in Mr. M. and T. A. nurse has suggested the interview because 'out of all the patients in the hospital, Mr. Pearsall is aware of his true condition.'

"Evie argues 'Why not?' and Art signals the crew to set up at Albro's spot—a chair by the shelf of the public telephone directory that Mr. Pearsall likes to lean on.

"Art, cross-legged on the floor, questions this man whose only identifying possession is the bracelet with his name limply hanging from his wrist. Mr. Pearsall resembles an El Greco portrait—bony hands, elongated face, flesh as taut as stretched canvas. Work? For over 20 years a top gold smelter in New York's diamond center. Age? Only 52. As the ten minute reel of film is about to run out, Mr. Pearsall admits, 'I'm dying of cancer . . . no hope . . . I'm suffering, so I wish Jesus would take me . . . I'm glad they told me the truth because a man should know.'

"The Barrons are excited and astounded by Mr. Pearsall's honesty; he accepts death without deception, without charades. They had originally planned to shoot only one reel, but Art changes his mid. He will film as much as Mr. Pearsall can take.

"Carol Marner pushes back her black braids once more to insert the ear set curved like a stethoscope with which she monitors the feeble heart beat of Mr. Pearsall's words. She waits for him to swallow a thumb-size cup of pain killer and then switches on the tape recorder.

"As Mr. Pearsall is talking about the life he's lived—regrets, good times—Art notices one of the birthday ladies wheeled past. She was carried out of the party hemorrhaging. Her case has worsened.

"*August 29.* As Steve Rotter is logging in rushes from the birthday party, the Barrons remember the interview with Mr. Pearsall and ask to see it. Their editor, Zena Voynow, has been complaining about the death house footage which deals with death only through hints and indirection. Where is the abrasive confrontation of one man groping for meaning in the face of his own extinction she wants to know.

"After the first reel of Albro Pearsall's interview, everyone's face is wet with tears. Here at last is the man who knows he is dying and will talk about it. The interview with Mr. Pearsall contains the bomb of truth that the death house footage desperately needs. Art makes a radical decision; to refocus the second half of his film on this one man, to interview Mr. Pearsall's cronies, family, fellow workmen, to trace down whatever photographs or movies remain of the houses he lived in, his parents, schools, childhood toys—to reconstruct the life of Albro Pearsall as he is dying.

"What has happened to Albro in the years prior to his admission to Calvary interests Art most because if the film is to realize his original conception, the death footage must emphasize the worthwhileness of life and love. Many months before, Arthur Barron made this promise to PBL in a proposal on *Birth and Death.*

"*Perhaps this is the best place to say I do not see this film as morbid . . . This film will not be sentimental about this man's death. It will not gloss over the pain, the grief, or the fear. But it will affirm the goodness and worth of life. And it will show, if we are very careful . . . in our choice of the man, that death can be faced with some courage and dignity, if one has worked, loved and been loved, if one believes life has been imbued with meaning. . . .*

"Art makes the casting change for the second half of the film knowing he has less than two weeks' shooting time left on the film, less than fourteen days to reconstruct the life of a man who may die any minute.

"*September 7.* It is still night outside when Gene and Arthur enter Mr. Pearsall's room located on the first floor annex. The nurse on duty notified the Barrons by phone that Mr. Pearsall is breathing his last. Immediately, Art sees that Mr. Pearsall's face is severely contorted and discolored. Without asking Gene, he leaves the room to tell Carol, now pregnant in her ninth month, 'You're not going in there.'

"Mitch Smith, assistant cameraman, takes sound for Gene. The soundman crouches on one knee then shifts to a standing position—trying to cover the event from every angle, knowing full well he can never return to reshoot this scene. His camera to his eye, Gene can maintain a distance from the death, can protect his feelings from what is really happening.

"Arthur has no camouflage. He watches the contorted features of this man who from the depths of his coma fights to stay alive. Albro's face, a web of strained muscles, shows the pull on the lifeline, the tug of war even of this man, 'prepared to die.' By comparison to Mr. M. who died last week, Albro struggles harder. Standing at the bedside of this dying man, Art reckons he has lived a 'full life'—marriage, sons, a continuity of line. He wants to make films that will stand up to those of Fellini and Flaherty, films that will carry the name ARTHUR BARRON beyond his lifetime, he wants a little longer . . . with Evie. And he thinks, staring at the dying man, "Better you than me . . . better . . . you . . . than . . . me.'

"Art signals a break and everyone is relieved just to walk out into the hall. In the corner of the corridor, a nurse is stacking wheelchairs. She pulls up the leather seat with a snapping sound and slaps the sides together. Side by side, the brown wheelchairs resemble a cordon of coffins, each ready for a consignment.

"A nurse comes out of Albro's room and announces he is dead. Art enters, glances at the corpse, but doesn't notice any difference from an hour ago. The moment of dying passed undistinguished from those before or after. And Albro's roommate, whose sensibilities and sleep were protected throughout by a curtain around his bed, never sees the doctor sign the death certificate, Albro wheeled to the morgue, or the kid undertaker in mourning tails and loafers pack the body in a zip-up sack. In the morning, the roommate only sees the empty-made-up bed. For him, Albro's death disappears like dirty laundry stuffed in a bag and quickly hidden from sight.

"In the hall, Art and crew wait for the death vigil to end as the nurse tries again to reach Albro's brother by phone. If the filmmakers have to stay through the day, dinner will be turkey with all the stuffings. Not even death has stopped their appetites.

"The record of the death of Albro Pearsall, the record of the pregnancy and delivery of Debbie North, these scenes are the Barron signature on film. David Oppenheim, PBL's Executive Producer in charge of Cultural Affairs, defines it:

" 'Arthur Barron is obsessed with personalizing his idas in live people and he succeeds in film because of this characteristic. Yet he manages to make a general, intellectual statement as well.'

"In his proposal to PBL, Arthur wrote:

"This is not a news film. It is not a report. . . . Its purpose is nothing more and nothing less than the purpose of all art: to inform the heart, to reveal what it is to be human. . . .' "

Barron has made significant changes in the film curriculum. As he said:

First, the film division has no connection with radio or television. There are no broadcasting studies offered in conjunction with the film program. We are separate .

Secondly, the hours required for graduation with an M.F.A. degree (Master of Fine Arts—author) in film have been increased from 42 to 60.

The courses are taken in sequence, meaning that students may not begin the program in mid-year. They have to begin in the fall and continue for four semesters. We are offering specialization in two major areas of film: directing or scholarship-criticism. We believe that the director is the key in film-making and consequently, we offer very little training for cameramen, soundmen and the like.

Students are expected to make films for government agencies or social welfare programs. They form their own production crews for these films. The directing students take courses in acting and all students shoot their beginning films in super eight millimeter.

We are looking for students who are interested in the total creative experience without being overwhelmed by exposure, cameras, focus or story line.

Barron has overhauled the entire film program at Columbia. The only film courses offered to undergraduates are film history and non-production courses. Columbia has no undergraduate program leading to a degree with a major in film making.

The equipment available to the graduate film makers at Columbia includes about a dozen Bolex cameras, some Bell and Howells, three Eclairs, an Oxberry animation stand, sound recording and mixing equipment, three editing units, three screening rooms, and a developing laboratory that the film makers share with the Columbia School of Journalism.

Barron has also hired additional faculty members and is continuing a program of re-building the faculty. Joining him for the 1969–1970 school year is Andrew Sarris, one of the leading film critics in the country. Sarris was formerly a faculty member of the New York University film program, downtown. His move to Columbia only means that he'll be taking different subways to work each day. Sarris has written film criticism for a variety of publications, including *The New York Times, The Chicago Trib-*

une, The Chicago Sun, The Washington Post, Saturday Review, Variety, Arts, Show, Film Comment, Film Quarterly, Film Society Review, Films and Filming, Movie, Moviegoer and *Cahiers du Cinema.* He is the author of several books on film. He will head the scholarship-criticism program under Barron.

Also joining the faculty will be Eleanor Perry, whose credits as a screenwriter include *David and Lisa, The Swimmer,* and *Last Summer.*

Rae Allen, who had one of the leads in the New York production of *Fiddler On The Roof,* will teach acting to the film students.

Some of the courses offered to the graduate film students are:

Film Production: Super eight millimeter, an introduction to the basic elements of film making. Technical (e.g. focus, exposure, camera movement, etc.) and Aesthetic (e.g. composition, mood, theme, etc.). Silent and Sound. Students will prepare assigned exercises and will also complete films on subjects of their own choice, and in styles of their own choice. Equipment and an allotment of film are provided;

History of the Motion Picture, a history of film from its beginnings to the present, with emphasis on the development of forms and techniques and on relationships to other arts and to social and political currents. Lectures, discussions, and film showings;

Analysis of Film, the techniques and aesthetics of the fiction film—through a "microscopic" analysis of selected films representing various cultures, theories, periods. Scripts will be studied in conjunction with the screenings and discussion will be from the point of view of the director and his range of aesthetic and technical choices;

The Documentary Film, principles and techniques of the documentary film from the past to the present. Emphasis on the special characteristics of documentary, as contrasted with fiction film. Case studies of selected films. Students will pursue individual writing or production projects. . . ;

Film Producing, a practical consideration of the legal, budgetary, union, sales, distribution, and administrative factors involved in producing a motion picture;

The Film Medium, analysis of the structure and functioning of the film industry, its place in society, its influence on society, its relation to other mass media. A sociological and social psychological perspective;

Master's Project, for students in the directing area of concentration, a sixteen millimeter film. For students in the scholarship-criticism area of concentration, a screen-play, research essay or major work of criticism. Students preparing a film may work alone or in a group;

The courses required of students majoring in directing are:

Film Equipment, Introduction to the motion picture camera, lenses, filters, lights, film, sound and recording equipment, editing equipment, animation stand, and other basic tools and material; their characteristics, and implications for the film maker;

Cinematography, an introduction to the craft, problems and techniques of the cinematographer through demonstrations and workshop exercises. The cinematographer's role in the production process;

Film Editing, workshop in the theories and techniques of film editing. Equipment and an allotment of sixteen millimeter film are provided;

Film Directing, directing the actor in relation to the camera. Directorial principles, techniques and range of responsibilities. Rehearsal and taping of exercises and scenes with instant playback on videotape equipment;

Screenwriting, analysis of the problems, forms, and techniques of screenwriting, and of the role of the writer in the motion picture field. Analysis of existing scripts, preparation of student exercises, and full scripts. Students' script material will be used in the directing and cinematography classes;

The Sound Track, technical and aesthetic problems relating to the sound track; acoustics, microphone placement; selection of equipment and material; on-location sound problems, transfer; mixing; laboratory processing. The dramatic role of music and sound effects;

Production Project, students and factulty will constitute themselves into a company for the production of a film. The faculty member will serve as executive producer, with students serving as producer, cameraman, soundman, editor, director, etc. The film, which may be documentary, fiction, or animation, will be exhibited or broadcast.

The courses required of the scholarship-criticism major are:

Film Aesthetics, a review and analysis of theories of film aesthetics. Attention to concepts of the frame, film time, space, light, reality and unreality, foreground and background, etc.;

Film Production, A step-by-step introduction to the complete film-making process: conceptualization, script, shooting, developing and printing, editing, mix, answer and fiinal print. The class will make a short 16 mm film as a team project. Visits to studios, laboratories, etc.;

Film Criticism, Analysis of major film criticism past and present. Development of a theory of film criticism on aesthetic grounds and related to social and political currents;

The Contemporary Film, A seminar on landmarks in contemporary cinema. Leading film critics, scholars, and film makers analyzed—and lead discussions of—works of current significance. Works discussed include films available in New York City theatres (attendance required) and some films screened in whole or part for the class;

Writing Project, a seminar in which students study research methods in film (e.g. stock footage research, content analysis, biographical and historical research, etc.) and in which they engage in individual writing of essays, scripts, reports, etc. In addition, students will help publish and edit a film journal and prepare a series of broadcasts for presentation on local radio and/or television.

As outlined in the division's bulletins, the semester-by-semester course work for the two areas of concentration leading to master's degrees in film in two years would be:

Directing	*Scholarship-Criticism*
First Semester	
Film Production: Super 8	Film Production: Super 8
History of Film I	History of Film I
Analysis of Film I	Analysis of Film I
Film Equipment	Film Aesthetics
Acting	Elective
Second Semester	
Cinematography	Film Production
Editing	Elective
History of Film II	History of Film II
Directing	Elective
Screenwriting	Film Criticism
Technical Proficiency Examinations	
Third Semester	
Sound	Contemporary Film
Documentary Film	Documentary Film
Analysis of Film II	Analysis of Film II
Production Project	Writing Project
Fourth Semester	
The Film Medium	The Film Medium
Film Producing	Film Poducing
Master's Film	Master's Essay
Comprehensive Examinations	

Under the guidance of Arthur Barron, and with the assistance of Andrew Sarris, Eleanor Perry, and the other members of the faculty, it should not be surprising to find the Columbia film program soon rated among the excellent programs in the country. If Barron's own films are any indications, the program at Columbit should become very, very good.

12.
New York University

THE INSTITUTE OF FILM AND TELEVISION
THE GRADUATE CINEMA PROGRAM

Exceptional film programs on both coasts are usually considered in pairs. On the west coast, the two logical schools are the University of Southern California and the University of California at Los Angeles. It is difficult to judge which is better. On the east coast, two schools are similarily paired—New York University and Boston University—but here the choice of the better school is easier. New York University offers a generally more comprehensive program; students interested in film making have the entire panorama of the New York megalopolis to shoot in, and advantages that can not be found in the Boston area.

Undergraduate film work at New York University is part of the Institute of Film and Television and courses are presented in class rooms in N.Y.U.'s Washington Square campus, in lower Manhattan.

The current catalogue described the undergraduate film program as:

> solidly based in the liberal arts. Studies in the sciences and humanities are required of all students to provide the background necessary for creative participation in a profession which influences attitudes, opinions, and ways of thinking in every aspect of human experience. Interwoven throughout the four-year curriculum with these liberal arts courses are studies in major areas of film and television. The film and television curriculum is structured and the courses designed to provide the student with (1) a variety of creative experience in both the conceptual and production phases of film and television, and the opportunity to develop (2) the technical skills for bringing these concepts to the audience, (3) an extensive critical and historical frame of reference, (4) an understanding of the relationship between society and the visual and sound

media, and (5) a personal philosophy which embraces the potential of these media as a means of expressing and communicating a wide range of human experience.

Underlying the undergraduate curriculum in the Institute of Film and Television is the belief that the individual's development as a creative artist is a continuing process. It does not begin nor does it end with college. The undergraduate experience is one phase in that continuing process, designed to be appropriate for the student who will go on to professional training in graduate school, or will serve a career apprenticeship in the film or television industries, will make his way as an independent film maker, or will find his place in some other professional area in which film and television play an important part.

Some of the cources offered for undergraduate film majors and their descriptions are:

Film History, . . . traces the development of motion pictures as an art form from birth as a literal visual record to its status in contemporary times. A feature film selected as representative of a type or concept is screened in each class meeting. Lecture and discussion deal with the individual films and also the concept in terms of the art, technique, and business of film. Form and technique are studied always in relation to context;

Aesthetic Principles of the Film, deals with the aesthetic principles of creative activity in motion pictures. Basic concern is with the standards for critical appraisal and judgment from both the creative and the audience points of view;

New Directions in the Cinema, surveys the avant-garde, experimental, underground, and abstract film and explores the potential of the medium. Class work consists of film screening, lectures, discussions, and parallel reading: The course is concerned with both the sociological and artistic significance of new directions in the cinema. From time to time, representative film makers screen their works and address the class;

Contemporary Cinema, the language of cinema as a distinct art form is considered in conjunction with its reflection of ideas and emotions of contemporary Europe, Japan, India, and America. The variety of the style is to be associated with the particular meaning sought by individual directors. Selected historical and critical readings and student writing parallel the films;

Studies in the Documentary: Film and Television, a study of the documentary beginning with Kino-Pravda and Flaherty and including Grierson's G.P.O. movement, the United States government sponsored films of the 1930's, the films of the National Film Board of Canada and the widening documentary and public affairs movement of television. In this course the term "documentary" is interpreted broadly to include any films or television programs intended to document, inform, educate or persuade;

Film Industry, a comprehensive survey of the contemporary motion-picture industry. Current practices in the production, distribution, and exhibition of films for theatrical, non-theatrical, and television release; labor and government relations;

The Language of Sight and Sound, The objective of this course is to develop the student's awareness of the potential of picture and sound as a means of communication and expression. The course provides the opportunity for recording and experience of perception, description, analysis, interpretation, and self-expression through the use of picture and sound. The basic techniques and equipment of both motion pictures and television production are examined and practiced;

Fundamentals of Film Making, provides the experience of working out conceptually and on film a wide variety of basic problems of film making. Students in the various laboratory periods rotate the functions of the production crew. The aim is to help the student develop a disciplined awareness of the *why* and *how* of form, techniques, and style in relation to content;

Motion Picture Production—Direction, a senior level course in motion picture production and direction. Students engage in production planning, preparation of shooting scripts and outlines, studio and location cinematography and sound recording, and editing. Emphasis is on creative film making and films representing a wide variety of types are completed during the year;

Sound for Film and Television, . . . is designed to familiarize students with the aesthetic values and expressive values of sound, sound juxtaposition, and the relationship between dialogue, effects and picture. Practical exercises deal with synchronous sound shooting, methods for recording wild sound, acoustic control, and sound mixes;

Music for Film and Television, . . . is designed to familiarize students with the aesthetic and expressive values of music in relation to sound and the picture. Laboratory practice deals with selection, recording, editing, and mixing of music;

Motion Picture Editing, principles and techniques of film editing for screen and television, with emphasis on artistic and aesthetic concepts. Laboratory practice with standard cutting room equipment. Creative expression in the film medium through individual projects;

Cinematography, principles and practices of cinematography. Laboratory exercises in use of professional equipment. Studio practice in interpretative lighting, composition, perspective and camera movement. The materials and techniques of color cinematography;

Production Design, A course dealing with creative and functional set design in terms of action and camera movement. A study of the uses of color, materials, special effects, rear screen projection, and graphics;

Directional Problems in Motion Pictures and Television, an analysis through lectures, readings and laboratory exercises of fundamental principles of direction—dramatic content and form, characterization, staging and a study of directional theories and practices as they apply to motion pictures and television;

Audio Workshop, an advanced course concerned with the planning and production of dramatic documentary, public service, and educational sound tapes. Students gain production experience both in the university studios and in the field;

Writing for Film and Television, a study of documentary and dramatic forms and styles. Students undertake writing projects in television and motion pictures.

As juniors and seniors, students are required to take about half their courses in either the "Group I" or "Group II" courses. Group I includes: *Contemporary Cinema; Aesthetic Principles of Film; Modern Drama; Studies in the Documentary; New Directions in Cinema; Mass Media in Contemporary Society; Studies in Audience and Programming; The Organizational Structure of Film and Television; and Advanced Individual Studies.*

The Group II courses are: *Television Production-Direction; Fundamentals of Filmmaking; Audio Workshop in Actuality and Studio Documentary; Writing for Motion Pictures and Television; Summer Motion Picture Workshop; Special Projects and Television Production-Direction;* and *Advanced Individual Study.*

During the 1968–69 school year, New York University had 312 students enrolled as undergraduate film majors and 55 students as graduate film majors.

There are two separate programs on the graduate level. First, there is the graduate program in the Institute of Film and Television. It is oriented toward different objectives from the undergraduate program. The graduate objectives, as listed in the N.Y.U. catalogues, are five:

1.) To provide students the opportunity to develop their creative talent through intensive class experiences and actual production experience using television cameras, 16 millimeter cameras and 35 millimeter cameras for both documentary and dramatic subject matter;

2.) To provide lectures nad seminars in aesthetic, historical and critical studies so that students may be aware of the best of the past and present as it may be applicable to the future;

3). Because individual responsibility in the professions of

film and television requires not only artistic expression but also entrepreneurial competence, the studies will provide students with the basic knowledge to deal creatively with professional structures and procedures;

4.) To familiarize students with the fundamental of design on which expression in film and television is based. Through research and laboratory experimentation, they will study the theories and artistic applications of light, space, sound, color, time and motion and the impact of these elements on the human mind;

5.) Through lectures, to introduce technological advances of the near and distant future, as a preparation for changes that lie ahead.

The classwork and production ratio of the graduate program at the Institute is unique in its structure. The catalogues explain:

> Courses are planned and the year is scheduled to provide a new approach to technical production studies. The first semester of the first year is divided into a ten-week study period and a four-week production period. The study period is devoted to script writing and pre-production planning for silent 16 mm minifilm projects, complemented by studies in camera technology and still photography. During the production period, each student directs one minifilm and participates in the crews of five other films as script writer, editor, producer, cameraman and assistant cameraman.
>
> This pattern is repeated during the second semester of the first year. The production period, however, is lengthened to seven weeks, during which time every student directs a short 16 mm sound film. During the study period, shortened to seven weeks, first-year students study sound camera technology and lighting technology while preparing scripts and budgets for the production period.
>
> Thus, at the end of the first year, all students have had actual experience directing, writing, editing, producing and shooting 16mm black and white silent and sound films, and each student has credits on twelve duifferent Institute productions. All work is done under the guidance of professional specialists in the above fields.
>
> In the second year, students continue work in 16mm film production but move on to studies in 35mm production and color film technology. The first semester is devoted to studies in and production of documentary films and the second semester to dramatic feature films.
>
> During the first semester, each student prepares an original documentary film script for production as class work for the course, Script. Similarily, a feature film script is prepared during the second semester. At the close of the seven-week study

period each semester, these scripts are submitted to a jury made up of faculty members, and four prizes in the form of production are awarded; first prize, a 35mm color film; second prize a 35mm black and white film; third prize a 16mm color film and fourth prize, a television production using the Institute's television studio for live taping plus some 16mm black and white film footage where desired. Thus four projects, each twenty minutes in length, are produced per semester.

At the end of two years' work, all Institute students have had classroom and production experience both in 16mm and 35mm and black and white and color work.

It must be noted that no graduate student can work in film or television while attending N.Y.U. without the permission of the director of the Institute. All films made by undergraduate or graduate students are owned by New York University.

The graduate courses offered by the Institute of Film and Television are:

Still Photography, Intensive studies in the aesthetics of still photography and in camera and laboratory techniques;

Cinematography-Editing I, Introduction to production and techniques for 16mm black and white films. Preparation for *Production Crews I,* production of two-minute films, giving each student the opportunity to work in different crew positions;

Production Crews I, Shooting, editing and group criticism of two-minute 16mm black and white silent films. Each student acts as director, producer, editor, writer, cameraman and assistant cameraman;

Production Crews II, Shooting, editing and group criticism of five-minute 16mm sound films with opticals;

Direction. Intensive study dealing with the film and/or the television director as he relates to actors, nonactors; staging for camera, planned and improvisational acting and its bearing on the camera. Students participate in special exercises and demonstrations;

Camera Technology, Emulsions, their testing, selection, sensitivity. Lighting in terms of footcandles. Balancing of interior and exterior lighting in black and white photography. Shooting of tests and teaching the basics of sensitometry of black and white reversal and negative-positive printing. Study of printing lights and visits to leading professional labs and studios. All class work done with 16mm Arriflex cameras in preparation for Production Crews I;

Directing I, Techniques in the directing of documentary films. How script content is communicated through the personal style of the student. Class viewing of several exemplary documentary films;

Directing II, Studies in the directing of theatrical films. The way in which script content is communicated through the personal style of the student; the casting of actors appropriate to the form; how to work with given actors once they are selected. Development of the personal style of the student, and how to apply this style to shooting scripts when on set;

Color Camera I, A study of realistic color definition. Color sensitometry for 35mm and 16mm emulsions and the techniques necesseary for realistic reproduction of color through technically perfect definition of contrast and density in the three basic color emulsions. Realistic form and documentary style. The class will shoot tests with 35mm cameras using the latest emulsions—7242, 5254, etc.

Color Camera II, The means of changing reality or how to use photographic techniques to create a non-realistic, subjective picture of the world on the screen. How to destroy reality when the end result reinforces the idea content of the script;

Production Crews III, The production of four documentary film scripts. Each student submits a documentary script to a jury at the end of the study period. Four prizes are given by the jury. First prize: permission to shoot a 35mm color film; second prize: permission to shoot a 35mm black and white film; third prize; permission to shoot a 16mm color film; fourth prize: permission to shoot a black and white television production using 16mm film footage and live studio taping. All four films are produced under the supervision of the faculty;

Production Crews IV, The same as *Production Crews III,* except that films produced are theatrical rather than documentary;

Light, Use of light for realistic and nonrealistic effects. Opticals, Creative use of different contrasts, densities, perspectives and depths of field. Shooting of tests in class using 16mm Eclair sound camera with Nagra tape recorder in preparation for *Production Crews II;*

Time and Motion, The application of time to image, composition, form and meaning. The application of movement to one or more objects in a field of vision. The effect of slow and fast motion on meaning;

Sight and Space, Changing ways of seeing properties of sight what we can and cannot see. Optical illusion. Composition, form, animate and inanimate objects, perspective, size, aspect ratio, emphasis;

History of Still Photography, The art of still photography. Its origins and development as seen in the works of its major exponents.

Through an agreement with the Museum of Modern Art, this course is taught at the Museum, offering students access to the Museum's archives of still photographs. John Szarkowski, Director of the Museum's department of photography, and Peter

C. Bunnell, Associate Curator, teach the course with the aid of other Museum staff members;

Expression, A survey workshop course exploring the techniques of writing in the various media open to the film and television writer: the narrative feature, the narrative short, the documentary, animation and live television;

Script I, Documentary script writing: the role of the writer in the documentary, including short educational films, television public affairs documentaries, entertainment documentaries and feature length documentaries for theatrical release. Emphasis is on techniques of editorial and visual research, structuring, writing to film and the uses of cinema vérité. Every student in this course prepares a documentary film script which is submitted to a faculty jury at the end of the study period. The jury selects four scripts for production.

Script II, Theatrical film script writing: study of important feature film scripts, screening of parts of important feature films and consideration of how the script writer changes reality into cinematic drama by using the literary style of the novelist or the visual style of the director. Every student in this cuorse, prepares a theatrical film script, which is submitted to a faculty jury at the end of the study period. The jury selects four scripts for production;

The Nature and Uses of Film and Television;

Pre-production, taught by different members of the Directors Guild of America; studies of the various considerations of the producer in preparation for the shooting of television shows, commercials, documentary and feature films. The economics of major film organizations and television networks, budgets, contracts, the value and uses of money, money-time equations, law principles applicable to films and television, audience—its influence and how it is influenced;

Film Production I, introduction to 35 millimeter color and black and white film stocks and opticals. Producing from costing to answer print. Direction from the editor's point of view, Laboratory work. Concentration on the documentary style film in preparation for *Production Crews II;*

Film Production II, feature film production: staging, editing, sound and image. Intensive studies in the developing of script into film and the editing of the film. Production preparation for *Production Crews IV.*

The second program on the graduate level is the Graduate Cinema Program, and it is administered through the Graduate School of the Arts and Sciences, instead of the Institute of Film and Television. The Graduate Cinema Program is intended to be a scholarly and critical program, as contrasted to the Institute's graduate program in practical film making. The Graduate Cinema Program is described as:

> designed to combine the academic tradition of responsible scholarship with the particular requirements of a unique and autonomous field of study. Its general purpose is to ground the student thoroughly in the principles, methods and objectives of film study; its ultimate goal is to prepare the successful graduate to pursue independent research, to contribute to an expanding body of knowledge and to assume competent leadership in a new academic discipline.
>
> Four major areas of concentration are fundamental to the structure of the Graduate Cinema Program: history, theory, aesthetics and criticism. These will be supplemented and augmented in time by the gradual addition of courses in important but subsidiary areas of study, with the aim and ambition of eventually developing a comprehensive program that will offer appropriate and adequate instruction in all significant aspects of cinematic art. The Program is conceived essentially as a liberal arts discipline and will pursue an interdisciplinary policy. It will therefore include and make provision for selected courses, both required and elective, in theatre and drama, art history, the social sciences and such other bodies and areas of knowledge as may be deemed relevant.
>
> The Graduate Cinema Program has concluded an agreement with the Museum of Modern Art offering qualified cinema students the opportunity of a one-year internship in the Museum's film department for training in curatorial work.

Courses offered are:

Aesthetics of the Cinema, A systematic study of the cinema as an autonomous art form, examining its specificity, formal principles, value criteria, fundamentals of style, etc. Extensive screenings;

The Art of Film Directors, A study of the personal contributions and styles of major directors, both American and European, to film history. Selected screenings;

The History of the American Film, The development of the cinema in America from 1895 to the present. Analysis of the contributions of leading directors and their work. Extensive screenings;

The Film and Modernism in the Arts, A consideration of the major aesthetic movements of this century as they have reflected and inflected the development of the cinema. Expressionism, Dadaism, Surrealism, Cubism, Neoclassicism, Constructivism and other styles as developed in other art forms are discussed in terms of their connection with film aesthetics and filmmaking. Selected screenings;

The Documentary Cinema, Examines the evolution of the film of fact and purpose, information and instruction, promotion and propaganda. Screenings and guest speakers;

Colloquium in Cinema Theory and Practice, A course offered by guest teachers and cinema personalities of distinction, invited for lectures and discussions in their respective fields of competence;

Theatre, Film, Narrative: Transformations of Style, Comparative studies in the dramatic, visual and fictional representation of reality, emphasizing relations of affinity, contrast and metamorphosis. Illustrations to be drawn from dramatic literature, the novel and the cinema;

History of the Cinema, A comprehensive survey of the historical development of the art of the cinema from 1895 to the present. Selected screenings;

Theory of the Cinema, Systematic critical study of the major works of formal theory, including the writings of Balasz, Eisenstein, Pudovkin, Arnheim, Kracauer, Bazin, et al. Readings from other sources. Selected screenings;

Film Criticism, principles and methods of film criticism. Critical analysis of selected films. Readings. Part 2: study and analysis of selected criticism in published form;

Seminar in Film Criticism;

Seminar in the Aesthetics of the Cinema;

Cinema Practicum, a course designed to meet especially the needs of the film scholar. Its aim is to acquaint the student with the specific crafts and processes peculiar to the cinema. Emphasis is not on professional proficiency but on theoretic and aesthetic understanding of film techniques and their importance to the cinema as a creative medium;

Film Literature, Bibliography and Research, is to acquaint the student with the vast body of film literature and criticism, much of it not yet available in English and much of it still in periodical form;

Advanced Individual Study.

The faculty of the Institute and the Graduate Cinema Program are as distinguished as any other film programs in the country. Current members of the Institute include: Joseph Anthony, who directed the television series *Profiles in Courage,* the films *The Matchmaker, Career,* and *All in a Night's Work,* and the stage plays *The Rainmaker, Marriage-go-round, The Best Man, Rhinoceros, Mary, Mary,* and *The Most Happy Fellow*; Fred Batka, who has experience as a still photographer and film director; Harold Flender, who has written a number of documentary scripts and published articles in *The Paris Review, Saturday Review, The*

Haig Manoogian, professor at New York University, is generally regarded with very high esteem by his students and former students. (Photo by the author)

Nation, The New Leader, and *Variety*, among others; Don M. Mankiewicz, who has written for a variety of films and television productions, including *Trial* (1956), *I Want to Live* (1958), *Playhouse 90, Profiles In Courage, The Defenders, Hawk, O'Brien, Ironside* (pilot segment) and others.

Robert Saudek,* Director of the Institute, has been an executive for N.B.C., vice-president of A.B.C., director of the Ford Foundation Television-Radio Workshop, founder and president of Robert Saudek Associates, which produced *Profiles in Courage, Omnibus, Leonard Bernstein and the New York Philharmonic*, and other specials; George H. Bouwman, head of the undergrad-

* On leave of absence during 1968–1969. He was a visiting Professor in the Carpenter Center at Harvard. On Sept. 10, 1969, the school announced that Leo Hurwitz would replace Saudek as chairman of the Institute. Hurwitz worked with Pare Lorenz and Paul Strand on many of the documentaries of the 1930s, including *The Plow That Broke the Plains* and *Heart of Spain*. He was later chief of news for CBS and director of film production for the U.N.

uate program, has won a CINE Golden Eagle for his films *Animation Goes to School* and *Discovery*; and Martin Scorsese who has been a writer-director for the films *What's a Nice Girl Like You Doing in a Place Like This?* (1963), *It's Not Just You, Murray* (1964), *The Big Shave* (1967), and *Who's That Knocking On My Door?* (1968).

Faculty members of the Graduate Cinema Program include: George Amberg, director, who has written *Marc Chagall, Jean Cocteau as Film Maker*, and *The World of Film*; George R. Hitchens, who has been the founder and editor of *Film Comment* magazine and associate editor of *Film Society Review*; and Arthur L. Mayer (Visiting Lecturer on Drama and Cinema), who has been director of advertising and publicity for Paramount Pictures and has written *The Movies* and *Merely Colossal.* He has published articles in *Saturday Review, Harper's, The New York Times*, and others and, prior to the 1969–1970 school year, when he moved to Columbia, Andrew Sarris was also a member of the graduate faculty.

The principal differences between the Graduate Cinema Program and the Institute of Film and Television were noted clearly in an article about film schools in the column "College," in the October 1968 issue of *Glamour* magazine:

> The Graduate Cinema Program, . . . is strictly an academic one. Students must have bachelors' degrees to gain admission; they study history, theory, aesthetics and criticism. Dr. Amberg believes it is the duty of the university to educate scholars of film, who can then become critics, teachers, curators for museums and libraries, etc.—not technical practitioners. "There should be professional schools for film-makers. An artist should not have to fulfill academic requirements. And the university should not give degrees for nonacademic work."
>
> "But many people disagree with me," said Dr. Amberg, pointing out that Robert Saudek's program at the Institute of Film and Television . . . is production-oriented. While Amberg's program offers an M.A., with a Ph.D. program to be added soon, Saudek's institute gives M.F.A.'s to college graduates and certificates to students with no previous degrees. At the Institute the small student body (this year they accepted thirty-four out of 350 applications) works on film-making for three years —the first in New York, the second in New York and Hollywood and the third in New York and Europe. The Institute stresses learning by doing and "aims to create a new breed of film-makers . . . informed, progressive, knowledgeable, young, ambitious leaders"—in Saudek's words.

The stress on "learning by doing," the aim of creating a new breed of film maker, and the experience of living and working in Manhattan gives the Institute a certain *elan,* a spirit visible at no other school. The now-dead magazine *eye* caught that spirit quite well in an article titled "NYU: The Ultimate Film School," which appeared in the April 1968 issue*:

> The "Normandie Room" on the second floor of the Central Plaza building in New York's East Village is a gem of Art Nouveau-riche. The pink mirrors, the yellow curtains, the golden Fred Astaire top hat which tips over the opulent red and yellow entrance have remained unchanged since the huge room was inaugurated as a banquet-bar mitz-vah ballroom in 1928.
>
> "Last September, a movie screen was set over the plush red bar, cutting tables and equipment were moved in, and bright white lights substituted for the hush-pink of yesterday. An anteroom, dominated by a long-haired, sylph-like maiden who glides in a silvery circle painted on a lavishly gilded window, became an office jammed with machinery and camera equipment. The "Normandie Room," where stars from Sir Laurence Olivier to Julie Andrews once rehearsed, became temporary headquarters for the new New York University Institute of Film and Television. Here, thirty-four outstanding students, among them five Phi Beta Kappas and several magna cum laudes, started work in their first year of the course, devoted to theory, history and processes involved in film-making.
>
> After six opening weeks studying theory of film, time and motion, history of motion pictures, and photography and television, the students were on their own. They divided themselves into groups of five or six and, under the direction of a student with some professional experience, had to produce a short film within six weeks. Each student fulfilled one particular role while making the film, then another after the film was shot. One would be cameraman, another sound man, etc.; after processing, one would supervise mixing the sound track, another would edit, and so on. Each of the students had a chance to specialize.
>
> They spent the first few days in the Normandie Room interviewing actors and actresses who agreed to work without pay for the experience and publicity. Building, in an apartment around the room, dividing it into closely guarded little sectors where the actors were tested. "Hey! That's my screen," someone would shout. "I've spent three hours fixing this up, where the hell do you think you're going with my screen?" Finally, when most of the casting was done, groups spread into different areas of the city to start rehearsals for the final shooting.

* * *

Only a few blocks away from the Central Plaza building, in

an apartment on East Eleventh Street, James Mannas has started work on his film *Kick*. The small room is crammed with equipment, sound blocks cover the ceiling and microphone wires trail out of people's bodies. A tall, heavyset Negro in sailor pants is swiping things off a table and shouting "No, goddammit, I can't do it. Baby, Baby, where's the money?" ("Careful, George, careful," calls out one of the crew, hastily removing the objects from the table. "Remember, it's not our apartment") and the actress sitting on the floor opposite him gets up and screams, "No! No money! No dope! Never again!" 'Who do you think you are, Nigger?" he snarls back at her. "High and mighty bitch. You remind me of those black bitches who send their men to the Man's jail for his own good.' '

Larry, a drug addict, has come home. His wife Adrienne realizes he needs a fix and pleads with him to let her help him stop. She finally arranges for a neighbor to lock them in for the night in an effort to kick his habit. He becomes feverish, cold; she tries to comfort him. They keep talking, remembering past days together, until gradually the worst is over and they break through to a new understanding of each other. The film ends with the coming of the dawn.

James Mannas, himself a Negro from New York, wrote and devised the film. Before entering New York University, he had taught photography to high school dropouts for Bedford-Stuyvesant Youth in Action.

* * *

Bob Cooperman's film takes place in a cold, destroyed ghost city. Charred skeleton buildings stand silently; there isn't a human being in sight. Inside the remains of a half-destroyed house lies what at first glance appears to be rubble. Closer inspection reveals heaps of gas masks and bedpans—an eerie juxtaposition of the instruments of chemical warfare and human frailty. In the background rise the forbidding silhouettes of hospital buildings. Death hangs in the air, frozen on a Satday afternoon.

The film is about life after an abortive nuclear war. And the set is all for real. Cooperman's crew went to the southernmost tip of Welfare Island, a decaying dump used only for firemen's practice, in view of pale hospitals for decaying humans. In the film, politicians are trying to stabilize a broken country and consolidate power through rhetoric. The story centers on one lonely man and his connections with the media. Most of the action takes place on his television set. When he finds his job is considered a "nonessential commodity" he leaves his girl friend instead of facing her with the news. She remains a zealous, unquestioning worker in the "Bureau of Relocation," but he takes off and joins the protests of the contaminated.

* * *

Back in the Normandie Room, Jeremy Kagan, a Harvard

scholar whose thesis was on Eisenstein, is at work on two animation films. One experiments with the use of color. A "being" with a long snout in a jungle-green/jungle-blue jungle swallows up the color from the plants. He moves on to a jungle-red/jungle-yellow jungle and again swallows, all the color mixing inside him. He moves everywhere, frantically sucking. As he takes the last drop, he swells right up, turns black until only two little eyes are visible, then explodes. Cartoons have almost replaced fables nowadays, in certain circumstances. The moral message here is that gluttony, absorbing everything indiscriminately, can only lead to self-destruction.

* * *

What is the connection between a punching bag and a Teletype? Or between a boxer and a girl who works for *The New York Times?* Sounds, sounds, identical sounds.

Terry Hustedt intends that these sounds connect two strangers who meet by chance one day when their hours of hammering at a typewriter or punching bag are over. Shots of their day zigzag between *The New York Times* machinery and the gymnasium at the YMCA. They bump into each other on a street corner and for an instant their eyes meet. The dream is for a moment, broken suddenly by the screech of a car's brakes. People rush to the accident. A policeman calls out, "Does anyone know this man?" But the girl doesn't really, so she keeps on walking.

Jeff Young, a Harvard Law School graduate, took his group to a posh Fifth Avenue apartment to start shooting *The Lonesome Death of Hattie Carroll,* a film based on the Bob Dylan ballad. A young Southern gentleman farmer, Billy Zanzinger, hits a Negro maid with his cane in a drunken brawl and kills her. Justice is administered: a six-month suspended sentence.

Technical problems were a real headache for the group. The New York view from the windows could hardly have looked less like the heavy Spanish moss and magnolia landscape of a plantation, and the ubiquitous mirrors produced a multitude of hot spots from the lights.

It took hours of manipulating the cameras round the chaise lounge and the delicate furniture to eliminate the reflections.

* * *

Mark Fine has turned a Chekhov story called *Grief* into a simple, sensitive and very moving film set in New York in the sixties. It concerns a man whose son has died, and who tries to tell someone about it. But no one wants to hear—all are too concerned with their own problems. The hero in the film is a hansom-cab driver who picks up various passengers on a cold winter night, none of whom understand or even try to understand his grief. He returns at the end of the night to the stable where he finds his friend Jack, another Cabbie. He tries to tell him ". . . but he finds only a tired, beaten face, though upturned and open-mouthed, lost in the passages of sleep, snoring or moaning as loudly as the rest of them." Finally, he goes and talks to his horse, the only one to whom he can relate his story.

* * *

The man responsible for all this flourishing activity is Robert Saudek, award-winning NBC producer and director of many television shows and films, who directs the Institute and teaches film and television. He admitted students on the basis of their interests, backgrounds and portfolios.

The NYU three-year program is unique in this country. The first year of study in New York is intended to expose the students to what Saudek calls "the rough-textured, virile style" of the city. To expose the students to top professionals in their fields, dinners are scheduled with producers and actors after each screening.

The class will go to Hollywood next year to learn the economics of film-making—how to plan efficiently, how to coordinate and how to deal with stars and contracts. Saudek considers Hollywood "one of the best-structured film centers in the world"; feels that students can learn a great deal by working closely with a great film director or company. During the third year, he hopes to send the most talented students to Europe to work with a European film director or to be attached to an institute of film or television. There they will find a more intellectual, often more creative, type of film-making.

The aim of the school is to create a new breed of film-makers. "There is a growing need in television and film for informed, progressive, knowledgeable, young, ambitious leadership," says Saudek. "The revolution in film and television must be accelerated, and these students can do it. I'd like to see them as future heads of MGM or NBC."

Albert Gregory, assistant professor of design, sums it up: "A feeling of excellence underlines the school." And his opinion is shared by nearly all its members, who realize the exciting opportunity the course presents. "We'll come out with a name," one student said. "There's a sensitivity here, a lack of the mediocrity found in most universities. There's no dogma or rules. There's action, less talk."

That same spirit carried over into an announcement of a film festival, scheduled late in the spring of 1969:

Movie Orgy—7 hours of Unbelievable Thrills, Violence, Nostalgia & Eyestrain—a mind-boggling barrage of Hollywood camp intercut with miles of extraneous footage culled from secret archives plus 2001 splices and miles of leader—an experience of mind-rotting celluloid hysteria—rated Z—not suitable for anyone. SEE thousands of actors in the roles that earned them obscurity. SEE the beautiful women attacked by the lust-crazed giant ape. SEE Roger Corman's greatest unknown classic. SEE the voluptuous Chiquita, Mexican Spitfire, lay a cunning trap for Hoppy and his pal Lucky. SEE Conway Twitty sing *That's Why We Go to College.* SEE coming attractions for pictures that don't come. SEE Nejla Ates, The Turkish Delight. SEE Ann-Margaret warn of the ever-present Communist conspiracy. SEE Giant Insects, Singing Cowboys, Maladjusted Indians, Bosomy Starlets, Alf Landon's historic plea for law and order, & More, More, More!

For all its excellence, New York University simply does not keep many records on its outstanding students and their films. Their files are haphazard at best, hopelessly inept at worst. Notable films in recent years, however, have been:

Expressway to Your Heart by Marc Stone, which won first prize in the experimental film category at the 1969 National Student Film Festival, and *Song for My Sister* by John Klein, which shared the second prize for a dramatic film at the same festival.

Hello, World by Barbara Battle received a CINE Golden Eagle award in 1965 and John Mavrogiannopoulous's *Plato in Amerika* received a similar Golden Eagle in 1966.

It's Not Just You, Murray, completed by Martin Scorsese when he was a student at N.Y.U., received an award at the San Francisco International Film Festival in 1964 and was honored at the National Student Film Festival in 1965.

Jeff Strickler's *Stillborn* received a CINE Golden Eagle Award in 1967 and an award at the San Francisco International Film Festival in 1966.

Lewis Teague's *It's About This Carpenter* gathered a number of awards including a Diploma of Merit at the Melbourne (Australia) Film Festival and the National Student Film Festival in 1965, the Edinburgh and San Francisco festivals in 1964, and a CINE Golden Eagle in 1964.

Arrivederci, Darling, That's My Advice to You by John Craddock was honored at the San Francisco Film Festival in 1963 and the National Student Film Festival in 1965 and received a CINE Golden Eagle in 1963.

Scorsese's *What's a Nice Girl . . .* was honored at the National Student Film Festival in 1965.

Daviel Kleinman's *The Applicant* won a CINE Golden Eagle in 1968, as did *Oupa* by Peter Rodis the same year.

There have been other significant winners, none of which New York University has bothered to record. The Institute's film makers generally win about three CINE Golden Eagles each year and several students place very high in the National Student Film Festival.

Generally, film program faculty members at any school only tolerate production courses. The students are demanding and the courses are tiring and simply more difficult to teach successfully than are scholarly or academic-type courses. One N.Y.U. professor who does not mind production courses and actually *prefers* to teach them is Haig Manoogian pronounced Hugh Ma-news-ian). "He is the beginning and the end, the be-all and the end-all of the N.Y.U. film program," Kenneth Golden has said. Golden was a former student of Manoogian's and now teaches in the Brandeis University film program. "He's the best," another student said. "He *is* the N.Y.U. program, personified."

"We try to teach the freshmen perception—to have a visual sense," Manoogian says. "During their sophomore years, we add the basic production techniques and when they are juniors, they receive more advanced teachings. We then teach them cinematography, lighting and direction and, as adjuncts, sound and music techniques. We try to structure the undergraduate program to be terminal when they graduate or to prepare them for additional graduate work in film."

Manoogian has taught at N.Y.U. for 23 years and when he began, he remembers, the equipment for the entire program consisted of one camera. "I won't say that we have enough equipment," he says, "we don't. We have an adequate supply for the basics, but need more senior level and advanced equipment."

Undergraduates in the Institute film in crews. During their beginning assignments, they shoot in crews of four. After their first assignment, the director leaves the crew to work on editing other films and the crews shoot longer films. The University pays for film within reasonable limits and does not encourage students to shoot footage past the maximum for each assignment.

Manoogian published the book *The Film-Makers Art* (New York: Basic Books) in 1966; in it he discusses the film *Tuesday* as an excellent example of student work at New York University:

> If anything has been proved thus far it is that there are no set routines or procedures for making a film. Aside from the vast artistic range possible in the film, the fact that operating budgets can be large or small—which has absolutely no bearing on artistic merit—in itself often dictates the way the film-maker must work. In addition, the subject matter itself practically demands that the film-maker make up new rules to fit his case as he goes along. This not only attests to the volatile and fluid nature of film, but amply supports Louis Kronenberger's state-

ment that "in a final sense, there are never any rules in art; there are only risks."

The following example of student work, therefore, is not intended to prescribe a procedural pattern. Rather it is to show that the one certainty of film-making is that it must be a labor of love. Beyond this, the exercise demonstrates a particular student's point of view as he took a short story he liked very much through a number of steps, breaking down its literary characteristics and visualizing them in terms of film.

The short story, *Blue Silk and Tuesday,* by Oliver C. Grannis, first appeared in the May 1959 issue of *Esquire* magazine.

BLUE SILK AND TUESDAY

Randolph leaned far far out over the window sill and gazed down at the sidewalk, four stories below. He allowed a bit of saliva to form in the top of his mouth, and then, slowly dropping his lower jam and relaxing his tongue, he let the saliva fall from his lips and splatter down on a white cat that had been chalked on the sidewalk by a ten-year-old artist who lived downstairs. The artist's name was Tuesday Reed, and she was standing only three feet from her chalk cat when she heard the ball of spit slap against its concrete fur. Tuesday didn't look up, because she knew it was Randolph who had spit, and she didn't stop to scold or even to think before ducking into the doorway of the apartment building, because she knew that Randolph had spit not at the cat but at her, and that next time he would be sure to hit her.

At least a dozen times, Randolph had spit on Tuesday Reed, who had moved to the neighborhood only nineteen days before. Randolph was twelve, but since boys don't grow up as fast as girls the age difference was just right. Tuesday's mother, who always looked ahead, thought secretly that Randolph might someday want to marry her daughter, and perhaps someday he might. Mrs. Reed had once been an artist too, making beautiful pot holders from colored elastic bands, but she had retired some time ago and preferred now to read mystery stories; and when she read she told Tuesday to play outside, but not to leave the sidewalk in front of the building. So, whenever Tuesday's mother was reading a mystery story, Tuesday was running the considerable risk of being spit upon by Randolph Horn.

Tuesday opened the hallway door just enough for her to squeeze through and slip back outside, under the protective arch that extended out about a foot over the doorway. She looked at her cat; it had a big wet spot about three inches wide right on its stomach. Pressing back against the door with the palms of her hands, she inched over to the side of the arch and looked up at Randolph's window. She just had time to pull her head back in before spit splashed down on the sidewalk, right at her feet. That was discouraging. It was impossible to get out to repair the damage that had been done to her chalk cat, to say nothing of taking the time to draw a new one. She scraped back along the wall to the door, opened it again and squeezed through into the foyer, where she pushed the second doorbell, and ringing it was the only way she could think of at the moment to get back at Randolph. She waited for the harsh buzz which somehow unlocked the glass door at the end of the hallway, but it didn't come, and even if it had she probably wouldn't have gone in. She took a piece of blue chalk from her dress pocket and began drawing owls on all the mailboxes except the Horns'. She left that one blank.

Upstairs, Randolph was still leaning out the window, trying to catch a glimpse of Tuesday sneaking around underneath the arch. And then he looked at the sidewalk and felt a little sorry that he had missed Tuesday and hit her cat instead, sorry not because it was her cat but simply because it was a cat, and he liked cats very much. He had his own cat, a live one, named Silk. Silk was a girl. Her mother had been a black cat with a white ear, her father a gray Angora. When the kittens were born, they had all been black with one white ear or one white paw, all except for Silk. She was a gray Angora. Weeks after all the others had stopped sucking, Silk was still trying to get milk from her mother, eating only as a very last measure the chopped liver and tuna fish the others ate. And weeks after the others had learned to use the sandbox, Silk was still learning, putting her front feet into the sandbox and going all over the floor. But the others were all given away, and Silk stayed on, even after her mother had gone—after she ran away or was run over by a truck or fell victim to any one of the other fates that befall cats who live in cities.

Right now, while Randolph was leaning out the window, Silk was walking back and forth along the mantel in the living room. There was a false fireplace with glazed yellow tiles, and over the fireplace was a marble mantel on which stood a rather large blue vase. The vase was shaped like an imitation of a Greek vase would be shaped, colored like an imitation of Wedgewood would be colored, and contained the ashes, or at least a part of them, of Mrs. Horn's uncle. Mrs. Horn's uncle was called Bernie, even today, after being dead for seven years, as it was because of Bernie that the Horns were able to live as well as they did on, or in spite of, Mr. Horn's earnings as a drapery salesman. So, the vase was very important, and no one was allowed to touch it, except to dust it. And no one ever did touch it, except for Silk, and she liked to rub her ribs against the white flowers on the side of the vase. That's what she was doing while Randolph was leaning out the window, trying to get a bead on Tuesday.

A blue uniform turned the corner and started down the row of apartment buildings in the direction of the doorway where Tuesday Reed crouched, drawing owls. Randolph ducked back into the room and grabbed something from the floor, something imaginary but nonetheless very heavy, something which caused him to grunt audibly when bending over to pick it up. He placed the heavy object on the window sill and waited for the policeman to walk directly beneath him. The uniform ambled along, pigeon-toed, swinging a stick, and stopped to admire the cat chalked on the sidewalk. The spit had long since dried. Randolph spread his feet apart to balance himself, put his hands squarely behind the weight he had placed on the window sill and pushed it out into space, throwing up his hands in a violent gesture of prayer. The weight hurtled down past four windows and struck him dead, but the policeman didn't notice. He gave the cat a final glance and continued his pigeon-toed beat, letting his night stick dangle from his wrist as he clasped his hands behind his blue back.

Randolph walked over to the mantel, picked up Silk and scratched her ears. He put her behind some books in the bookcase, watched her crawl out and then put her back again, doing this three or four times until Silk didn't bother coming out any more; then he went to the kitchen, got a cookie, and went back to the window. Tuesday had come out of hiding, had quickly drawn a bird right on the cat's back, and had slipped back into the doorway again, all while Randolph was playing with Silk and getting a cookie. The bird was almost as big as the cat, and had stripes running all the way from its head to the ends of its feathers. And the cat had been improved upon, getting a tail and a second eye. The tail was curved up and around, and the bird, which was riding backwards, could easily have reached out and pecked it. Randolph was quite angry. He was going to spit on the bird, but because he had just eaten a cookie, he couldn't get any spit; so he went to the bathroom and drank a glass of water.

When he got back, an umbrella had been drawn over the bird's head, and the umbrella had red stripes, which only made it worse. Randolph took careful aim. He wanted to hit the bird, but he missed and all he hit was a very empty space on the sidewalk about two feet away from either the bird or the cat; and, before he had time to get any more spit, Tuesday had run out from her doorway and drawn a blue circle around the spot on the sidewalk, marking his failure for the whole world to see. Randolph was still sucking in his cheeks and frantically pushing his tongue up against the top of his mouth when Tuesday was back in her haven.

Randolph had heard of men who lock themselves in apartments and then go berserk, shooting at men, women, policemen, and even children, shooting until they run out of ammunition or they're subdued by tear gas. It was a good idea. He went to the door of the apartment, locked it, and proceeded to pile up in front of the door every piece of furniture he could move. Finally, with a sofa, two armchairs, a coffee table and three telephone books, he quit and returned to the window. While he was gone, Tuesday had drawn two horses, three stars, a tree, and a heart with some initials in it, but he couldn't read the initials.

He took careful aim and hit one of the horses right in the head; he hit the tree, missed twice, hit the umbrella, missed again, hit the blue circle Tuesday had drawn around his other miss, and, finally, hit a woman who was walking down the street with a bag of groceries. He hit her on the head. The woman reached up and touched her head; she looked at her hand, touched her head again and looked at her hand again. She made a face and wiped her hand on her coat, and then she looked up and saw Randolph, his mouth working. She jumped in under the archway, beside Tuesday, and was again scored against, this time on the shoe. Tuesday scrambled out, ran in a quick circle around her art, and returned to the protection of her archway, all before Randolph could get off another one. She smiled smugly at the woman who was still wiping her hand on her coat. A man wearing a bowler and a pinstriped suit walked underneath the window and, when he looked up to see where whatever it was that had hit him on the shoulder had come from, he dropped the bowler. And when he picked it up, he noticed a large, round wet spot right on the crown. He too joined Tuesday under the archway. They were joined by a woman in a fox fur, and all of them waited for the policeman to come back, which he did.

The policeman stood back on the sidewalk and looked up at the window. Silk had joined Randolph at the window sill and they looked back at the policeman. Silk looked over at Randolph who worked his mouth for a moment and then hit the third button from the top on the policeman's tunic.

The policeman joined the others, and Tuesday was dispatched next door to get Randolph's mother, where she was visiting. Randolph's mother, the policeman, the man in the bowler, the woman with the fox fur, and Tuesday climbed the steps to the fourth floor. The woman wiping her hand on her coat stayed downstairs.

They knocked on the door. Mrs. Horn looked through the keyhole, and she saw Silk sitting on one of the armchairs, her eyes on the doorknob. The man in the bowler asked if he might look through the keyhole, but no one paid any attention to him. The policeman took a knife with a screwdriver from his pocket and began taking the lock apart. Silk stayed on the armchair, her head tilted to one side, watching the door, and Randolph kept his post at the window, managing to hit the chalk cat once more. He turned around and saw the furniture slowly giving away before the opening door. He took one last desperate shot, ran to the fireplace, grabbed the blue vase and ran back to the window. Silk jumped for the mantel as the policeman muscled his way into the room, Randolph's mother behind him. She emitted a muffled squeal when she saw the sacred blue vase in her son's hand, and as the policeman's arm gathered up the already limp Randolph and the vase dropped from sight, she rushed from the apartment.

Mrs. Horn stumbled down the four flights of steps, through the foyer and past the owls chalked on all the mailboxes but hers. She went out onto the sidewalk and looked, looked at the blue vase which was scattered for about ten yards in each direction, and looked for some sign of the last remains of Bernie, but it was impossible to distinguish between dust, ash and chalk. And nobody seemed to notice Tuesday as she skipped out wearing a bowler, drew a hasty circle around a fragment of blue pottery and disappeared around the corner.

The first draft of the story as a written-out film was dubbed a treatment.

Treatment

Spittin' Image (Possible title)

Titles are chalked in a child's scrawl on a city sidewalk. Under the titles music is sung by a little girl (Tuesday) to the accompaniment of a single instrument. The mood created by the titles and the singing is one of childish gaiety on a balmy summer day. As the camera progresses down the sidewalk to reveal all the titles, Tuesday Reed Loves Randolph Horn (in chalk), we eventually reach the hand of the artist—a child's hand, hard at work, drawing a large cat on the sidewalk. We finally see the artist herself—a ten-year-old girl diligently filling in the outline of the cat's body with white chalk.

The girl is in a summer dress—an attractive child. She has a lap full of colored chalks from which she selects artistically the implements for her creation.

We cut up to a long view from the street of a window on the fourth floor of the building in front of which the girl is working. A twelve-year-old boy, is leaning out of the window, looking down at the girl drawing on the sidewalk.

A closer view of his face shows that he is ruminating like a mischievous camel, working his cheeks until he has a large ball of saliva in his mouth. He has an expression of conducting an interesting experiment. Taking aim, he lets the saliva drop to the sidewalk below. He watches with concern to see where it lands.

It splats on the cement cat. The little girl jumps up and with her hands over her head dashes to the protection of the doorway. The chalk that was in her lap has scattered all over the sidewalk.

She cautiously moves to the edge of the doorway and peeks up toward the boy in the fourth-floor window. The boy has let fly another ball of saliva. The girl jumps back just as the second missile hits on the top step near her foot. She pulls back her foot and inspects it distastefully. She is satisfied that he missed.

Randolph leans a little farther out the window, trying to see into the archway where Tuesday is hiding. He shows little or no expression except patiently waiting for his target to reappear.

Tuesday, standing in the doorway, looks out at her cat and the disarray of artist's materials with frustration. As the huge wad that Randolph had been saving for her is disgorged again on her chalk cat, she clenches her fists in anger and looks menacingly up in the direction of her enemy. She sticks her tongue out futilely.

Then she goes into the foyer to the row of mailboxes and door buzzers. Angrily she takes a piece of chalk from the pocket of her dress and begins writing on one of the mailboxes to extend on down the wall:

Tuesday Reed Hates Randolph Horn Hates Randolph Horn Hates Randolph Horn Hates Randolph Horn

Upstairs in the living room of his apartment, Randolph is leaning out the window. Randolph's mother walks into the room, sees the cat on the mantlepiece, rubbing against an ugly vase-like urn (or some other breakable monstrosity). The mother snatches the cat and hands her to Randolph. She scolds Randolph, pointing to the vase (or monstrosity), to show her concern for the safety of the object. Then she carefully, fastidiously wipes an imaginary speck of dust from it. She picks up a fantastic handbag, goes to Randolph, kisses him mushily, smoothes his hair in an overly protective manner. As soon as she turns her back, Randolph deliberately musses his hair up again. The mother waves goodbye to him at the door and goes out.

Randolph goes back to the window and looks down at the sidewalk. He is shocked at what he sees. Tuesday is furiously at work on her art again, which has now expanded. She has drawn a bird on the cat's back, and the cat has been improved upon, getting a tail and a second eye. She also has added two owls and a palm tree.

Randolph is working up another ball of spit and is about to let it fly, when his mother comes out of the doorway. She walks up to Tuesday, admires the art with broad gestures as if exclaiming, "Oh! how beautiful!" She pats the little girl on the head and moves off.

A policeman approaches. Mrs. Horn nods to the policeman, who salutes her with a smile. Mrs. Horn goes off down the street.

The policeman stops to admire Tuesday's art work. Randolph ducks back into the room in a blind rage. He grabs a heavy object from the floor—something completely imaginary but nonetheless very heavy. He pretends to be straining as he carries it to the window sill. He shoves it out into space. He turns back, his eyes closed with malicious glee, his hands held together in a wild prayer. He opens his eyes hopefully and peers out the window to see what his imaginary weight has done to his victims. He sighs as he sees the cop move on down the street, allowing Tuesday to resume her creation. The cop continues his pigeon-toed beat, letting his night stick dangle from his wrist, clasping his hands behind his back.

Randolph, dejected, works up some more saliva, lets it fly, and watches as it falls. It misses Tuesday's art work by a mile. Tuesday skips over to the blot which missed, draws a circle around it, and with a triumphant look up to Randolph, runs into the doorway before Randolph can retaliate.

Tuesday runs into the foyer, rings the buzzer to Randolph's apartment to signal her victory. Randolph listens to the bell with annoyance. He shrugs and takes a cookie from a bowl. It is crumbly and dries up his mouth. He picks up the cat and offers her a cookies. The cat sniffs and turns away. He puts the cat on top of the treasured vase (or monstrosity) and smiles as the cat nearly knocks it over by leaping off.

He wanders back to the window and looks down. Tuesday's art has now achieved its full-blown glory. Many animals and designs have been added, completely covering the area in front of the building. She has long since blotted out the heart which had said *Tuesday Reed Loves Randolph Horn* and in its place she has drawn a tombstone with the simple inscription, *Randolph*. The perpetrator of this infamy is nowhere in sight.

Randolph's mouth is constricted with cookie crumbs. He tries unsuccessfully to work up some saliva. Tuesday dances out suddenly and laughs at him. He is unable to do anything. He spits on his chin. He stares down in disgust for a moment and then becomes inspired. Tuesday touches up her art work nonchalantly. From out of nowhere a great spray of water rains down on the sidewalk. Alarmed, but untouched, Tuesday jumps up and looks up with disdain. Randolph holds an empty glass furiously. Tuesday begins to chant derisively, showing that she knows his aim has become wild with mounting rage.

Randolph disappears from the window. Tuesday gets a skip-rope from the doorway and begins to skip happily.

In this first treatment two scenes are of key importance: one, in which Randolph's mother straightens his hair, which Randolph then musses; two, in which Randolph picks up an imaginary object and hurls it at the policeman below. Still, in spite of the flowing visual quality in the description of the incident, the importance of the two key scenes appears lessened as they fail to relate to the central situation.

The latter half of the story appears precipitiously, as if the end had to come. The treatment had lost much of the subtle and underlying richness of the original story.

A second treatment was written, both to offset the weaknesses already mentioned and to include detail to flesh out the characters involved.

Treatment

(Second Draft—showing elaboration of ending)

Randolph takes the cookie out of his mouth, tries to spit on the art work below, then throws the cookie down in disgust at being unable to work up the necessary saliva. He tries desperately to spit again, and manages instead to spit on his chin. Tuesday sees his plight and stops skipping rope long enough to laugh hilariously as she points at him, then goes back to skipping rope. After a moment she glances up, stops skipping rope. She watches as Randolph's hand appears, holding a pan of water, which he turns over carefully, and lets the water deluge the art work. His face then appears, haughtily staring back at his foe.

* Tuesday bursts into a derisive chant, pointing down at her art work. Randolph, his aplomb momentarily shaken, peers over the window sill to see what his pan of water has done and is dismayed to see that there is a long streak of water down the front of the building and that none of it has damaged Tuesday's art work after all.

* Randolph, his fury mounting, disappears from the window. He snatches up the feather duster and wildly begins ripping feathers out of it until it is plucked bald, with feathers floating all over the room. The cat looks at him curiously. Then with the handle of the plucked feather duster, which he imaginatively converts into a machine gun tucked at his waist, he sprays everything in sight with a hail of bullets, his teeth chattering in

* Designates scenes that were cut.

imitative firing. He reserves the last of his imaginary ammunition for a special burst of fire at the door which slammed so rudely when his mother left.

Randolph decides to barricade that door. He drops his imaginary machine gun and pushes a piece of furniture against the door. He gets another piece of furniture and piles it on.

Then he goes to the kitchen, rummages around and gets out a dozen waxed bags which are used to put sandwiches in. He gets out a dishpan and as he fills each sandwich bag with the right amount of water from the faucet, he twists its top, and with a devilish smile arranges a neat grouping of these lovely missiles in place, in the dishpan. He now carries his dishpan full of ammunition to the window sill. Setting it down carefully, he looks out to find his foe.

Tuesday is now back on this side of the street, skipping rope not far from her art work. Randolph takes out his first sandwich bag of water. He holds it delicately and lets it drop. He hits a chalk horse. Another one, carefully aimed, hits a tree. Another one hits the umbrella, dangerously close to Tuesday herself, who dashes in alarm to the safety of the doorway, where she watches the devastating bombardment taking place.

Randolph continues with unerring accuracy. He hits an owl, misses once, hits the blue circle Tuesday had drawn around his earlier miss, hits a woman who unexpectedly appears from the corner with a bag of groceries. The woman drops the groceries with a smash onto the sidewalk and joins Tuesday in the doorway, looking up with consternation, then out to her oranges and tin cans rolling around the street. Tuesday waits until the next missile has splashed onto the sidewalk, then she scrambles out, sticks a thumb in each ear and wags her hands up at Randolph, scrambling back to safety as she sees the next bag of water descending. A man in a bowler rounds the corner just in time to receive the bag squarely on his proudly adorned head. The man takes off his bowler, examines it incredulously, looks up, and with a shriek, joins Tuesday and the woman in the doorway. A bag narrowly misses.

Randolph sees he is running low on ammunition. How to hold them off while he refills. He dashes to the kitchen, pulling a toy balloon out of his pocket. Slipping a rubber band looped around the end a couple of times, he stretches the neck of the balloon with a rubber band to hold it tightly onto the faucet; under it is a pan. He sets the water running into the balloon moderately.

Meanwhile, the man and woman and Tuesday are moving hesitantly out from the doorway. Should they make a run for it? No—they dash back as they see Randolph's face reappear at the window with a wax bag of water in his hand.

Randolph smiles grimly and runs back to see how his balloon is doing. Not ready yet. He dashes back, sees his besieged victims trying to explain to a woman in a fancy fur-piece that they cannot step aside to let her in and that she had better step aside herself. She ignores their pleas—to her sudden sorrow, for Randolph has let his last wax bag fly. Drenched, she tries to join the group in the safety of the doorway.

Randolph dashes back to the kitchen. The balloon has swelled with water until it fills the pan. Randolph shuts off the water, carefully removes the neck of the balloon, knots it, and lifts the pan in which it rests out of the sink.

The pigeon-toed cop is returning along his beat, oblivious to the mayhem ahead. Randolph is leaving the kitchen with his blockbuster cradled in his arms. The cop swings his night stick, carefree. Randolph approaches the window. The cop curiously looks at the debris littering the sidewalk ahead, then sees the people grouped in the doorway. Randolph is at the window. The cop says, "What the hell's going on. . . ." The people wave at him frantically.

SPLASH! ! !

The cop does a slow burn, then looks up. Randolph and the cat are looking down curiously at the people below—Randolph's face taking on a gradual realization of the enormity of his warfare.

The people in the doorway step aside for the cop, who enters just as Randolph's mother appears on the scene demanding to know what is going on. Everyone ascends the stairs in a chattering, gesticulating mass. The cop knocks on the door. No answer. Randolph's mother takes out her key and unlocks the door. It still won't open. She pushes the cop aside and peeks through the keyhole. She can't see anything. The man in the bowler asks if he can look through the keyhole. Nobody pays any attention to him. The cop takes a knife with a screwdriver from his pocket and begins taking the lock apart.

Inside, Randolph is frantic as he looks at the door. He sees the furniture gradually sliding as the people outside force their weight against the door. Desperately looking around for something else to weight down the door, he can find nothing. So he backs up and takes the urn containing Great-uncle Bernie. He holds the urn in his hands, threatening to drop it, as the people break into the room. The cop starts for Randolph, but the mother throws up her hands to her mouth and stops, frozen by seeing Uncle Bernie's remains about to go out the window. And out they go, just as the cop grabs Randolph. The urn crashes on the pavement below.

The mother makes her way through the people and furniture back down the stairs. The mother takes a look at the rubble in the area in front of the building. She stands there, staring with disbelief, and somehow doesn't even know what to do when Tuesday, wearing the bowler, comes skipping out of the doorway.

The mother watches Tuesday dazedly as she skips over to a piece of the broken urn, draws a circle around it, and skips off down the street, singing the same songs she sang in the beginning.

In reviewing the second treatment, the student decided that a number of scenes expanded the story to the point of dissipating it. These were cut. The ending, which appeared unnecessarily complex with the meaning of the scene lost in the shuffle of action, was rewritten.

The student, being generally satisfied now with his approach to the story, moved ahead to shot planning. Before the actual shots were laid out, however, the student found it helpful to outline the course of the action. These notes follow the treatment, but select key action only. Full meaning of the scenes would be found, of course, by referring to the treatment. After several starts, the final outline shaped up as follows:

*Outline**

Introduction (The Game Begins)

1. Tuesday at work.
2. Randolph in window spits.
3. Tuesday surprised into doorway.
4. Randolph versus Tuesday—he spits again; she is helpless.
5. Randolph waits . . . spits, hits the cat.
6. Tuesday angry, reacts by writing on wall.

Development (Game Interrupted)

7. Randolph in window waiting to continue game.
8. Mother enters, Randolph almost caught in act of spitting.
9. Mother scolds and puts him to work.
10. Mother removes cat, arranges room, leaves, re-enters, says goodbye to Randolph.
11. Randolph musses his hair, disposes of feather duster.
12. Randolph starts to work up spit for Tuesday, but Mother appears.
13. Mother compliments Tuesday and leaves.
14. Randolph starts to spit again, but cop appears.
15. Cop and Tuesday.
16. Randolph "shoots" cop.
17. Enters fantasy of barricading door (gangster, etc.).
18. Tired, he eats a cookie, and pets cat.

* The outline not only pulled out the essential points of the story treatment, but also introduced changes in refinements.

Complication, Exploitation (Game Renews)

19. Tuesday, having filled pavement with art, is bored. Where's Randolph? Finally, she calls up to him.
20. He appears at the window, she taunts, he spits and misses.
21. She circles his miss and taunts him.
22. He tries to spit again, hits his chin. Picks up vase of flowers and dumps it.
23. She picked up flowers and ridicules him with a dance. (Water only went down side of building.)
24. Randolph disappears from the window.
25. Suspense. Tuesday wondering where he went. Arranges flowers. Keeps looking at empty window. Expands drawing around flowers.
26. Meanwhile, Randolph is unsuccessfully filling paper bag. Frustrated, finally discovers sandwich bags. Loads up arsenal.
27. Randolph appears at window and aims first bomb.
28. New weapon astonishes Tuesday. Another bomb scores hit, and dismays her. Barrage unexpectedly complicated by hitting lady with fur-piece (or fancy hat).

Crisis Development (Movement toward Climax)

29. Lady joins Tuesday in the doorway. Tuesday laughing.
30. Man in bowler passes oblivious to situation, gets clobbered, looks up, screams, dives into doorway just as another missile hits where he stood.
31. Randolph, drunk with power now, waits patiently for a victim.
32. Wet group in doorway see lady with bags of groceries, they gesture frantically. She pauses in wonder; too late—she gets hit. Reaction. Joins group in doorway.
33. Cat and mouse game as hesitant group tries to escape and keeps returning to shelter when Randolph drops bomb.
34. Cop enters picture. Cop gets hit (work out details). Tuesday goes into hysterical laughter.

Denouement

35. Tuesday gasps as she sees Randolph's mother arrive; cop still reacting. The six of them go upstairs.
36. Randolph backing away from window, facing door. Frozen. Begins building up his barricade desperately. Phone books, etc.
37. Crowd arrives at the door; Randolph pushes against the opening door. Barricade gives way. The cop crashes in.
38. Randolph is at the point of no return, wraps his arm around vase. Mother seeing this attempts to restrain the

cop. As cop grabs him, Randolph drops the vase out the window.

39. Mother shrieks and heads back downstairs. She arrives to see the ruined urn splattered all over the sidewalk.
40. The mother is incredulous as Tuesday comes out from behind her, wearing the bowler hat. She draws a chalk circle around one of the fragments of the urn, and skips off down the street.

The student next developed a shooting script: a visualization of the shots as he imagined them. After a conference with the instructor in charge, still another shooting script was prepared. Further discussion and evaluation led to yet another shooting script. And beyond this, still searching for refinement, came the last shooting script. Each time changes were made in order to control the camera work and in a sense to set the editing pattern so that the character and theme values of the story would be brought into a favorable proportion.

The various shooting scripts, in progressive order, were labeled as follows: (1) Shooting Script, (2) First Final Shooting Script, (3) Second Final Shooting Script, (4) Third Final Shooting Script.

After the film had been shot and edited a log was made of the shots as they actually appeared in the film. Those changes that came about during the shooting, as well as the multiple changes brought about through cutting, may be spotted by comparing the log with the shooting script. Although these changes on the surface may seem purely technical, in that a pan may have been dropped for a direct cut, for example, the motivation is anything but technical. In the cutting the story has been intensified and proportioned, with shots relating to each other to reveal greater insight into character and motive. Note that the 76 planned shots worked out through shooting and editing to total 166.

Third Final Shooting Script	*Post-Production Script*
	1. FADE IN (40 frames): Title superimposed on an empty sidewalk. Title: The Motion Picture Workshop of New York University Presents 5 ft.

1. Title: based on an original story by Oliver C. Grannis	2. DISSOLVE TO: Super as above. Title: TUESDAY 5 ft.
2. Credits: Actors	3. DISSOLVE TO: Super as above. Title: based on a story by Oliver C. Grannis 4 ft.
3. Credit: Instructor	4. DISSOLVE TO: Super as above. Title: a film by Robert Guy Barrows Carlos M. Colon-Torres A. Robert Karl C. Kennon Robertson Hugh Rogers Gabriele Wunderlich 5 ft.
4. Credit: Instructor FADE OUT	5. DISSOLVE TO: Super as above. Title: Instructor Leo Hurwitz 4 ft. FADE OUT (40 frames)

FADE IN:

5. EXTERIOR—CITY SIDEWALK—DAY—CLOSE SHOT—PAN TO GIRL'S HAND A chalk heart drawn by the child on the sidewalk with the words: TUESDAY REED LOVES RANDOLPH HORN Pan slowly across sidewalk to pick up Tuesday's hand, drawing an animal with chalk on the sidewalk.	6. MEDIUM CLOSE—EXTERIOR SIDEWALK: DAY A chalk heart drawn on a sidewalk with the childish inscription inside the heart: "TUESDAY LOVES RANDOLPH." The camera pans to the full figure of Tuesday drawing a striped cat on the sidewalk next to the heart. 6 ft. 25 frames

6. CLOSE-UP—TUESDAY'S FACE
She is totally absorbed in her work, humming a tune which we have heard from the opening. She looks down into her lap from time to time as she selects from there new pieces of chalk to work with.

7. CLOSE-UP—TUESDAY'S FACE —OBLIQUE ANGLE
She is absorbed in her drawing. 1 ft. 36 frames

8. MEDIUM FULL SHOT FROM ABOVE—TUESDAY DRAWING
We see her working on the cat. We can read the inscription in the heart again. 5 ft. 23 frames

9. CLOSE-UP—TUESDAY'S FACE
Continuation of shot 7. She blows dust off the drawing. 3 ft. 36 frames

10. LONG SHOT — FROM HIGH ABOVE—TUESDAY DRAWING
From third-floor window. Much higher than shot 8. 2 ft. 7 frames

7. MEDIUM CLOSE SHOT—RANDOLPH IN WINDOW
The boy is chewing from a stick of licorice, thoughtfully looking down on Tuesday. He thinks about it, then works up some saliva, takes aim—and spits.

11. LONG SHOT—FROM SIDEWALK —RANDOLPH IN WINDOW
We see the small figure of a boy high up in the third floor window. He looks down without moving. 2 ft. 27 frames

12. MEDIUM SHOT — TUESDAY DRAWING
She draws unaware of the boy above. 2 ft. 22 frames

	13. FULL SHOT—TUESDAY As a man's legs pass by close to the camera, Tuesday turns and looks up at the window above. 1 ft. 24 frames
	14. LONG SHOT—FROM SIDEWALK —RANDOLPH IN WINDOW Similar to shot 11. 1 ft. 10 frames
	15. MEDIUM SHOT — RANDOLPH IN WINDOW He looks down. He seems about to do something. 2 ft. 7 frames
7A. TUESDAY DRAWING—FROM RANDOLPH'S POINT OF VIEW	16. LONG SHOT — FROM HIGH ABOVE—TUESDAY DRAWING Similar to shot 10. 2 ft. 17 frames
	17. MEDIUM SHOT — RANDOLPH IN WINDOW—SIDE VIEW He leans forward, works his mouth and spits. 1 ft. 34 frames
8. CLOSE - UP — TUESDAY'S HAND	18. CLOSE-UP—TUESDAY'S HAND DRAWING HEAD OF CHALK CAT 31 frames
9. CLOSE - UP — TUESDAY'S FACE	19. CLOSE-UP—TUESDAY'S FACE With sudden disgust, she jumps up. 19 frames
10. CLOSE-UP—TUESDAY'S LAP— THEN PAN TO HER FACE As she rises the chalk falls from her lap. The camera pans up to her face, looking up. She sees something above and dashes out of frame.	20. CLOSE-UP — TUESDAY'S FEET NEAR THE CAT'S HEAD As she jumps up, the chalk spills from her lap onto the cat near where the glob of spit landed. 30 frames

11. FULL SHOT—DOORWAY
Tuesday enters frame and stands in doorway. She peers up.

12. LONG SHOT — RANDOLPH IN WINDOW (ALTERNATE: PAN SLOWLY UP TO RANDOLPH)
Randolph leans very far out to peer down. He chews and spits.

13. CLOSE SHOT—SPIT LANDS ON STEP NEAR TUESDAY'S FOOT
Foot moves out, steps on blob and rubs it out angrily.

14. LONG SHOT—RANDOLPH'S POINT OF VIEW—PAN FROM TUESDAY TO DRAWING
Tuesday's head peers out, then quickly withdraws. Pan to drawings.

21. LONG SHOT — FROM RANDOLPH'S POINT OF VIEW — TUESDAY AT WALL
The little girl runs to the building wall, directly under Randolph, but out of his sight because of the window ledges. 31 frames

22. FULL SHOT—FROM SIDEWALK —TUESDAY AT WALL
She runs and stands with her back to the wall, looking up. 2 ft. 1 frame

23. MEDIUM SHOT—RANDOLPH
He looks down, trying to find the girl. He spits again. 29 frames

24. FULL SHOT—TUESDAY WITH HER BACK TO BUILDING
She ducks 28 frames

25. MEDIUM SHOT — RANDOLPH IN WINDOW
Still trying to sight the girl below. 2 ft. 38 frames

26. CLOSE-UP — TUESDAY'S FACE AGAINST THE BUILDING
She looks up—furious 2 ft. 5 frames

15. CLOSE-UP — RANDOLPH IN WINDOW
Calmly, he changes his aim, spitting at drawings instead of girl.

16. CLOSE-UP—CHALK ANIMAL ON SIDEWALK
A blob of spit lands on the chalk animal

17. CLOSE-UP—TUESDAY'S FACE IN DOORWAY
She looks out at her cat, and up toward Randolph angrily.

18. FULL SHOT— TUESDAY IN DOORWAY. PAN TO ACTION
She runs out and with her foot rubs out the spit on her drawings, then runs back, opens door and enters foyer.

27. MEDIUM SHOT — RANDOLPH IN WINDOW
He pulls a licorice stick from his back pocket and chews. 2 ft. 9 frames

28. RANDOLPH CHEWS AND SPITS
1 ft. 32 frames

29. CLOSE-UP—HEAD OF CHALK CAT—GLOB OF BLACK SPIT LANDS 1 ft. 33 frames

30. CLOSE-UP — TUESDAY'S FACE AGAINST BUILDING
She looks out at cat and up at Randolph—furious
2 ft. 7 frames

31. FULL SHOT — RANDOLPH IN WINDOW
He looks down, trying to see Tuesday, then spits again. 1 ft. 28 frames

32. GLOB OF SPIT HITS SIDEWALK
1 ft. 10 frames

33. FULL SHOT—TUESDAY RUNS OUT
She runs from the wall, picks up a piece of chalk, and bends down to draw a circle around the glob of spit. 2 ft. 34 frames

34. CLOSE-UP TUESDAY'S HAND
Circles the spit on the sidewalk. 31 frames

35. FULL SHOT — COMPLETING THE ACTION
She finishes the circle, drops the chalk and runs to the doorway. Camera PANS to follow her. 26 frames

36. FULL SHOT—NEW ANGLE
Tuesday arriving in doorway. 2 ft. 21 frames

37. MEDIUM SHOT—RANDOLPH IN WINDOW
Looking for Tuesday. 2ft. 26 frames

38. MEDIUM SHOT—TUESDAY IN DOORWAY
Looking up angrily at Randolph. 2 ft. 21 frames

39. MEDIUM SHOT—RANDOLPH IN WINDOW
He spits again 27 frames

40. CLOSE-UP—SIDEWALK
Spit lands on a different Chalk drawing. 37 frames

41. FULL SHOT—TUESDAY UNDER LEDGE
She runs out to the ledge to look up. 2 ft. 15 frames

42. CLOSE-UP—TUESDAY
Full face as she looks up. 36 frames

43. FULL SHOT—TUESDAY
Tuesday runs out to her chalk drawings again. 1 ft. 1 frame

19. INTERIOR FOYER MEDIUM SHOT—TUESDAY WRITING ON WALL
The angry girl has taken a piece of chalk from her dress pocket and writes on the wall: "Tuesday Hates Randolph." She draws an arrow to his mailbox.

20. INTERIOR LIVING ROOM—MEDIUM SHOT—RANDOLPH'S BACK AT THE WINDOW
Randolph is leaning far out, trying to find Tuesday.

21. MEDIUM CLOSE SHOT—MOTHER ENTERING FROM ANOTHER ROOM
The mother wears a hat, dressed to go shopping. She stops as she sees her son and exclaims, "Randolph!"

44. FULL SHOT—FROM ABOVE—RANDOLPH'S POINT OF VIEW
Tuesday picks up a piece of chalk and draws a big X through the heart with the inscription "Tuesday Loves Randolph." 5 ft. 34 frames

45. MEDIUM SHOT—RANDOLPH IN WINDOW
He watches Tuesday. 1 ft. 8 frames

46. MEDIUM SHOT—TUESDAY BACKS IN DOORWAY—OPENS DOOR
She enters the vestibule, takes out a piece of chalk and begins to write on the wall under the mailboxes, "Tuesday Hates . . . " 15 ft. 33 frames

47. INTERIOR—LIVING ROOM—RANDOLPH'S APARTMENT—MEDIUM SHOT
The mother, hat on and purse in hand to go shopping, enters living room, looks up, sees her son and exclaims, "Randolph!" She heads toward camera and passes out of frame. 2 ft. 4 frames

48. REVERSE ANGLE — MEDIUM SHOT—RANDOLPH'S RACK
Randolph is leaning out the window. He straightens up and wheels to face his mother who enters the frame. We see her body and arm and she takes the

22. MEDIUM SHOT—RANDOLPH AT WINDOW
The boy wheels to face his mother; stuffs licorice in pocket.

23. MEDIUM TWO-SHOT—RANDOLPH, THEN MOTHER
The mother comes up to Randolph and points to a cleaning implement nearby. He nods and possibly picks it up.

boy's shoulder. He looks up at her as she scolds. 4 ft. 19 frames

49. COMPLETION OF SHOT 46—TUESDAY IN VESTIBULE
The girl finishes writing "Tuesday Hates Randolph," then draws an arrow to one of the mailboxes, discovers it is the wrong mailbox, rubs out the first arrow and draws a second one. 5 ft. 39 frames

50. MEDIUM TWO-SHOT — RANDOLPH AND MOTHER
The mother reaches out of frame to take a carpet sweeper by the handle and demonstrate to Randolph how to use it. 2 ft. 24 frames

51. CLOSE-UP — RANDOLPH AND MOTHER'S FEET
The carpet sweeper moves to and fro. 1 ft. 23 frames

52. COMPLETION OF SHOT 50—RANDOLPH AND MOTHER
She finishes the demonstration and hands him the sweeper. 3 ft. 7 frames

24. CLOSE SHOT—TABLE (IN BACKGROUND OF PREVIOUS SHOT)
Randolph's cat jumps onto the table containing an urn on which is inscribed, "R.I.P. BELOVED UNCLE BERNARD HORN — 1883–1932."
Next to the urn is a framed photograph of Uncle Bernie.

53. CLOSE-UP—VERY LOW ANGLE UP TO TABLE WITH URN
The cat jumps onto the table next to the urn. 1 ft. 11 frames

54. MEDIUM TWO-SHOT — RANDOLPH AND MOTHER
The cat is on the table behind the mother. 2 ft. 3 frames

25. CLOSE-UP—MOTHER'S FACE
She sees the cat on the table, and moves out of frame to get it.

55. CLOSE-UP—VERY LOW ANGLE —CAT, THEN MOTHER'S FACE
The mother's face swoops down as she picks up the cat. 1 ft. 24 frames

26. FULL SHOT — RANDOLPH AND MOTHER
Mother grabs cat on table and hands it to Randolph, scolding him.

56. MEDIUM TWO-SHOT — OVER MOTHER'S SHOULDER — RANDOLPH
The mother hands the cat to Randolph, who looks up at her. Mother then walks out of frame. Randolph's face turns to watch her as she leaves. 7 ft. 17 frames

27. MEDIUM CLOSE-UP—HIGH ANGLE — MOTHER'S POINT OF VIEW
Randolph looks up with the cat in one hand and the cleaning implement in the other. He nods that he understands her orders.

57. FULL SHOT—MOTHER WALKING AWAY FROM CAMERA TOWARD DOOR
When she gets to the door, she turns and looks back at Randolph. 4 ft. 14 frames

28. MEDIUM CLOSE-UP — LOW ANGLE—FROM RANDOLPH'S POINT OF VIEW
    The mother bends down to kiss him, smiling sweetly.

29. MEDIUM SHOT—RANDOLPH AND MOTHER
    She kisses his forehead and smoothes his hair. She turns head past camera toward the door.

30. MEDIUM CLOSE SHOT — RANDOLPH
    He watches her go. *Sound effect: door slam.* (May need 30-A: shot of mother turning back at door to blow kiss, then slam door.) Randolph deliberately musses up his hair, then lets the cat down on the forbidden table. He tosses aside the cleaning implement and smiles as he watches the cat. Intercut shot 24: taking licorice out of his pocket.

58. MEDIUM SHOT — RANDOLPH HOLDING CAT
    He forces a smile to his mother at the door. 1 ft. 10 frames

59. FULL SHOT — MOTHER AT DOOR
    She smiles at Randolph, then turns and goes out the door. 4 ft. 35 frames

60. MEDIUM SHOT — RANDOLPH WITH CAT
    He puts the cat on table which urn stands on. 2 ft. 14 frames

61. CLOSE-UP—PHOTO
    Photo is of Uncle Bernie, on the wall above the table. 1 ft. 20 frames

62. MEDIUM SHOT — RANDOLPH AND CAT
    At the table with the urn, Randolph pets the cat, then pushes the sweeper across the room. 6 ft. 24 frames

63. CLOSE-UP—PHOTO OF UNCLE BERNIE
Tighter close-up than shot 61. 1 ft. 37 frames

64. FULL SHOT — RANDOLPH GOING TO WINDOW
He pulls out a stick of licorice from his back pocket, jerks a bite out of it, and goes away from camera to window to look out. 2 ft. 34 frames

31. LONG SHOT—STREET BELOW — RANDOLPH'S POINT OF VIEW
Tuesday is again drawing on sidewalk — a drawing has been added. The mother comes out of the doorway below and stops to admire Tuesday's art, exclaiming, "Oh, how beautiful!" Tuesday looks up and smiles. The mother starts to leave.

65. LONG SHOT—FROM RANDOLPH'S POINT OF VIEW—TUESDAY ON SIDEWALK — THEN MOTHER — THEN COP
Tuesday sits on sidewalk drawing; Mother comes out of building; goes to Tuesday, pats her on the head, and walks away; as mother walks away, she meets cop who salutes her, then cop walks over to look at Tuesday's drawings. 7 ft. 3 frames

31A. TUESDAY — CLOSE-UP — SMILING AT MOTHER

31B. CLOSE-UP IN WINDOW — WATCHING, FRUSTRATED, THEN ABOUT TO SPIT BUT STOPS, THEN SWALLOWING SPIT

32. MEDIUM CLOSE — COP'S FACE — FROM TUESDAY'S POINT OF VIEW
The cop gives official approval of Tuesday's art work.

66. CLOSE-UP — TUESDAY'S FACE
She smiles up at the cop. 37 frames

33. CLOSE-UP — TUESDAY — FROM COP'S POINT OF VIEW
She smiles up at cop. Intercut Randolph about to spit (31B). Tuesday looks past the cop to see Randolph, then quickly ducks behind the cop's legs. She draws an outline around each of the cop's shoes. Intercut cop's face smiling down (32). The cop's feet step out of the outlines, leaving new designs.

33A. LONG SHOT—RANDOLPH IN WINDOW — FROM TUESDAY'S POINT OF VIEW
He points his thumb and forefinger, making a pistol.

67. MEDIUM LONG SHOT—FROM SIDEWALK — RANDOLPH LOOKING DOWN FROM WINDOW
He looks down without moving; he seems angry. 1 ft. 38 frames

68. LONG SHOT — FROM RANDOLPH'S POINT OF VIEW—COP AND TUESDAY BELOW
Continuation of shot 65. Cop walks around behind Tuesday. 3 ft. 1 frame

69. INTERIOR — MEDIUM SHOT—RANDOLPH LOOKING OUT WINDOW
The boy straightens up as he sees cop walk behind Tuesday. 2 ft. 37 frames

70. FULL SHOT — EXTERIOR — COP'S LEGS—FULL FIGURE OF TUESDAY
The girl turns around on the sidewalk and draws a chalk circle around each of the cop's feet, then looks up at him, smiling. 6 ft. 9 frames.

71. CLOSE-UP—COP'S FACE
He grins down at the girl and lifts his cap slightly. 1 ft. 31 frames.

34. INTERIOR—LIVING ROOM—RANDOLPH AT WINDOW —MEDIUM SHOT

Randolph, his thumb and forefinger making a pistol, aiming at the cop, mouths "Pow! Pow!" Then he wheels toward camera and fires a few more shots, pulling a second imaginary pistol from an imaginary holster. (Try using the "weight" from original story.)

35. NEW ANGLE — RANDOLPH BEHIND A CHAIR

He keeps firing his imaginary revolvers toward the door, crouching behind a chair. He jumps up and races toward the door.

36. NEW ANGLE — RANDOLPH BARRICADING THE DOOR

At the door, he takes a piece of furniture, barricades the door, then backs away, covering door with his "pistols." Then he blows smoke out of each barrel and pockets each of his "guns" in the holsters, victoriously, the grim cowboy.

72. INTERIOR—RANDOLPH LOOKING OUT WINDOW

Continuation of shot 69. Randolph makes a "pistol" with his forefinger and shoots down at the cop below, then wheels into the room and fires at something outside the frame. 4 ft. 39 frames

73. MEDIUM SHOT — RANDOLPH AT COUCH "SHOOTING"—CAT ON BACK OF COUCH

Randolph continues to "shoot" at something imaginary, then ducks at the foot of the couch, as if being fired upon. 8 ft. 11 frames.

74. MEDIUM SHOT—PAN TO FULL SHOT — RANDOLPH RUNNING TO DOOR

Randolph, "shooting," runs past couch to chair, then to door, opens it, shoots out into hall, closes door, barricades it with a chair, turns back into room and fires toward window, then blows the "smoke" from his "pistol." 7 ft. 17 frames

75. EXTERIOR—CLOSE-UP—TUESDAY'S FACE

She is drawing on sidewalk again. 3 ft. 4 frames

37. NEW ANGLE — RANDOLPH GETTING COOKIE
He gets a cookie from a bowl, picks up the cat, and squats on the floor, with cat in his lap.

38. EXTERIOR — TUESDAY ON SIDEWALK
Tuesday at work, looks up toward window. Where's Randolph? She stops drawing and just sits there, looking up plaintively. She sighs, watching the empty window.

76. INTERIOR—MEDIUM SHOT—GETTING COOKIE FROM CUPBOARD
He looks for and finds a cookie, then walks past camera, eating. 10 ft. 17 frames

77. FULL SHOT—PAN TO FOLLOW ACTION—RANDOLPH GETS CAT
Randolph comes from hallway into living room, picks up cat from couch, gives cat a bite of cookie, then sits on floor with cat. The boy looks idly across the room. 13 ft. 27 frames

78. CLOSE-UP—UNCLE BERNIE—PHOTO ON WALL
Photo of Bernie, austere. 2 ft. 1 frame

79. CLOSE-UP—URN
Urn of Bernie's ashes on table. 2 ft. 13 frames

80. CLOSE-UP — TIGHTER THAN 78
Photo of uncle on wall. 2 ft. 21 frames

81. MEDIUM SHOT — RANDOLPH GETS UP AND GOES TO WINDOW—PAN TO FOLLOW
Randolph still holding cat, and with cookie in mouth, gets up and goes to window to look out. 6 ft. 18 frames

39. EXTERIOR — RANDOLPH COMES TO WINDOW
Randolph looks down at Tuesday, cookie in mouth, cat in arms.

82. EXTERIOR—MEDIUM SHOT—RANDOLPH WITH CAT — STANDING IN WINDOW LOOKING OUT
Petting the cat, Randolph looks down at the sidewalk. He lets the cat out of his hands. 3 ft. 28 frames

83. CLOSE-UP—TUESDAY—LOOK-AT RANDOLPH
Her hand to her mouth, the girl anticipates something. 2 ft. 33 frames

84. LONG SHOT — FROM SIDEWALK UP — RANDOLPH IN WINDOW
Randolph blows out the cookie crumbs from his mouth angrily. 1 ft. 7 frames

85. CLOSE-UP — TUESDAY'S FACE
She giggles. 1 ft. 12 frames

86. LONG SHOT—FROM SIDEWALK UP—RANDOLPH IN WINDOW
He spits some more crumbs. 1 ft. 37 frames

87. CLOSE-UP — TUESDAY'S FACE
She laughs up at him. 1 ft. 19 frames

88. MEDIUM SHOT — RANDOLPH IN WINDOW
He wipes his mouth with his arm. 2 ft. 9 frames

89. LONG SHOT—FROM SIDEWALK UP
Randolph wipes mouth again. 2 ft. 9 frames

40. MEDIUM CLOSE—TUESDAY
She sticks out her tongue and stands, moving out of frame.

41. CLOSER SHOT—RANDOLPH AT WINDOW
He lets cat go, takes cookie out of mouth, and tries to spit. It dribbles over his chin. He is humiliated. He disappears from window for a moment (or simply reaches into room) and returns with a vase of flowers. Dumps contents out the window.

41A. FOLLOW FLOWERS FROM VASE TO SIDEWALK

41B. INTERCUT: TUESDAY — MEDIUM SHOT — LAUGHING AT RANDOLPH

42. FULL SHOT—TUESDAY IN DOORWAY—PAN TO FOLLOW ACTION
She runs to get one of the flowers, which she sticks in her hair; looks up defiantly at Randolph. Intercut the empty window (part of 38). She puts her hands on hips and waits.

90. MEDIUM SHOT—TUESDAY
She stands up, coming into frame, and makes an ugly face with her tongue sticking out at Randolph. 1 ft. 25 frames

91. CLOSE-UP—EMPTY WINDOW
3 ft. 30 frames

DISSOLVE TP:

92. FULL SHOT—TUESDAY SITTING ON SIDEWALK DRAWING
She stops drawing, turns and leans back so that she can look up at window. 4 ft. 15 frames

92. CLOSE-UP — EMPTY WINDOW
1 ft. 31 frames

94. COMPLETION OF SHOT 92
Tuesday sighs and returns to her drawing. 2 ft. 12 frames

43. NEW ANGLE—TUESDAY ON SIDEWALK — CLOSE SHOT —PAN TO DRAWING

Tuesday moves into frame by sitting down to draw some more. Pan slowly to the animal she begins to draw.

44. CLOSE-UP — THE SAME DRAWING LATER — IT IS NEARLY COMPLETE

A water bomb lands smack in the drawing near Tuesday's hand. The hand moves quickly out of frame

45. FULL SHOT — TUESDAY DASHING INTO DOORWAY— MOVES INTO FRAME

She looks up and sees: shot 46. She quickly withdraws.

95. CLOSE-UP — EMPTY WINDOW

1 ft. 34 frames

96. FULL SHOT — TUESDAY PAN TO FOLLOW ACTION

She is arranging her various colored chalks by one of her drawings. Picks up her chalk, moves to a new spot and begins to draw a rabbit. 4 ft. 10 frames

97. LONG SHOT—FROM SIDEWALK UP—THE EMPTY WINDOW

1 ft. 4 frames

98. CLOSE-UP—TUESDAY'S HAND

Drawing the rabbit. 13 ft. 25 frames

99. CLOSE-UP—FROM EXTERIOR— LOOKING PROFILE AT RANDOLPH'S WINDOW

Hand extended holding a bag of water. 36 frames

100. CLOSE-UP — COMPLETION OF SHOT 98

Hand drawing rabbit. Bag of water lands. 39 frames

101. FULL SHOT—TUESDAY RUNNING TO DOOR—PAN TO FOLLOW HER

The girl jumps up and runs to the steps leading down to the door of the apartment building. As she runs, a second water bag lands on the sidewalk. She jumps up and down angrily. 2 ft. 18 frames

102. LONG SHOT — FROM RANDOLPH'S POINT OF VIEW—TUESDAY ON STEPS
The girl looks up, then disappears out of bottom of frame to safety of doorway. 2 ft. 17 frames

46. MEDIUM CLOSE-UP — RANDOLPH AT WINDOW
Randolph holds a dishpan from which he takes a water bomb and delicately lets it drop. Intercut Tuesday in doorway looking out, watching bombs land (more of 45).

103. LONG SHOT — FROM SIDEWALK UP — RANDOLPH IN WINDOW
The boy has a dishpan from which he takes a bag of water. 1 ft. 4 frames

104. MEDIUM CLOSE-UP — INTERIOR — LOOKING AT RANDOLPH IN WINDOW
Randolph takes a bag of water from dishpan. 1 ft. 10 frames

105. LONG SHOT — RANDOLPH'S POINT OF VIEW
Bag falling toward sidewalk. 33 frames

46. A,B,C. CLOSE-UPS — BOMBS LANDING

106. CLOSE-UP — BAG SPLATTERING
Hits next to circle around spit. 1 ft. 29 frames

46D. BOMBS FALLING — FROM RANDOLPH'S POINT OF VIEW

47. MEDIUM CLOSE—TUESDAY IN DOORWAY—WOMAN WITH HAT COMES INTO FRAME
Tuesday watches

48. MEDIUM CLOSE—RANDOLPH AT WINDOW, THEN LEAVES
Randolph sees he has run out of ammunition. He leaves window.

48A. CLOSE-UP — EMPTY DISHPAN

49. CLOSE TWO SHOT — TUESDAY, THEN WOMAN INTO FRAME
Tuesday frantically beckons the woman in the fancy hat, who comes into frame, asking what is wrong. Tuesday points. The woman looks up. Intercut the empty window (part of 38).

107. MEDIUM SHOT—EXTERIOR—RANDOLPH IN WINDOW
Takes bag from dishpan. 2 ft. 35 frames

108. LONG SHOT — RANDOLPH'S POINT OF VIEW
One bag, then a second lands on the chalk heart below. 3 ft. 3 frames

109. MEDIUM SHOT—EXTERIOR—RANDOLPH IN WINDOW
Dropping more bags. 11 ft. 38 frames

110. MEDIUM SHOT—TUESDAY IN DOORWAY
Looks up at Randolph. 1 ft. 25 frames

111. FULL SHOT—A NEW DOORWAY NEARBY
A lady in a big hat comes up the three steps to the sidewalk, taking a handkerchief from her purse and touching it to her lips. 2 ft. 33 frames

112. MEDIUM SHOT—TUESDAY IN DOORWAY — MORE OF SHOT 110
The girl sees the lady coming and puts her hand to her face as she anticipates the lady getting hit by a water bag. 29 frames

The woman sympathizes with Tuesday, then starts to move out. Intercut Randolph arriving at window with dishpan of bombs. As Randolph drops a bomb, the woman is saying goodbye to Tuesday, waving as she walks from the door. The bomb lands on her fancy hat.

113. MEDIUM SHOT — LADY IN HAT

The lady sees Tuesday and waves to her. A water bag hits her on the big hat. The lady runs out of frame. 1 ft. 11 frames

114. FULL SHOT—LADY RUNS TO JOIN TUESDAY—PAN TO FOLLOW

The lady is galvanized into running to join Tuesday in the doorway, where she tries to brush the water off her dress. 4 ft.

50. CLOSE-UP — RANDOLPH IN WINDOW

He claps his hand over his mouth, realizing what he's done.

115. MEDIUM SHOT — RANDOLPH IN WINDOW

Dropping bags of water. 2 ft. 24 frames

51. NEW ANGLE—TUESDAY AND WOMAN IN DOORWAY

The woman runs back into frame, angrily trying to dry herself.

52. INTERIOR TO STREET—RANDOLPH'S POINT OF VIEW (SEE 50)
We can see a man in a bowler hat coming into range. Intercut Randolph's face taking on a new look (more of 50), as he decides this time it might be fun to hit that bowler hat on purpose instead of accidentally. He aims a water bomb.

116. FULL SHOT—A MAN IN BOWLER HAT APPROACHES
The man walks along reading a book, unaware of what he is walking into. He walks right up to the camera to a full close-up. Book title: *Catcher in the Rye.* 3 ft. 35 frames

117. MEDIUM SHOT—NEW ANGLE—MAN IN BOWLER
Continues walking to bull's-eye area. 1 ft. 10 frames

118. CLOSE-UP—FACE OF MAN IN BOWLER
The man stops and smiles at something he is reading. 1 ft. 11 frames

53. CLOSE-UP—WATER BOMB—RANDOLPH'S FACE IN BACKGROUND
He holds the bomb delicately. Intercut more of the man approaching from Randolph's point of view (52). The bomb is released. Intercut more of 51; Tuesday and woman look up as they see the man approaching. The woman starts to say something. But the bomb hits the man squarely on the bowler. He freezes, takes off his hat, looks up,

119. MEDIUM SHOT—NEW ANGLE—MAN IN BOWLER
As he pauses, smiling at the book, a water bag hits his bowler hat, knocking it askew and crushing in the top. 2 ft. 7 frames

lets out a shriek and joins the woman and Tuesday in the doorway. A new bomb narrowly misses.

54. NEW ANGLE—MAN, WOMAN, TUESDAY IN DOORWAY, THEN COP
The woman sympathizes with the man who is trying to regain his dignity. Tuesday is trying to keep from laughing.

120. MEDIUM SHOT — RANDOLPH AT WINDOW
He laughs and takes another water bag from the dishpan. 1 ft. 3 frames

121. CLOSE-UP — MAN TAKING OFF HAT
The surprised man takes off his hat, now crushed. He looks at it, looks up, sees Randolph, and hastily runs out of frame. 3 ft. 32 frames

122. MEDIUM SHOT—SIDE ANGLE —RANDOLPH IN WINDOW
He drops another water bag. 37 frames

123. CLOSE-UP—WATER BAG LANDING
Lands on sidewalk next to iron cellar plate. 1 ft. 40 frames

124. MEDIUM SHOT—SIDE ANGLE —RANDOLPH IN WINDOW
Laughing, enjoying himself. 1 ft. 33 frames

125. MEDIUM THREE SHOT— MAN, LADY, TUESDAY IN DOORWAY
The man and lady angrily look up at Randolph. Tuesday watches, crouching behind the lady. 6 ft. 32 frames

The cop comes up to them.

126. LONG SHOT—FROM RANDOLPH'S POINT OF VIEW—THE THREE COME UP TO THE STEPS
The man, the lady, and Tuesday cautiously go up the steps to the sidewalk. A bomb sails down and lands in front of them on the sidewalk. The three turn and descend again to the safety of the doorway. 7 ft. 19 frames

127. INTERIOR—MEDIUM SHOT—RANDOLPH AT WINDOW LOOKING OUT
He sees that his dishpan is empty of water bombs. He dumps the remaining water in the dishpan out the window, turns into the room and heads out of the frame toward the kitchen. 2 ft. 10 frames

128. MEDIUM THREE-SHOT—MAN, LADY, TUESDAY IN DOORWAY
Continuation of shot 125. The angry people see someone coming. 1 ft. 2 frames

129. LONG SHOT — FROM RANDOLPH'S WINDOW — COP APPROACHING
As the cop approaches from far down the sidewalk, the camera tilts with his approach to bring him nearer to the

55. CLOSE-UP—COP
He asks what's going on.

56. REVERSE—MEDIUM SHOT—MAN, WOMAN, TUESDAY
They all talk at once, pointing and complaining.

57. CLOSE-UP—BROKEN WATER BAGS ON DRAWINGS ON SIDEWALK, ETC.

58. NEW ANGLE—TO INCLUDE COP, WOMAN, MAN, TUESDAY
The cop steps into the doorway and looks at the mailboxes to read the names. He gets out his book to write some notes as the others step on the sidewalk to point up at Randolph. Intercut Randolph looking down at people, taking aim (Shot 46). They scurry for shelter. The cop steps out from the doorway to look up.

building. He sees something is wrong and quickens his pace. 5 ft. 24 frames

130. MEDIUM THREE-SHOT—MAN, LADY, TUESDAY, THEN THE COP
The man anxiously beckons the cop to hurry to them. The cop's back enters the frame as he goes down the steps to face them in the doorway to listen to their anxious story. The man points up to the window. The cop looks up. 9 ft. 3 frames

131. CLOSE-UP — RANDOLPH'S WINDOW
Only the cat is seen there on the window sill. 2 ft. 5 frames

132. FULL SHOT — COP, MAN, LADY, TUESDAY
The cop gestures that no one is up there. The others come up the steps toward the sidewalk to see for themselves. 2 ft. 25 frames

59. CLOSE-UP — COP LOOKING UP

He sees a bomb coming down and tries to duck —too late. It splashes on his shoulder (or some part of body).

60. SHOT OF ADULTS ENTERING DOORWAY

60A. MEDIUM SHOT—RANDOLPH'S MOTHER APPROACHING

60B. SHOT OF MOTHER FROM RANDOLPH'S POINT OF VIEW

61. FULL SHOT—FOUR ADULTS AND TUESDAY

The mother pushes her way through the others, and with cop, they all enter the doorway of the building. The mother carries a hat box or some other luxury item; her shopping was trivial.

62. CLOSE-UP — RANDOLPH'S FACE IN WINDOW

He is absolutely horrified.

133. SIDE VIEW — MEDIUM SHOT RANDOLPH AT WINDOW

First the empty window; then Randolph suddenly appears with the dishpan and sails a fresh water bag out without looking down. 1 ft.

134. LONG SHOT — RANDOLPH'S POINT OF VIEW — THREE ADULTS AND TUESDAY BELOW

The bag sails down. The cop ducks—too late—it hits his back. The three adults and Tuesday head back down steps to doorway. 2 ft. 6 frames

135. LONG SHOT—MOTHER

She is seen coming up the street toward the camera. 4 ft. 14 frames

136. INTERIOR — RANDOLPH AT WINDOW LOOKING OUT

He claps his hand to his mouth, turns into the room, sets the dishpan on the floor and runs out of frame toward door. 4 ft. 15 frames

63. INTERIOR LIVING ROOM — MEDIUM SHOT—RANDOLPH AT WINDOW
Randolph turns into the room, looking at door he barricaded. He sets down the dishpan, looks right and left, wildly trying to figure a way out of this mess.

137. CLOSE-UP — THE DOORKNOB WITH CHAIR BARRICADING— THEN RANDOLPH'S FACE
Randolph's face and hands come into frame as he presses against the door to keep anyone from entering. 1 ft. 23 frames

138. FULL SHOT—MOTHER
She is standing on the sidewalk looking at the watery mess. 2 ft. 18 frames

139. MEDIUM SHOT — THE SIDEWALK
Bags and water splashed all over. 1 ft. 23 frames

140. CLOSE-UP — RANDOLPH PUSHING AGAINST DOORKNOB
Continuation of shot 137. The boy pushes, then turns, going out of frame for a second, returns and sits in the chair with his back to the door, eyes tightly closed, mouth screwed up. 2 ft. 26 frames

141. FULL SHOT—MOTHER
She runs down the steps and into the door of the building. 2 ft. 15 frames

142. INTERIOR FULL SHOT—ADULTS COMING UP THE STAIRS IN HALLWAY—PAN TO FOLLOW
From above looking down into the stairwell, we see the adults running up the stairs toward the apartment: first comes the cop, then the lady, then the man in the hat, then the mother, who passes the man and knocks his hat off with a package she has. The man stops, is torn between his lost hat and the boy upstairs. Camera holds on him. He forgets the hat and runs out of frame. 7 ft. 18 frames

64. NEW ANGLE — RANDOLPH ADDING TO BARRICADE
He pushes a chair into place at the door, then looks around desperately. All he can find handy are two phone books which he adds to the barricade.

143. FULL SHOT—RANDOLPH IN CHAIR WITH BACK TO DOOR
The boy opens his eyes, decides to get something, runs out of frame; camera holds on empty chair; boy runs back into frame with a flimsy little table which he piles onto the chair; then he runs out of other side of frame and returns with a phone book which he adds to the barricade, hesitates, goes back out of frame. 6 ft. 25 frames

65. NEW ANGLE — RANDOLPH BACKING TOWARD WINDOW
As he backs away, he sees the urn (insert shot 24, without cat), and impulsively grabs the urn, hugging it to his bosom.

66. INTERIOR — LANDING OUTSIDE APARTMENT — FULL SHOT
The four adults and Tuesday arrive, puffing. The man in the bowler loses his hat in the rush. He tries to recover it. They rush past the camera toward the door. Intercut 65; Randolph with the urn.

144. CLOSE-UP—COP'S FACE FOLLOWED BY LADY'S FACE AS THEY APPROACH DOOR
They are outside and just reach the door. 1 ft. 2 frames

145. MEDIUM SHOT — BARRICADE DOOR
Randolph returns with a second phone book; finally he backs toward camera and out of frame. 5 ft. 16 frames

146. FULL SHOT TOWARD WINDOW
Randolph runs into frame, across room toward table, picks up urn and clutches it to his breast. 2 ft. 33 frames

147. CLOSE-UP — COP'S FACE THEN LADY'S
Mother pushes lady aside to come up by cop. 1 ft. 2 frames

67. MEDIUM SHOT — FROM RANDOLPH'S POINT OF VIEW—COP AND MOTHER ENTERING

The cop pushes the barricade aside, forcing door open. Mother is right behind him; others in background. Cop starts toward Randolph; Mother grabs cop's arm as she sees: cut of shot 65—the boy at window with urn. Randolph in desperation holds the urn out the window, threatening to drop it. The cop, dragging the mother, continues toward Randolph. Out the window goes the urn as the cop grabs Randolph.

148. FULL SHOT — THE BARRICADE

The cop pushes the barricade aside as he opens the door. He enters room, followed by mother, lady, and man. They all head into the room toward camera. Mother grabs cop's arm. 3 ft. 18 frames

149. FULL SHOT—RANDOLPH

Randolph holding the urn steps toward the window. 1 ft. 6 frames

150. MEDIUM TWO-SHOT — COP AND MOTHER

The mother looks horrified and drops her package. 1 ft. 26 frames

151. EXTERIOR — LONG SHOT — FROM SIDEWALK LOOKING UP

Randolph in the window, and holding the urn, looks out. 21 frames

152. MEDIUM TWO-SHOT — COP AND MOTHER (MAN AND LADY IN BACKGROUND)

The mother turns, runs back out the apartment and down the steps. 2 ft. 11 frames

68. EXTERIOR LONG SHOT FROM STREET LOOKING UP AT WINDOW
The urn comes hurtling down until it blacks out the frame.

153. EXTERIOR LONG SHOT—CONTINUATION OF SHOT 151
Randolph heaves the urn out the window. Camera pans down with it. 1 ft. 12 frames

69. CLOSE-UP — URN CRASHES ON PAVEMENT

154. CLOSE-UP—URN
Crashes on the sidewalk. 16 frames

155. CLOSE-UP—URN FRAGMENTS
These fly across the sidewalk. 14 frames

156. CLOSE-UP—URN FRAGMENT
Another fragment goes skidding. 20 frames

157. CLOSE-UP—URN FRAGMENTS
More fragments go skidding. 31 frames

70. INTERIOR MEDIUM CLOSE SHOT — MOTHER MAKING EXIT
Crowding her way through heads and shoulders, she gets out door.

158. INTERIOR—MEDIUM SHOT—COP RUNS AND GRABS RANDOLPH—PAN TO FOLLOW
The cop runs across the room and grabs Randolph in his arms. The boy kicks and flails in cop's arms. 2 ft. 27 frames

159. EXTERIOR — CLOSE - UP — FRAGMENT
A final fragment skids and rocks to rest. 1 ft. 25 frames

71. EXTERIOR—MEDIUM SHOT —MOTHER IN DOORWAY
Mother appears in doorway and surveys the sidewalk.

72. PAN SLOWLY ACROSS DEBRIS ON SIDEWALK

73. NEW ANGLE—TUESDAY APPEARS BEHIND THE MOTHER
With bowler hat on her head, Tuesday pops out from behind dazed mother and skips out to the broken pottery.

74. CLOSE - UP — TUESDAY'S HAND DRAWING CIRCLE AROUND BROKEN FRAGMENT

75. FULL SHOT — TUESDAY SKIPPING DOWN THE STREET
Camera holds on the little girl wearing the bowler, skipping off happily down the street until she is almost out of sight. We can faintly hear the tune she was humming in the beginning.

160. FULL SHOT — DOORWAY — MOTHER COMES OUT AND UP STEPS TO LOOK
She stops on the steps and her hands come to her face as she takes in the horror of the broken urn. 5 ft. 21 frames

161. CLOSE-UP — THE BROKEN URN FADE IN: Superimposed photo of Uncle Bernie over the urn fragments. FADE OUT. 6 ft. 25 frames

162. MEDIUM SHOT—MOTHER ON STEPS LOOKING AT URN
Tuesday comes out from behind the mother; wearing bowler hat, she comes up the steps. 4 ft. 9 frames

163. CLOSE-UP—FRAGMENT WITH LETTERS: "R.I.P." Girl's hand draws chalk circle around this fragment. 1 ft. 15 frames

164. FULL SHOT—TUESDAY—PAN TO FOLLOW—ENDS IN LONG SHOT
Tuesday finishes the circle, stands up and skips off down the street to the corner, where she takes off her bowler hat and waves with it as she continues to skip around the corner out of sight. 8 ft. 20 frames

FADE OUT

FADE IN

76. THE END. A project of N.Y.U. Workshop, etc.	165.	TITLE: SUPERIMPOSED ON SIDEWALK AS FOR BEGINNING TITLES Cast *Tuesday* Patty D'Arbanville *Randolph* Noah Lamy *Mother* Elizabeth White *Cop* James Anderson *Lady in Hat* Terry Heyl *Man* Lou Cutelli. 6 ft.
	166.	DISSOLVE TO TITLE: The End A project of The Motion Picture Workshop of New York University 1960. 3 ft. FADE OUT

The shooting was well handled and some extremely fine shots were taken, particularly of Randolph. This was accomplished by shooting from a rooftop across the street (using telephoto lenses), from windows above Randolph, and from still another window adjacent to Randolph's.

The directing of the players was equally well done; the performances of the boy and girl were strikingly good. They were neighborhood children with no professional training of any kind. The production was scripted, planned, shot, edited, and completed in six weeks' time, so that the pressures were often greater than in a professional production.

"Although in some places dialogue could have been used to advantage, the shots were so self-descriptive that there was no real need for it. Also, the students had their hands full working out and securing the visualization. The elimination of complicated sound equipment to some extent simplified the field work. A full musical track was added in the sound studio.

The film was shot on 16-mm black-and-white reversal stock, set up on A and B rolls in the printing."

13.
Harvard University

THE CARPENTER CENTER; THE BRATTLE THEATER

Film at Harvard consists of two areas; the token offerings in film as part of the Carpenter Center for the Visual Arts on campus, and the showings presented by the Brattle Theater, perhaps the nation's foremost art house off campus.

The Carpenter Center, which includes visual and environmental studies, includes several film courses. The philosophy of the Center has been stated in academic language as abstruse as any:

> In an education which helps the individual toward the fullest possible realization of his potential integrated within the framework of society, visual and visually creative experience and exploration share a relevant place with conceptual and verbal experience, investigation and creation. Visual and conceptual concerns are not mutually exclusive but enhance each other since image, word and concept are linked on many levels. A full complement of thought must accompany visual experience just as the visual environment must be considered the result of processes that can be methodically observed, analyzed and interpreted. At the same time the realm of thought and word needs to be tied back continuously to all sensuous realities of the human environment including the visual.
>
> A gratifying recognition of this fact was implied in the decision of Harvard's Faculty of Arts and Sciences to create a new Department of Visual and Environmental Studies. After July 1, 1968, it replaced the former Department of Architectural Sciences and the former Program of Visual Studies which had been administered by a Faculty Committee for the Practice of the Visual Arts.
>
> This development must be seen as part of a process that began at least as far back as 1954 when President Pusey appointed a committee ". . . to help determine the future course of the arts at Harvard" because the University felt the need

The only building in this country designed by Le Corbusier is the Carpenter Center for the Visual Arts. It is the home of the film dept. at Harvard. (Photo by the author)

to look critically at the place of the visual and performing arts in the total picture of its educational policy. As a consequence of the findings of this committee and of reactions to them, the Loeb Drama Center and the Carpenter Center for the Visual Arts came into being, the latter with the intent of bringing together in one building related activities such as film-making and visual design which till then had been carried on independently in various parts of the University. The construction of the Carpenter Center for the Visual Arts was made possible by a generous gift from Alfred St. Vrain Carpenter '05, and the building was opened in May 1963. It is the only work of architecture which Le Corbusier designed in the U.S.A.

In the Visual and Environmental Studies program, students may take some of the following courses:

Introduction to Visual Design; Fundamentals of Light and Communication, a course designed to expose the student to the full range of concerns and possibilities of the Light and Communication area; an initial experience with light-sensitive media which relates their characteristics to examination of environmental issues. Exercises in still photography, animation and television are paired with weekly lectures and demonstrations. Some topics covered in these lectures are light and perception; the eye and the camera; the discovery of light-sensitive materials; persistence of vision and the illusion of motion; the cognitive bases of film editing; sound and image. *Design in the Visual Environment; Introduction to a Psychology of Visual Studies: Perception and Expression in Art and Design; Principles of Graphic Design; Form From Technology; Still Photography; Image and Communication; Space, Structure and Urban Design in Ancient Times; Space, Structure and Urban Design in the Middle Ages; Renaissance and Baroque Architecture in Italy;* and *Space, Structure and Urban Design in Modern Times.*

Optional courses related to Visual and Environmental Studies include: *Psychological Anthropology; Games and Strategy* (in the Economics department); *Urban Politics; Impact of Technology on America, 1850–1950* (in the History department); *Development of the Modern City; Automatic Computing; Sensation; Perception; Social Psychology*; and *The Modern Industrial Society.*

The film courses offered in the Carpenter Center are four: *Light and Communication*—Documentary, described as a "workshop concerned with the elements of cinematographic communications: light, motion, time, space, and form. Through a series of lectures, demonstrations, and exercises, students will acquire both technical skills and conceptual awareness of the motion picture medium."

In Harvard's animation class, ". . . students will deal with line and color animation through lectures, demonstrations, and exercises. The workshop is an extension of graphic techniques into a time dimension. Emphasis will be placed on the relevance of animation to the communications process." An extension of the same course may be taken the following semester.

A seminar in *Communications Media* is also offered and it is described as "a critical case-study discussion of the media of visual communication with special considerations given to television and its environmental implications."

Robert Gardner, coordinator of the Light and Communications Workshops in the Center, said:

> the studies in photography and motion picture offered in the Carpenter Center are not the first offered at Harvard; there has been film study as part of anthropology courses since 1958. In 1963, however, classes were begun in animation, film-making

and still photography. In 1969, we have begun to put together a department consisting of courses that previously were optional. Our policy is not to become a typical design school, but to offer courses which teach the student to appreciate and grasp his environment.

We have one-hundred to one-hundred-fifty students in our film courses, which is the capacity of the courses. We subsidize them to about $200–$300 in film and processing, cameras and lights.

We never have enough cameras, the film work is entirely in sixteen millimeter. Currently we have six or seven Bolex cameras, which each student can use one day out of three; two Airflex sixteens and two Airflex 35's, which are rarely used. We also have three Bell and Howells and ten CineRoyals.

Our object is not to turn out craftsmen, but to educate the students' vision and give them a new tool with which to see the world, to appreciate the world. We want to be formative in this medium; the students can apply the insights they gain here after they leave . . .

Harvard does offer complete mixing and recording equipment, but does not believe in the crew concept, nor is it very desirous of obtaining composite prints from student films. The object here is more to make a film to see what happens through the lens, and get it to the editing stage to see what it means to edit a film.

From Derek Lamb's *House Moving,* a pixilation film.

From *Clay Or The Origin Of Species,* an animated clay film completed by Eliot Noyes, Jr. It was nominated for an Academy Award.

One of the most recent films, however, did get to the composite stage and eventually was nominated for an Academy Award. The film was *Clay,* or *The Origin Of Species,* a ten-minute, black-and-white study in animated clay techniques by Eliot Noyes, Jr.

Other exceptional films have been: *Sand,* or *Peter And The Wolf,* by Caroline Leaf, a ten-minute, black-and-white study in animated sand;* *House Moving,* a pixillation film by Derek Lamb, who is a lecturer in Visual Studies; *The Shout It Out Alphabet Film* by Lynn Smith, a ten-minute, color example of college animation; *The Great Sail,* a color and sound film by Robert Gardner in pixillation and cinema vérité.*

Perhaps to film enthusiasts, of more importance than the Carpenter Center is the Brattle Theater, off-campus but near the Harvard Yard. The Brattle Theater has pioneered the importation of exceptional foreign films for distribution in this country.

* *Sand* won the Special Jury Award for Animation at the Chicago Film Festival, Nov. 25, 1969.

* All five films are available for rental showings from Image Resources, Inc., 267 West 25th St., New York, N.Y. 10001

From *Sand Or Peter And The Wolf,* an animated sand film by Caroline Leaf.

The owners of the theater were the original owners of the Janus Films Company (now sold to others). The Brattle continues to lead the country in the excellence and scope of its presentations.

The revival of interest in films starring the late Humphrey Bogart was begun, to a large extent, at the Brattle Theater, although the national revival was begun much later.

C. I. "Cy" Harvey, owner of the theater, said. "The Brattle was built in Febrary, 1953 and was patterned after the Film Museum in Paris. The theater shows films that are not readily accessible for showings. We are booked months in advance and have a library of one hundred or more films which we show regularly, including films by Bergman, Eisenstein and Renoir.

"We screen films in series, according to director, period, national origin or stars. The Janus film operation, which we began in 1956, also books these same type films into theaters throughout the country."

Harvey attended the Sorbonne from 1949–1950 on a Fullbright and studied comparative literature and cinema techniques.

From *The Great Sail* in film pixilation and cinema vérité by Robert Gardner.

The Brattle Theater, near Harvard, began the Bogart revival in the early 1960s. In addition to a fine program of films, the Theater complex also includes the Truc shops, foreign and domestic (sign at lower left of building), a series of speciality shops in the basement of the building. (Photo by the author)

Upon returning to this country and discovering that "comparative literature couldn't fill my stomach," he began the Brattle. Harvey added a coffee house under the theater and has slowly expanded the basement areas into a series of boutiques. "We'd like to have families and students spend their evenings here," he said. "After the theater, they can have coffee in the Club Casablanca, under the theater, then browse in the shops we have set up and open at night."

All the shops are small boutiques and gift shops, operated under the name Truc, Inc. Harvey supervises the design of the shops and orders all the merchandise. The shops have thoroughly delightful decors, and smells from several of them waft through the corridors. The shops carry names typically boutique: Club Casablanca, The Poster Gallery (which sells expensive posters

From Lynn Smith's *The Shout It Out Alphabet Film*. It was a project in collage animation.

as well as the inexpensive pop-posters) ; The Hamlet Coffee Shop, and The Blue Parrot Coffee House.

The design of the theater-boutiques has been imitated elsewhere, but the reputation for fine film programming that the Brattle has cannot be copied. The theater has 340 seats and is usually filled to capacity, particularly for the special series, which the Brattle runs at regular intervals.

Among the programs advertised in Brattle pamphlets for Harvard students have been:

"Renoir in the 30's: *Rules of the Game; Boudu Saved From Drowning; Toni* plus *A Day in the Country* and *La Marseillaise;*

"Eisenstein, Films and Fragments: *Alexander Nevsky; Time In The Sun; Ten Days That Shook The World* and *Bezhin Meadow;*

"Kurosawa, Shakespeare, Shimura, Samurai: *Throne of Blood; Ikiru* and *Sanjuro;*

"Jean Vigo: *Zero for Conduct* and *L'Atalante*;

"Antonioni Week: *Eclipse, LaNotte* and *Red Desert;*

"Fellini Week: *Juliet of the Spirits* and *8½;*

"Italian Film Series: *Yesterday, Today and Tomorrow; Boccaccio '70; Bell Antonio; Seduced and Abandoned; The Fiances; The Easy Life; 8½; La Viaccia; Two Women; Rocco and His Brothers; Red Desert* and *Let's Talk About Women.*"

"Hommage to Nikolai Cherkassov" included *Peter The Great,* parts I and II; *Ivan The Terrible,* parts I and II; *Moussorgsky*; and *Alexander Nevsky.*

A Russian film festival once included the following films in two weeks: *The Battleship Potemkin; Chapayev; We Are From Kronstadt; Peter The Great,* parts I and II; *Childhood of Maxim Gorky; Alexander Nevsky; Volga-Volga; Ivan The Terrible,* parts I and II; *The Inspector General; The Forty-First; The Captain's Daughter*; and *Poem of the Sea.*

An "April Film Orgy" offered the following films on a day-to-day basis: *Citizen Kane; Ballad of a Soldier; The Bed; Cleo From 5 to 7; Nights of Cabiria; The Lovers*; Luis Bunuel's *Viridiana; The Bridge; Inspector Maigret*; John Ford's *The Informer*; Antonioni's *L'Avventura; Gunga Din; Lust For Life,* with Kirk Douglas; *The Proud and the Beautiful; Tunes of Glory; Sparrows Can't Sing; Gate of Hell; Miss Julie; We Are All Murderers; Mr. Hulot's Holiday*; and *Utamaro.*

And, of course, there are the Bogart festivals, which continue to be favorites of the Harvard crowd. A recent series included: *Casablanca; The Maltese Falcon; Treasure of the Sierra Madre, The Big Sleep; Key Largo; Beat The Devil; The Oklahoma Kid,* with Bogart as a cowboy dressed entirely in black; and *High Sierra.*

Many Boston area film makers believe that if Harvard ever wished to create a film department with no connections to the Carpenter Center, the film program could well be one of the best in the country. The salary scale that Harvard could offer faculty members and the prestige of teaching at Harvard might mean the creation of a film department second to none. So far, Harvard has shown no inclination toward creating such a department. Thus, primary film activity in the Boston area will continue to remain at Boston University and at Brandeis.

14.
Boston University

WEINKAUF; SUROWIECKI; ROBERTS

Most members of the university film community acknowledge that the two best film programs on the eastern seaboard are New York University and Boston University. This is correct. Boston University does have a fine program, existing amiably within a School of Public Communications. The School also includes public relations, journalism, and broadcasting. It was created in 1947 and has, since then, offered masters degrees in the three divisions. In 1963, a fourth specialization was added, that of Communications Research.

On the undergraduate level, students are required to take a combined film-television major. About half of the students in the undergraduate program are unofficially film majors.

Some of the courses offered during the 1969–1970 academic year to undergraduates were:

> *Broadcasting and Film in the United States*, development of the cinema, radio and television from their beginnings until the present. Cultural role of the media in American society. Institutional structures and communication processes; *The Sound Studio*, basic approach to sound as used in radio, television and film; *Film-Making: Theory and Practice*, provides basic experience and understanding of communications through film. Whole class sessions, including illustrated lectures and small group sessions involving instruction in basic techniques of film making. Super eight millimeter equipment and some materials provided; *Film Production*, planning transformation of an idea into film: initial analysis, film, script, preproduction planning, nature of production processes. Production of a short film by each student. Students *must* (authors italics) provide basic sixteen millimeter equipment and materials; *Feature Film*, an exploration of the most notable feature films with attention given to influential authors and directors. Screen-

ings, lectures, discussions and papers; *Dramatic Film Directing,* the planning, scripting and production of dramatic films. Each student produces a film under faculty supervision; *Functional Film,* examination of classic and modern films of a documentary nature: films that are artistic attempts to inform, educate and entertain, and *Experimental Film,* intensive study of the work of film makers who are removing or extending boundaries of the medium.

On the graduate level, students may option for either a concentration in film criticism or film production. The courses leading to the master of science degree in film are:

Film Production. Preparatory course in practical aspects of film production, required of beginning students in Film; *History of Film.* Development of the cinema, emphasizing role of film as a social art affected by and affecting the society of its time; *Theory of the Cinema.* "Basic narrative techniques of the cinema; origins in pictorial art and in literature. The illusion of movement, the frame, the viewpoint on the subject; the concept of the "scene." Fragmentation and resynthesis of the "scene"; nature of the "master scene." The art and practice of "montage." Study of various specific modes of cinematic communication as exemplified in selected films: and *Screen Education.* Examination of "the screen," i.e., film and television, in terms of screen language and its role in the educational process. Philosophic assumptions of screen education, communication and the screen language, and methods of screen teaching considered.

Film Studies I. In first part of three-semester sequence in Film Studies emphasis on selected areas of film history and theory, supplemented by advanced work in production:

Film History: Selected movements in development of film theory and technique studied in detail, e.g., early Russian film as influenced by Eisenstein and Pudovkin. Students expected to acquire a scholarly and critical understanding of main currents that influenced the growth of film and to explore in depth selected areas of cinematic history.

Film Theory: Analytical study of evolution and current state of screen dramaturgy. Literary and pictorial origins of film dramaturgy; relationships to theatre, the novel and radio and television dramaturgy. Development of contemporary dramatic forms and structures peculiar to the cinema. Cinematic metaphor and symbolism within the dramatic context. Application of theory to practical problems in screen dramaturgy and film criticism:

Production: Advanced training and experience in use of

cameras and sound equipment. The editing process, including cutting, mixing, negative cutting, syncing, and titling.

Film Studies II. The second part of Film Studies sequence stresses the socio-economic aspects of film, as well as analytical studies in film medium and creative experience in film making.

Sociology of Film: Film as communication related to general theories of communication. Studies of the film, audience; relationship of film to other media, especially television; films of persuasion, dissent, protest, and social investigation placed in societal context. Developing a sociology of film.

Economics of the Film Industries: Examination of institutional structure of Hollywood, especially ownership and control patterns and influence of economics on product of the film industry. Independent and specialized film operations in United States. Factors affecting modes of distribution and exhibition. The non-American film industries.

Problems in Production: Budgeting and administering film operations up to medium sized investment. Preparation of outlines, treatments, and synopses for proposed films; developing a shooting script with complete production planning. Organizing technical personnel and directing performances.

Film Studies III. Emphasis placed, in third part of Film Studies sequence, on scholarly investigation, creative writing, and experimental film making according to student's interest:

Theoretical: Selected portions of general film theory studied in relationship to specific problems of film production, film criticism, and analysis.

Creative Writing: Creation of films in script form, both original and adaptations, based upon techniques in dramaturgy common to all forms of narrative communication, and on film dramaturgy, i.e., the specific art of screen narrative peculiar to film as medium of communication.

Experimental: Studying work of film makers who have extended or are extending boundaries of the medium. Exploring creative potential of film through personal engagement in film making.

Peter Chvany, an instructor in the School of Public Communication, who holds a masters degree in education as well as in film, said:

During the 1968–1969 school year, there were about 150 undergraduates in the Film-TV Program and about half of them were film majors. On the graduate level, we have about 25 graduate students, with about ten to fifteen in their second year. Boston holds generally to the single film-maker concept. In the undergraduate program, we have three courses in production: *Film-Making, Theory and Practice; Film Production* and *Dramatic Film Production.* In the first course, students film in super eight; in the second course, they make exercise films or short films and in the *Dramatic Film Production* course, we do use the crew concept and students shoot their films in crews of four or five. This course is generally for seniors.

On the graduate level, the courses are planned so that only the first semester is scheduled; the remaining three semesters of the two-year program are left unscheduled so that the students may use all of that year-and-one-half, if they have to, to complete their thesis film project. Generally the graduate students shoot their films in crews, but Boston University recently found that it is no longer economically feasible to supply students with film. They must pay for all that they use.

As a point of comparison with the production of other film programs, about 25 films reach the composite or answer print stage at Boston University each year.

And as is usually the case, especially with large departments, Boston has found that the equipment available to film students is inadequate. During the 1968–1969 school year, there were avail-

Peter Chvany, an instructor in the Boston University film program, shoots in a downtown Boston street.

able several Bell and Howells, one Auricon, a CineSpecial, and a Nagra recorder. There were also eight full-time faculty members in the film program and two part-time members during that year.

Generally the major point of criticism usually voiced about Boston's program is that all the faculty members and their guidance is aimed toward film aesthetics; some of the graduate students and more of the undergraduates offer the complaint that they know everything about film and criticism, but no one has ever taught them how to load various types of cameras. The criticism is apparently justified, but students ought to remember that there are some aspects of the mechanics of film work that they ought to learn on their own, particularly that of the equipment they hope to master.

Listed here are some of the exceptional films made recently at Boston University.

A Question of Color by Richard Bartlett is a satire on the film *Hiroshima, Mon Amour.*

Altar Boy by Dexter McDonald is a short film about a young altar boy as he leaves home to go to church, dresses, and prepares to assist in giving Mass. The freckle-faced youth dons the garb of an altar boy, almost leaving his youthful freshness behind. It is ten minutes long, in black and white; it was completed in 1964.

McDonald also made *Confession* in 1965, a film about a little

Peter Chvany lectures during a film course.

boy and girl who arrive at a church to give their confessions. The little girl is very quiet, polite and reverent, while the young boy rebels at some of the traditions he must follow.

The Devil's Pool by Roman Slezas is a drama of murder, confession, and renunciation, involving a young priest in a European rural setting. The film, which Slezas completed in 1964, runs one-half hour, in black and white and sound.

Face Junk, also by Richard Bartlett, is a graphic and sometimes hilarious statement about the use and application of cosmetics. Bartlett has used extreme close-ups and the viewers often find themselves struggling through a valley-sized eyelid, forging over tears and mascara, and slipping over grease paint. It is rather like *Ritual,* made at the University of Southern California. *Face Junk* is ten minutes long, in color and sound; it was a finalist in the Experimental Film category of the National Student Film Festival in 1967.

Festival by Gunther Pfaff is a candid comment on the Arts Festival held each year on the Boston Common. Watching people watching art objects is more fun than watching the art objects. *Festival* is 20 minutes long, in black and white; it was completed in 1964.

Fun At The Circus by Ray Priest is not about the conventional circus, complete with animals, but about the sights and sounds of Boston. A traffic policeman directs the crowds like a lion tamer. In the background, a side-show barker calls out patter to attract an audience. *Fun At The Circus* is ten minutes long, in black and white and sound; it was completed in 1964.

Gayle, a documentary made by Terry Hickey, concerns a blind and deaf girl who is involved in the contemporary world, and who is a student of literature, French, and current affairs. It is 20 minutes long, in black and white; it was completed at the Perkins School for the Blind in 1966.

Get Yourself A Pre-College Boy was written and directed by high school students in New Orleans as an experiment in screen education under the direction of Ray Richardson, a Boston University undergraduate who spent a summer in the south. It is a 20-minute comedy reminiscent of Mack Sennett.

King Bagel is about "King Bagel," who makes bagels for a living. In addition to making the bagels, he throws in philosophy regarding his neighbors, his customers, his wife, his children, and his work. It was completed in 1965 by Werner Bundschuh and is ten minutes long, in black and white and sound.

Match Girl by Andrew Mayer won first prize in the 1966 National Student Film Festival and is owned by the British Film

Institute. It is the classic fable of the penniless match girl, re-told by one of Andy Warhol's retinue of campy super-stars.

Mayer said, of the film:

"I started out knowing I was going to do a film based on Hans Christian Andersen's tale of the poor little match girl, which had been filmed by Renoir in 1927. However, this got mixed up in my mind with a poor little rich girl story about a successful but lonely fashion model who idealizes herself as a story book character. Out of this confusion comes one of the themes of the film: that what is most illusive can also be most real. Thus, when the girl hallucinates, she is watching Hitchcock's *Vertigo,* a film which revolves around similar ideas. Besides the character of the girl, interpreted by model Vivian Kurz, there is a sort of Prince Charming, played by poet Gerard Malanga, also trying to maintain a certain image of himself. Andy Warhol appears as a witch or overlord of the pop milieu in which the action takes place. The grandmother in the story is replaced by Marilyn Monroe as a sort of fairy godmother to the girl."

And James Stoller, writing in New York's *The Village Voice,* said

". . . an arabesque from Hans Christian Andersen, in the footsteps also of Renoir, using Warhol and Malanga and in gorgeous color with many reflections and many reminders of other works we have seen, is somewhat less incredible. It is merely prodigious. I felt some preciousness here, also a sense of trying to have things too many ways, but may have been confusing the seen with the seer. At its best it affirms again how Mayer has been able to transform his visions and thoughts into film which is literate (not just literary) as well as sensuous, and in which form and even a sense of the dramatic play major parts."

Mechanism by Peter Novak is a beautiful trip through the inside of a clock—the gears, wheels, springs, and levers. It is ten minutes long, in color.

Solus by John Bartholomew was selected best in Contemporary Photography and Cinematography by REFOCUS at the University of Iowa in 1967. It is ten minutes long, in black and white, and has been described as: "early in the morning a motorcyclist travels around Beacon Hill in Boston. There is a sharp contrast between the fast-moving, loud motorcycle and the quiet 'Proper Bostonians' getting ready to go to work. In the background, a girl sings a Brazilian folk-tune."

One of the exceptional students at Boston University has been David Weinkauf, who received his master of science degree in June of 1965, submitting as his thesis film the documentary *As*

Long As It Holds Out. It was one of his earliest films. Since completing it, he has done *Impressions,* a documentary on nursing (1966); *Nurture the Seed,* a documentary on teaching the mentally retarded (1967); *Face to Face—Walt Whitman: A Hundred Years Hence* (1968), an experimental documentary based on Whitman's poem, "Crossing Brooklyn Ferry"; and *Franklin: Autobiography and Beyond* (1968), an educational film about Philadelphia in Franklin's time.

Since his graduation from Boston University, Weinkauf taught at the University of South Dakota for one year, 1965–1966, and organized the Film Unit at Edinboro State College in Pennsylvania, where he continues to teach. Recently, he negotiated a television equipment donation for Edinboro State College worth $111,225 and has been negotiating a second donation worth $60,000.

As Long As It Holds Out was filmed during the summer of 1964 at Holl's Inn, a summer resort near Inlet, New York.

Weinkauf had worked at the resort during previous summers and was thus acquainted with its topography and its management. He has written extensively about *As Long As It Holds Out,*

Opening credits from *As Long As It Holds Out* by David Weinkauf.

both prior to and after the actual filming. Before he began, he submitted a prospectus for acceptance as a thesis film, and after the film was completed, he detailed his problems and his feelings about it. Both periods of work on the film are worth noting:

> The subject for my thesis film is a hotelman from Germany with fifty one years of hotel experience, thirty years, of which, as owner and operator of his own resort-hotel in the Central Adirondacks. This person is atypical. His attitudes and feelings toward the hotel business are European-oriented. He has, however, been able to combine European and American management procedures to produce a good business despite stiff competition.
>
> I propose to look at the problems involved in running a seasonal resort-hotel by directing attention to this person's lifelong experiences. The film will be specific. It will focus on one man's life and hotel. Although generalizations about hotel business are not intended, they may arise out of the material as it is constructed. I have already "scouted" for the material, having

The sense of cinema vérité is established in this shot, early in *As Long As It Holds Out.* The woman is surprised by the camera.

previously worked for the above mentioned hotelman.

Visually, the film will show my subject at work before, during and after the summer season, with the emphasis on the "during." I propose to use the "cinema vérité" technique a good deal of the time. "Wild sound" recording will be a problem, but will be used whenever possible. Only available light will be used with the "cinema vérité" technique. There will be times, however, when the camera setups and angles will be chosen for specific purposes. When this happens, more attention will be given to sound and "low-key" lighting.

The sound track will consist mainly of commentary by my subject. "Wild track" sound will be inserted when it does not conflict with my subject's commentary, it serves a useful purpose and it can be obtained. Music will be used to create atmosphere in sequences without commentary or "wild sound" recording. Two sequences in which music will be used, will be the first and last, mentioned later.

Since most of the filmic material will depend on spontaneity, only a basic outline of the film's beginning, middle and end can now be made. The film will open on two or three workman preparing the hotel for its opening. The weather conditions will, hopefully, be dull, drab and cold. An alternative would be a series of shots showing the mess around the hotel prior to opening. In either case, I want to show the work involved in opening the hotel. More important, I want to create a feeling of irritation.

In recording what goes on during the season, the camera will serve many functions. In its subjective function, the camera will follow my subject around the hotel. At times, it will stop to glimpse at the help and guests. In some cases, the camera will serve a "parallel commentative" function. For example, when my subject speaks of things left undone, various shots of unpainted structures, ripped umbrella shades, broken oars, etc., will be included. The camera will also record unexpected happenings such as power failures, accidents, fires, etc.

One sequence within the main body of the film will contrast the present with the past (the past being 1934 to 1940). This will be accomplished by the use of old photographs and home movies. One approach to the sequence might be to have my subject looking at and talking about old photographs. Another might be to have people looking at my subject's home movies. The flicker of the projector, in this case, would be seen before the inserts of the home movies. The inserts would be selected from eight reels of 16 millimeter color film and printed at a laboratory later.

The end of the film could be done in one of several ways. The first might be to show several employees taking down the huge road signs near the hotel and storing them away. Another way might be to construct a montage of shots showing various things being stored away for winter. A third way might be to show my subject addressing cards and letters for the following season.

My proposed budget of four hundred dollars will include costs of additional film stock, work prints, audio tape, postage, optical effects, answer and release prints and other related costs. The length of the film will be no less than five hundred, nor more than seven hundred feet. The shooting ratio will be three to one. Since I will be working as assistant manager of the hotel this summer, I will have to send film out to be processed. Because of this, work prints will be made of all film shot.

Weinkauf was not able to realize his estimate of a three-to-one shooting ratio. He shot 2,400 feet of film and edited that down to a final print of 385 feet. Although his estimate of a budget of 400 dollars was also surpassed, it was not surpassed by much. His final figures for expenditures of $447.97 are quite reasonable, considering the problems that he had during the shooting (which he notes in his subsequent writings). Many bigger productions

This scene was illuminated with only a 60-watt light bulb. From *As Long As It Holds Out* by David Weinkauf.

should do as well in keeping to their original budget. His figures for the film were:

1800′	Double-X and Plus-X negative film (supplied by Boston University)	———
200′	Plus-X negative film	3.44
400′	Double-X negative film	19.44
200′	High-contrast film	2.00
2600′	Processing	80.00
2510′	Work prints	99.40
2355′	Edge numbers	28.80
3600′	Audio tape (1200′ reels)	5.97
2400′	Audio tape (300′ reels)	6.00
1200′	Magnetic film (supplied by Boston (University)	———
600′	White leader	6.00
100′	Black leader	2.75
400′	Black leader (supplied by Boston (University)	———
	Three track mix	15.00
5	Photo enlargements and processing	6.00
	Postage	1.66
	Reels and cans	7.94
5	Title cells (hot press)	14.00
1	Can Permacell	6.75
380′	Optical transfer	33.25
379′	Optical transfer	33.16
385′	Composite answer print (A & B roll printing)	26.95
8	Dissolves	24.00
385′	Composite release print	22.00
385′	Composite release print	22.00
	Pre-print preparation	7.50
	TOTAL	$ 474.01

After completing *As Long As It Holds Out,* he noted:

Film is such a fluid medium that the distance from original idea to final presentation is a great one. Since there are many variables inherent in the creative process, the original idea and the final film are virtually two different things. This is true in, *As Long As It Holds Out*. Even though some of my original ideas were incorporated in the final film, the overall pattern was greatly different from the original conception.

One reason for the difference was the lack of a detailed shooting script. My original idea was to make a film that would show a hotelman's life over a period of a year. In actual shooting,

A close-up of the owner of the hotel featured in Weinkauf's *As Long As It Holds Out*.

I found that a film about the man running the hotel during the summer season only would be sufficient. I wish now I had prepared a more detailed script in terms of overall pattern, allowing for the same flexibility of sequences, but concentrating on my subject during this more limited period of time.

I set out to illustrate the problems and frustrations of a man who had been in the hotel business for half a century and who was the main force behind his current business. I planned to shoot with the "cinema vérité" technique and ended up using it more out of necessity than anything else. The camera was to serve a recording function in showing things as they happened and a narrative function in commenting on what was being seen. I found out in actual practice how difficult it was to separate the two functions. In recording reality, a comment upon that reality is inherent in what is being seen. If, for example, my subject is conscious of and irritated by the camera's presence, this makes a comment both about the shooting situation and the character of my subject.

An awareness of the camera's presence is, perhaps, the key factor in establishing "cinema vérité" as a shooting technique.

The owner of Hobb's Inn checks the plumbing during *As Long As It Holds Out.*

The "cinema vérité" camera has to establish itself as a third person present within the environment of the overall filmic situation. The establishment of the camera as a dominant character has to come early in the film so the audience is not taken by surprise half-way through the film. The role of my camera was established in the first shot of the film. At the beginning of the shot, no-one was aware of the camera. Then, to the right of the frame, a woman suddenly noticed the camera and showed her surprise in a distinct facial expression. From this shot on, the camera was established as a character in the film and the "cinema vérité" technique was under way. Throughout the film, my subject was conscious of the camera and several times showed his awareness and irritation. But, if it were not for the early establishment of the camera, the shots of my subject showing his irritation and awareness might have been difficult to understand.

My research for the film was based on experience with the hotel and the man who was to be my subject. I had worked at the hotel during three earlier summers and was scheduled to work as assistant manager while shooting the film. I had not worked at the hotel two summers before this. Hence, some things were changed when I arrived in June. This situation did not affect, to any great degree, the structure of my film. What did affect my situation was the fact that I had to work as assistant manager while shooting it.

Shooting began during the first part of June when the hotel was being readied for opening. I originally planned to shoot about two hundred to three hundred feet of film on the pre-season activities, but for reasons I am not at liberty to mention, shooting could not begin until the season was under way. This situation drastically changed my original outline and I realized then that the film would have to concentrate on the season itself. I rewrote my original idea and kept notes on what I was doing. By the middle of the summer, I had a pretty good idea of the kind of footage I would come home with.

Since I had no time to set up lights, I overcame the problems of adequate light by working with Double-X negative film and shooting at A.S.A. 400. Focus was extremely critical, but I was able to get shots by using as little as one sixty watt bulb. Once only, I used lights to highlight two girls singing. As a result, the shots were too bright and did not fit too well with the rest of the film. Fortunately, the exposure of the shot was corrected in printing.

Because of the mobile nature of my shooting, I was forced to have a simple system of focus and exposure. Throughout the summer, I took exposure readings and kept notes should a case arise where I had no time to worry about exposure. I also simplified my meter by taping a conversion scale on its side. All I then had to do was to get the light value reading and the corresponding lens opening. Most of the time I worked with the lens wide open inside the hotel and stopped down all the way outdoors when the sun was bright. My setting for focus was usually eight feet. I found this distance adequate for follow-focusing purposes.

I used a simple pattern of shooting since my job as assistant manager sometimes hampered my activities with the camera. In using two different films (indoor and outdoor film) I was forced to empty my camera after each shooting period and before the next. This accounted for the vast amount of footage (twenty-three hundred feet) shot. Each morning I placed the camera (loaded with film I expected to use) under my desk. Throughout each day, my procedure would be to grab the camera, follow my subject and shoot what happened. More often than not, this procedure worked well. I managed to get, for example, actual shots of my subject checking equipment, checking people into the hotel and supervising work. One time, as I predicted in my original plan, a pump broke down and had to be fixed immediately so that a flood would not occur. Naturally, my subject had to supervise and participate in the repair procedure. And, naturally, my camera and I had to shoot the whole event. I had just started shooting when my job took me away from the hotel. I had taken only two shots. When I got back, a new pump had been installed and the event was lost. Other times, I followed my subject only to have nothing happen. Film taken in these cases had to be discarded.

Sound recording was a real problem. I managed to record background noises and voices which were of great value later on. These presented no problems. The problems arose when I attempted to shoot synchronous sound without sync sound equipment. I tried it in three sequences, one of which was discarded completely. In one case, the bar sequence, I used one tape recorder for the public address signal and another for background noise. The tape recording of the public address noise was not good since it produced sixty decibels of hum. The battery-operated tape recorder produced a track which was technically good, but extraneous noises due to bad acoustics were present. I recorded the check-in sequence with a battery-operated tape recorder. The unblimped camera was mounted on a tripod and positioned at least ten feet in front of and in back of the subjects. The problems of post synchronization will be discussed later.

During shooting, I made sure that I was legally protected when photographing guests. When there was a prospect of filming guests, I made sure each signed a simple release. On the weekend when I was to shoot the dining room scene, for example, I had each check-in and each guest sign such a release. With one or two exceptions, all of the guests consented. I had to stay out of the way of those who did not. I remember that one of the guests who refused to sign was sitting close to where the dining room shooting was to take place. Because of this, I had to set up the camera in such a way that he would not be filmed.

When the shooting was finished, I had to wait a month or so for all of the work prints to be made up. Since I was in the woods, and three hundred miles from the labs, every foot of the negative had to be printed. This greatly added to the cost of work prints. Since the labs were sometimes slow, I did not see the bulk of work prints until I returned to Boston late in September. Because of this, I had to reshoot about one hundred feet of film. The narration was done at two stages of the film's development. Since the first time was before editing, I include an account of the process here. I have to mention again that it was only through persistent and slow coaxing that my subject eventually consented to having his voice taped. But, even when the taping sessions were under way, he was constantly on his guard. He insisted that I prepare something before taping. I complied by drawing up a list of sixty questions. This only complicated matters since he constantly referred to his written notes. The first taping session was held the day after the hotel closed. Both of us were tired and, as a result, the taping session suffered somewhat. The second occurred in January after he was more relaxed and after he had seen the first rough cut of the film. During the session, he loosened up somewhat, but remained on his guard. At one point in the recording, he forgot the recorder was running and made some off-hand remarks about people. This was the type of narration I had hoped for, but never obtained until this time. If I could have hidden a microphone and talked with him conversationally, the resulting narration would have been up to my expectations.

By the beginning of November, I had assembled the total footage into twenty-one sequences, most of which were not used in the final film. The order of sequences, at this point, did not matter. A selection was made based on what would work and what wouldn't. The material left was then assembled according to rhythmic continuity in an attempt to keep the climaxes and tensions evenly spread. This did not always work since the first half flowed nicely without really saying anything. The second half was a hodgepodge that got nowhere. I left this method of construction for a while and concentrated on rearranging shots within the sequences.

During the time the rough cut was being assembled, and rearranged, I began work on the synchronous sound sequences. In doing so, I noticed a big difference in the speed between picture and track. I expected some difference, but not a consistent difference. To correct the situation, I used the variable speed motor on the moviola in transferring the track to the film recorder, thus speeding up the track to fit the picture. In the check-in sequence, the system worked despite slight differences between picture and track and a slight loss of equality. The system would not work with the sequence involving the girl singers. The resulting sound was terrible. To overcome this, I cut the closeup of the girls short enough to be in sync with the existing track. The shot was very short, but the sync seemed to remain throughout. I discovered that my camera had run consistently slow throughout filming. If it had run up to speed, most of the problems would have been taken care of.

When the sync sound sequences were fit into the film, the overall order of sequences began to show itself. Some sequences were edited independent of the sound while others had to be edited with the sound. In many respects, the fine cut was actually a simultaneous cut of both picture and sound.

During the fine cut, tensions and climaxes were built in or brought out in the use of "cinema vérité" as a technique. Tensions occurred whenever the camera, as a character of the film, conflicts with the people and objects in its path. The varying distances between the subject and the camera produce tension. Tensions are also inherent in shots themselves. In a sequence of dull room shots, a canted shot of empty coathangers produced some tension and, coupled with the narrative track, proved to be a climax of the film.

Climaxes within the film were built out of the direct relationship between picture and sound. In the pre-title dining room sequence, for example, the overall flow was constant, but leading to some climax. The climax, itself, was reached when my subject said, ". . . that we cannot make it pay," over a shot of hands erasing an entry from the day book. The sequence was brought to a climax because the above statement was so unlike the preceding statement which stressed the easy-going enjoyable aspects of the dining room and the visuals which showed everything going so well. The statement, however, was not the only element that brought the sequence to a distinct climax. Immediately after the statement, the sound track went silent while an extreme long shot of the hotel appeared on the screen. The effect was one of stopping the action or interrupting the rhythm of the film to give the audience enough time to contemplate the preceding statement and the forthcoming film.

The same type of climax was used in the pumps sequence where the statement was, "Most breakdowns happen when the equipment is at its hardest use like on a weekend when you can get no service at all." The soundtrack dropped to outside noises while the shot showed my subject walking through the woods. This technique of building a climax and "straight-away cutting" to something else not only served to highlight the climax, but also provided a smooth transition.

In the editing process, I found a direct relationship between picture and sound. The visuals, which were not outstanding in themselves, were given life when put next to the tracks. When my subject said, "During the war, any room could be rented," the previously mentioned visual of the empty coathangers had some meaning. This is not to say that picture and track did not have meanings in themselves. It is to say that when put together, both had more strength than before.

It was decided late in the editing process that the dining room sequence should be substituted for the existing pre-title sequence in order to lead the audience into a nice, pleasant atmosphere before bringing in the pessimistic feelings of my subject. The switch worked, and the titles provided just the right amount of time for the audience to unwind from my subject's last phrase. When the sequences were finally in order, picture and track were trimmed to allow for just the amount of material needed to get important points across.

In editing sound, I worked with three independent tracks because of increased flexibility. I worked with background sound, narration and sync sound tracks. The narration track was changed many times during the editing process, even after the other tracks were almost completed. Since there were specific sounds underneath the narration and since these sounds had to correspond to specific visuals, the two tracks could not be combined until the entire film was edited. When all three tracks were edited and the visuals were fine cut, a mix was performed and for the first time, I saw a composite picture. After this, visuals were rearranged along with the soundtrack. This was possible since the rearranging did not affect the mix in any way.

In my original prospectus, I proposed a budget of four hundred dollars to cover costs of additional film stock, work prints, audio tape, postage, optical effects, answer and release prints and other related costs. When final prints are completed, I shall have exceeded my original figure by seventy-eight dollars. In considering the extra cost, it should be noted that two hundred feet of film were given to a camera repair shop to check a defect in my camera after shooting. Because of this, I had to buy additional footage to make titles. Another unexpected expense was a second optical transfer to replace the first which was badly done. Also, if I had been near a laboratory during shooting, I could have cut the cost of work prints by almost fifty dollars. Considering, however, that I accomplished most technical aims I originally proposed, the extra seventy-eight dollars is not an extravagant figure.

I have mixed emotions about the film. On the one hand, I realize my lack of ability in directing and shooting. This lack of ability is partly due to a difficult task in convincing a subject of my objectives in making the film. Second, I shot in such a manner that a good deal of the camerawork was concerned with things as they happened. In a way, this was good since it fit the mood of the film. Several times, however, I was shooting blind and nothing hapened. I see, on the other hand, my ability in the technical means of editing. Out of any work done on the film, sound and editing took the most time and were the most satisfying.

I learned a lot from making *As Long As It Holds Out,* but I still have a lot to learn. I have to go back several steps and direct my thinking to visuals alone. I have to see what each shot means. In *As Long As It Holds Out,* my knowledge of events outside the frame no longer had any validity once I started concentrating on the visuals through the editing process. I have also to redirect my thinking in terms of rhythmic continuity as opposed to visual continuity. Too many times, I worried about how different shots would go together in terms of clothing, positions, etc., not realizing that the overall flow of the film overrides all other considerations. It is in this rhythmic continuity that visual continuity is suppressed to the point where it has no validity. Above all, I must limit my material by discarding that which is not needed.

As Long As It Holds Out, as far as I am concerned, is my first film. It presents a chunk of life and makes some social commentary upon it, although this was not my original intention. The cinematography leaves much to be desired. Editing and the use of sound are the two elements best developed. Perhaps if I had a subject who had more time to cooperate with me and spend time with the film, many of the defects in the film would have been corrected, and, ironically, the social commentary might not have come through. It is hard to speculate, however, on what could or could not have been done with the film. It is over and done with. I have now to think about my next film.

The problems of being young and in college, in a world of conflict and uncertainty, have been used by film makers as fit subjects for study. Often these films are quite successful, more successful in their own genre than, for instance, Mike Nichol's study of post-college traumas, *The Graduate.* Another Boston University graduate student who has taken a somewhat satirical look at the best of times and the worst of times is John Surowiecki, who has completed his master's thesis film, *The Physical.*

When this writer interviewed Surowiecki in June of 1969, he had only one-quarter of the film completed. He explained then: "I graduated from the University of Connecticut in June of 1966, with a major in English. I then began graduate work in film at the Boston University in September of 1966. My thesis proposal for *The Physical* was accepted in June of 1968. I had problems with the film beginning at about that point. I ran out of money and had to drop out of school for a while and, at the same time, one of my main characters, a student who was to play all the various F.B.I. agents, was busted (arrested) on a narcotics charge. I worked at various jobs, the latest as a writer and researcher for the Smithsonian Institution's Astro-Physical Observatory and will return to Boston University in the fall of 1969. I hope to complete *The Physical* and graduate sometime in 1970 or 1971. I have the film to complete and ten credit hours of classes to take for the degree."

One of Surowiecki's earlier films, *Candy,* shared the first prize in the Brown University Film Festival in 1966. *Candy* was based on the Terry Southern-Mason Hoffenberg sex novel of the same name, although Surowiecki changed the focus of the plot; instead of centering on the heroine of the book, a nubile and all-too-eager teenager, Surowiecki centered his film on the character of the retarded hunchback, who appears for a brief time toward the end of the book.

In *The Physical,* Surowiecki mirrors the bathos that all students feel when they face that most ignominious of ordeals, the Selective Service physical exam.

THE PHYSICAL

by John Surowiecki

TYPE	VISUALS	DIALOGUE	SOUND
SCENE I:	INTRODUCTION		
Titles	——	——	——
#1–6: l.s.	Factories at dawn.	"	piano music
#7: l.s.	Group of men coming out of factory. AL DUCK is among them. Slow zoom to AL.	"	
#8: m.s.	AL walking (front). Cam. handheld.	"	
#9: l.s.	AL walks l. to r.	"	
#10: xls	Street: AL goes into one of the houses.	"	
#11: m.s.	House door: AL opens it; walks in.	AL: (*inside*) Hi mom. I'm home.	fade to nature
#12: c.u.	MOM: camera follows her in profile; she meets and kisses AL.	AL: (*kisses* MOM) I'm hungry.	

Shot	Video	Audio	Music
#13: l.s.	AL sits down at table and reads newspaper. MOM gives him breakfast.	MOM: Listen AL, I got something in the mail yesterday.	
		AL: Yeah? Who's it from.	
#14: c.u.	MOM: worried.	MOM: The government.	
#15: m.s.	Cam. on table; MOM to AL's left. AL takes letter and reads it.	AL: Let me see. (*reads*) It's from the Army.	
#16: c.u.	MOM: worried.	——	
#17: c.u.	AL: confident	AL: (*looks at* MOM) Aw mom, you don't have to worry. They're not going to take me. I've got a hernia, remember?	
#18: c.u.	MOM: worried	——	natural
#19: c.u.	AL: slightly less confident.	——	

SCENE II: FIRST SERGEANT

Shot	Video	Audio	Music
#20: l.s.	AL: walking up a driveway to a large Gothic building; he goes inside.	——	piano

Shot	Visual	Sound
#21: mls	Inside: from above (stairs in back of Sgt's desk). AL stops in front of Sgt's desk.	AL: (*cheerful*) Good natural morning. SGT: (*gruff*) Get in line. (*belches*)
#22: mcu	SGT: desk in foreground.	AL: But there's no one here. SGT: No back talk. Just get in line.
#23: mcu	AL: shrugs, moves back a step.	SGT: You got a pencil? AL: Yeah, I think so (*fumbles for a pencil, produces one*). SGT: Fill this out. (AL *gets paper*).
#24: xls	From above: AL writes leaning over desk.	——
#25: c.u.	SGT.	SGT: Your name Al Duck? AL: That's right. SGT: (*gives paper back to* AL) Do it again. We don't take nicknames here. AL: But it isn't a nickname. SGT: Al's not a nickname?

Shot	Camera	Dialogue	Sound
		AL: It's my real name, what can I say?	
		SGT: It's your real name?	
#26: c.u.	AL: confused	AL: Yeah.	
#27: c.u.	SGT: cool	SGT: No. (*pause*) Your name is Albert. (*writes on paper*) A-l-b-u-r-t.	
#28: mcu	AL: SGT in foregr'nd, AL resigns himself	AL: Wha? (*he shrugs*)	natural
#29: scu	SGT.	SGT: Albert Duck, 10 Westmoreland Drive, Hershey, Pa. Hgt.: 6 ft. Wgt.: 172 lbs. Have you ever been arrested?	
	pan to AL in focus	AL: Not yet (*laughs, then stops quickly*).	
		SGT: Have you ever had psychiatric help, syphillus, yaws, dyspepsia, emphysema, the mange, ricketts, cancer, suicidal tendencies, polio, tuberculosis, diphtheria, typhoid, beriberi, heart disease, acne, or any ailment of the upper, lower or middle tracts?	
		AL: No, but I do have a hernia.	

#30:			
c.u.	SGT: frustrated	SGT: Now did I ask you that? You're okay. Follow the white line to your next station. (*stamps paper and gives it to* AL. . .)	
#31:			
l.s.	AL: from above, he walks up stairs following white line.	——	piano
#32:			
l.s.	White line out of focus in f-gr'nd. Camera on floor, Al walks toward camera.	——	

SCENE III: THE URINE DOCTOR

#33:			
m.s.	AL enters room. Cam. follows him as he walks to table of Urine Doctor who is talking to an armless man.	U.DR.: (*to armless man*) You're okay, go to the next station.	natural
#34:			
m.s.	From in back of U.D. AL and armless man exchange greetings.	MAN: Hi. AL: Hi.	
#35:			
c.u.	U.D. camera pans to AL and changes focus as AL leaves the room.	U.D.: Good afternoon. I am the urine doctor. Will you please fill this bottle? (*hands* AL *qt. jar*) You may go outside for privacy.	natural

Shot	Description	Dialogue
#36: l.s.	Outside: zoom to AL's face.	—
#37: mls	A group of girls posing for a photographer (Pepsi advertisement)	—
#38: m.s.	Inside: AL enters.	AL: I can't go out there. There are girls out there. U.D.: You a trouble-maker or something? Get out there.
#39: l.s.	Outside: AL leaves building.	—
#40: m.s.	Girls, giggling, they are holding Pepsi bottles. Cam. pans to AL who is hiding behind a tree.	—
#41: c.u.	From below: qt. bottle . . . AL unzips pants.	—
#42: c.u.	AL (profile desperate.	AL: (*muttering*) Come on, Jesus . . . son of a . . . come out . . . Jeeeeesus.
#43: mls	From rear: girls move up to tree, photog. follows.	—

#44:			
xcu	Pepsi bottle: girls harassing AL in background.	——	
#45:			
xcu	Pepsi bottle: AL runs away from girls, picks up Pepsi bottle.	——	
#46:			
m.s.	AL picks up bottle pours Pepsi into qt. bottle. Girls come toward him from rear. He rushes into building, camera follows.	——	natural
#47:			
mls	Inside: AL enters, camera pans quickly to U.D. who is talking to a pregnant woman.	——	
#48:			
m.s.	AL: puts dirt from plant into qt. bottle.	——	
#49:			
m.s.	From behind U.D., woman leaves, AL takes her place before desk, gives U.D. qt. bottle.	——	
#50:			
c.u.	U.D. (profile) holds qt. bottle up to light.	AL: You're not *really* going to draft that lady, are you? U.D.: Of course not, we want the child. AL: But what if it's a girl?	

Shot	Visual	Dialogue	Sound
		U.D.: (*casually*) We send it to Sweden. (*refers to qt. bottle*) Have you been eating right?	
#51: mls	AL & U.D. at desk.	AL: It could be my hernia. U.D.: You have a hernia? AL: Yes, and it hurts.	
#52: c.u.	AL.	U.D.: Really? That's quite interesting. The lady before you has a hernia . . . You're not pregnant, are you? AL: No. (*offended*)	
#53: m.s.	U.D. tests urine with chemicals.	U.D.: Hmmm that's good. (*more official*) Although you seem to be slightly diabetic, you pass. Go to your next station. (*stamps paper*)	
#54: c.u.	AL staring dumbly.	—	
#55: c.u.	white line . . . camera follows it up stairs.		piano
#56: l.s.	From above, AL following white line.	—	piano

Shot	Picture	Sound
#57: mls	Cam. on top of stairs AL walks up following white line.	——

SCENE IV: THE MENTAL TEST

Shot	Picture	Sound
#58: xcu	Mental Tester's face	M.T.: We're gonna natural take a mental test ta see if youz are fit for da army.
#59: l.s.	AL sits among testees, others include women and children. Pan.	M.T.: Is dare anyone here who don't understand American? (*everyone shakes head no*) Good. You got 20 minutes . . .
#60: m.s.	M.T. passes tests out	M.T.: . . . to answer the questions although you can finish quicker if you want.
#61: c.u.	AL gets test	AL: (*thinking*) SECTION A, VOCABULARY. LET'S SEE. THE KNIFE.
#62: m.s.	AL holding knife.	CUTS THE . . .
#63: m.s.	AL cuts house with knife	HOUSE? . . .
#64: mcu	AL holding dog & knife	THE DOG? . . .

Shot	Video	Audio	
#65: m.s.	AL cutting bread	THE BREAD?	
#66: c.u.	AL in reality (profile)	AL: (*ponders*) MUST BE THE HOUSE. (*writes on test paper*). NUMBER TWO: THE MAN . . . READS THE . . .	
#67: m.s.	AL in easy chair (pipe etc.) reading knife	THE KNIFE.	
#68: m.s.	AL as student reading cabbage	THE CABBAGE?	
#69: mcu	AL reading book upside down	THE BOOK?	
#70: c.u.	AL in reality	AL: (*ponders*) MUST BE THE CABBAGE. (*writes on paper*) NUMBER 3: THE DOG RUNS, IGNITES, DEDUCTS . . . WHAT IS THIS (*fills in other answers without thinking about them*) SECTION B: SPATIAL RELATIONS. LET'S SEE. THIS CONSTRUCTION . . .	natural
#71: m.s.	AL in front of table holding a cardboard cube (black). AL moves along table to diagram of a pyramid. To a diagram of	IS THE SAME AS THIS DIAGRAM?	

	a pentagram. To a diagram of a solid oblong.	THIS DIAGRAM?
	He looks at oblong diagram, ducks under table, comes up with a globe, shakes head no. Does same for other 2: 2nd diagram he comes up with a complex solid figure, the last with a statue of an ape.	OR THIS DIAGRAM?
#72:		
c.u.	AL in reality.	AL: WHAT KINDA GARBAGE IS THIS? (*fills out entire test.*) M.T.: (AL *looks up*) *I* know it ain't 20 minutes yet . . .
#73:		
mcu	M.T.	M.T.: . . . but is anyone finished with the test?
#74:		
mls	Fast motion: group raises hands	——
#75:		
m.s.	M.T. (profile): gets up and collects papers. Stops at one boy.	M.T.: Hey, what's da matter, you didn't fill in nuthin? BOY: No speak English. M.T.: Stupid bastard, didn't I ask if anybody spoke American? BOY: No speak.

		M.T.: Damn Italians.	
#76: c.u.	From below: M.T. turns to camera (AL).	M.T.: And YOU. I saw the way you took that test. You tryin to be cute, buddy?	natural
#77: c.u.	AL: Mouth open, shakes head no.	M.T.: If you're smart enough to play stupid, you're smart enough to pass this test. Here, wise guy, (*hands* AL *test*) perfect score.	

SCENE V: MUSIC

#78: mls	From white line to AL walking into room.	——	piano
#79: m.s.	AL and eye doctor . . . pan to wall with a huge letter E, the eye test, AL passes.	——	
#80: c.u. l.s.	AL ascends narrow staircase, cut intermittently to tower (pan up) from outside.	——	
#81: m.s.	AL in Psychiatrist's office. He lies down on couch. Psych. reaches for his leg, AL leaves.	——	

Shot	Action	Sound
#82:		
c.u. l.s.	reverse of #80, AL descends staircase.	—
#82:		
c.u.	AL, hand with bell ringing in his ear, feigns deafness. Hand snaps fingers in AL's ear: AL hears nothing. Gun is placed near AL's ear, AL no longer feigns deafness.	—
#83:		
mcu	White line ends at wall, bumps into the wall.	—
#84:		
c.u.	A kitchen: cook hands out slop to AL. Cook is smoking, ash falls into food. Cam. pans to AL who looks sick.	—
#85:		
mcu	AL's legs from knees down; his pants are at his feet.	VOICE: O.K. Cough. (AL *coughs*) V.: Cough again. (AL *does*) Does it hurt when you cough? AL: Sure it does, I have a hernia. V.: You do? Well then go immediately to Hernia Headquarters and Information Center.
		natural

SCENE VI: THE ARMLESS MAN

Shot	Action	Dialogue
#86: l.s.	A park: AL walks and sits down on a park bench next to armless man.	—
#87: c.u.	AL: looks over to A.M. Cam. shifts to A.M.	AL: Hi. A.M.: Hi.
#88: l.s.	Both on bench.	—
#89: xls	Bench, corner of screen.	—
#90: m.s.	AL and A.M.	AL: (*blurts out*) Say, are you taking your physical for the draft? A.M.: Yes, aren't you? AL: Yeah, I'm going to the Hernia Building right now. They'll let me go. (*pause*) Say, they aren't going to accept you, are they? A.M.: Hell no (AL *sighs in relief*), I've got something wrong with my ears (AL *looks worried again*). AL: Oh.
#91: l.s.	Bench.	

Shot	Picture	Dialogue	
#92: xls	Bench.		
#93: c.u.	AL.	AL: Say I hate to sound crude or anything, but why didn't they reject you because of your arms?	
		A.M.: Because they don't have doctor who checks arms.	
	Pan to A.M.	AL: They don't?	
		A.M.: I think they used to, but he died.	
		AL: Oh.	natural
#94: l.s.	Bench from passing car.	——	
#95: xcu	Flower, bench out of focus.	——	
#96: m.s.	Profile: both men.	AL: What's wrong with your ears?	
		A.M.: (*pause, A.M. looks at* AL) I don't know.	
#97: l.s.	AL leaves, waves goodbye.	——	

SCENE VII: HERNIA BUILDING

#98:

m.s.	Film projector out of focus, seats in f-gr'nd. AL sits down.	VOICE: All those with hernia problems raise their hands. (AL *does*) O.K. Good. First we'll see a short film on the various types of hernia treatments just to get
	Lights out projector on.	you familiar. Lights out please.

HERNIA TREATMENT FILM: OPENS WITH TITLE: U.S. ARMY HERNIA TREATMENT. IN IT, A DOCTOR WILL DEMONSTRATE FOUR KINDS OF TREATMENTS UTILIZING A PAIR OF IRON CLAWS (USED TO STOKE FIREPLACES) AND INVISIBLE TESTICLES. NARRATOR WILL DESCRIBE THE TECHNIQUES (E. G. OVER AND UNDER TECHNIQUE, SNOWBALL TECHNIQUE, ETC.) OVER BEETHOVEN'S FIFTH SYMPHONY.

#99:

m.s.	Film ends, AL in dark, lights go on.	VOICE: O.K. will those people with hernias
	Everyone except AL runs out of room.	please line up in the back of the room.

#100:

c.u.	profile of hernia dr., he walks toward AL. Pan goes past H.D. to c.u. of AL.	H.D.: Well, I guess you're the only one here.
		AL: (*wary*) Yeah, I guess so.
		H.D.: Well we can begin your treatment now and you'll be ready for the Army in no time.
		AL: Ready for the army?

Shot	Picture		Dialogue	Sound
#101:				
c.u.	H.D.		H.D.: Sure you'll be fit as a fiddle by this afternoon.	
#102:				
c.u.	AL		AL: You mean my hernia won't keep me out of . . .	
#103:				
c.u.	H.D.		H.D.: Keep you out? Hell no, there isn't a hernia alive we can't cure (*chuckles*) Well, shall we go, the sooner the better.	natural
#104:				
m.s.	Profile: AL backs away, bumps into chair, leaves room, running. H.D. follows to doorway, goes to phone.		——	piano
#105-#116:	AL ESCAPING, BEING CHASED BY F.B.I. (2).			

SCENE VIII: THE ALLEY

Shot	Picture		Dialogue	Sound
#117:				
l.s.	An alley, AL runs in.		——	natural
#118:				
m.s.	From above: he looks around corner of alley.		"	
#119:				
c.u.	AL looks around corner of building (full face).		"	

Shot	Description	
#120: mls	FBI #1 climbing fence.	"
#121: c.u.	same as #119	"
#122: l.s.	From above: AL runs down length of alley to find it boarded up on other side.	"
#123: c.u.	AL: through fence, He peeks out, then pulls face back.	"
#124: mls	FBI #2 through fence.	"
#125: l.s.	Same as #122, but in other direction.	"
#126: mls	From above: AL huddles in alley. Lights cigarette.	"
#127: c.u.	From in back of AL (cam . . . h-held) he moves out from corner of building, FBI #1 is crouched right in front of AL. FBI is startled, shoots AL in face. AL staggers (he is on his knees) and places his left hand to his face (his right, with cigarette, is holding on to building for support).	"

Shot	Action	Dialogue	Sound
#128: xcu	Cigarette: as AL collapses his hand falls to his side, cigarette falls into pocket which holds his draft papers.	——	natural
#129: mcu	From in back of FBI #1, AL places other hand over his face . . . he crawls back on his knees, collapses in kneeling position.	——	
#130: l.s.	AL in kneeling collapse, smoke is rising from his pocket.	——	
#131: c.u.	FBI #1: scared. Blows whistle. Blows again.		
#132: xcu	Pocket: smoke pouring out	——	piano
#133: l.s.	AL: smoke rising.	——	
#134: mls	FBI #2 running toward cam.	——	
#135: mcu	FBI #1 gets up and runs, cam. follows . . . both meet, #1 points toward alley.		

Shot	Visual	Dialogue	Sound
#136: l.s.	Alley: smoke over top.	——	
#137:- #140:	Shots of AL in flames.		
#141: l.s.	Ground level: FBI men run toward alley.	——	
#142: m.s.	From above: Charred corpse in Buddha position: FBI men standing over it: #2 bends down and picks up a card, after fire is put out.	FBI #2: Look at this. The only thing that wasn't burned: his draft card.	natural
#143: c.u.	FBI #1: silent.	——	
		#2: What happened here, anyway?	
		#1: Nothing. He was trying to get away and I shot him.	
#144: m.s.	AL's corpse.	*#2:* Well, at least we know it's Al Duck.	
		#1: So, what are we going to do?	
		#2: What can we do? We have to bring him back. We have to bring something back.	natural

Shot	Description	Dialogue	Music
#145: l.s.	From above: #2 picks up corpse, carries it away.	none	piano
#146: l.s.	FBI men walk up driveway to Gothic building.		
#147: mls	Through partially closed doors, FBI men holding corpse, talk with officer.		
#148: c.u.	Outside: AL's corpse, men carry it to car, and inside car, they drive away.		
#149: l.s.	Car on highway.		
#150: m.s.	A table in an open field.		

SCENE IX: THE EXECUTION

Shot	Description	Dialogue	Music
#151: c.u.	Officer (in #147) stern.		
#152: m.s.	Table: corpse is placed on table by FBI #1.		
#153: c.u.	Officer nods yes.		

#154: m.s.	#1 takes hanky and ties it around where AL's eyes would have been.		
#155: l.s.	Profile: table, pan to firing squad, officer and FBI #2.		
#156: c.u.	Officer nods.		
#157: c.u.	FBI #1 makes sour face.		
#158: c.u.	Officer: stern face.		
#159: m.s.	FBI #1 complies: walks toward table (cam. follows) and offers corpse a cigarette; he then turns to Officer and shakes his head no.	——	piano
#160: c.u.	Officer smiling . . . pan of firing squad.	——	
#161: xls	Entire scene. From above.	——	
#162: mcu	Corpse.	——	
#163: xls	Entire scene. from above.	OFF.: READY	natural

Shot	Description	Sound
#164: m.s.	Profile: firing squad. FBI #1 joins others.	——
#165: l.z.	Entire scene.	——
#166: c.u.	Corpse.	——
#167: xls	Entire scene. From above.	OFF.: AIM. . . .
#168: c.u.	FBI #1: nervous.	——
#169: l.s.	Entire scene.	——
#170: m.s.	AL.	——
#171: c.u.	Pan of firing squad, rifles aimed.	——
#172: c.u.	Officer, smiles	——
#173: xls	From above: entire scene.	OFF.: . . . FIRE . . .

TITLE: THE END — silence

BOSTON UNIVERSITY, 1968 ——

A thesis film much different than any other produced recently is Tom Roberts's *The Anniversary Special,* completed in the late summer of 1969. Roberts, who received his bachelor's degree in the classics from Holy Cross College in 1966, frankly admits that he enjoys writing musical comedies, an admission that might be greeted with less than complete enthusiasm at some other film

Tom Lane appears as Warren Oak in *The Anniversary Special.* Lane here reads *The New York Times* during a break in the filming.

schools. *The Anniversary Special* was filmed from April to July of 1968, and re-takes of some scenes were completed during the summer of 1969. Roberts shot 12,000 feet of film with a Bolex camera and a modified Oricon, and edited that footage to a completed 58-minute film of approximately 2,000 feet.

As Roberts noted, "I planned *The Anniversary Special* as en-

Mary Dale Foley is Frankie Randall in *The Anniversary Special* by Tom Roberts.

tertainment. I like making entertaining films. I think that *The Anniversary Special* is very Antonioni-esque, although some scenes or sequences may not be handled as well as possible. I see my films as entertaining, but not superficial; light films that don't bludgeon the viewer with a message. It might sound frivolous, but I like to make films that make audiences smile."

Tom Roberts sets up a shot during the filming of his *The Anniversary Special.*

Roberts, like Surowiecki, delights in bits of wry humor; Surowiecki in his view of the draft, Roberts in his view of college life in general and classroom techniques in particular, "On Monday, we'll take up gonorrhea." His Self Basting Turkey might well be a cross between some of the typical psychedelic lyrics of the 1960s and the nonsense song, "The Lobster Quadrille," from Carroll's *Alice's Adventures In Wonderland.*

James Kocot is Roger Shetland in *The Anniversary Special.*

(*The Anniversary Special*—script and dialogue—is printed in full at the end of this chapter.)

The student films from Boston University don't generally receive the recognition that similar films do at other schools, like U.S.C. or U.C.L.A. The Boston administration does not encour-

Tom Lane appears as Warren Oak and Ann Marie Shea is Doris Phelps in Tom Roberts' *The Anniversary Special.*

age "playing the (film) festival game," as one graduate student phrased it. Although Boston University is generally regarded as one of the best schools in the country for film, film publicity that comes from there is apt to be minimal.

Robert S. Steele, associate professor of film at B.U., was quoted in the October 28, 1968 *Boston Evening Globe* (in an article "Hub Reels as Film Makers 'Do Their Thing' ") as saying that 64 percent of film-goers are under 25 years old and many of them are disenchanted with television. "They reject television as a crass, materialistic, controlled medium. Of course, film today is vogueish. It is the thing to be in or doing."

"Really, I think that many of these young film-makers and students lack maturity and discipline. Many of them are not well read enough to be English majors and others, for instance, do not want to spend the time studying in a scientific course. Film looks like an easy thing and I am sure that lethargy and indolence brings a lot of them into film-making."

But, he added, there is no question of the sincerity and the total devotion to film of many of his students.

THE ANNIVERSARY SPECIAL*

by Tom Roberts

CHARACTERS

Doris Phelps
Scott Landau
Hilary Weinberg
Roger Shetland
Warren Oak
Tony Azalea
Frankie Randall
Angela LaFleur
Evelyn Langtree
The Self Basting Turkey
Hamburg
Mr. Langtree
Polycarp
Priest
Student
The Man
His Mother
Thomas Aquinas

INTERIOR, DAY

1. CU Doris Phelps and Scott Landau kiss.	*Sync sound:* *Heavy Breathing.*
	A bell rings.
They part. Zoom out to show that they are at the head of a crowded classroom. She arranges her hair and her suit. Scott passes blackboard on which is written:	*Sync sound:* DORIS: Thank you, Scott.

COMMUNICABLE
DISEASES
measles
mumps
mononucleosis

Doris speaks to the class. Hilary Weinberg crosses frame, carrying Doris' coat. Track down front row of desks, pan to Roger Shetland and Warren Oak, seated in second row.	DORIS: On Monday, we'll take up gonorrhea.
	ROGERS You gotta admit, she tries to make geography interesting.
	WARREN: Especially if you're Scott Almighty.

EXTERIOR, DAY

2. LS Scott exits classroom building and goes off left. Other students follow him, including Warren and Roger, who approach to MS. Roger is in the midst of talking.	*Sync sound:*
	ROGER: . . . not let her catch you asleep again. She didn't like it.
	WARREN: Who could care about Mozambique? Let's wait for Hilary.

ROGER: No. I gotta go to musicology.

Freeze frame

The opening two bars of Beethoven's Fifth Symphony.

The action resumes. Pan with Roger as he walks left. Stop pan, Roger exits frame, zoom in and pull focus to MS Scott talking with Tony Azalea. Scott smiles from one side of his mouth.

ROGER: See you.

3. MCU Warren attempts the same smile. Hilary enters the frame in profile. Warren stops trying. They exit frame.

Sync sound:
HILARY: Who are you now, John Garfield?

4. ELS from the end of the road on which the students are walking. As they approach the camera, they are in the order of their departure from the setting of shots 2 and 3: Roger, Scott and Tony, Warren and Hilary, and Doris.

Voice over:
BANJO SINGER (*sings*):
Oh, the Yale College chaplain
Is preaching sacret smut.
H. L. Hunt should put a stop
To this rebellion, but
Everyone is waiting for,
Dating for,
Mating for,
Baccalaureating for the
Anniversary Special.

Titles are supered.

Smoking marijuana's
Become the public craze.
LSD is tasteless, though.
I'd sooner mayonnaise.
Everyone is waiting for,
Dating for,
Mating for,
Inarticulating for the
Anniversary Special.

Bargain rates requested
Are fully in effect.
Bishop Pike is threatening
To found another sect.
Everyone is waiting for,
Dating for,
Mating for,
Undenominating for the
Anniversary Special.

Scott exits frame left. Warren and Hilary approach to two shot. Hilary watches Scott. He nudges Warren and they both look off in the same direction.

H. Rap Brown's decided
To lay siege to New York.
Kennedy wants Westchester
To change its name to Cork
Everyone is waiting for,
Dating for,
Mating for,
Insubordinating for,
Catherine the Greating for
Nova Scotiating for
The Anniversary Special.

5. Zoom in as Scott and Frankie Randall (a girl) run into an embrace at 32 f.p.s.

Voice over:
HILARY: That's vulgar.

6. CU Doris Phelps looks angry.

7. CU Warren looks on vacantly.

Voice over:
DORIS: Warren . . .

EXTERIOR, DAY

8. CU Scott and Frankie. Scott pulls on a lacrosse helmet, turns and runs out of focus.

Voice over:
DORIS: . . . Warren Oak.

WARREN: Yes. Would you repeat the question.

9. LS, hand held, lacrosse game.

DORIS: Some environmental aspects of Mozambique.

10. CU Frankie

11. CU Warren

WARREN: Very nice . . . time of year . . . the rain on the rhubarb . . . natives celebrate . . .

12. CU Frankie	Saturnalia . . . capital Mescaline thronged . . . merchants . . .
13. LS, hand held, lacrosse game	hemp . . . or . . . vanilla . . . or . . .
14. CU Frankie	
15. CU Warren	
16. CU Frankie	(*Hilary begins to speak over shot 16, then continues, in sync, with his own appearance in shot 17.*)
	Sync sound:
INTERIOR, DAY	
	HILARY: I had never before seen anyone literally asleep on his feet. At first I thought you might be doing a Sandy Dennis, but I wondered . . .
17. MS Hilary crosses the room that he and Warren share. He stops at his desk and pours sherry from a decanter into a small glass. He holds out the glass. Pan left with his arm to Warren, asleep on his bed.	HILARY: Sherry?
Dissolve to	
EXTERIOR, DAY	
18. High Angle LS Warren runs along railroad track toward camera.	
(Shots 19 through 26 are supered over shot 18.)	
Fade in	
19. MCU Frankie, zoom out to show her sitting in a tree.	(*Soprano sings for the duration of shots 18 through 26.*)
20. Low Angle MS Roger slides frontwards down a bannister.	*Voice over*: SOPPRANO:

21. MS, eight frames, Warren has his hand on Angela Lafleur's shoulder.

Girl walking slow says hello
It's beautiful this time of year
Caressing my cheek is her tear
She can't hear, but she must know

22. LS Hilary skateboards from left to right.

Dissolve to

23. LS Frankie runs down wide stone steps from right to left.

24. MS, eight frames, Warren has his hand on Angela's shoulder.

25. MS Doris in profile. She drops her shoulder strap.

26. Low angle zoom into Frankie walking across an old bridge.

Shot 18 fades out.

Shot 26 dissolves to

(The rhythm becomes more staccato. A male chorus takes over for the duration of shots 27 through 32.)

27. MS Warren's hand begins on Angela's shoulder and slowly moves down her arm.

(Shots 28 through 31 are supered over shot 27.)

Voice over:
MALE CHORUS:
The shattered glass
The green boy sitting mute
The weed of crime bears bitter fruit
Fruit doesn't pay

28. LS pan industrial type setting to sudden CU Warren looking into camera.

29. CU Scott, tilt up as he chins himself on a tree limb.

30. MCU Tony bites a cork from a bottle and drinks.

31. CU Warren with a cigarette, zoom out to billboard he leans on.

    Shot 27 fades out.

    Shot 31 dissolves to

32. High angle zoom out and tilt up to Warren running away down the railroad tracks.

    Dissolve to

(The softer music returns and the Soprano continues from shot 33 through shot 42.)

33. Low angle MCU Frankie with her hair blowing in slow motion.

    (Shots 34 through 41 are supered over shot 33.)

    Fade in

Voice over:

SOPRANO:

Flowers can't see the way she
Floats like my sleep about her hair

34. High angle MS Warren and Frankie lie head to head across the frame.

SOPRANO:

She speaks about the flower I wear
Keep my prayer from being free

35. LS eight frames of shot 5, Scott and Frankie run into an embrace.

36. LS Warren swings around a pole to the left.

37. LS Frankie swings around the same pole to the right.

38. LS Warren swings around the pole to the left.

39. LS Frankie swings around the pole to the right.

    (Shots 36 through 39 are each 24 frames long.)

40. CU Frankie in profile. Pan across white background to CU Warren facing her in profile.

41. LS eight frames of shot 5. Scott and Frankie run into an embrace.

(Shot 33 fades out.)

42. MS Warren kisses Angela. They exit frame left.

43. MS Warren kisses Frankie. They exit frame right. Scott enters from the left and snarls into camera.

(*Male chorus returns through shot 50.*)

44. MCU Warren backed against a brick wall. He is frightened.

Voice over:
MALE CHORUS:
She spits up blood
No arm he can't salute
The weed of crime bears bitter
fruit . . .

45. Swish pan circle of angry faces.

46. MS Tony steps in from right frame and snarls.

47. CU Warren against brick wall.

48. Swish pan angry faces.

49. ECU Warren against brick wall.

(*Roger interrupts the chorus to wake Warren.*)

50. Swish pan angry faces.

Voice over:
ROGER: Warren.

INTERIOR, EVENING

51. MS Warren sits up into the frame. He is just wak-

ing up. Pan to Roger in the open door.	*Sync sound*: ROGER: Evelyn's downstairs. *Voice over*: WARREN: Okay.
INTERIOR, NIGHT	
52. MCU Evelyn Langtree waits for Warren. Zoom out to LS. She looks at her watch. Warren charges in and sits next to her.	*Sync sound.* WARREN: Ev, I'm late . . . EVELYN: Hello, Warren Oak. WARREN: . . . and I'm sorry, but . . . EVELYN: You're late. WARREN: I'll make up for it. How's your mother? EVELYN: How late does the dance go? Oh, she's fine. WARREN: Till one. I'm glad of that.
53. MCU Evelyn	EVELYN: You mean that, Warren Oak?
54. LS Evelyn reaches for Warren's hand. Evelyn drops Warren's hand.	WARREN: Mean what, Ev? Your mother . . . ? You know what you mean to me, Ev.
55. ECU Warren's eyes.	
56. ECU Evelyn's eyes.	
57. ECU Warren's mouth.	
58. ECU Evelyn's mouth, slightly ajar.	

59. ECU Warren's mouth, slightly ajar.

60. ECU Evelyn's eyes closing.

61. ECU Warren's fingers stroke Evelyn's fingers

Voice over:
One strum of an electric guitar.

INTERIOR, NIGHT

62. CU Hand strums electric guitar.

Post sync:
Another strum of electric guitar.

63. LS The Self Basting Turkey begin to sing on a small stage. Couples dance in front of them.

(Shots 64 through 74 will be taken in documentary style at a staged dance, and so the description here is only cursory and included merely for basic visual continuity in this script.)

Voice over:
THE SELF BASTING TURKEY:
Groovy Eskimo lady,
What makes you so blue?
Is it just a disguise
When you lower your eyes to look at your shoe? Yeah
Could it be you're just getting cold?
Groovy Eskimo lady,
What's gone wrong with you

64. Scott and Frankie dance.

65. Roger and Marjorie Hamilton dance.

66. The Turkey sings.

Groovy is what you are,
My groovy movie star.
Eskimo you turn me on
Apropos sine qua non.
You turn me on.

67. Warren and Evelyn dance.

68. Another couple dances.

69. Hilary sips sherry on the sidelines with an elaborately coiffed post-deb.

70. Hamburg and Susan Darwin dance.

Groovy Eskimo lady,
Are they prejudiced
'Cause they say there's no space
When they look at your face?
Can't we all coexist? Yeah

71. The Turkey sings.	There are things we've always been told.
72. Warren and Evelyn dance.	Groovy Eskimo lady, Doesn't that get you
73. Scott and Frankie dance.	pissed?
74. The Turkey plays on its stage as couples dance in front.	Groovy is what you are, My groovy movie star. Cold weather solidify My groovy Eskimo pie Solidify Groovy Eskimo lady Groovy Eskimo lady Groovy Eskimo lady Groovy Eskimo lady
FADE OUT.	FADE OUT.
EXTERIOR, NIGHT	
75. LS Warren slams the door of his car and takes Evelyn up the path to her house. They go up the front stairs and out of camera view. This shot remains for several seconds.	*Wild sound:* *car door slams.* *Muffled voices* *Heavy breathing* *Evelyn sighs* *Warren moans*
76. MS Warren's feet and Evelyn's feet face each other. Tilt up slowly. Evelyn has her far hand on her hip. Her near hand is on Warren's shoulder. Warren is leaning slightly sideways to fit the key into the lock.	*An irregular clicking noise* (*These noises continue through shot 77.*)
77. MCU Warren tries to concentrate on the key, but he keeps looking back at Evelyn.	

78. LS The door flies open and Mr. Langtree stands in his pajamas, glaring at Warren. Evelyn looks at her father.

79. CU Evelyn's head turning to look at her father.

80. CU Mr. Langtree looks from Evelyn to Warren.

81. POV Warren looks up and smiles wanly.

82. MS Warren straightens up and faces Evelyn, who looks back at him.

Sync sound:
EVELYN: Good night, Warren Oak.

WARREN: Good night, Evelyn.

83. CU They shake hands.

EXTERIOR, NIGHT

84. CU Warren, through the windshield of his moving car. He is upset.

85. CU Warren through side window.

86. CU Warren from passenger side seat.

87. LS Warren's car goes around corner.

88. CU Warren through windshield.

89. LS sun rise, from inside car, through windshield, Warren's head in foreground.

Voice over:
WARREN: *(sings)*
Love is someplace I have never been
What's the matter with me
Always playing, but I never win.
What's the matter with me
Where is someone who'll take me to
A world where everything's right?
I am one of the chosen few
Who go to sleep every night
Alone, when I might
Do things that shocked me long ago.

90. LS In early morning light, Warren's car pulls into campus parking lot and turns into empty space. Warren gets out and trudges up stairs.	WARREN: What's the matter with me The matter with me? How the hell should I know *"What's the Matter with Me?" music continues.*
91. MS Warren reaches the top of the stairs and continues trudging. Camera tracks in front of him. Warren stops and looks up to his left.	*"What's the Matter with Me?" music crossfades into organ music.*
92. POV Zoom up to golden cross atop lofty chapel, just catching the sun's first rays.	
93. LS Warren in front of the chapel.	
94. CU Warren's upraised head. He looks just below the cross.	
95. POV Low angle MCU inscription on chapel frieze: INTROIBO AD ALTARE DEI	*Voice over:* WARREN: "Give me your tired . . ."
96. LS Warren climbs the chapel steps. Slow zoom in as he tries one side of double door. It is locked.	*Wild sound.*
97. CU Warren is desperate.	
98. MS Warren grabs the other handle and the door opens easily.	

99. CU Warren is a little disappointed.

INTERIOR, DAY

100. LS Warren enters the chapel and walks down the middle aisle. Pan with him as he walks. *The organ music continues*

101. CU statue of St. Joseph.

102. LS Warren walks down the middle aisle.

103. CU statue of Mary.

104. LS Warren walks down the middle aisle.

105. CU statue of St. Francis talking to the birds.

106. High angle LS from choir loft, Warren stops at the end of the aisle. He starts off to his right.

107. CU tabernacle

108. CU sanctuary lamp

109. LS from side of chapel, Warren approaches, looking up at something out of the frame. He stops right in front of it. He puts on his glasses to read inscription.

110. CU inscription:
SAINT POLYCARP
Patron Saint of Stevedores

111. CU Warren looks up, removing his glasses.	
112. Low angle POV statue of Polycarp.	
113. High angle MS Warren kneels at the altar rail and looks up at the statue.	
114. Low angle POV statue of Polycarp.	
115. High angle MS Warren looks up and pleads.	*Sync sound:* WARREN: Why?
He buries his head in his arms and begins to sob.	*Voice over:* POLYCARP: Why not?
Warren straightens up and looks around. Lastly, he looks up into the camera.	*Sync Sound:* WARREN: Was that you?
116. Low angle POV statue of Polycarp.	
117. High angle MS Warren shakes his head to clear it.	WARREN: I must need sleep
	POLYCARP: You need more than that.
Warren looks into the camera again.	
118. Low angle POV statue of Polycarp.	
Dissolve to	
119. Low angle POV Polycarp in the flesh and on the pedestal.	
120. MS from the side, Warren looks straight ahead and talks to himself. Polycarp appears in the frame, sits	*Sync sound:* WARREN: I'm having a vision. I'm having a vision. I wish I were dead. I'm having a vision.

on the altar rail and swings his feet onto Warren's side.	
121. MS reverse angle, Polycarp pulls Warren to his feet and holds him by the shoulder. Warren's mouth hangs open and he shakes wildly as Polycarp moves his shoulders for emphasis.	POLYCARP: Listen, Warren. We both just happened to be here at the same time. Understand? It's a coincidence. WARREN: It's a vision.
122. High angle LS from Choir loft Polycarp and Warren start up the middle aisle.	
123. CU statue of St. Francis	
124. CU statue of Mary	
125. CU statue of St. Joseph	
126. MS They stop in the middle aisle. Polycarp looks around. Warren tries to follow his gaze, but he is still stupefied.	POLYCARP: What a dump. Isn't there somewhere else we can go? WARREN: You're a vision and you've come to help me.
127. LS A priest darts out of the shadows into the sanctuary. He levels an accusing finger at the camera.	PRIEST: I know what you two are up to. Out of my church. Out.
128. MS Polycarp and Warren are turned to look at their accuser.	WARREN: It must be your clothes. POLYCARP: You know the old saying.
They both nod. They turn and start for the exit.	

EXTERIOR, DAY

129. CU inscription on gravestone: ORLANDO WHITNEY NORCROSS and his wife PHEBE ELLEN SIBLEY	*Voice over:* POLYCARP: Orlando Whitney Norcross. WARREN: And Phebe Ellen Sibley.
130. LS Warren is seated on a stone bench in the temple-like Norcross tomb. Polycarp leans against a pillar, looking out over the cemetery.	*Sync sound:* POLYCARP: Nice place. come here often? WARREN: Come here to dream. POLYCARP: Dream? Dream what? WARREN: Dream I'm someone else.
Polycarp points to the inscription.	POLYCARP: Like Orlando Whitney Norcross?
Warren laughs.	WARREN: No. POLYCARP: More like Scott Landau?
131. MCU Warren looks away. He is embarrassed. He steals a quick look at Polycarp.	WARREN: No.
132. POV Polycarp stares back at Warren.	
133. MCU Warren tries to change the subject to Polycarp's new costume. He looks back up to Polycarp. He laughs self-consciously. Warren begins to daydream.	WARREN: Never wear white socks with . . . Well, something like Scott. Scott Almighty.

134. MCU Polycarp tries to get Warren's wandering attention.	POLYCARP: Warren?
135. MS Warren does not hear Polycarp. He begins to live a daydream. His lips synchronize with the pre-recorded song.	*Voice over:* WARREN *(sings):* Suppose I were lifeguard In muscles attired,
EXTERIOR, DAY	
136. CU Warren in pith helmet, zoom out to him on lifeguard stand, wearing bathing suit and jersey labelled LIFEGUARD He no longer lip syncs the song	*Voice over:* WARREN: *(sings).* Who sat there on the beach just getting tanned.
137. High angle POV pan with two girls in bikinis walking along the edge of the water.	Wouldn't it be treat To date
138. CU Warren lowers one eyelid.	Bikinis,
139. LS pan with Frankie as she runs along the beach. She is also in a bikini. She reaches Warren, who is posing, flexing whatever bicep he manages to summon up.	Spending nights on beds of golden sand?
140. CU Frankie looks up admiringly. Then she looks straight ahead with horror.	And then I could be happy
141. POV zoom into Scott floundering in the water.	So handsome, admired,

142. LS Warren emerges from the water with Scott over his shoulder.	And everything I seem to prefer.
143. CU Warren. Frankie enters frame right and kisses his cheek.	One,
144. CU Warren. Frankie enters frame left and kisses his cheek.	two,
145. CU Warren lying down in profile, face up. Frankie enters frame top and kisses the visor of his helmet.	three —
146. MS Scott is being lowered from Warren's shoulder onto the sand. He enters from frame top, hits the sand and emits a spout of water from his mouth.	I'm popular.
EXTERIOR, DAY	
147. CU Warren, in the cemetery, his eyes closed. He lip syncs the words.	*Voice over:* WARREN *(sings):* If you see a
EXTERIOR, DAY	
148. CU inscription on jersey: LIFEGUARD Zoom out to show someone else wearing the jersey and pith helmet. This lifeguard looks more authentic than Warren. Pan and tilt down to Warren at the base of the stand. He is building a sand castle.	*Voice over:* WARREN *(sings)* Lifeguard Muscular and knife-scarred You can bet your B.V.D.'s That isn't me,

EXTERIOR, DAY

149. CU Warren, in the cemetery, he lips syncs the words.

Voice over:
WARREN *(sings):*
Even though I'd like to.

EXTERIOR, DAY

150. MS Warren in helmet and jersey pounds his chest with his fists.

EXTERIOR, DAY

151. MS Warren sitting on the stone bench in the Norcross tomb, lip syncs the words.

Voice over:
WARREN *(sings):*
But if I were a lifeguard

EXTERIOR, DAY

152. MS a more realistic Warren as lifeguard. He wears a heavy sweatshirt and his glasses. His arms are folded.

Voice over:
WARREN *(sings):*
I'd stand straight and watch hard

153. LS Warren patrols edge of water at left side of frame. Right side of frame shows many bathers wading into the water. One of the bather's feet go out from under him, and another grabs his foot in pain.

Lest undertow or sting rays occur.

EXTERIOR, DAY

154. MS Warren on the stone bench. Polycarp stands in profile behind him. Warren lip syncs the words.

Voice over:
WARREN *(sings):*
One, two, three — I'm popular.

155. MCU Polycarp in profile. Warren in background. Warren raises his head.	*Sync sound:* POLYCARP: Warren. Can you swim?
Pull focus to Warren. He shakes his head.	WARREN: No.
156. CU Warren has another idea. He lip syncs the words.	*Voice over:* WARREN *(sings)*: Suppose I were a gangster
EXTERIOR, DAY	
157. CU Warren, zoom out to two shot of him and Frankie. He is dressed in a suit and vest and he is wearing a hat. She is wearing a microdress and a beret. They both hold guns.	Who worked with a beauty
158. The rear wheel of a car peels out.	
159. LS Warren drives convertible away from camera. Frankie kneels in the back seat, shooting with both guns.	WARREN *(sings)*: The Ten Most Wanted's first most wanted team.
160. MS Bank teller puts money into paper bag held by Frankie. Zoom out to LS Warren, with a gun in his left hand, shakes hands with the frightened customers, one of whom is a flower-hatted Doris Phelps. Tony Azalea is dressed as a uniformed guard.	Holding up a bank, We'd thank our victims,
161. MS Warren approaches Doris and kisses her on	So they could hold us in high esteem.

the cheek. Doris faints and Tony catches her.	
162. LS hand-held camera follows Warren and Frankie as they leave the bank. They get into the same convertible as in shot 159 and drive away. On the back of the car is a large picture of each and a long sign saying: WE'RE NUMBER ONE	And since we'd be a legend We'd feel it our duty To save our reputation from slur.
163. LS The convertible speeds across the frame from right to left.	One,
164. LS The convertible speeds across the frame from left to right.	two,
165. High angle LS looking straight down onto the road. The convertible speeds from the top of the frame to the bottom of the frame.	three,
166. LS tracking from another car, through the convertible's windshield, Warren and Frankie laugh it up.	I'm popular.
167. LS The convertible speeds across the frame from right to left. When it has left, focus is on Roger dressed as a farmer in front of a store window. Window has many signs and some pictures in it. Roger looks after the car, zoom in to MCU Roger as he realizes who was in the	Everywhere our picture Makes the legend richer.

car and looks at the window.	
168. CU large photo of Warren and Frankie in store window. Tilt up past inscription above picture. WANTED DEAD OR ALIVE REWARD to Scott in cowboy hat and tin star — modern rural law enforcement.	Spite of him we still survive
EXTERIOR, DAY	
169. MCU Warren has his chin resting on his hand. He lip syncs the words.	*Voice over:* WARREN *(sings):* Dead or alive: That's the way they want
EXTERIOR, DAY	
170. LS six frames, Warren and Frankie sprawled on the ground.	
171. LS six frames, Warren and Frankie stand grinning.	
172. LS six frames, Warren and Frankie on the ground.	
173. LS six frames, Warren and Frankie stand grinning.	
174. LS six frames, Warren and Frankie on the ground.	
175. MS Scott, dressed as a sheriff, in profile behind a sparse bush. He levels his gun.	*Voice over:* WARREN *(sings):* and then without a warning

176. MCU twelve frames, Doris in flowery hat (cf. #161) averts her face.	We're shot
177. MCU twelve frames, Roger as a farmer (cf. #167) gapes.	down one
178. CU Scott's smoking gun exits frame bottom.	morning But
179. High angle CU Warren's dead hand, pan to Frankie's dead hand holding a flower.	even as our bones
180. CU Dirt hits a gravestone inscribed LOVE.	they inter

EXTERIOR, DAY

181. LS Warren, through two gravestones. He lip syncs the words.	*Voice over:* WARREN *(sings):* One,
182. MS Warren, from same position	two,
183. CU Warren, from same position.	three — I'm popular.
184. MS Polycarp leans against the pillar. He does not share Warren's enthusiasm.	*Sync sound:* POLYCARP: Kinda gruesome
185. MCU Warren in profile, Polycarp in soft focus. Warren nods affirmatively. Then he looks off in front of him. He lip syncs the words.	*Voice over:* WARREN *(sings):* Suppose I were a ski bum

EXTERIOR, DAY

186. CU Two skis, headed from right to left, edge to a stop and spray snow into the camera.	In Aspen
187. CU Two skis stop in the opposite direction.	or Chile.
188. ELS skiing slope crowded with people. Zoom into LS of Warren skiing down the hill perfectly.	I'd spend my days on skis my nights on gin.
189. MS Warren, in same outfit, slaps his skis together to clean them. When they are apart again, he looks directly into camera.	I could have affairs With pairs
190. POV zoom into MS Frankie, also in skiing clothes. She looks into camera and slowly pulls down the zipper of her parka.	of stretch pants, Zipping down those hills
191. MCU Warren slowly pulls off his ski hat.	like Erroll Flynn
192. CU girl in ski clothes	And every girl
193. CU girl in ski clothes.	will whisper
194. ECU Frankie smiles	"Oh, Warren,
195. POV skis moving along snow.	you thrill me.
196. MCU pan with Warren as he walks down a row of girls who are between him and camera.	And each one wants the next to be her.
197. MS Warren on a bench with his right arm around Frankie.	One,

198. MS same as above, now Angela sits to Warren's left. His left arm is around her.	two,
199. MS same as above, now Evelyn stands behind Warren with her head just above his. He looks up at Evelyn and then grins at camera.	three— I' popular.
200. POV skiing down a trail	Flying down a ski trail
201. CU Warren, moving.	Right beside.
202. POV skiing down a trail.	a female Is the plot
203. Fast zoom into tree trunk.	of all my dreams
204. CU Frankie closes her eyes	Somehow
205. LS Warren has come to a stop around a tree.	it seems
EXTERIOR, DAY	
206. MCU Warren in the cemetery, his chin in his hand. He lip syncs the words.	*Voice over:* WARREN *(sings):* That's the time I wake up
EXTERIOR, DAY	
207. LS Warren standing still on skis. He falls on his side.	
EXTERIOR, DAY	
208. MCU Warren at the front of the Norcross tomb. He lip syncs the words. Slow zoom out to LS. Polycarp is stretched out on the ground with his arms around Warren's ankles.	*Voice over:* WARREN *(sings):* I know I'm not a ski bum, A gangster, a lifeguard. But proudly I could say if I were, "One, two, three— I'm popular."

EXTERIOR, DAY	
209. Zoom out to ELS, low angle, Warren on mountainous rocks.	*Voice over:* WARREN *(sings):* In Colorado
EXTERIOR, DAY	
210. LS Warren stands on a gravestone. He lip syncs the word.	*Voice over:* WARREN *(sings):* Popular
EXTERIOR, DAY	
211. LS Warren dances with a whitehaired lady.	*Voice over:* WARREN *(sings):* With golden agers
EXTERIOR, DAY	
212. LS Warren sits atop a large marble sphere amid the graves. He lip syncs the word.	*Voice over:* WARREN *(sings):* Popular
EXTERIOR, DAY	
213. High angle ELS Warren stands in the middle of an excavated pit holding a ukelele.	*Voice over:* WARREN *(sings):* Like Arthur Godfrey
EXTERIOR, DAY	
214. MCU Warren, in profile, lying face up on the ground. He lip syncs the word. Zoom out to show him in the middle of the empty cemetery.	*Voice over:* WARREN *(sings):* Popular.
215. MCU Polycarp leans on a gravestone.	*Sync sound:* POLYCARP: That's what you really want? To be like Scott Landau?

216. LS Warren and Polycarp face each other. Warren is on the bench in the Norcross tomb, Polycarp leans on a grave opposite him.	WARREN: Scott Landau. It'd be a nice change. POLYCARP: It's a nice change to get away from that rat race. WARREN: Heaven? POLYCARP: You can have it. Do you know what it's like when everyone's perfect? After a couple of centuries, it begins to get to you. WARREN: How did you get down here?
Polycarp becomes wistful. He notices Warren's quizzical look.	POLYCARP: Today's my anniversary. It seems like yesterday . . . But it wasn't. It was eighteen hundred years ago that I worked my way into heaven. WARREN: How? POLYCARP: A Roman cookout.
Warren laughs.	WARREN: What do they serve at a Roman cookout? POLYCARP: That day they had one bishop, five virgins and me.
217. CU Warren is horrified.	WARREN: You mean . . .?
218. MS Polycarp stands up.	POLYCARP: Yeah. Wanna see my scars. No, forget it. That won't help.
219. ELS Polycarp starts off through the gravestones. Warren stands and follows him.	*Voice over:* WARREN: Nothing can help me. POLYCARP: Don't ever say that.

	WARREN: Can you make me like Scott?
	POLYCARP: Like Scott? I can turn you into Scott.
	WARREN: Oh, do it.
	POLYCARP: No, you're not ready for . . .
	WARREN: Please do it.
	POLYCARP: Only in cases of extreme hardship are miracles . . .
	WARREN: You've gotta do it.
Polycarp stops and turns to Warren.	POLYCARP: I don't have to do anything.
220. MCU Polycarp.	*Sync sound:* POLYCARP: Remember, I am a saint.
221. MS Two shot of Warren and Polycarp.	WARREN: You're no saint.
	POLYCARP: Don't ever say that.
	WARREN: What are you anyway?
	POLYCARP: Don't push me.
	WARREN: Saint. Huh.
222. ECU Polycarp closes his eyes and begins to mumble.	*Polycarp mumbles.*
223. LS Warren backs away from Polycarp.	*Polycarp mumbles.*

224. ECU Polycarp stops mumbling and his eyes open very wide.

225. LS Warren stands still. Dissolve to

226. LS Exactely the same shot except that Scott stands in Warren's place, in Warren's clothes.

(NOTE: At this point in the film, Warren Oak is changed into Scott Landau. The conditions of this change are that Warren achieves only the appearance of Scott, while he (Warren) retains his own personality. In the production of the film, this means that the actor who has played Scott as a somewhat unthinking hulk, begins now to portray Warren's attempt to imitate Scott, which is a very inadequate imitation. The person whom the audience has come to identify as Scott Landau now begins to act like Warren Oak. The name "Scott' in the script will indicate this character who has Scott's body but Warren's actions and reactions. The other characters, with the exception of Polycarp, continue to treat this new Scott as they did the old one.)

227. MS Polycarp is having second thoughts.	*sync sound:* POLYCARP: I hope I haven't gone too far.	
228. LS Scott notices that his arms are too long for the jacket. He looks at his hands. It is still Warren's voice. Scott lip syncs the words.	*Voice over:* WARREN: Scott? I'm Scott?	
229. MS Polycarp	*Sync sound:* POLYCARP: I've gone too far.	
230. ELS Polycarp and Scott each carries on a conversation with himself. Both of them are upset. They are both talking at once. It is still Warren's voice in Scott's body.	*Voice over:* POLYCARP: I never stop and think. All the time. You'd think I'd learn.	WARREN: Like a dream But it's true Still something I need. Bigger clothes.

	Probably over my quota. And trouble. I'm in big trouble. Now that he's Scott, what do I do with the other one? Shoulda stayed in heaven.	gotta get some of his clothes And the voice That's it. still need voice.

Shot	Sound
231. MS Polycarp continues his monologue. Scott, with Warren's voice, interrupts him from offscreen. Their lines overlap.	*Sync sound:* POLYCARP: What do I do with Scott? WARREN *(off):* I'm Scott. POLYCARP: Keep out of this. WARREN *(off):* But I still need the voice. You forgot the voice.
Polycarp confuses himself.	POLYCARP: Make Scott Warren. WARREN *(off):* I'm Warren. POLYCARP: That'll keep me safe for a while. WARREN *(off):* I want that voice.
Polycarp looks off at Scott.	POLYCARP: All right. Take the voice.
232. High angle MS pan across shallow water of a pond to reflection of Scott kneeling to look at himself. Tilt up to Scott. He notices a scar on his cheek that	*Voice over:* *Scott (sings):* Sean Connery retire. My ratings are higher. At last the world will have to concur:

he hadn't seen from a distance, but then he decides he likes it.	
233. LS Scott swings on a tree limb.	One,
234. LS Scott pushes at the pillars of the Norcross tomb.	two,
235. MS frame at a ninety degree angle. Scott has his shoulders against the sphere on which Warren sat in shot 212. The angle makes it appear that he is holding up the sphere.	three—
236. MSC Scott smiles. Tilt down as he rests his head on the base of a gravestone. The top of his head is at frame right.	I'm popular.
Dissolve to	
INTERIOR, DAY	
237. MCU Tony is asleep in his bed. His head is at frame left. His mouth is open. He opens his eyes. He sits up. Hand-held camera keeps him in MCU throughout. He gets up and starts across the room to the bathroom. He looks down at Scott's bed. Camera pans down to Warren asleep in Scott's bed. Pan back to Tony. He continues on. He realizes that that was not Scott in Scott's bed, but	*Wild sound.*

creepy Warren Oak. Tony does a take. He turns, walks back to his bed, gets in and pulls the covers over his head.

(NOTE: As Warren took over Scott's body, Scott reciprocates by being changed into Warren. Just as above, Scott receives only the appearance of Warren, while he retains his own personality. This means that the actor who has played Warren as hesitant and super-sensitive now begins to duplicate the actions of the actor who has been playing Scott. Whereas the character Warren tries to act like the body he inhabits, Scott continues to act as he has previously, although his appearance has been altered. The name "Warren" in the script indicates this character who has Warren's body and voice, but Scott's personality. The other characters, with the exception of Polycarp, continue to treat this new Warren as they did the old one.)

238. CU Warren wakes up. *Wild sound.*

239. CU Warren's feet hit the floor.

240. CU Warren's face as he stands up.

241. CU Warren's feet. His limber torso is inadequate to accommodate Scott's more ample underpants and they fall to a position surrounding his feet.

242. CU Warren reacts to his recent loss.

243. CU Warren's feet surrounded by the underpants. His hands enter from frame top and retrieve the pants. Hands and pants exit frame top together. The pants, however, return for a solo engagement.

244. MCU Warren bends out of frame to retrieve the pants and goes into the bathroom holding them up. Hand-held camera follows him and keeps him in MCU. He passes the sink and steps back in front of it. He stares at the mirror. He reacts.

245. CU Warren's feet. The pants drop in for a limited return engagement.

246. MCU Warren pinches the skin on his face to make sure that it is real. He opens the medicine cabinet door and removes his razor. He opens it to take out the blade, when he is startled. Warren drops his razor into the sink. He looks into the bedroom.

Voice over:
POLYCARP: *(off)* Stop that.

FX: *Razor drops into sink*

247. CU Tony asleep.

248. MCU Warren picks up the razor, but as soon as it enters the frame, Polycarp blasts again. Warren again drops the razor and looks into the bedroom.

Voice over:
POLYCARP *(off):* Put that down.

FX: *Razor drops into sink*

249. POV Polycarp, in all his heavenly raiment, sits on Scott's bed.

250. CU Warren's feet. His hands enter frame top and pull up the underpants resting there.

251. MCU Warren is overcome. He lip syncs the words within quotation marks.	*Voice over:* POLYCARP: "Who are you?" he asks me.
252. MS Polycarp stands up and goes into the bathroom. He sits Warren down on the toilet and rambles on.	
He lip syncs the words within quotation marks and talks unsynchronously throughout the rest. Warren lip syncs the words within quotation marks. Polycarp lip syncs the words within quotation marks. Warren lip syncs the words within quotation marks. Warren stands up to grab Polycarp, but Polycarp intercepts the thrust and forces the astonished transplant to the floor. Warren leans against the wall. Polycarp sits on the vacated toilet to continue. Zoom in to Polycarp.	*Voice over:* POLYCARP: Then I start using my head. "I am the great and glorious Wizard of Oz," I tell him. Okay with him. "Where's my body?" he asks. So I explain to him that once, when he was eleven years old and just becoming aware of the full extent of his magnetic charm, he wondered what life must be like for poor cross-eyed Lester Meister across the street, who had none of his countless friends and peerless gifts. "Better late than never," I tell him. "Your wish is come true." He thinks back and, smart boy, realizes that this is not poor cross-eyed "Lester Meister" but is poor dull eyed "Warren Oak," and in any case, whatever happened to the beautiful blue-eyed Scott Landau that last night got into the bed he just got out of. He becomes a bit churlish and calls on some strength that his new arms don't have in stock. Victory comes once again to the forces of right. At last he understands. But now I'm confused. The lot of the saintly, I suppose.

EXTERIOR, DAY

253. LS Hand-held camera precedes Warren down the steps of Scott's dorm. He is wearing Scott's clothes, much too big for him, and he has a toothbrush in his breast pocket. He is angry. Swish pan to Scott approaching from Warren's dorm. His clothes are too small and he, too, has a toothbrush in his breast pocket. He is sheepish.	*Wild sound.*
254. High angle ELS They approach one another.	
255. CU, hand held, Warren is angry.	
256. CU, hand held, Scott is sheepish.	
257. LS They approach one another.	
258. CU, hand held, sheepish Scott.	
259. CU, hand held, angry Warren.	
260. High angle ELS They pass one another and hurl epithets across their emotional abyss.	*Voice over:* WARREN: Coward. SCOTT: Bully. WARREN: Worm. SCOTT: Ox. WARREN: Faggot.

SCOTT: Narcissist.

261. CU, hand held, Warren is angrier than ever.

262. CU, hand held, Scott is somewhat uncertain, but happy that at least he had the last word.

INTERIOR, DAY

263. MCU Tony wakes up again. He gets up and crosses the room, preceded by hand-held camera. He glances at Scott's bed. Pan to show it is empty. Pan back to Tony. He goes into the bathroom. Camera stops at MCU Scott in the shower. Scott smiles and turns his face into the water.

FX: *A running shower.*

Voice over:
TONY *(off):* When I dream I don't mess around.

INTERIOR, DAY

264. MS Warren comes in the door of Warren and Hilary's room. He glances around.

265. POV pan from Hilary just sitting up in bed, past Warren's still made bed, to the desk with Hilary's decanter of sherry on it.

Voice over:
HILARY *(off):* You haven been to bed yet. What'd you do, catch a late show?

266. MS Warren slams the door. Pan as he crosses to the desk and picks up the decanter.

FX: *Door slams.*

Voice over:
HILARY *(off):* Ah, my morning sherry.

267. MS Hilary holds up his glass. Warren's hand holding the decanter enters frame and decants the sherry onto Hilary's head. Hilary sputters and jumps from the bed.

Voice over:
Hilary sputters.

268. Low angle LS Warren sits down on the bed with the decanter as Hilary paces back and forth in front of the camera. Zoom into Warren. He sneers a Scott sneer but manages only to look like John Garfield.

HILARY: You've turned into some sort of . . . of Fascist.

Dissolve to

EXTERIOR, DAY

269. CU Scott smiles a Warren smile.

270. High angle LS Scott and Frankie drift in a boat on a lake. They both seem happy.

271. ELS Scott and Frankie in the boat. Pan to Polycarp sitting against a tree on shore. He is watching them with binoculars. He has a pear in his mouth and a newspaper on his lap. He puts the binoculars down. Zoom in slowly as he bites into the pear and throws away the core. He raises the newspaper in front of him and reads aloud from it. His mouth is hidden by the paper.

Voice over:
POLYCARP: I wonder if this is a sin?

POLYCARP: "The New York Times" "All the News That's Fit to Print" "Kills Eight Children; Shoots Self" "Riots Rip Pittsburgh; Mayor Declares Disaster Area Disaster Area."

272. LS from the side, Polycarp throws the newspaper over his shoulder. He picks up the second half of the Times, zoom in slowly.	POLYCARP: That's not fit to print. I can get all that at home.
273. Zoom in slowly to MCU Polycarp with paper in front of him. His mouth is hidden again.	POLYCARP: Why do they hide this? *(sings)* Scarsdale lady reads Dickens To refugee orphans with gout.
274. LS Pan Polycarp as he walks through the woods reading the paper.	POLYCARP *(sings):* The Wollman Arena Is under subpoena
275. ELS Polycarp walks across a field reading the paper.	POLYCARP *(sings):* Calcutta is having a drought.

INTERIOR, DAY

276. LS Roger and a very disinterested Warren play chess. Warren wears glasses. Hilary sits on the side. Hilary lip syncs the words.	*Voice over:* HILARY *(sings):* My grandmother living in Paris Is thinking of buying the Louvre. The Plaza Cotillion Is spending a million On champagne alone.
277. MS Roger looks across the board. He lip syncs the words.	ROGER: It's your move.

EXTERIOR, DAY

278. High angle LS Scott and Frankie float in the boat.	*Voice over:* SCOTT *(sings):* Happiness seemed To come only when I dream But, I'm happy, happy now.

279. High angle LS Polycarp walks along grass reading the paper. Zoom out to ELS. He is in a football stadium.

POLYCARP *(sings)*:
Stony Brook lifeguards
assemble
For winter reunion by sea

280. Low angle LS Polycarp walks down flight of wooden steps, reading the paper.

POLYCARP *(sings)*:
The Duchess of Windsor
Claims exercise thins her

281. LS Polycarp walks past park benches, reading the paper.

POLYCARP *(sings)*:
Bronx Zoo receives new
chimpanzee.

282. LS Scott and Frankie in the boat.

SCOTT *(sings)*:
I'd always heard
Making wishes was absurd,
But I'm happy, happy now.

INTERIOR, DAY

283. LS The chess game continues. Warren is bored, Roger is intent on the game and Hilary is still talking. Hilary lip syncs the words.

Voice over:
HILARY *(sings)*:
The Porters have moved out
of Larchmont
And live at The Club in
Great Neck.
My uncle in Venice
Is building a tennis
Court on the Canal.

284. CU Roger looks across the board. He lip syncs the words.

ROGER: You're in check.

EXTERIOR, DAY

285. LS Pan with Polycarp as he walks along a crowded street, still reading the paper.

Voice over:
POLYCARP *(sings)*:
The Mayor of Milwaukee has
X-rays
For source of his post-nasal
drips.

286. LS Polycarp walks between two rows of cars in a parking lot, reading the paper.

POLYCARP *(sings):*
And Baby Jane Holzer
Says shaving consoles her.

287. LS Polycarp walks along the beach, reading the paper. Fast zoom in to him. He looks quizzingly into camera.

POLYCARP *(sings):*
The Plaza abolishes tips.

288. LS Polycarp in front of the water. He picks up a branch and uses it as a cane to strut his stuff. He lip syncs the words.

POLYCARP *(sings):*
After martyrdom on a hot barbecue,
My sainthood must entitle me to

POLYCARP *(sings):*
Spend the life I'm leading
Reading The New York Times

289. CU Polycarp. He lip syncs the words.

POLYCARP *(sings):*
Can't wait for Sunday.

290. LS Polycarp finishes up by sinking to one knee and spreading his arms. He lip syncs the words. He looks off left.

POLYCARP *(sings):*
I love the Times,
The New York Times.

291. LS The boat containing Scott and Frankie floats to the shore. Scott steps out and pulls onto dry land with great effort. Frankie steps out and they walk together down the beach away from Polycarp.

Wild sound.

292. MS Hand-held track with Scott and Frankie as they walk. Frankie trips over something.

293. LS Tony and Angela sit up out of the bushes. Frankie has tripped over their legs. They stand up. No one says anything. Scott and Tony stare at each other dumbly. Frankie examines the skin on her elbow. Angela begins to get irritated by the silence.

Sync sound:
ANGELA: What is this charades?

Tony looks at Angela. Then he speaks to Scott.

TONY: Going to Hamburg's To the party?

Scott feigns nonchalance.

SCOTT: Yeah, Thinking about it.

TONY: See you there, huh?

Dissolve to

EXTERIOR, NIGHT

294. CU Polycarp's feet. Tilt up to his face. He is peeking in the window of Hamburg's house.

Wild sound:
Party noises.

INTERIOR, NIGHT

295. MS Frankie sits alone in a giant armchair. She shifts about uncomfortably.

Wild sound:
Party noises.

296. MS Scott leans against a wall, looking off at Frankie nervously. Couples pass in front of him.

297. MS Frankie sits in the armchair.

298. MS Scott leans against the wall. Tony comes in beside him. They do not speak. Tony also looks off at Frankie, then he exits the frame.

299. LS A group of party goers participate in some new and wholesome parlor game. Pull focus and pan as Scott enters frame CU. He is walking around looking for something.

300. LS Scott closes one door in a hallway after having looked inside. He looks at other doors in the hall, goes to one and opens it.

301. POV Tony sits fully dressed and puffing on a cigar in a full bathtub. He waves. Across from him sits a girl facing away. She turns around. It is Frankie. Zoom in to her.

INTERIOR, NIGHT

302. LS The door to Scott's room opens and Scott sneaks in. He motions outside, reaches out and pulls Frankie into the room. She is chewing gum. She walks out of frame. He checks the outside knob to make sure that the door is locked and then closes it. He turns to face Frankie.

Voice over:
FRANKIE: What a boring party.

FX: Refrigerator door opens.

303. LS Frankie rummages through the refrigerator.

Voice over:
FRANKIE: How about a beer?

	SCOTT: Later
Scott enters frame and goes to Frankie. Holding her shoulder, he turns her around to face him. He smiles the Scott half-smile at her. She leers back at him and pushes the refrigerator door with her elbow.	
304. CU Scott, Frankie in soft focus in foreground. She moves out of the frame. He goes to follow her, but comes up short.	FX: *Refrigerator door closes.*
305. LS Scott comes up short with his tie caught in the refrigerator door.	
306. High angle MS Frankie lies down on Scott's bed. She is still chewing gum. Scott enters frame and sits on the bed. He puts his hand to his mouth.	FX: *Refrigerator door opens and closes.*
307. MCU Scott, hand to mouth and eyes freaking out.	
308. High angle MS Scott rolls over and half obscures Frankie. Her head is visible over his shoulder.	
309. CU Scott closes his eyes.	
310. High angle MS Scott wavers. Frankie's gum emerges from her mouth in an ever growing pink bubble. Scott chooses this moment to kiss her.	

311. MS from the side, Scott connects squarely with the bubble. Gum splats all over both their faces. Frankie gets off the bed and out of frame, knocking Scott off balance. He slowly slides off the other side of the bed.	*Voice over:* FRANKIE: I'm having a beer, now.
	FX: *Refrigerator door opens.*
312. LS Frankie takes a can of beer out of the refrigerator and closes the door. Scott enters, picking bubble gum from his face. Scott looks at the door and freezes.	FX: *Refrigerator door closes.* *A knock on the door of the room.*
313. CU Scott, frozen with fear.	
314. MCU Frankie holds her beer and her ground. She is used to raids.	FX: *More insistent knock on door.*
315. CU Scott panics.	
316. LS Scott grabs Frankie just as she opens the can. Beer sprays all over the room. Pan as Scott drags Frankie into the bedroom, pushes her into the closet and closes the door. He opens the door and pulls the steaming Frankie back out of the closet and looks for somewhere else to hide her.	FX: *The knocking becomes a steady pounding.*

EXTERIOR, NIGHT

317. LS Warren climbs the stairs to Scott's dorm. As he comes up, a student passes him going down. Warren remembers that he is at the wrong dorm and turns and walks back down the steps. Warren hears the commotion and turns to look.	*Voice over:* STUDENT: Hi, Warren. *Voice over:* FRANKIE: You creep. SCOTT: Shhh.
318. POV zoom in to Scott lowering Frankie out of his first floor window to the ground.	
319. MCU Warren smiles and twirls a piece of hair with his fingers.	
INTERIOR, NIGHT	
320. LS Scott rushes to the door and turns the knob. Doris Phelps throws the door open, pushing Scott behind it. She does not see him at first, then she notices him quavering behind the door. She pulls him into the middle of the room and slams the door. Scott tries to answer, but he can't make any noise at all. Doris becomes pleasant for a moment as she sniffs the room's tangy scent, but her anger comes back for a final word.	*Sync sound:* DORIS: Don't try hiding from me. How old is she? Twelve? Fifteen? And where were you at 7:30? DORIS: Mmm. I like your deodorant. DORIS: I hate to be kept waiting. Doesn't matter, we'll get it over with here. You have bubble gum on your face.
Doris slips out of her skirt and hands it to Scott.	
Scott starts to wipe the affected area of his face	DORIS: Hang that up.

with the skirt. She walks into the bedroom. She turns to Scott. She twirls a piece of her hair in her fingers and disappears within. Scott rushes to the bedroom door and closes it. He buries his face in the dress, then realizes what it is and throws it onto the desk. He looks upward in an appeal.

DORIS: I am in a hurry.

SCOTT: You didn't say it was gonna be like this.

Doris sticks her head out the door. She is impatient. She opens the door and holds it with one hand. The other she places on her hip.

DORIS: Let's go, baby. I have forty exams to correct. You're not the only lump in my mattress.

Jump cut to

321. LS Doris, with her head sticking out the door. She again opens the door and assumes the same pose.

DORIS: You're not the only plane in my hangar.

Jump cut to

322. LS Doris, with her head sticking out the door. She opens it and resumes the same pose.

DORIS: You're not the only bulb in my socket.

323. LS Doris, with her head sticking out the door. She opens it and resumes the same pose.

DORIS: You're not the only fly in my ointment.

Jump cut to

324. LS Doris, with her head sticking out the door. She opens it and resumes the same pose. She starts back in and then turns, remembering one more thing. She closes the door.

DORIS: You're not the only meat in my freezer.

DORIS: Oh, and . . . Don't forget the crushed ice.

325. LS Scott pleads upward once more. Polycarp appears, seated on the back of Scott's chair. He stands and picks up the skirt, brandishing it at Scott. Polycarp paces.

SCOTT: Where are you when I need you?

POLYCRAP: Can't you handle anything by yourself?

SCOTT: But her . . .

POLYCARP: Only a woman. Now, go in and tell her to get out.

He hands the skirt to Scott.

Scott hands the skirt back to Polycarp.

SCOTT: You.

The skirt goes back to Scott.

POLYCARP: You wanted to be Scott.

Skirt to Polycarp.

SCOTT: You're the saint.

They look at each other. Polycarp takes a deep breath.

POLYCARP: All right. I'll handle it.

Polycarp opens the door and goes in.

DORIS *(off)*: Who the hell are you?

The door closes. Scott sits at the desk and plays with a pencil. For quite a while.

326. MS Frankie sits with her back against a pillow on Warren's bed. She sips a glass of sherry. Warren sits on the edge of the bed, filling his glass with sherry.

"What's the Matter with Me?" music.

He replaces the decanter and sits back.

327. MCU Warren looks out lasciviously over his glass.

328. MCU Frankie snickers into her sherry.

329. CU Warren still looks lascivious.

330. CU Frankie still snickers.

331. ECU Warren raises one eyebrow, just a soupcon.

332. ECU Frankie licks the rim of her glass.

333. CU Their hands put the sherry glasses on the desk next to the decanter.

INTERIOR, NIGHT

334. LS Scott still sits at the desk playing with a pencil. He looks at the wall in front of him, trying to see what is happening on the other side. The door opens and Polycarp edges out, closing it behind him. He is smiling. Scott stands. Polycarp crosses to Scott, takes him by the arm and shepherds him to the door. He opens the door and nudges Scott outside.

Voice over:
Muffled conversation and laughter of Doris and Polycarp.

Sync sound:
POLYCARP: I'll take care of everything. Don't you worry about a thing. That's my thing—to worry.

335. LS Scott stands in the hall. Polycarp is in the door.

POLYCARP: Say, where do they keep the ice?

Black out. Fade in

EXTERIOR, DAY

336. High angle LS glimmering water. Boat floats into frame carrying Doris and Polycarp.

INTERIOR, NIGHT

337. LS Pan a row theatre seats filled with expectant play goers. Midway down the row are Evelyn and Warren. Evelyn reads the program. Warren looks around, very bored. The house lights dim.

EXTERIOR, DAY

338. MCU Scott enters frame bottom and exits frame top doing a push up. He does two more, and each becomes progressively lower.

INTERIOR, DAY

339. LS Scott and Tony watch television. Scott is exhausted. Tony is excited over whatever is on. He stands and cheers, punches Scott on the shoulder and points at the set. Scott falls off the chair.

EXTERIOR, DAY

340. MCU Scott continues push ups. On the third one he barely makes it into the frame. Zoom out as he collapses on the ground.

(Polycarp sings from shot 336 through shot 342.)

Voice over:
POLYCARP *(sings):*
Subways, highways,
Everything moving fast

In the world of today.
Building supers, wearing minis,
The world of today's
Where it's at.
Oho, take trips and don't wash
And you'll be out of sight
Today the world is
The world of tonight.
Don't get up tight.
Yesterday is dead.
Tomorrow is here
In the world of today.

341. MCU Boat floats from left to right. Just above the top of the boat is visible, first, Doris' head, then, Polycarp's head.

INTERIOR, NIGHT

342. LS Pan same theatre row as in shot 337. Same audience is applauding politely. Warren and Evelyn's seats are empty. Pan continues past them to the gentleman in the next seat. He is not applauding. In his lap are a pair of feet, and the lady in front of him has a pair on her shoulder.

INTERIOR, DAY

343. LS Hilary stands at the door of his room, surrounded by a spate of luggage. He fumbles with it, finally gets it all in his grasp and calls out of frame to Warren.

Sync sound:
WARREN *(off):* Want some help?

HILARY: No, thank you. Goodbye, Warren.

344. MS Warren on Warren's bed reads Playboy. Pan to desk. The decanter is there, shattered.

EXTERIOR, DAY

345. LS Doris and Polycarp picnic on the grass. She tosses a grape into his mouth. Zoom out to ELS.

Voice over:
POLYCARP: My goodness.

DORIS: No fair bragging.

INTERIOR, DAY

346. LS Scott rests his head on his desk. His arms hang limp. Tony enters, slaps Scott on the back and goes to the refrigerator. As he is slapped, Scott's head bounces on the desk. Tony forages in the refrigerator. He holds a piece of cheese and bites off pieces as he speaks. He offers his cheese stump to Scott. Scott turns his face away from view. Tony goes back to the refrigerator. Scott's head bounces back around to face the camera.	*Sync sound:* TONY: It's great out there Like a . . . like a spring day. SCOTT: It is a spring day TONY: You take my ch. . . No, here it is, Wanna play some ball? Cheese? TONY: Hey, we're out of ice.

EXTERIOR, DAY

347. LS hand held, Scott, Tony and several others play an informal football game. During the play, Scott runs in circles and finally bumps into someone.	*Wild sound*
348. ELS Warren and Roger walk along the road beside the field. Roger notices the game off right.	*Voice over:* ROGER: That should've taught me to keep away from avant-garde dentists. Hey look, there's Scotty Dumd giving his jock a workout
Warren points off left.	WARREN: Which one is . . .
Roger turns him the right way. Warren puts on his glasses.	ROGER: Warren, they're over here. Put on your glasses.
349. POV Zoom in to Scott dropping a pass.	WARREN: I've had it. I'm getting in the game.
350. ELS Warren runs onto the field and joins the players.	ROGER: But Warren, . . . football?

351. CU Tony sneers.

352. CU Hamburg laughs.

EXTERIOR, DAY

353. LS Doris and Polycarp stand in front of a mangy buffalo at the zoo.

Voice over:
DORIS: No, seriously, Pol some of my best friends are saints.

EXTERIOR, DAY

354. LS, hand held, Tony gets the ball. Scott goes out for a pass, covered by Warren. The pass comes, high and slow. As it comes down, Warren jumps in front of Scott, intercepts the pass, and knocks Scott onto the ground. Warren races down the sidelines for a touchdown.

Wild sound.

355. High angle LS Scott picks himself up and walks off the field.

EXTERIOR, DAY

356. Zoom in slowly to MS Hilary and Evelyn sit on a bench on the campus.

Sync sound:
HILARY: It's almost as though Warren were possessed. I have a cousin in Welles Hills who insists that she's lived before.

EVELYN: As what?

HILARY: She changes continually. Now she claims she was Jesse Owens.

EVELYN: But he's still alive.

HILARY: You know who he is? She is not very clever with

names. She thinks Gertrude Stein swam the English Channel.

EVELYN: Where is Warren Oak today?

Hilary grimaces.

HILARY: Roger just told me he's playing football. Football. Have you noticed how he does things now that he never knew existed before.

357. CU Evelyn blushes.

EVELYN: Yes.

EXTERIOR, DAY

358. LS Scott walks away in a field Tilt up to the blue blue sky.

(The Man and His Mother converse over the shot of the sky.) Voice over:

MAN: Worse all the time. What should I do?

MOTHER: Always with the problems.

MAN: What's a mother for?

MOTHER: So, what do you want?

MAN: Just a simple solution.

MOTHER: Solution. Who am I, Ann Landers? Ask your father.

MAN: At the wedding, did I . . .

MOTHER: All right. Send someone down there.

MAN: Send who?

MOTHER: The Spook?

		MAN: He stays
		MOTHER: Then Fatty What's His-Name.
		MAN: Aquinas.
		MOTHER: That one. Give him a knockwurst to go and tell him to be back by supper.
		MAN: Without you, Mom. where would I be?
		MOTHER: I hate to think.
	Tilt down to field. Acquinas approaches from a distance. He is a large person wearing flowing white robes.	TINKER: EVERS and CHANCE *(sing):* Oh, he's a deus ex machina He's a truth maniacina. He's an apple-eating, vice-defeating, old hypochondriac
	He reaches LS distance and stops. He lip syncs the words approximately. He takes an apple out of his tunic.	*Voice over:* AQUINAS: I have come to right the ship of state, and I intend to begin as soon as I finish this apple.
	He bites into the apple.	FX: *Biting into apple and chewing.*
	EXTERIOR, DAY	
359.	LS Scott wanders through the cemetery.	FX: *Biting into apple and chewing.*
	EXTERIOR, DAY	
360.	LS Aquinas produces another apple from his tunic. He bites into the apple.	*Voice over:* AQUINAS: . . . as soon as I finish this apple.

FX: *Biting into apple and chewing.*

EXTERIOR, DAY

361. LS The lacrosse team practices. Zoom in and pull focus to Warren across the field, walking with his hands in his pockets.

FX: *Bitting into apple (twice) and chewing.*

EXTERIOR, DAY

362. LS Aquinas produces yet another apple from his tunic. He bites into it. Tilt down. His sandalled feet are surrounded by an orchard of apple cores.

Voice over:
AQUINAS: . . . as soon as I finish this apple.

FX: *Biting into apple (three times) and chewing.*

EXTERIOR, DAY

363. LS, slow motion, Polycarp pushes Doris on a swing. She swings forward, then backward, then forward again. At the top of her forward arc,

FX: *Biting into apple and chewing.*

Fade out

Freeze frame.

EXTERIOR, DAY

364. LS Aquinas reaches into his prolific tunic and produces a banana.

Voice over:
AQUANIS: I think I'll try a banana this time.

THE MAN: Remember, Thomas by six o'clock.

Aquinas folds his hands around the banana and bows his head.

AQUINAS: Lord.

THE MAN: Thomas?

	AQUINAS: What is for supper?
EXTERIOR, DAY	
365. MCU Doris sits in a field. She is bored. Pull focus to Polycarp behind her, nodding gravely. Pull focus to Aquinas, behind him, reading aloud from a paperback.	Somber, "The World of Today" Music.
366. ELS Doris, Polycarp and Aquinas walk along the top of a rise.	*Voice over:* AQUINAS: You'll have to choose between God and Doris Phelps. POLYCARP: That's no choice. Doris giggles.
367. CU Scott	
368. CU Warren	
369. CU Doris	
370. ELS Doris, Polycarp and Aquinas walk along the rise.	*Voice over:* POLYCARP: Back by supper, huh? They sure know how to keep you loyal.
They join hands and begin to dance.	POLYCARP and AQUINAS *(sing)* Life is much more fun to When you're in the state of grace.
371. MCU Warren looks up	Even penance can be swell
372. ELS Doris, Polycarp and Aquinas	So confess or go to hell. Exercise discretion When you enter the confession
373. MCU Scott looks up.	And you'll find out that mind is not at ease
374. ELS Doris, Polycarp and Aquinas dance along the rise.	But cry out with contrition And you'll find that your position

375. MCU Frankie turns away.	Is much higher to inspire men like these
376. ELS Doris, Polycarp and Aquinas dance along the rise.	You'll wonder where temptation went When you receive that sacrament. Confess your sins like crazy And feel fresh as a daisy Be you Christian, be you Jew, You will know that God loves you. DORIS: You should try these modern costumes. AQUINAS: No. DORIS: Not enough time? POLYCARP: Not enough cloth.
377. LS Scott runs toward the camera.	SCOTT: Wait, I want to be Warren again.
378. CU Polycarp	
379. LS Warren runs toward the camera.	WARREN: It's no joke any more.
380. CU Aquinas, pull focus to clock in tower reading 5:45.	
381. High angle LS Doris, Polycarp, Aquinas, Warren and Scott talk quickly among themselves.	AQUINAS: We'll miss supper POLYCARP: Please, Ox, this one last miracle. AQUINAS: But hurry.
382. CU Polycarp, in profile, chants	*(Polycarp chants very quickly in Latin from shot 382 through shot 439.)*

383. CU eight frames Scott

384. CU eight frames Warren

POLYCARP *(chants):*
Hanc tam praecipitem
divisionem libido facieba
iam dudum enim
amoliri cupiebam custode

385. CU eight frames Scott

386. CU eight frames Doris

387. CU eight frames Scott

388. MS Aquinas tugs at Polycarp's sleeve.

389. CU looks confusedly left and right

390. CU six frames Warren

391. CU six frames Scott

392. CU six frames Warren

393. CU six frames Scott

394. CU six frames Warren

395. CU six frames Scott

396. CU six frames Warren

397. CU six frames Scott

398. CU six frames Warren

399. CU six frames Scott

400. CU six frames Doris

401. CU six frames Scott

402. CU six frames Doris

403. CU six frames Scott

404. CU six frames Doris

405. CU six frames Scott

406. CU six frames Doris

407. CU six frames Scott

408. CU Polycarp chanting very uncertainly.

409. MS Aquinas pours pills from a bottle into his hand and gulps them down.

410. CU six frames Scott

411. CU six frames Warren

412. CU six frames Scott

413. CU six frames Warren

414. CU six frames Scott

415. CU six frames Doris

416. CU six frames Scott

417. CU six frames Doris

418. CU six frames Scott

419. Low angle MS Clock reads 5:55

420. MS Aquinas pulls Polycarp by the arm.

421. CU four frames Warren

422. CU four frames Scott

423. CU four frames Warren

424. CU four frames Scott

425. CU four frames Warren

426. CU four frames Scott

427. CU four frames Warren

428. CU four frames Scott

429. CU four frames Warren

430. CU four frames Scott

431. CU four frames Doris

432. CU four frames Scott

433. CU four frames Doris

434. CU four frames Scott

435. CU four frames Doris

436. CU four frames Scott

437. CU four frames Doris

438. CU four frames Scott

439. High LS Aquinas drags Polycarp away from Warren, Scott and Doris. Aquinas and Polycarp go out of the frame.	*Polycarp cuts off his chant. Organ music begins.*
440. Low angle LS stone stairway. Aquinas and Polycarp approach it from right and left respectively. They ascend the stairs. Two thirds of the way up, they fade out. The stairway remains.	CHORUS *(sings)*: Where art thou, O Joy, Whom men seek without cease? Wherefore dost thou slake me? Doth it bring thee peace To mislead and destroy? Where are the snows? When am I free? God knows.

Fade out	*The organ continues.*
INTERIOR, DAY	
441. LS Black becomes the inside of the chapel doors. They open, admitting a bright stroke of light. A dark figure enters.	*The organ continues.*
442. Low angle CU reinstated statue of Polycarp.	
443. High angle MS Doris kneels at the altar rail. Doris shakes her head, no.	*Voice over:* POLYCARP *(sotto voce)*: It's all over, Doris
444. Low angle CU statue of Polycarp.	POLYCARP: I'm telling you Doris, this is the end.
445. High angle MS Doris begins to speak angrily. It is not her voice that is heard. She lip syncs the words. Pan to burning candle.	SCOTT: It better not be. CHORUS: God knows. Amen.

Super title:

THE END

Fade out.

15.
Brandeis University

A BEGINNING PROGRAM; DAVID KEITH HARDY, KENNETH GOLDEN

The combination of a new and bright campus, liberal administration, competent faculty, and energetic students should make the Brandeis University film program one of the finer small school programs within the next few years.

Brandeis, which has a total enrollment of 2,800, is located in the Boston suburb of Waltham, Massachusetts. It has only recently begun an undergraduate film program, and during the 1968–1969 school year, it established the course of study for a graduate program in film. Perhaps the best asset that Brandeis has, in film, is David Keith Hardy.

In 1965, Hardy presented a course at Stanford University on "The Making of a Documentary." In 1966, Brandeis University asked him to present the same course and subsequently appointed him a professor of Theater Arts and Director of the Morse Center for the Study of Communication.

Prior to his appointment at Brandeis, Hardy held a variety of positions in various forms of media. He received his bachelors degree from Trinity College in Dublin, Ireland. During the Second World War he was a Captain in the British Royal Marine Corps and saw action behind the lines in Europe, Burma, and China. One of his assignments in the Marines was the reactivation of Radio Hong Kong and, at the same time, he served as correspondent for the B.B.C. for China and Southeast Asia. He then went on to work for A.B.C., N.B.C., National Educational Television, C.B.S., and the Australian Broadcasting Commission. He produced the televised series "Close-Up," "David Brinkley's Journal," and other programs. Among his documentaries are: *Cambodia—The Peaceful Paradox,* a one-hour report on Cambodia and its ruler Prince Norodom Sihanouk; *The Essential Nehru,* which was

David Keith Hardy, the director of the film program at Brandeis University, Waltham, Mass. He has worked for *Life, Look,* and *NBC.* (Photo by the author)

broadcast two weeks before Nehru's death; and *India—Writings in the Sand,* a one-hour color report on the problems of population in India and the steps being taken to introduce new methods of birth control there.

In this country, he has been Director of Special Projects for Time, Inc., was of the founding editors of *Sports Illustrated* magazine, and produced the series "World We Live In" for *Life.* He has also been the director of the Motion Picture Division for *Look* and, in 1950, he helped produce the Mike Todd-Lowell Thomas production of *Cinerama.*

Hardy, an engaging man with an Irish accent, has contributed articles on film making and world affairs to a wide variety of magazines including *The Saturday Review, Reader's Digest, This Week, Asia, The New York Times Sunday Magazine,* and *The Times* of London.

Under his direction, the film programs on both the undergraduate and graduate level at Brandeis are being strengthened. Currently, some of the undergraduate courses are:

Film Workshop, an intensive course in film production from concept to final print including treatment, writing, photography, lighting, sound recording, editing, sound mixing, and laboratory procedure and cinemagraphic objectives. Students work in small units to produce films for release in the fields of education and public television.

Introduction to Film, an inquiry into the principles and theory of motion picture and its uses in education, television, and the cinema. The course will examine many types of film including documentaries, features, propaganda and advertising with emphasis on film history.

On the graduate level during the 1968–1969 school year were:

Introduction to Film; Film In Research, a seminar and workshop on the use of film in research projects open to students who wish to use film, tape and photographs to undertake scholarly research on topics in their major field of interest;

Film Analysis I . . . viewing and discussion of fifteen films to stimulate understanding and appreciation of essentials of the media. An attempt to discover the capacities of film and to suggest the properties that must be investigated in preparation for criticism;

Film Analysis II, intensive study of three film makers (Bergman, Antonioni, and Godard) with an eye to developing a concept of cinematic style. An analysis of cinematic techniques. An analysis of how the vocabulary of film criticism has developed as the technique has developed.

In late April 1969, Hardy presented for approval by the Graduate Council a plan of study for a graduate level major titled "Theater Arts—Film." He noted that

"such a program would eventually accept a maximum of 15 graduate students a year. The standards for admission would be those general requirements of the Graduate School. In addition, the department would require the submission of films, film scripts, or other equivalent evidence of talent and suitability from applicants.

Each student will be responsible for writing, directing, producing, photographing and editing films. One film would be made in the first year, and the second film in the second year. As a general rule, one of these films will be made by the student as a work of personal expression. The second film will normally be made on contract for an outside non-commercial granting agency, such as Educational Television, a government agency, or such sponsor. The final completed release print of the films will constitute the student's thesis for granting a degree.

Students are required to assist in the shooting of films by their colleagues. They may also be required to crew on such film-making projects as the Dretzin Living Biographies, television shows in production on campus, or at local television stations, such as WGBH-TV, channel two (the flagship station of the nations' educational television system) and their work in such productions will receive academic credit and count toward their final degree.

Each student must take one *Film Production* course, one *Film Aesthetics* course and either a *Directing, Acting, Design* or *Writing* course in Theater Arts, each year.

This plan of study was approved by the Graduate Council and went into effect at the beginning of the 1969–1970 school year.

The Dretzin Living Biographies, which Hardy mentioned in the study plan, is a project of the entire film program at Brandeis and is a series of film biographies of noted world figures. Both faculty and students work on the production of these films, which are produced on and off-campus.

Subjects of the films have included: Dr. Grete Bibring, noted psychoanalyst who was taught by Freud; President Eamon de Valera of Ireland; Prime Minister David Ben Gurion of Israel; and the sculptress Louise Nevelson. As an example of the student-faculty work on the series, the film on Dr. Bibring was completed in 1968, during these long shooting sessions on campus, where she was interviewed by Hardy. Then the film was given to film major Marty Ostrow, of Elmont, Long Island, to edit and complete. He did so during 1969.

Hardy's chief assistant in the Morse Center is Kenneth Golden, who, at the age of 25, earns a bit more than $12,000 each year at Brandeis. Golden received his master's degree in 1969 in film from New York University and his work there was principally under Haig Manoogian.

During the late spring of 1969, both the undergraduate and graduate programs in film were either in a state of change (as in the undergraduate program) or in a state of development (Hardy's study plan for the graduate film major). Golden said of the undergraduate program then:

> We are trying to get away from a one class-one professor type structure. The 1969–1970 school year should be fluid in its

One of the bright young men in film is Kenneth Golden, who has his master's degree in film from New York University and who is now assistant director of the Morse Center for the Study of Communication at Brandeis University. Behind him is the Spingold Theater on the Brandeis campus. (Photo by the author)

approach. We hope to have nucleus groups of film makers here, graded into beginning, intermediate and advanced groups. The beginning groups will use super-eight millimeter equipment because we want them to have all their early mistakes done cheaply in super eight. The films that they make will serve as the basis for the selection of students for the intermediate and advanced programs, where they will be shooting in sixteen millimeter. We'd like to go by a "guru" approach, of letting the students make films on their own and letting them come to faculty members for guidance when they have to. We'd like to let some students jump past the beginning classes into the intermediate or advanced classes if they show enough talent to by-pass the first courses.

During the 1968–1969 school year, there were approximately 150 undergraduates and five graduate students in the film program (the dearth of many graduate students was simply because of the indecisions concerning a formal plan of study toward a graduate degree in film). The film program offices are in the four-year-old Spingold Theater Arts Center, although classrooms and editing facilities are located in a small building that acts as the stage for a Greek theater, built on the side of a hill on campus.

Marty Ostrow, who completed the Living Biography film on Grete Bibring, is an excellent example of the students at Brandeis. In addition to the Bibring film, he has also completed *Willard,* a ten-minute study of a crippled panhandler, who he encountered in the Boston area. During the summer of 1966, Ostrow taught a film course in the Upward Bound program at Fisk University in Nashville, Tennessee. During that time, he also filmed *Della and the Snakes,* an impressionistic study of a 98-year-old southern black woman. While in high school, he filmed *Erudition,* a film critical of his school and the lack of direction that was fostered there. As he says, he "fooled around with eight-millimeter film" at a film workshop at the 92nd Street Y.M.H.A. in New York City during his high school days, and then came to Brandeis specifically for film. He hopes to complete his degree requirements during 1970 and continue for graduate work at Brandeis.

In May of 1969, Brandeis held its first public screenings, a two-day program of films by the faculty and students. The program, "My Movie," was a success; it made a profit of $1,200 and 800 spectators attended—most from the other film schools in the Boston area, who came out of curiosity for the newer Brandeis program.

Some of the films shown were:

What Students Perceive, a film critical of high school programs, filmed partially in Columbus, Ohio, and sponsored by the United States Commission on Civil Rights.

Dr. David Seegal, Carlos P. Romulo and *Dr. Grete Bibring,* excerpts from the Living Biographies series.

India, impressions of that country by Ira Brenner.

Ostrow's *Willard, Della and the Snakes,* and several others, notably *Roger Vogtman,* a study of a sculptor; *Of Endless Wonder,* about a painter; *Sparkgap,* a visual and textual expression of American society; *The Virtuoso,* which is surrealistic; and *Ringmasters,* an electronic film. Perhaps the highlight of the show was *Lemme Kishya,* a parody of the French "New Wave" films.

Of more than 40 films, 15 were judged exceptional and plans were made after the festival to show one film each week on a variety of Boston area television stations, including the educational channel, WGBH.

Although the programs and facilities at Brandeis may seem

The Spingold Theater is the home of the film department on the Brandeis University campus, although most film work is done in another building. The Spingold Theater houses offices, three different theaters, dance studios, rehearsal halls, editing facilities, TV studio, workshops, dressing rooms, and classrooms. (Courtesy of Brandeis University)

inadequate compared with other bigger, more established schools, the next few years should result in expansion and advancement for the Brandeis program. The consensus seems to be that among major urban areas in this country, the Boston area, involving the Brandeis program, Harvard's Carpenter Center, and Boston University's program, should have great potential for film making. And of these three schools, the one with the best chance of excellence seems currently undeveloped regarding film making on campus, but the potential for continued excellence in the three schools is certainly planted. Of the three, Brandeis ought to emerge as the leader.

16.

Syracuse University

FILM FORUM; "STALAG 17" FILM MAKING

Syracuse University is one of the few large universities that has a dominant interest in film showings and very little interest in film making. It is exceptional because the film program, Film Forum, not only makes a profit, but is able to subsidize students for film projects of their own.

The Film Forum at Syracuse is operated under the direction of the United Campus Christian Fellowship. The director of the film program is the Reverend Norman O. Keim, and under his guidance, the program has shown a wide variety of films, purchased its own equipment, and as mentioned, subsidized student work.

As the Reverend Keim has said,

> The Film Forum has been in existence since the 1967–1968 school year. At this time, we had 15,000 paid admissions to film showings (Syracuse has a total enrollment of approximately 14,000 students—author.). In the 1968–1969 school year, we had 50,000 paid admissions to our films and during the 1969–1970 year, we hope to double that to about 100,000 tickets sold.
>
> We began the programs in sixteen millimeter and in January of 1967, we were able to buy 35 millimeter projection equipment from a theater in West Point, New York. About the same time, Syracuse University bought the Regent Theater near downtown Syracuse for dramatic productions and for first-run films and the Film Forum runs selections there between plays. When we can't use the Regent, the Film Forum uses the Gifford Auditorium, on campus.

In March of 1969, the Film Forum presented three grants of $250 each to campus film makers to aid in their productions. A panel of three judges—Martin Fass, coordinator for public information at University College; Timothy R. Wilson, writer-director in the motion picture program at the Center for Instructional Communications; and Richard Cressey, owner of the C-T Film Center, in Syracuse—selected the winning projects. The grants were awarded to Bruce McCurdy, Stanley P. Sztaba, and Bruce J. Thompson.

McCurdy, of Easthampton, Connecticut, was in the Center for Instructional Communications and used the grant to help complete *College,* a short animated film. He also used part of the grant to work on an animation project for J. S. Bach's "Fantasia."

Stanley Sztaba, who is from Maryknoll, New York, and who was enrolled in the television-radio department, used his grant to produce *On the Cities,* a multi-media, multi-image program about the problems and the future of cities.

And Bruce J. Thompson, from Braintree, Massachusetts, used his grant to produce a black-and-white documentary, *The Move,* concerned with the problems of relocating elderly people displaced by urban renewal. Thompson was in the University's School of Social Work.

Actor Rod Steiger makes a point during a guest appearance at Syracuse University.

Rod Steiger gestures during his appearance at Syracuse University.

"All rights to completed films will remain in the hands of the film-makers," Rev. Keim said. "There will be no restriction in subject matter and no editorial supervision or censorship."

It was the second year in a row that the Film Forum presented grants to students. Similar awards were given the previous year.

A typical schedule of Film Forum for the school year is the 1969 program, which included showings of: *Charly*, with Cliff Robertson and Claire Bloom; *Shame*, which won the National Film Critics' Award for the Best Actress (Liv Uhllman); both shown at the Regent Theater. *Dr. Zhivago, The Illustrated Man, Closely Watched Trains, Elvira Madigan, Zita,* and Francis Ford Coppola's *You're A Big Boy Now* were shown at Gifford Auditorium, as were *The Graduate, Wild In The Streets, Love Affair Or The Tragedy of A Switchboard Operator, Hour of the Wolf, Personna, Bonnie And Clyde,* and *Petulia.*

For the third year in a row, the Film Forum held a "Retrospective," featuring the films of one actor. For two days during the 1969 festival, Rod Steiger appeared on the campus, while the Retrospective honored his achievements in film. Some of his past

Actress Claire Bloom talks to students at Syracuse University

Dr. William Pearson Tolley, Chancellor of Syracuse University, presents the University Centennial Medal to actor Rod Steiger and his ex-wife, actress Claire Bloom.

films shown included *The Sergeant, On The Waterfront, The Mark, The Big Knife, The Loved One* (with Steiger in the role of Mr. Joyboy), *Across The Bridge, In The Heat of The Night* (for which Steiger won an Academy Award), *No Way To Treat A Lady,* and *The Pawnbroker.*

Steiger's wife, actress Claire Bloom (they have since been divorced), also appeared at the Retrospective. Her latest film (at the time), *Charly,* was given its Syracuse premiere and both Steiger and Miss Bloom attended university classes. Miss Bloom taught a class in Shakespearian drama and she and Steiger met with film students and attended a class in Freshman English taught by poet-teacher Phillip Booth. Later during their visit, both Steiger and Miss Bloom were presented University Centennial Medals for their work in film.

Before he left the campus, Steiger said, "I realize now how unfairly young people on campuses have been misrepresented by the press. It's given everyone the idea that college students are a cross between pot addicts and Hell's Angels. College students have good manners and good ideas. Today's generation is on its toes and will notice any dishonesty on my part."

Rod Steiger, deep in thought, during his Syracuse appearance.

Rev. Norman O. Keim, the director of the Syracuse University Film Forum, walks with Rod Steiger.

One year earlier, the Film Forum presented a Henry Fonda Retrospective, and screened films that traced Fonda's career. They included: *The Trail of the Lonesome Pine* (1936); *Jesse James,* which also featured the late Tyrone Power (1939); *Grapes of Wrath,* which won Fonda an Academy Award for his portrayal of Tom Joad (1940); *The Lady Eve* (1941); *The Ox-Bow Incident* (1943); *My Darling Clementine* (1946); *Mr. Roberts* (1955); *The Wrong Man,* directed by Alfred Hitchcock (1957); *12 Angry Men* (1957); and *The Best Man* (1964). Fonda also attended classes and met with interested students. The film *Yours, Mine and Ours,* with Fonda and Lucille Ball, was given its Syracuse premiere during his visit.

The 1970 Retrospective honored Alan J. Pakula. His films shown during the festival included: *Stalking Moon, To Kill A Mockingbird, Love With a Proper Stranger, Fear Strikes Out,* and *The Sterile Cuckoo.*

In 1966, a fore-runner of the Film Forum was a Bogart Festival presented by the United Campus Christian Fellowship. It included five of Bogart's best films:*The Caine Mutiny, The African Queen, Treasure of the Sierre Madre, The Maltese Falcon,* and *Casablanca.*

Film making on the Syracuse campus is relegated to what is now known as the "Stalag 17" barracks. Under the guidance of Lee McConkey, of the Center for Instructional Communications, the film students have taken over several ancient World War Two-vintage barracks near the University's round Fieldhouse. During the war, the barracks were used for classified research, and they were surrounded by barbed-wire fences that held signs stating RESTRICTED AREA. AUTHORIZED PERSONNEL ONLY.

Inside the barracks, the film students now work in small rooms, with plasterboard walls and tired swivel chairs. It is drab and bleak, but they appear to tolerate it. There is a certain amount of wry humor and resignation associated with the fences and the barbed-wire and the signs, and the students enjoy that. The bar-

The film program at Syracuse University is carried on behind barbed wire and "Restricted" signs left over from government research projects. The film faculty and staff often refer to the buildings as "Stalag 17." (Photo by the author)

racks are isolated from the main campus in a quiet area near the outskirts of the city and the students and staff enjoy the relative freedom found there. They often refer to the fences and the signs and claim justifiably that there is no film program in the country with facilities quite like theirs—a moot point.

The "Restricted Area" atmosphere at Syracuse carries over into other aspects of the film program as well; the film making is listed in the university catalogue as the Center for Instructional Communications, and it, in turn, is listed under the Department of Instructional Technology, which is a part of the School of Education.

The Center had, during the 1968–1969 school year, five courses in production, two in history and aesthetics, and five in production for graduate students.

According to Lee McConkey, who received his doctorate in communications from Michigan State University, there are usually 100 students in the production courses during any given semester; 20 in Script Writing, 20 in Animation, and 15 in Directing. Of all those students, he added, it is lucky if there are three good films completed every year.

The department staff, too, is fragmented in such a way that there is less than one fulltime faculty member for 150 students. Dr. John Tyo, of the Center, is officially listed as having a one-half-time teaching assignment and a one-half-time production assignment. McConkey has a one-quarter-time teaching load and a three-quarters production assignment. Tim Wilson does no teaching but has a three-quarter-time production assignment in the Center. Stewart Sandaw, a doctoral candidate in communication, is also on the staff for film production. The combined total for Tyo and McConkey of three-quarters of a full teaching assignment for 150 students strikes the faculty and staff as most bizarre, but it is totally in keeping with the RESTRICTED AREA notices on the fences.

Within the drama department, however, students are able to take additional courses in film. Dan Krempel teaches directing, history of the theater, and a course formerly titled Cinema appreciation, re-titled *Development of Film Art* in 1969. It was formerly considered a "Mickey Mouse" course, a snap, an easy "A," but that has changed. Krempel demands heavy reading. The first half of the course is devoted to silent films and the advent of sound. The second half concerns the sound film. The course is limited to juniors and seniors and requires students to attend one hour of lectures and one hour of film screenings each week.

Students are also able to take summer courses in production, as well as allied courses in message design, drama on radio-TV.

Surveying the barracks and the plasterboard walls, Lee McConkey told this writer, "We seldom have enough equipment, or facilities, for that matter, faculty members. The University cries 'poor mouth,' but it recently bought the Regent Theater for the use of the Drama Department and the university also bought a Syracuse country club which it operates as a private business. Syracuse also owns considerable property in downtown New York City, but apparently doesn't have enough money for the film programs."

The comment is justified. Syracuse's film program, such as it is, is considerably under-staffed and under-equipped for the number of students it serves.

Nonetheless, some exceptional films are produced at Syracuse. Some of them have been: *Ivory Flicks,* a twelve-minute, black-and white film by Ann Chablers, completed for the course *Motion Picture I: Basics of Motion Picture Reproduction. Ivory Flicks* is a strange, convoluted film about a girl in a bathtub.

Once A Year is a five-minute film, in black and white, by Jerry

Setting up for shooting *The Evolution of Learning Spaces,* a fantasy by Lee McConkey, are (at left) Ron Bouverat, the set designer, and Bruce MacCurdy, the puppet designer and animator.

From the film *The Evolution of Learning Spaces*. Bruce MacCurdy was the puppet designer and animator; Stuart Sandow was the location director; Ron Bouverat was the graphics designer; Vaughn Bode, titles; and Fred Knirk was the producer for the film.

Tararian and Charles Dunn, and *What Turns Tommy On/Off* by G. William Jones is three and one-half minutes long.

The Parting by Tillman Ragan is a boy-girl love affair in black-and-white. *Against The Wall* is also a short film—three minutes—with sound by Mike Brinn.

Annabel Lee, filmed in a cemetery by Keith Jackson, follows the Edgan Allen Poe poem of lost love. It is four minutes long.

What The Hell Are You Doing? a social commentary on war, poverty, and "all the world's problems" was completed by Jon Keeble and is three minutes long.

The Allnighter, a film about a student studying all night for upcoming final exams, was done by Michael Weber and is five minutes long.

Stepping Stones to Historical Footnotes was a project for the Animation class. It was a cell animation study that totalled 7,000

Kevin. . is a 17-minute experience during which the viewer learns a ten year-old's thoughts and desires. Born blind, Kevin's sensitive impressions of the world around him leave the viewer "drained" with a strong desire to help him and others like him. Kevin was produced by Syracuse graduate student Malcolm Tarlofsky. (Distributed by Churchill Films)

". . . I feel the bark of MR. TREE, and he's got a bad body. The bark is all rough, and I say . . . he's not taking care of his body. He's been hit by lightning three times, you know. He's got lightning scars, but he's still standing tall out there. MR. TREE has been taking lots of beatings, getting well over 1,000 volts into him . . ." from *Kevin*, an award-winning film by Malcolm Tarlofsky. *Kevin* is a sensitive study of a 10-year-old blind boy. (Distributed by Churchill Films)

drawings and, like *What The Hell. . . .*, is a commentary on war, poverty, and other problems. It contains a considerable amount of humor, exposing all the great clichés of world thinking.

Semper Fidelis is a four-minute kinestasis film, consisting of World War One stills, accompanied by a sound track of the 1914 record "Do It Again." *Semper Fidelis* was completed by David Rend and Arthur Daniels.

*Cube Olés** is a study of three-dimensional cubes, each painted different shades and colors. The sound track is bullfight sounds. It was also done for the animation class by Richard Thomas and Carol A. Lee.

Jabberwocky is a Da-Da-esque study of the Lewis Carroll poem and a three-minute color film by six members of the animation class.

But perhaps the best film to be produced at Syracuse in the last few years is *Kevin*, a 17-minute black and white film produced by former graduate student Malcolm Tarlofksy on contract for the Central New York Eye Bank Association as a fund-raising film.

Kevin is a study of a ten-year-old boy blind from birth.

". . . I felt the bark of MR. TREE, and he's got a bad body. The bark is all rough, and I say . . . he's not taking care of his body. He's been hit by lightning three times, you know. He's got lightning scars, but he's still standing tall out there. MR. TREE has been taking lots of beatings, getting well over 1,000 volts into him . . ."

It is a poignant film that drives the viewer to help the boy (and hopefully others like him). Tarlofksy lived with his subject for some time before shooting and the results are lyrical and moving. *Kevin* has been awarded the first prize in the Rensselaer Polytechnic Institute Film Festival and the First Prize-Gold Camera Award in the U.S. Industrial Film Festival in Chicago. Similar first prizes have been won at the Atlanta International Film Festival, the American Film Festival, and the Columbus, South Carolina, Film Festival. *Kevin* was completed in 1968 and, as a contract film completed by a student, it is superb.

As a film school, Syracuse leaves much to be desired, in equipment, faculty, and most of all administrative encouragement. The Film Forum is self-sustaining and profitable, but the film making, on the other hand, will probably remain much as it is. Aspiring film students should be cognizant of the warnings: RESTRICTED AREA. And they would do well to consider other film programs that are not behind barbed-wire fences.

---

* *Cube Olés* won the first prize for animation in *Esquire* magazine's First International College Film Festival, as announced in the August 1970 issue.

An Abridged Lexicon of Film Terms

A AND B ROLLS—system of preparing original film in two strips instead of one; A and B rolls are convenient when special effects, such as titles, must be inserted. Obligatory in 16 millimeter, option in 35 millimeter, depending on the effects that the film maker wants

ACE—spotlight rated at 1000 watts

ANIMATION—the technical process of making drawings or inanimate objects appear to move on the screen

ANSWER PRINT—the first complete print of a film; so-called because they are first shown to producers, who then give their answer whether the film is complete as is or needs more editing or other changes. *See also* COMPOSITE

APERTURE—the changeable opening in a camera lens; light passes through the aperture onto the film

ASA—a film rating system established by the American Standards Association; film with a high ASA rating generally takes a faster exposure than lower rated film; still film with an ASA rating of 400, for instance (Kodak Tri-X), might need exposure of 1/250th of a second, whereas film with an ASA rating of 80 (Kodak Kodacolor), might need exposure of 1/125th of a second or lower for the same shot, all other factors being equal. The same guidelines apply to movie film

ASSEMBLE—to place sections of film in the correct order, as they would appear in the completed film

ARC LIGHT—a carbon lamp used to illuminate sets

ARRANGE—to adapt written music to voices or instruments

BACK PROJECTION—to project scenes behind actors, to be picked up by a second camera; scenes of actors inside taxicabs, for instance, involve back projection. Shots of highway traffic are back projected behind the actors to give the illusion that they are in fact in a taxi

BARN DOORS—flaps on light units to keep light in specific areas of a set and out of unwanted areas

BLIMP—protective covering surrounding a camera unit to prevent the sound of an operating camera from being picked up and recorded on the sound track, accidentally

BLOOP—the sound of a splice on an optical soundtrack
BLOOPING INK—black ink used to cover a splice and thereby eliminate a bloop
BOOK—to schedule a film into a theater
BOOM—an extension used to hold a microphone over an actor
BOOSTER—lights used when shooting outdoors, to supplement sunlight
BUDGET—the schedule showing when various scenes of a film are to be shot; or, the financial schedule of a film—actor's salaries, technician's salaries, and all other cost factors
CAMERA ANGLE—the relationship of the camera to the scene that is to be photographed; low, camera below action; high, camera above action, on ceiling, etc.
CAST—all members of a movie who will act in front of the cameras
CELLS—single transparent sheets used for cartooning
CINEMA VÉRITÉ—a shooting style of unplanned observation of an event in progress
CLAPBOARD—a set of hinged slates that are snapped together at the beginning of a take; the editor will later match the sight of the sticks together with the sound of the slap to establish the synchronized soundtrack for the take. The clapboards will often include a small blackboard on which the take number and film identification are noted.
CLOSE-UP—*see* SHOT
CODE NUMBERS—*see* EDGE NUMBERS
COMPOSITE—film containing both the picture and soundtrack
CONTACT PRINTING—a system of printing film emulsion-to-emulsion
CONTRAST—the difference between the intensity of blacks and whites on film
COOKIE—a cut-out that is placed in front of a light to soften it; cookies are made of various designs
CRAB DOLLY—a small camera platform on wheels that can be moved by hand in any direction
CRANE—to move a camera above or below a scene during shooting
CREDITS—the sections of a film listing the producer, director, cast, crew, etc.
CREW—all members of a film company who work behind the cameras
CUT—a single strip of film; To cut: to transfer instantly from one shot to the next
CUTTING BENCH—*see* EDITING BENCH
DAILIES—*see* RUSHES
DEUCE—spotlight rated at 2000 watts

DEVELOP—the chemical process of treating exposed film to make the image visible
DIRECTOR—the person who controls the action during shooting sessions
DISSOLVE—to gradually fade out one shot while gradually fading-in another
DOCUMENTARY—a film that has as its main objective the qualities of information, persuasion, documentation, or education
DOUBLE SYSTEM—a system of film making in which the picture is exposed while the sound is being recorded with another unit
DUBBING—to edit in a sound track to an existing film; to add orchestration or voice tracks
EDGE NUMBERS—numbers placed on fresh film at intervals of one foot to aid in identification during processing and editing
EDITING BENCH—table where the film editor works, usually equipped with a viewer or moviola, splicers, gloves, glue, etc.
EFFECTS—an all-purpose term that includes wipes, fades, cuts, and other methods of replacing one shot with another
EMULSION SPEED—*see* ASA
EXPOSED FILM—film that has not been developed or printed
EXPOSURE METER—a precision instrument that gauges the amount of light in an area to be photographed; there are two types of exposure meters: incident light meters, registering the light *on* a subject, and reflected light meters, registering the amount of light *reflected from* the subject to be photographed
FADE IN—film that goes from black to image
FADE OUT—film that goes from image to black
FILTERS—colored or tinted glass that is placed in front of the camera lens to change the contrast of the film; those are *contrast* filters. Other filters can cut down glare or change the density of light
FLASH—*see* SHOT
FLIP—a wipe that turns over; *see* WIPE
FILM RATIO—the amount of footage filmed to the amount in the final release print
FOCUS—the point at which a sharp image is formed on the film; if all parts of the photographed scene are blurred, the shot is out-of-focus
FOOTAGE—exposed film measured in feet
FRAME—a single picture in a strip of film
FREEZE FRAME—repetitions of the same frame, which adds the quality of still photography, when needed
FROZEN WORK PRINT—a print that is so complete that no more work need be done on it
HEAD—the beginning of a reel of film; when film is ready for

projection, it is said to be "heads up." The end of the reel, then, is the TAIL

HOT SPOT—a portion of film that is accidentally overexposed due to a reflection into the lens.

HARD TICKET SHOW—a reserved-seat film, or a film with a higher-than-normal admission price

INTERLOCK—a system of interconnecting projectors and recorders that insure synchronized sound and image

KEG LIGHT—spotlight rated at 750 watts

KEY LIGHT—the principal light for a scene

KINESTASIS—a method of shooting a film from a series of still photographs

LAY IN—to add various material during editing; the sound, titles, etc.

LEADER—plain film, usually black or white, added to a completed film to compensate for the additional lengths required for threading through a projector

LIGHTING—illuminating a scene for photographic purposes

LIGHT METER—*see* EXPOSURE METER

LIGHT SOUND—sound that is recorded during shooting

LOCATION—a film made outside a permanent studio

LOOP FILM—a film that has been spliced together and is run through a projector continuously, without re-winding

MARRIED PRINT—film with both image and sound on one strip

MICROPHONE—precision instrument capable of transmitting sound from scene to tape

MIX—to make a single track of two or more tracks of sound

MOVIEOLA—trade name of a machine used to edit image and sound, either together or separately

MUSIC TRACK—sound track containing music, to be mixed with other tracks or used separately

NARRATION—spoken comment to accompany images

NEGATIVE—exposed film with reversed light values; whites in negative form are black; dark shades are light. When the negative is printed, the values become positive; whites are white and blacks are black

NEGATIVE COST—the total cost of an entire film

OPTICALS—*see* EFFECTS

ORIGINAL FOOTAGE—the amount of film that the cameraman uses initially

OUTLINE—a brief summary of a motion picture

OUT-TAKE—section of film that is not used in the final print; OUT-TAKES are rejected for a variety of reasons: an actor's mistake; a hot-spot; an error of some other kind, or simply because the editor wanted a different version of the sequence or none at all.

Also called TRIM

OVEREXPOSURE—a scene that is photographed accidentally or deliberately with too much light, resulting in film that is over-all too white

OVERLAP—to repeat part of the same action in a series of different shots

PAN—*see* SHOT

PANCAKE—actors' make-up that darkens skin tones

PERFORATIONS—regularly-spaced holes on the edge of film that are used to pull the film through a projector

PLAYBACK—to listen to a previously recorded track or tape

POSITIVE—a print with light values consistent, i.e., whites and blacks as they are regularly; a print made from a negative

POINT-OF-VIEW—a camera angle used to simulate the view as seen by an actor; i.e., scenes shot through the cockpit of an airplane might be used to simulate the view of the pilot

PRODUCER—the person financially responsible for the finished film

PROJECTION ROOM—small room in which films are viewed for consultation by film makers, film company officials, or others

PROP—any object needed by an actor during a particular scene

PROPERTY—any piece of literary work that may be used as a basis for a film

RAW STOCK—fresh film that has not been exposed

RELEASE PRINT—final version of a completed film that can be scheduled for screenings

RE-TAKE—to shoot a scene over, to correct mistakes

REVERSAL FILM—a film stock that is processed for a positive image instead of a normal negative image

ROUGH CUT—an unpolished film that needs more editing and completion

RUNNING SHOT—*see* SHOT

RUSHES—all the film shot on the previous shooting day

SCORE—a musical work for film; to score; to record that music for a film

SCREENPLAY—the written form of a piece of literary material to be filmed; usually includes dialogue, set instructions, etc.

SCRIPT—a duplicated form of the screenplay used in the day-by-day shooting

SHOT—the division of a film into sections according to camera angle; there are many varieties of shots. Some of the most common and their abbreviations are:

> CLOSE-UP—of a person, usually head or head and shoulders; abbreviated CU
>
> DOLLY—a shot in which the camera moves from one place to another; also called trucking or tracking

FLASH—a shot that appears for only a few frames; its effects are usually subliminal, as the viewer does not fully comprehend what he has seen

HIGH SHOT—a shot taken from above the subject; at or near the ceiling, for instance, in an interior scene

LONG SHOT—a shot in which the subject appears in the distance or on the horizon; abbreviated LS

LOW SHOT—a shot taken from below the subject

MEDIUM CLOSE SHOT—between the range of a close-up and a medium shot; abbreviated MCS

MEDIUM SHOT—a shot that shows the entire subject; abbreviated MS

MEDIUM LONG SHOT—between the range of a medium and a long shot

PAN SHOT—is a shot in which the camera moves from side to side

RUNNING SHOT—a shot in which the camera follows the action

ZOOM SHOT—a shot taken with a zoom lens

There are variations of these abbreviations: E.C.U. is an Extreme Close-up; E.L.S. is an Extreme Long Shot, etc.

SLUGS—pieces of blank film inserted to replace worn or damaged sections of film

SOUND STAGE—studio stage specially constructed for filming with sound, usually padded and insulated to prevent outside noises from being recorded and to eliminate the use of a blimped camera

SOUND TRACK—the thin band on the left side of film that contains the sound to accompany the film

SPEED—*see* ASA. Also refers to running speed of recorders; when a recorder comes up to correct running speed, the soundman usually shouts "Speed"

SPLICE—to glue two sections of film together

STILLS—photographs used to illustrate or advertise a film

PRODUCTION STILLS—show members of the crew or cameras positioned for shooting

STOCK FOOTAGE—pre-filmed segments that can be used for a variety of different films; a library of scenes

STORYBOARD—to diagram a film, scene by scene, using drawings or illustrations showing position of actors, cameras, etc.; a STORYBOARD will also indicate the shot that the director will use

SUPER-IMPOSE—to lay one piece of film over another and print both together

SYNCHRONIZATION—(commonly abbreviated sync and pronounced "sink") the process of matching image and sound, so that actors appear to speak at the right time; OUT-OF-SYNC refers to sound that comes at the wrong time, before or after the actor's mouth moves

TAIL—*see* HEAD

TAKE—total amount of film used for one scene without stopping

TILT—to move the camera up and down, as a person nods his head

TITLES—*see* CREDITS

TRIMS—*see* OUT-TAKE

TURRET—revolving part of the front of a camera carrying a variety of lens, which may be positioned over the camera, for various lens effects

VIEWER—small instrument used by editors for viewing film that generally has no sound added

WILD SOUND—sound that has been recorded and will be added to film later

WIPE—an optical effect of a second shot replacing a first on the screen; there are many varieties of wipes

WORKPRINT—a positive print of a film used for editing purposes

Index